BRIDGESPOTTING

A GUIDE TO BRIDGES THAT CONNECT PEOPLE, PLACES, AND TIMES

Bob Dover

Bridgespotting: A Guide to Bridges That Connect People, Places, and Times
© 2022, Bob Dover. All rights reserved.
Published by Sewell Pond Press, Columbia, MD

ISBN 978-1-7379003-0-6 (paperback)
ISBN 978-1-7379003-1-3 (eBook)
Library of Congress Control Number: 2022903133

www.robertdover.com

This book is intended to provide accurate information with regard to its subject matter and reflects the opinion and perspective of the author. However, in times of rapid change, ensuring all information provided is entirely accurate and up-to-date at all times is not always possible. Therefore, the author and publisher accept no responsibility for inaccuracies or omissions and specifically disclaim any liability, loss or risk, personal, professional or otherwise, which may be incurred as a consequence, directly or indirectly, of the use and/or application of any of the contents of this book.

Publication managed by AuthorImprints.com

TABLE OF CONTENTS

FOREWORD

BRIDGES SPEAK TO US.

In my 50-year career designing bridges, I have learned that bridges speak to us about the places they are and the places they take us. They speak to us about the skill of their designers and the courage of their builders. Above all, they speak to us about the values and aspirations of the communities, organizations, and institutions that build them.

With this book, Bob Dover encourages us to listen to what they have to tell us, by simply walking across more than 600 memorable bridges. Crossing a bridge as a pedestrian is a dramatically different experience than in a moving vehicle. For starters, it exposes you to the actual size of the bridge. Bridges are much larger than they seem from a car or train. Directly experiencing that fact can be both exhilarating and a little bit intimidating, and you have more time to think about it. In a car, you will cross a mile-wide river in a minute or two. Walking will take you at least 20. In that additional time, you will learn all kinds of things.

For one thing, you will understand how wide the Seine, or the Thames, or the Mississippi really is, and you will get to watch the boats and barges as they ply the waters below. You will understand how deep the Royal Gorge really is, and experience for yourself the thrill of acrophobia. Your bridge projects you into the space above the river or the gorge, a location that no one else can occupy, and gives you a unique vision of the world.

From your vantage point, you will get an exclusive view of the skyline, or the cathedral, or the rock formations of the canyon's walls.

While you are there, you will learn all kinds of things about the history of the place. After all, many cities are where they are because of a crossing of some kind. That's why they are called Cambridge, or Hartford. When you learn that all of the bridges over the Liffey River in Dublin are named for Irish patriots, you will have also learned something about the Irish Revolution. Many bridges, such as Prague's Charles Bridge, commemorate important events in local history. Finally, you will learn something from the other people using the bridge. Your common experience of crossing the bridge is a great conversation starter. Some of the others will be fellow tourists, but some will be residents who will provide a local's response to the bridge and the community traditions that have grown up around it. Conversely, some will have chosen to walk the bridge as an opportunity for contemplation. Observing the sole crossers is a unique kind of people-watching.

You will also learn that bridges can be quite controversial if they are too crowded, or in bad shape, or especially if they need to be replaced. Almost always, the root of the controversy is a difference of opinion between the public agency that owns the bridge and the public that uses and loves the bridge about what should be done. The public, meaning the people who ultimately own (and pay for) the bridge, almost always wins. If you care about particular bridges, you may want to get involved in such controversies. In his last chapter, Bob offers some ideas about how to do so.

This book makes all of these experiences accessible and enjoyable, even in anticipation, if you haven't yet made it to the bridge itself. Better yet, this book will encourage you get to all of the bridges, to experience them for their own sake and, at the same time, to learn more about the places they are. Enjoy!

Fred Gottemoeller, PE, RA
Principal, Bridgescape LLC
Author of *Bridgescape, The Art of Designing Bridges*

INTRODUCTION

FOR MORE THAN 35 YEARS, I have been fortunate to travel extensively, both for work and pleasure, all over the United States, Canada, and Europe. I love to visit places for the full effect of their natural setting, history, and culture, and this has always included walking across the local bridges. I had no particular interest or expertise in bridge engineering or the history of bridges. Instead, the major attraction was that a position on the bridge, elevated above the city streets and separated from the buildings and trees, usually provided the best available view of the city skyline or waterfront. I had never traveled to a place just so that I could walk across a bridge. It was simply that, if a bridge with sidewalks happened to be close by, I always made it a point to check out the view. However, it never occurred to me that "tourist bridges" existed or that I was, even casually, a "bridgespotter."

This changed a few years ago on a trip to Prague, where it is impossible to ignore the sheer numbers and enthusiasm of the tourists on Charles Bridge. I decided to visit a few more tourist bridges and, before long, I was reading books, pursuing internet research, talking with local people on the bridges, and consulting with experts to identify additional tourist bridges to visit.

Early Morning Tourists on Charles Bridge

Over the next few years, I walked across more than 600 prominent bridges in more than a dozen countries throughout North America and Europe. I hit every landmark bridge that was accessible to pedestrians, bridges in almost every major tourist center, and hundreds of historic, decorated, and recreational bridges in smaller cities, parks, and rural areas.

In the beginning, I knew there were a few bridges that, like Charles Bridge, attracted sightseers due to their prominent location in the middle of a major tourist center. However, I also soon learned that there were plenty of people visiting smaller bridges outside of tourist centers, leading me to understand that something else was going on. The more bridges I walked across, the more I realized that I was not alone. I began to notice the people sitting on the benches, people looking out at the scenery, people taking photographs, people being walked by their dogs, people reading the historical information and dedications on bronze plaques, and people enjoying the decorations and artwork.

These were not local residents using the bridge to cross the river in the course of their daily business. They were either tourists, or people using the bridge as an outdoor recreation space. Some of the bridges were so popular that I needed to wait in a line for my turn to cross, or had to fight with the selfie-takers for elbow room to look out over the view. I learned about cases where local authorities limited pedestrian access on sunny weekend days, or even closed a bridge down due to fears that people would get trampled during a stampede of bridge tourists. Even in the most obscure, less-traveled places, in the dead of winter, I could go to an out-of-the-way bridge at 6:00 a.m. in the freezing cold and find other bridgespotters already on it, waiting for the fog to lift and the sun angle to be just so, to capture that perfect picture.

Then, even more unexpected than the presence of bridge tourists, I began to observe how they interacted with each other. Total strangers chatting at an overlook high above San Francisco Bay. A couple asking me to take their picture as they attached their padlock to the railing of the Pont de l'Archevêché in Paris. A van with Minnesota license plates pulling up to the Chiselville Covered Bridge in Vermont in the rain, disgorging seven smiling senior citizens who take selfies before climbing back in the van exclaiming, "Five down! Three to go!" One group of kids using the steep slope of the approaches of the Bob Kerrey Bridge in Omaha for downhill roller blade races while another group listens to a tour guide describing how Lewis and Clark passed this point on their way to the Pacific Ocean more than 200 years ago. Thirty rowdy people on a bus in downtown Mackinaw City at 5:00 a.m. on Labor Day, yelling out of the windows at passersby to come and fill up the last few empty seats so that we could leave to go walk across the Mackinac Bridge with 33,000 other people. In the end, the project turned out not to be about bridges. It was about the people on the bridges.

There was one major frustration associated with the pursuit of the project. This was the enormous lack of available background information to support the bridge visits. We are curious about bridges, and there are hundreds of books and websites on them available. We read these because they are prominent features of our city skyline and were important contributors to the historic and economic development of our communities.

There are books that are focused on a single, iconic landmark bridge. Others discuss groups of bridges sharing common features such as type of structure, construction material, designer, or geographic location. These books all tell interesting stories about why they were built, the engineering challenges and technological innovations, the back-room political dealings, and the irresistible personalities who defied public opposition to make their vision a reality. The books also have lovely photographs showing how these beautiful works of public art enrich their local landscape or cityscape.

While this is all good, these books have one flaw in common. With only a few exceptions, they are almost completely detached from the concept of visiting, enjoying, and appreciating the bridge yourself on foot, as a tourist, for recreation, or in pursuit of a hobby. The lovely photographs turn out to be aerial photographs showing a view of the bridge that you will never get to see, unless you have access to a helicopter.

The obvious reason for this is that most bridges are not accessible to pedestrians. Most of the bridges in our communities serve only to carry high-speed traffic from Point A to Point B, and the only way we can visit the bridge is to drive over it at 60 miles an hour.

Another reason is more subtle. Because we have grown accustomed to thinking of bridges as having only one high-speed, river-crossing function, we have largely forgotten the pre-automobile, slower-speed functions of bridges. Although we drive across our local bridge daily, it generally does not occur to us that there is something interesting to see and do there because visiting on foot is just not part of our normal experience of bridges.

This is the purpose of this book – to tell the stories about the bridges visited by tourists, recreationists, and hobbyists. To explain why people visit, and to describe how to get there to see it for yourself. To encourage you to walk across at your own pace, look at the details of the construction, take in the scenery, and understand why it was constructed here and not over there. To show how the bridge influenced the location and settlement patterns of the city around it. To describe how it supports the economic, cultural, and social life of its local community. To demonstrate how the presence of the bridge influenced, and even caused, important events that have changed world history. To help you get up close and personal with some of the large and high-speed bridges you have already seen from a distance, and to tell you about many amazing slow-speed bridges hidden in smaller towns and rural areas. To suggest some things at each bridge, whether it is historical plaques, or decorations, or construction details, or bridge-focused events and festivals that you want to make sure to see.

On many of your vacations, you will be walking across these bridges anyway as you pursue other activities. On your business trips, you may find that your hotel is just across the street from an unexpected historic bridge. Having learned their stories in advance, you will hopefully be inspired to take five minutes out of your day, while on your way from one museum to another, to enhance your enjoyment of the city by learning how the bridge has influenced its historic, cultural, and economic fabric.

Many criteria can be used to assess the "tourist-ness" of a bridge. The first, and most obvious, is simple familiarity. When shown a picture of the bridge, does a large segment of the population know it by sight?

A second measure is the extent to which the community has attempted to attract and accommodate visitors. Is there a parking lot provided for people to park their cars while they visit the bridge on foot? Have they installed plaques describing the historical importance of the location? Are there benches for visitors to stop and enjoy the view? Is there a bridge-specific website providing information on the bridge and how to visit it? Is there a dedicated visitor center, complete with a snack bar and gift shop? Do the local hotels offer maps and pamphlets describing the bridges that can be visited by guests during their stay? Have you started to notice stylized images of the bridge appearing around town, being used as logos for local businesses, or emblazoned on city-owned road signs and vehicles?

A third major indicator is not as obvious but can be judged if you are willing to sit and watch the people for a while. Are there people on it, just hanging out? Not walking across quickly, with their head down, to get to the other side. Instead, are they strolling and looking at the scenery? Are they stopping to look at the decorations or the construction details? Are they reading the memorial dedications and historical plaques? Are they sitting on a bench reading a book, or chatting with friends while the kids run on ahead? Are they jogging, biking, roller blading, walking the dog, or otherwise enjoying the bridge? Are they part of a group following a tour guide, listening to stories about the bridge and the nearby sights? Are strangers trading stories with one another about other bridges they have visited?

Aside from these qualitative criteria, there is one indicator that did not exist until recently, but which is now almost a direct, quantitative measurement of the level of tourist interest in bridges. This is the phenomenon of love padlocks.

Twelve, maybe even five years ago in most places, there were no padlocks. Apparently, the love padlock fad started on the Ponte Milvio in Rome, the result of a book and a movie depicting the practice. The ceremony involves a young couple in love. They procure a padlock and write their names and the date on the lock using a marker, paint, or, in some cases, fancy engraving. A padlockable location is then selected, usually on a railing of appropriate size, but sometimes on other pieces of the structure such as a metal support for lighting fixtures or lampposts, or narrow components of sculptures. The padlock is attached. Photographs are taken to commemorate the occasion. Some attempt is made to record the exact location so that the same lock can be tracked down years later. Then, the key is thrown into the river. This ritual apparently symbolizes the unbreakable nature of the attachment between the lovers or, in some cases, is supposed to guarantee that they will return together someday to the same spot.

This would be a cute story, worthy of a single, brief mention in a book on the tourist attractions of bridges, except for one thing. It has caught on like crazy. The presence, number, and extravagance of the padlocks are now almost a direct barometer of tourist interest in particular bridges.

Paris became so overrun, on multiple bridges, that authorities have removed padlockable metal railings and replaced them with plexiglas. There are thousands of padlocks on a small pedestrian bridge underneath Charles Bridge in Prague. In Florence, there is a fine for placing padlocks on the Ponte Vecchio, but it does not appear to have stopped many people. Padlocks have broken out onto places other than bridges. In Vienna, which does not have a good padlockable bridge in its central tourist area, padlocks can be found on the grillwork of the windows near the top of the South Tower of the Stephansdom. In the United States, there are quite a few on the Brooklyn Bridge, thousands on the Roberto Clemente Bridge in Pittsburgh, a few on the Purple People Bridge in Cincinnati, and you will quite often see one or two strays in isolated locations on other bridges.

A website, waymarking.com, dedicated to tracking unique and interesting locations, has a category for love padlocks listing more than 200 padlocked sites, mostly bridges. After seven years of hiking across more than 600 bridges, it now seems unusual to cross a major bridge or visit a tourist area without finding a padlock.

Once you learn about the various attractions of bridges and observe the people, these once-subtle indicators will become increasingly obvious to you and, whether you intended it or not, you will have joined the community of people who have a common interest in visiting bridges. People who have taken time out of their day to admire the view of the Connecticut River Gorge from French King Bridge, snap pictures of the Marienbrücke from Neuschwanstein and vice-versa, buy a refrigerator magnet at the Clifton Bridge gift shop, trigger their vertigo by looking up at the Ravenel Bridge towers while gripping the railing white-knuckled, or stroll among the angels on the Ponte Sant'Angelo.

Perhaps you will watch as a solo walker at the northern end of the Golden Gate Bridge pumps his fist into the air, not expecting anyone watching, as he adds this key possession to his collection. Maybe you will see a woman on the 2,000 year-old Romerbrücke walking slower than the other pedestrians, admiring the stonework, pausing to take a picture of the stone crucifix in the middle of the bridge, and then turning to walk back into central Trier in the same direction from which she came. Or you may arrive at the DuSable Bridge in Chicago at 7:00 a.m. on a Saturday morning in July and find two or three people already out on it, taking pictures of the surrounding Art Deco architecture.

You may find yourself on a tiny, nondescript wooden bridge in the middle of the woods near Tunbridge Wells and notice that every person who crosses the bridge stops to lean over the railing on the upstream side of the bridge, drop a stick into the stream, and then run to the other side of the bridge to watch their stick emerge. Not some of the people, but *every* person. You may decide to take a walk way over the Hudson on the Walkway over the Hudson on a cold, rainy weekday in October and notice that the parking lot is not only full, but all of the cars display out-of-state license plates.

You might notice a weird, spiral-type design on the "Welcome to Madrid" sign coming into Madrid, Iowa, and then realize that the exact same design is displayed on multiple road signs, on the town's water tower, and on the banner head of the local newspaper. While watching the old MGM musical *On the Town*, you might notice that the first tourist sight that Frank Sinatra and Gene Kelly choose to visit on their 24-hour shore leave in New York is the Brooklyn Bridge. Maybe you will find yourself standing in a short line in the middle of Charles Bridge waiting for your turn to touch the bronze image of St. John of Nepomuk, not sure why, but everyone else seems to be doing it. You might stroll on the Purple People Bridge in Cincinnati and slowly become aware that, yes, there are more than a few people on the bridge who are wearing purple T-shirts.

Or you may see a single padlock attached to the railing on the Court Street Bridge in Binghamton and, understanding how it got there, you suddenly have links to people you have never met and to places you have never been.

A NOTE ON THE PEOPLE WHO VISIT BRIDGES

The word "tourist," as used throughout this book, is intended as a broad, catch-all term that encompasses all of the various reasons that people visit bridges. Many bridges attract and serve casual tourists. Some are appealing destinations because they are historic or were constructed with innovative engineering. Others are pleasantly decorated or provide scenic views. Many bridges are located in the middle of a major tourist area, and their attraction is derived from this central location.

In addition to attracting casual tourists, bridges are also visited by people for other reasons. Many are outfitted with features that support recreation for the local residents. Some are the focus of hobbyists who have specific interests that intersect, somehow, with bridges. Other bridges are used to host community or religious celebrations and commemorations. A bridge where people offered up their lives for a cause 700 years ago may be a historic tourist attraction, whereas a different bridge where people offered up their lives for a cause 55 years ago may be a shrine, especially if that cause is still being fought for today.

With all of these various reasons to visit bridges, it was tempting to title the book "*Bridgespotting: A Guide to Bridges for Tourists, Bicyclists, Hikers, Hobbyists, Celebrants, Shoppers, Worshippers, Lovers, Sports Fans, Dog Owners, Photographers, Pilgrims, and Anyone Else Who Wants to Walk Across a Bridge*," but that was clearly not feasible. Although the word "tourists" is generally used throughout the book to represent all of these various types of visitors, the casualness usually associated with that word is not intended to cheapen the experience of those who visit bridges for these other non-casual reasons.

A NOTE ON ORGANIZATION

For most individual tourist bridges, it is reasonable to organize them by theme, according to their different types of attractions, and that is how this book is generally organized. Each chapter and sub-chapter discusses a feature or characteristic that attracts tourism or recreation to a group of bridges, briefly describes a few of the smaller or less prominent examples, and then provides a more detailed description of one or two of the more prominent examples. While many bridges present more than one theme, and tough decisions needed to be made regarding the categorization of some of them, it is usually quite easy to identify the one, primary reason that people visit.

Two facets of bridge tourism require deviation from this framework. The first deviation is necessary because some bridges are so awesome, with multiple attractions, that they cannot be assigned to one category over another. These bridges are all historic, *and* decorated, *and* scenic, *and* centrally located in important tourist destinations. To properly reflect the iconic status of these bridges, it is not sufficient to discuss their size in one chapter, their engineering in another, their height in a third, and their use for biking and hiking trails in a fourth. To split the attractions of these bridges into their separate parts would be to diminish their overall attraction to tourists. Chapter 1 is set aside to discuss these iconic bridges.

The second deviation is needed because you will often find two or more interesting bridges of different types of attractions right next to each other. If you are focusing your trip on historic suspension bridges, you might prefer to march right past a modern sculptural bridge without even a glance. Or, because the other bridge is just a three minute-walk away and you have some extra time, you may want to stop for a look. The most important objective of this book is to support your own visits to these bridges, and it would be negligent to fail to point out, when discussing one interesting bridge, that you can see others just a short walk away. Therefore, after the individual tourist bridges have been discussed in Chapters 1 through 8, Chapter 9 puts some of them back into their geographic context with other nearby bridges and compiles them into bridge tours. This allows you to knock off five, ten, even 20 bridges of different types in a single, manic bridge day. Or even 100. It has been done.

A NOTE ON TIMING

With very few exceptions, the bridges discussed in the book were directly visited by the author between 2013 and 2021. Information from the site visits was supplemented later by websites, books, and interviews with knowledgeable experts, and this was all important to fill in details. But to serve as a travel guide, the site visit experiences are the key. Direct observations and information from plaques directly on the bridge are probably a more reliable source of information than websites, many of which were found to contain errors during the research for the book. More importantly, focusing the book from the perspective of the site visits provides details that are not available in other source materials, such as ways to access the bridge or small details of interest to look for.

Unfortunately, because conditions change over time, focusing the book from the perspective of the site visits also places a shelf life on the information provided here. The book can only represent the conditions that were in place at the time of the author's visit and may not be perfectly reflective of what you will see when you visit several years later. This issue is not just hypothetical. Many bridges in the book were actually visited two or more times over several years, and differences that are relevant to the tourist experience were documented.

A major example is the 1904 Pond Eddy Bridge in Pennsylvania. This bridge was visited in 2013 and, as the last revisions were being made to the book in 2021, it was learned that the bridge was demolished and replaced with a new bridge in 2018. The Waldo-Hancock Bridge in Maine has also been demolished since site visits began in early 2013. However, other important tourist or recreational bridges, such as the Pont Napoleon in Lille and the Kenneth F. Burns Bridge in Massachusetts, were newly constructed in that period. Between 2013 and 2016, the love padlock craze grew in the United States, with previously unlocked bridges such as Roberto Clemente in Pittsburgh becoming overrun. In the same time frame, it seems that a few European cities started to tire of dealing with the padlocks, and began removing and banning them. Perhaps the biggest change was in the lighting of bridges at night. In 2013, bridge lighting, if done at all, was relatively primitive. However, by 2017, cities were competing with one another to see who could present the most elaborate outdoor light displays, using their bridges as the canvas.

While these differences show the risks that come with basing the book on personal observations and visits, they also demonstrate how the use of bridges for tourism, recreation, and decoration changes over time. As you use this book to plan your visits, it is recommended that you check websites in advance to verify that what you wish to see is still there, and still accessible.

CHAPTER 1

LANDMARK BRIDGES

THE PROPER PLACE TO BEGIN is with the tourist bridges that you already know. These are the iconic, landmark bridges that are instantly recognized by millions of people. You have seen them on the covers of tourist guidebooks and travel posters, or on the screen savers of your co-workers who just returned from vacation. You have seen brief glimpses of them in movies or television shows. You may have even seen these bridges in person, from a distance, or while crossing in a car or train. However, even though you know them by sight, you may not know that these are more than just prominent landmarks to be viewed from a distance. These are visitable tourist attractions, complete with parking lots and bus stops, gift shops, museums, and pedestrian access, and crawling with tourists taking pictures any time of the day and often well into the night.

A common theme among most bridges, even those special ones discussed in this book, is that though they may be pleasant places to visit if you happen to be nearby, almost none would merit a substantial trip for the sole purpose of doing a tourist visit unless you are one of the more enthusiastic bridgespotters. The iconic bridges are exceptions. If you have any remote interest in bridges, these have to be at the top of your priority list, and visiting them can be a highlight of any trip to their city. It is well worth traveling long distances to see them, and disappointing to consider that large numbers of tourists see them only from a distance without even knowing that walking across, going inside the interior spaces, or visiting the gift shop is an option.

Many bridges are local, state, or national landmarks, with their image featured in travel advertisements, or even struck into the coinage of the country. But the number of iconic, landmark bridges that are instantly recognizable to millions of people is remarkably small—it is probably limited to fewer than ten bridges in the entire world.

GOLDEN GATE BRIDGE, SAN FRANCISCO

Possibly the most recognizable bridge in the world, the Golden Gate Bridge is the perfect example of a bridge for which the various tourist attractions are almost too numerous to mention. It is a historic bridge at a historic location, in a popular tourist city, and it has a stunningly beautiful Art Deco design. It is not only accessible to pedestrians, but has dedicated parking lots and bus stops, a gift shop and snack bar, and guided tours. It is high enough over San Francisco Bay to please any thrill-seeker, offers incredible scenery, and the sidewalk connects to regional hiking and biking trails.

The Golden Gate Bridge was built in 1937 and, until 1964 when it was surpassed by the Verrazzano Narrows Bridge, was the longest single-span suspension bridge in the world. The middle span is 4,200 feet (about 0.8 miles) long, and the entire length is about 1.7 miles. The road surface of US Highway 101 is suspended by steel cables 220 feet above the water surface. The towers supporting the cables extend about 750 feet above the water, or more than 500 feet above the road surface.

If these parameters make it sound like every feature of the bridge is on a gigantic scale, then the correct impression has been made. This bridge is such an attraction in its own right, with more than ten million annual visitors, that the Golden Gate Bridge Highway and Transportation District operates a visitor center, called the Bridge Pavilion, at the southern end of the bridge. The Bridge Pavilion provides historical displays, offers tours, operates a shop selling bridge-related souvenirs, and has a small snack bar. The district also maintains a website, www.goldengatebridge. org, which provides visitor information such as the locations of viewing areas, tour information, open hours, and ways to get to the bridge.

Walking the bridge is just one part of the experience of the Golden Gate Bridge. Simply looking at it, and admiring the beautiful Art Deco architecture of the towers, is an experience in itself. To be fully appreciated, this needs to be done at various times of day, from various angles, and in different kinds of weather. Unless you have done research in advance, you may not even know that the Golden Gate Bridge is open to pedestrians. Seeing it from a distance is probably all that most visitors experience, because the bridge is a few miles away from downtown and the major tourist areas. This distance is too far for the casual tourist to just stroll over for a closer look, and maybe to notice that there are people up there. To walk the bridge, you must make a deliberate effort to drive or take a bus to one of the available parking areas at the Bridge Pavilion or Fort Point on the south end, or the Marin Headlands Visitor Center on the north end. These are small parking areas, so the district's website strongly encourages traveling by bus instead. The website provides detailed instructions on which buses to take from various points both north and south of the bridge.

The areas on both ends of the bridge are important tourist and recreation destinations on their own. Although the bridge itself is owned by the Transportation District, the property at both ends is managed by the National Park Service as the Golden Gate National Recreation Area. Besides the bridge, the recreation area operates numerous points of interest, including Alcatraz Island in the middle of the bay, and Fort Point and the Presidio on the southern shore. On the northern shore in Marin County, the recreation area operates the Lands End and Marin Headlands Visitor Centers and the Muir Woods National Monument. However, other than Fort Point, which is located directly under the south cable anchorage, the other sites are not within easy walking distance of the Bridge Pavilion.

Before discussing the amazing views available from the bridge, it is important to also point out some views you may have been hoping to see, but which are not available. Mainly, the Pacific Ocean. The pedestrian sidewalk is on the eastern, bay side of the bridge. The view of the ocean to the west is partially obstructed by having to look past six lanes of traffic and the railings and cables on the other side.

The other views, though, are not obstructed. The hills of the Marin Headlands area are on the north end, and views of the forested hills of the Presidio dominate the south end. But the most pleasurable views are to the east, which provides a completely unobstructed view of downtown San Francisco, San Francisco Bay, its islands (Alcatraz, Angel Island, and Treasure Island), the Bay Bridge, Berkeley and Oakland on the far shore, and the Coast Range Mountains beyond. The bay is busy with boats, ranging from enormous tankers and container ships to crisscrossing ferries and pleasure boats. If you can withstand the vertigo, one of the thrills is to position yourself on the crest and watch an enormous tanker approach from the bay, and then pass directly beneath you, 200 feet below. If you watch the water carefully for a while, you may be lucky enough to see seals swimming by.

The view of downtown is fantastic. Because San Francisco is so hilly, downtown covers a hill slope directly facing the bridge. As a result, the downtown view is not just a flat view of the front row of buildings blocking everything behind. Instead, the skyscrapers cover the hill slope, each one rising higher than the one in front of it, so that the whole downtown area is displayed to viewers on the bridge. Although it is a few miles away, it is amazing how clear and close it seems.

The architecture of the bridge, including its iconic orange-red color, is well-known. The primary place to provide decorative flourishes on suspension bridges is on the towers themselves. On many suspension bridges, the towers are plain, with one or more unadorned steel crosspieces serving as support for the two sides. On the Golden Gate, there are four crosspiece supports, each sculpted with stepped insets to frame the arch, and each faced with vertical pyramidal shapes. The bottom two arches are rectangular, and the same size as each other. The top two arches are smaller, making the towers tapered, which amplifies their apparent height. The railings and lampposts are in the same style, fashioned out of orange-red steel I-beam girders.

A couple notes on photographs, which you almost certainly will be taking. The first recommendation, if the weather is fine, is to make sure to take plenty of photographs immediately. This is because, no matter how perfect the weather looks, fog can blow in unexpectedly. It is easily possible to walk out on a bright sunny day with great views and then walk back in a thick fog, shivering while listening to the foghorns. You do not want to wait and miss your chance for good pictures.

The second recommendation is to consider waiting to take your pictures until you are on the northern half of the bridge. This is because the southern half is so jam-packed with tourists and bikers that the pictures are just not pleasurable. You can get great pictures of the views to the east at any time. However, to get unobstructed pictures of the towers, you need to step into the bike lane of the sidewalk, and there is hardly a moment when a bike is not coming at you. On the southern half, any pictures you take of the bridge itself are likely to be dominated by the hordes of people around you. Once you get past the halfway point, most of the walkers have turned back, and you can get better pictures with much less trouble.

BROOKLYN BRIDGE, NEW YORK CITY

The three bridges connecting Lower Manhattan to Brooklyn across the East River were all prominent players in the setting of new records for length and the first use of new bridge technologies that occurred in the United States from the 1840s to the 1960s. These bridges are the Brooklyn, Manhattan, and Williamsburg bridges, and taken together they comprise a multi-bridge seminar in early suspension bridge technology.

The Brooklyn Bridge is the earliest of the three. It was the world's longest suspension bridge when built, holding that distinction for 20 years from 1883 to 1903. It was also the first steel cable suspension bridge in the world, and the tallest man-made structure in the Western Hemisphere when it was completed. The Brooklyn Bridge was the final bridge designed by John Roebling, who was also associated with the Waco Suspension Bridge in Texas, the Roebling Bridge in Cincinnati, and the Delaware Aqueduct in Pennsylvania, all of which can still be walked today. Two of his other bridges in Pittsburgh and one at Niagara Falls no longer exist. John Roebling's name comes up whenever early suspension bridges are mentioned.

The stories of its construction are legendary. When conducting surveys of the Brooklyn Bridge site in 1869, Roebling was injured in an accident and died three weeks later. The final design and engineering were taken over by his son, Washington Roebling. Like many of the construction workers on the Brooklyn Bridge, Washington Roebling fell victim to the bends while visiting work inside the caissons on the floor of the East River, and he remained disabled for life. After he became incapacitated, his wife, Emily Warren Roebling, continued work on the project, and she is honored with a plaque on the bridge today. Construction took 14 years, and the bridge opened to the public in 1883.

The suspension technique used on the Brooklyn Bridge is extremely complex. As readily recognizable as the bridge is in photographs and films, these images are confusing because they do not show the simple, clean arc and vertical cable structure we are accustomed to seeing on modern suspension bridges. Instead, the cables form an apparently random net, with individual cables crossing each other at wild angles. Once you are on the bridge, armed with your knowledge of suspension and cable-stay bridge technologies, it all becomes clear. This is because the structure of the Brooklyn Bridge is a hybrid between a classical suspension bridge, which has vertical support cables, and a fan-shaped cable-stayed bridge, which has angled cables. In this manner, the deck is attached to the towers by two separate, independent cable systems.

The visual effect that this creates is striking. First, there is a vertical set of cables, each cable parallel to the next. Superimposed on this is a diagonal set of cables, but with each cable crossing the vertical set at a different angle. If the Brooklyn Bridge had a single deck, this complex pattern, when viewed from the side, would be superimposed over a second set of cables—there would be one set on each side of the deck. However, the bridge does not have a single deck. It has two decks, running side-by-side, each supported by two sets of cables. Therefore, the view from the side is actually looking through four sets of vertical cables and four sets of fan-shaped diagonal cables. The visual image, through eight sets of cables at weird angles, is dizzying. It all makes sense once you can study the connections at the top of the towers from up close.

The Brooklyn Bridge is one of the few bridges where the majority of pedestrians are tourists, visiting specifically to walk across the famous bridge. The western entrance to the pedestrian and bike path is located at the southeast corner of City Hall, at the corner of Centre Street and Chambers Street. There is a small plaza located just across the street from the entrance, and it serves as a gathering place for tour groups to listen to historical stories about the Roeblings before they embark across the bridge. The plaza can be accessed by the Brooklyn Bridge-City Hall station on the 4-5-6-J-M-Z subway lines.

Tourists Approaching Brooklyn Bridge

Very unusual among bridges, the pedestrian sidewalk and bike path is located in the middle of the bridge, and not on its edges. It is also elevated above the traffic lanes. At each tower, the sidewalk splits and passes through the arch-shaped openings on either side of the central part of the tower. The sidewalk widens out into a plaza with historical and informational plaques, hawkers selling bottled water and souvenirs, and dozens of tourists taking pictures. The position of the sidewalk in the middle of the bridge makes it difficult to get unobstructed views or photographs because, on either side, you are looking at this view through four sets of oddly-angled suspension cables.

Although the views are obstructed, there are numerous prominent landmarks visible from the bridge. From various points on the bridge there are expansive views of Lower Manhattan, dominated by the new Freedom Tower. Governor's Island and the Statue of Liberty are visible in the harbor south of the bridge, with views of the Verrazzano Narrows Bridge in the distance. Looking north along Manhattan Island, there are views of the Empire State Building and Chrysler Building. Crossing the river about a quarter-mile to the north is the lovely Manhattan Bridge. Directly to the east is the Brooklyn skyline, with Brooklyn Bridge Park lining the river.

Even with the obstructed views, the Brooklyn Bridge is an event to walk across. Just being in the middle of this iconic structure, along with hundreds of other people enjoying it for the same reason, makes it worth the trip.

TOWER BRIDGE, LONDON

The two massive, gothic-looking towers of Tower Bridge, which spans the Thames on the east end of London, are one of the most iconic visual landmarks of this city full of iconic landmarks. The towers are so large and impressive that, if they were situated in the middle of the city and not associated with any bridge, would still be a major tourist attraction just for being large and interesting towers.

The name of Tower Bridge is a little enigmatic, at least for those who have not visited. First, the phrase "London Bridge" is more widely known than "Tower Bridge," so people who have not visited have been known to jump to the conclusion that this is London Bridge. This is incorrect, because London Bridge is the low-profile, nondescript bridge just to the west.

The second misconception is that the bridge's name derives from its structure, of which the two 200 foot-high towers are the prominent visual feature. This is also incorrect. In fact, the name derives from the location of the bridge at the Tower of London, with the northern landing of the bridge literally a few feet away from the eleventh century walls of the famous castle.

Built in the early 1890s, the Tower Bridge structure is complex, being a composite of several types of construction. The central span is a double-bascule drawbridge supported between the two massive central towers. The lower part of the towers house the counterweights needed to raise the spans, and the upper part of the towers serves as the anchor point for girders that form the adjacent suspension-supported spans that flank the drawbridge. The two towers are connected to each other at their tops by enclosed walkways.

A visually striking feature of the two suspension segments is that the suspension is asymmetrical. We are accustomed to seeing suspension bridges being completely symmetrical, with the main cable being anchored at the same height on each end and the low point of the drooping cable being exactly halfway between the two anchors. On Tower Bridge, the two suspension segments are anchored at a high elevation on the two main towers and then at a much lower elevation on the two smaller towers situated near the banks of the river. This presents a draped appearance, framing the central towers the same way the pulled-back curtain frames the main stage in a theater.

This entire complex structure is elaborately decorated. The two large central towers and two small flanking towers are faced with two different types of stone for decorative effect. The walls of the towers are constructed of rough-faced granite, while the carved arches and crenulations are made of a smooth-faced limestone. Both stones are a tan-gray color that was obviously chosen to blend in with the walls of the Tower, more than 800 years older. The stonework has been used to create a riot of turrets, crenulations, spires, gargoyles, and every other possible castle-like feature on the tops of the towers. In fact, the White Tower at the base of the bridge, which was an actual working castle in its day, pales in comparison to the bridge in terms of our modern conception of what a castle should look like.

To continue with the description, remove thoughts of castles and medieval knights from your mind and bring your attention to the Industrial Age. This is because the remainder of the bridge, outside of the towers, does not adhere to the stone-gothic theme. Instead, the bridge decks, suspension infrastructure, and ornate metal parapets are all of a hand-riveted steel-girder appearance. To ensure that these are not confused with the gothic-themed towers, the steel parts of the bridge have all been clothed in bright white and pale blue paint, with details highlighted in red and black. This scheme is also, on its own, attractive.

One interesting feature of Tower Bridge is not something it has, but something it lacks. The metal railing on the drawbridge portion is faced with a steel mesh about the perfect size for the attachment of love padlocks. During a visit in 2013 there were a few padlocks, maybe 15, widely spaced. However, after being exposed to tens of thousands of padlocks on other prominent bridges in Europe, it seems incomprehensible that Tower Bridge, as centrally located and iconic as it is, is not overloaded with padlocks. There is space for thousands of them. Perhaps it is illegal in London, or padlocks are removed periodically.

Like the Golden Gate, Tower Bridge is a tourist attraction that draws thousands of visitors at any given time. The area can be accessed from the Tower Hill Underground Station, and a visit to the bridge should be combined with a visit to the Tower. You can easily spend all day at the Tower, famous for being the location of the British Crown Jewels. Readers with an interest already know snippets of the 900-year history of the Tower, and numerous books provide the full details. A few highlights include the White Tower constructed by William the Conqueror, the two princes murdered within its walls, the beheading of Anne Boleyn, and the imprisonment of Rudolph Hess during World War II.

Just as important as walking across the bridge is visiting the publicly accessible areas within the towers and the arches. A small tourist pavilion is located inside the base of the northern tower, off the western sidewalk, which would be the first location approached when walking onto the bridge from the Tower of London. A visitor's desk there sells tickets for access to the towers and the Engine Rooms. Note that the video screen behind the ticket desk displays the times of upcoming openings of the drawbridge, which are known well in advance. You have come all this way to see the bridge, so you might as well as see it in action.

From the ticket desk, a lift carries you to the top of the tower, releasing you into a large, dimly lit space crisscrossed with riveted steel girders. A small theater set-up shows a short presentation depicting how the bridge design was selected, with actors portraying the architects trying to convince another actor portraying Queen Victoria of the superiority of their proposed design.

Following the film, the tour leads out onto the walkway, suspended about 100 feet above the bridge deck. The walkway is enclosed in glass, protecting you from the wind and cold. The first walkway you enter is that on the eastern, downstream side of the bridge. As Tower Bridge is located at the eastern end of the historic and touristic section of London, no prominent landmarks are visible from the first walkway. The view is impressive, though, showing the London Docks, Canary Wharf, and the more recent industrial and commercial developments of London. The walkway is also lined with displays showing photographs and discussing features of many of the prominent bridges of the world.

At the end of the walkway is the entrance to the south tower, which has a similar-sized, dimly lit space. In this tower, a film describing the construction of the bridge is shown. From this room, there is an entrance to the western walkway, which faces all of the famous historic sights and landmarks of London. On the right is the Tower, with the new office towers of the City behind. Prominent among these is the famous Gherkin Building, named for its odd shape and blue-green color. Further west along the north shore, Sir Christopher Wren's Monument and St. Paul's Cathedral are prominent. Numerous bridges can be seen on the Thames in the upstream direction, including London Bridge, Southwark Bridge, the Millennium Footbridge, and Blackfriars Railway Bridge. The prominent landmark on the Southwark bank, to the left, is the gigantic new glass building called "The Shard," constructed in 2013, and now the tallest building in Europe. Once viewing is complete, your tour continues down the staircase of the south tower, leading back out to the bridge sidewalk.

As if Tower Bridge needed more attractions, it also has a museum that displays the original equipment used to operate the movable span. The Engine Rooms are located within the structure of the stone arch on the south bank, just off the Southwark-side promenade at the end of the bridge. The Engine Rooms are probably seen only by a small fraction of the people who visit the bridge, but they are a highlight.

All moveable bridges must solve the problem of how to supply the motive power to move enormous pieces of the bridge to open and close the span. Starting in the twentieth century and up to today, this has been done with electric motors, which was not an option in 1894. At that time, steam power was possible, but it required enormous boilers and engines. To open a span in the middle of the river, the boilers and engines would also have to be in the middle of the river.

The solution for Tower Bridge was elegant, being one of the first uses of hydraulic power, which can be transmitted over large distances through pipes and hoses. The boilers and engines were sited on the south bank, where they were fed by coal from barges. The engines then converted the steam energy into a hydraulic system, which was transmitted out to the central part of the bridge where it was used to drive the bascule. Although the hydraulic system is no longer used, all of the components are still there, brightly painted. The ticket purchased to enter the towers on Tower Bridge includes admission to the Engine Rooms.

PONTE VECCHIO, FLORENCE

Ponte Vecchio, which spans the Arno River in the center of Florence, Italy, is one of the most iconic, recognizable bridges in the world. The bridge structure itself is a fairly boring-looking gray stone bridge, not large, but stacked with brightly-colored yellow and red houses clinging, overhanging, and generally looking like they are about to fall off into the river.

The locations of the Ponte Vecchio and the city of Florence were influenced by the size of the Arno River. The bridge and city were sited at the narrowest point on the river, where it was easiest to build a bridge. The narrowest part of a river is advantageous because it reduces the length of the bridge that has to be built. However, the narrowest stretches of rivers are also the location of the fastest flowing water, an effect that is intensified during floods. Therefore, while building bridges in these locations is relatively easy, the bridges also tend to be frequently wiped out. It is thought that the Romans had built a bridge here, and the first mention of a bridge at this location in historical records dates back to 996. Bridges constructed at this location were destroyed by floods in 1117 and 1333. The current bridge, constructed in 1345, has survived additional floods and wars for more than 650 years.

The bridge itself is nondescript. It consists of three arches resting on two piers in the middle of the river, all made out of local stone. The stone surface is flat, undecorated, and not particularly attractive. Actually, it looks dirty and old. The bridge is not large, being only about 300 feet long and 15 feet above river level. The bridge structure itself is not what catches your eye when viewing it from a distance, and is not visible at all to you when you are standing on it.

Instead, the bonus feature of this bridge is the shops and apartments, in narrow two- and three-story structures that line both sides of the bridge and overhang the sides. The buildings originally housed butcher shops. Then, in 1593, the ruling Medici, Ferdinand, decided that the practice of throwing wastes from the butcher operations over the edge into the river was unappealing, and he decreed that the butcher shops be replaced by goldsmiths.

More than 500 years later, almost all of the shops are still occupied by high-end jewelry stores that do a brisk business year-round. The shops are on the first floors of the buildings, and small apartments with tiny balconies are found on the second and third floors. The structure of the buildings, being directly connected to the other buildings on the river banks, blends in so well with the surrounding neighborhoods that it is easy to cross onto the bridge and walk out to the middle of it without actually realizing that you are on a bridge, especially at night.

In the middle of the bridge, the shops make way for overlooks on both sides. This central plaza is the only place where you can get to the sides of the bridge to view the river and the buildings along the riverbank. Because the buildings come right down to river's edge, the cityscape and surrounding hills are not visible, and the view is limited to the narrow, flat river and the riverfronts of the buildings. Other bridges on the Arno are visible on both sides, but none is as visually striking as the shops on the Ponte Vecchio.

If the shops sound like an interesting use of the deck of a bridge, they are just the beginning. The bridge connects the well-known medieval town area of Florence, the site of the Duomo, with the equally interesting Oltrarno neighborhood on the south side of the river. The Oltrarno is the site of the Palazzo Pitti, the renaissance home of the ruling Medici family. By 1565, the Medici had apparently grown tired of mingling with the little people when taking the carriage ride across the Ponte Vecchio from the Palazzo Pitti on the south bank to their offices at the Palazzo Vecchio on the north bank. They ordered the construction of the Vasari Corridor, a private, enclosed passageway designed by Giorgio Vasari.

Construction of the corridor was complicated by the fact that there was already a bustling city sitting in between the two destinations, not to mention a river. A normal solution, especially for an all-powerful ruling family, would have been to knock down a few buildings and then construct a covered corridor at ground level. This is not what they did. Instead, they simply strung the corridor over the tops of the existing buildings, including the shops on the Ponte Vecchio. In areas where there were no buildings, such as the central plaza on the bridge and along the north bank of the Arno, the corridor is held up on arcades, maintaining its elevation above the streets. The corridor is not open to the public, which is unfortunate because its novel appearance beckons those tourists who feel the need to peek inside every unusual nook and cranny.

Other than the architecture itself, the only other artistic decoration on the bridge is a bust of Benvenuto Cellini, the Renaissance Florentine goldsmith, artist, and otherwise colorful character celebrated in the Berlioz opera. The bust is located on the central plaza on the eastern, downstream side of the bridge. The grate surrounding the Cellini bust is a popular place to leave love padlocks, but they can also be found on other metal gratings throughout the bridge. While this practice is encouraged by shopkeepers selling padlocks, it is discouraged by the municipal government to the extent that there is a fine for leaving padlocks. This has not stopped many people, as can be seen by the hundreds of locks on the bridge at any given time. The city frequently removes the locks, only to make way for more.

The combination of the dull, dirty gray bridge, the brightly colored two- and three-story shops, and then the smooth, clean beige walls of the Vasari Corridor gives the bridge the appearance of having three completely different generations and styles of construction plopped one on top of another. In any newer building, this haphazard mix of styles, materials, and colors in a single structure would immediately cause a community outcry objecting to the resulting visual discordance. However, in an older structure, and one in which the three separate styles of structures were constructed hundreds of years apart, the effect is utterly charming. The novelty of the Ponte Vecchio was apparently so impressive to the Germans during World War II that it was the only bridge over the Arno, and one of the few in Italy, that was not destroyed during their retreat in the face of the advance of American troops. Instead of demolishing the bridge, the Germans destroyed all of the buildings at either end of the bridge, effectively blocking the streets approaching the bridge.

The bridge's appeal is enhanced by its central location. The Ponte Vecchio is steps away from many of the most important historic, cultural, and artistic treasures of the world. Any college course in the history of Western art usually begins in Florence in the twelfth and thirteenth centuries, and stays there through the sixteenth century. These works were executed largely by artists born or trained in Florence, completed in Florence and, in many cases, are still displayed in their original intended location within a short walking distance of the Ponte Vecchio. Although the artistic and cultural tourist sights are mostly located on the north bank of the river, there are more than enough treasures just off the southern end of Ponte Vecchio to place the bridge squarely in the middle of the action. This means you will likely cross the bridge multiple times as you go from one amazing church, palace, or museum to another.

CHARLES BRIDGE, PRAGUE

This book discusses bridges that are beautiful in their architecture, and some that are beautiful in their decoration. It discusses historic bridges that are not just old, but that have served to turn historical events. It discusses bridges that provide stunning views of their river, city, or surrounding landscape. And it discusses bridges located within a few minutes' walk from must-see historic and cultural sights.

Charles Bridge has all of these, to an enormous degree. Admittedly, there are older bridges around. Charles Bridge is not even the oldest stone bridge in Czechia (formerly the Czech Republic). However, the areas in which Charles Bridge excels, and the things that make it such a special place, include the decoration, its place in history and mythology, the views from the bridge, and the proximity of the bridge to other major tourist attractions. It is not simply beautifully decorated, but it is probably the most elaborately decorated of all bridges. It is not simply old, but it is as historically interesting as any bridge. It does not simply provide a nice view of the surrounding area, but it provides some of the best views of any bridge, except maybe the Golden Gate. It is not simply close to amazing cultural and historic sights, but the number and interest of them far exceed those of any of the other bridge.

Previous wooden bridges had been located at this site on the Vltava River since about the tenth century. A stone bridge, called the Judith Bridge, was built by 1170, but destroyed by flooding in 1342. Shortly thereafter, Charles IV became the King of Bohemia and Holy Roman Emperor and made Prague the capital of the empire. He then went on a massive building spree during which much of modern-day Prague, including Charles Bridge, was constructed. The bridge was designed by Petr Parler, the most prominent architect in Prague at that time. Parler designed Charles Bridge, St. Vitus Cathedral, the Prague New Town area, and parts of the Royal Palace within Prague Castle.

The bridge itself was completed by the 1390s. It is constructed of 16 sandstone arches, and about 1,500 feet long and 30 feet wide. Parts of the bridge have been destroyed by floods and rebuilt over the years. The bridge surface is composed of cobblestone, and the sides are flanked by sandstone parapets. The roadway, now a pedestrian promenade, sits about 40 feet above the surface of the Vltava River. Vehicle traffic was stopped in the 1960s, leaving a pedestrian-only link between Prague's Old Town to the east and the Mala Strana neighborhood and Prague Castle to the west.

The first feature that makes Charles Bridge different and special is its statues. Starting in the late seventeenth century, the parapets lining both sides of the bridge were decorated with statues depicting religious and historical figures. The pedestals on which they sit are about six feet high above the road surface, and each statue is about eight to ten feet high, so the statues seem enormous, towering over the crowds of tourists. Most statues represent a single figure, usually a saint, but several depict groups.

Most are full figures carved from sandstone, but there are a few bronze figures.

The statues are not simply art, but represent saints and other important persons and events in Bohemian history. These include Saints Cyril and Methodius, who Christianized the Slavs; Saint John of Nepomuk, who was martyred by being thrown off the bridge in 1393; and Saints Ludmila, Vitus, and Wenceslas, all significant in the history and mythology of the founding of Prague and Bohemia. Most of the statues are actually replacements of the originals, which have been moved for protection from the elements and are now displayed in various indoor locations in the city. While this sounds like a disappointment, it really is not. The overall effect of the replacement statues while strolling the bridge is still enormously powerful, and you can see the originals if that is important to you.

The oldest statue on the bridge is that of Saint John of Nepomuk, from 1683. Made of bronze, the saint's head is encircled by a halo of five stars, which were miraculously seen in the Vltava when his body was fished out of the water. The location from which he was thrown is also memorialized with a bronze cross placed among the cobblestones on the road surface. There are actually three depictions of Saint John of Nepomuk on the bridge, with the statue being the largest. At the base of the statue are two bronze plaques, and in the one on the right, the actual act is shown, with St. John flailing his arms as he is thrown over the edge. This view includes a detailed landscape showing Prague Castle in the distance.

Separately, there is another bronze plaque showing Saint John floating in the river in front of the bridge, his head surrounded by the five stars. A legend has it that touching Saint John will bring good luck or grant wishes. However, it is not clear which of the two plaques performs this service, so both have been touched thousands of times, rubbing the patina on the bronze to a shiny gold. Through its association with Saint John of Nepomuk, Charles Bridge has also been featured in artworks throughout Europe that depict his martyrdom. An excellent example is in the Peterskirche in Vienna, where Saint John is shown being thrown off the bridge, through which pass the flowing waters of the Vltava.

Numerous resources, including online websites and books that can be purchased throughout the city, provide detailed descriptions and histories of the statues. This is certainly one way to enjoy the statues, by learning about the sculptors, the iconography, and the donors. But they also can be enjoyed by just strolling, and seeing what catches your eye. It is guaranteed to be something different every time you cross.

There is additional impressive decoration of Charles Bridge on the towers placed at either end. On the western bank, two towers flank a pointed arch, through which the roadway passes. This gate served to guard the entrance to Mala Strana and the route to Prague Castle. The smaller of the towers remains from the Judith Bridge, while the larger tower and arch were connected to it during the construction of the current bridge. The towers are made of the same sandstone as the bridge and are topped with decorative turrets.

The tower on the eastern bank, guarding the entrance to the Old Town, is much larger and more ornate. It is about 50 feet high, with statues decorating the landward side. This tower is accessible to visitors, serving as a museum of the bridge's history. It is also worth seeing because of the amazing ornamental ceiling decorations in some of its rooms. More importantly, you can climb to the top and enjoy an incredible view of the city, Castle, and bridge from the balcony.

The martyrdom of Saint John of Nepomuk is only one of the events of historical and mythological importance to the Czech people to have occurred on the bridge. The bridge also featured prominently in the Protestant revolts against the Catholic Hapsburg monarchy in the 1620s. Following the Battle of White Mountain in which the revolt was crushed, 27 Protestant councilors were executed on Old Town Square a short distance from the bridge. The heads of the councilors were then displayed on the bridge to serve as a warning to other would-be rebels. The bridge was also a central focus of the Swedish occupation of Prague in 1648, at the end of the Thirty Years' War. The bridge was the site of heavy fighting as the Swedes tried to enter the Old Town. As a result, the statues and other decorations on the bridge-side of the tower were removed and carried away, leaving this side of the tower bare-looking even today.

The bridge is not only important in Prague's past, but is also prophesied to play a role in Prague's future. A prominent figure in Prague's mythology is St. Vaclav, a Duke of Bohemia in the tenth century. Vaclav was murdered in the mid-930s, and he was immediately celebrated as a martyr and saint. He became a national hero, and is memorialized in statues and legends throughout Bohemia. One legend has it that the statue of St. Va-clav, located at the southern end of Wenceslas Square near the National Museum, will come to life at the time of greatest need for the Czech peo-ple. He will cross Charles Bridge and his horse will stumble over a stone, revealing a legendary sword that will be used to kill the enemies of the Czech people, resulting in peace and prosperity.

The views available from Charles Bridge are among the best of any bridge in the world. Prague is not within a region of high mountains, but it is hilly, and much of the iconic architecture of the city can be seen from the bridge. The least impressive view from the bridge is probably to the east, toward the Old Town, and even that is stunning. The view to the east includes the tower at the entrance to the Old Town, as well as spires of the Church of the Holy Savior, Old Town Hall, the Tyn Church, and the other buildings of the Old Town, most of which date to the tenth and eleventh centuries.

To the south, the view looks upriver on the Vltava, which at this loca-tion is a flat, shallow river approximately 1,000 feet wide. The east bank is lined with 150 year-old apartment houses facing the river, leading south to a hill that is the location of the Vyšehrad fortress. On the west bank, the buildings of Kampa Island, a part of the Mala Strana neighborhood, come down to the edge of the river. Behind them, further to the west, is pictur-esque Petrin Hill, topped by the Petrin Observation Tower.

The most impressive view is to the northwest, toward the Castle and, within the Castle walls, St. Vitus Cathedral. Prague Castle is the largest castle complex in the world and, because it is located on top of a substan-tial hill, it is prominently visible from many parts of Prague, including Charles Bridge. One of the greatest pleasures of Prague is visiting Charles Bridge near sundown and watching the lights of the Castle take effect as the city around it darkens.

Maybe the most appealing feature of Charles Bridge is how integral it is to a visit to Prague. Most bridges will be a one-time destination, and there is only one chance to get it right. You will have a bridge on your tourist to-do list, and you will go out of your way to see it—but only once.

If it is raining or foggy, you are out of luck. Even if the weather cooperates and everything works perfectly, you will still only get a portion of the experiences available on that bridge. If you go during the daytime to see a great view of the mountains, you will miss the sunset, or the beauty of the bridge lit up at night. The one-time bridges are largely hit or miss.

Because it is so central to the city, Charles Bridge is not hit or miss. It is a hit every time. The Prague sights are located in a compact area, and the historic core of the city is balanced, being evenly distributed on both sides of the Vltava. You are likely to be within a short walk of the bridge at all times during your visit. In a single day, you will probably walk across in the morning to visit the Castle or art museums, back in the afternoon to have a drink on Old Town Square, again in the evening for dinner in Mala Strana, and then at night to see the Castle all lit up. The result is that Charles Bridge is not just another tourist sight to be visited as much as it is the central focus of a visit in a way that applies to no other bridge in any other city.

Early in the morning, you can have the bridge almost to yourself, watching vendors set up their wares in preparation for the day. Sunset and nighttime are also relatively uncrowded. These may be the best times to watch the river, enjoy the view of the city, and observe the statues at a leisurely pace. Mid-morning and through the mid-afternoon, though, are crazy. It is almost a carnival atmosphere, with the bridge packed shoulder-to-shoulder, from end to end, with literally thousands of people strolling at one time. If the bridge could only be crossed once, and it had to be crossed through these crowds, the effect would likely be negative. It becomes difficult to enjoy the statues and the views, being hemmed in and jostled the entire time. However, because you will have plenty of other opportunities to cross when it is much less crowded, the mid-afternoon crush is just a different experience to be enjoyed, for the people-watching. You can join in, or at least watch, the throngs in strolling the bridge, taking pictures, inspecting the statues, lining up to touch St. John of Nepomuk, shopping for souvenirs, or enjoying incredibly talented street performers.

With all of these tourists and a prominent bridge you could guess, correctly, that Prague is going to have some love padlocks. There are a large number of them on the railing at the square at the eastern entrance to the bridge, near the statue of Charles IV. In 2013 there were a quite a few pad-locks on Charles Bridge itself, connected to the grillwork on the bronze plaque of St. John of Nepomuk floating in the river, but these had been removed by 2017. The rest of the structure of Charles Bridge is not pad-lockable, because it is all stonework. Also, for a reason that is not clear, there are dozens of padlocks on the Vyšehrad Bridge, an unappealing rail-road bridge a couple miles upstream. You could visit these other sights and think, yes, padlocks have come to Prague, but they are under control.

This is not correct. They are not under control. You just need to know where to look for them. That is on two tiny pedestrian bridges connecting Kampa Island to Mala Strana, one located almost directly underneath one of the arches of Charles Bridge. Near the western end of Charles Bridge, about 80 percent of the way across, the bridge crosses Kampa Island. The view of the narrow channel separating Kampa Island from the bank on the south side of the bridge includes a picturesque mill wheel, so most of the tourists on the bridge are focused on this southern side. On the northern side, if you stand right at the wall and lean over to look directly straight down, you will find this tiny bridge over the narrow channel, weighed down with hundreds, maybe thousands of love padlocks. You can visit it by taking stairs down to the island, and then doubling back under the arch of Charles Bridge. Alternatively, you can exit off the western end of the bridge into Mala Strana, then turn right and follow the winding city streets back toward the river. You will find the padlocks on the ornate metal railing, in the shadow of the larger bridge. At any time of the day, you will find tour groups being led here to see them.

CHAPTER 2
HISTORIC BRIDGES

AN ATTRACTION COMMON AMONG MANY tourist sights is their appeal to visitors with an interest in history, and old bridges are no exception. If a bridge ever merits a mention in the tourist guidebook for the city you are visiting, it is probably because it is located in the center of the town near the other historic attractions. Whether it is to admire old architectural and decorative styles, indulge an interest in the development of engineering and technology, feel the residual force of historic events, or simply marvel at something that has somehow survived intact for centuries, old bridges attract tourists in much the same way as historic churches, castles, museums, and palaces.

Visiting an old bridge is a way to study the entire history of the area. It explains why the location was originally settled, and then expanded into a community. It shows where the early transportation routes were. It provides hints regarding the configuration of rivers, creeks, and harbors in the area before these were reengineered with docks, dams, weirs, locks, canals, and levees. It tells you what the early industries were, and the availability of building materials in the local area. Newer, larger bridges now bypass the area, but these relics are left for us to investigate on foot along with the surrounding historic streets, churches, and shops.

An important issue to consider when pondering the history of a bridge is that they tend to be more fragile than other types of historic structures over long periods, so their odds of survival are much lower. A tour of historic bridges is partly a function of where they were built, but it is also just as much a reflection of places where bridges were not destroyed.

By definition, a bridge is intended to cross a wide amount of empty space while, at the same time, minimizing its contact with the ground. Bridges are also directly exposed to the forces of flowing water, ice, and wind, and have their foundations constructed in water-logged sediments. As a result, bridges are inherently less stable than other structures, and therefore more prone to collapse.

Bridges may sink into the mud, which doomed London Bridge in the 1960s. Their decks can be swept away if floodwaters rise high enough, as happened at multiple bridge locations along the Delaware River in 1841, 1903, and 1955. Entire sections of a bridge can be picked up like toys and carried downstream by ice floes, as happened at Walnut Street Bridge in Harrisburg in 1996. Finally, bridges are uniquely exposed to high winds, an effect that famously destroyed Galloping Gertie, also known as the Tacoma Narrows Bridge, just a few months after it opened in 1940.

Castles, cathedrals, houses, and any other structures can be made more stable simply by making the walls wider to increase the amount of contact between the structure and the earth, and by constructing them on dry bedrock. Castles and cathedrals are a pile of rocks sitting on the ground, while a bridge that has stood for centuries defies gravity.

Another factor contributing to the ephemeral nature of bridges is that transportation technology changes. Originally designed for carts and horses, the bridges then needed to support carriages, then automobiles, then trucks, then bigger and heavier trucks, and often light-rail trains and trams. In most cases, when a bridge becomes obsolete and a new, larger bridge needs to be built, the old bridge is demolished to make way for the new. There was a reason that the old bridge was built at that location—the crossing width was narrow, or the subsurface made for a solid foundation. The reasons that this location was good for the construction of the old bridge are the same reasons that it is still good for the new one, so the old bridge has to go.

The same concept of changing transportation technology applies to the boat traffic passing under the bridge. Old stone arch bridges were constructed with arch openings wide and high enough to allow barges and boats to pass beneath the bridge. However, bridges like the thirteenth century St. Servaasbrug in Maastricht and nineteenth century Stone Arch in Minneapolis are a hindrance to the larger commercial ships and barges in the twentieth and twenty-first centuries. In these cases, a portion of the original bridge was demolished and replaced with an unattractive modern section, leaving only a fragment of the original bridge looking small and incongruous in comparison.

A third reason for the scarcity of historic bridges is that bridges are deliberately destroyed during periods of war, to limit the mobility of enemies and/or to disrupt the commercial activities that support their economies. This is a major factor governing the distribution of historic bridges in Europe. In general, the United Kingdom and Ireland retain their historic bridges because there have been no major land battles there since the advent of mechanized warfare. Take an after-dinner walk along the tiny River Avon in Salisbury, go around the corner, and the bridge carrying Crane Street looks sort of old. There are no historical exhibits or date plaques, but look it up on the internet and, sure enough, it is old—more than 500 years old.

On the other hand, Germany, Italy, France, Hungary, and other countries that were the center of massive troop movements and tank battles in the twentieth century generally have few remaining historic bridges. Those that have survived, including Charles Bridge in Prague, Ponte Vecchio in Florence, and even the bridges of Paris, remain either because a narrow sliver of German-occupied land still separated the American and Russian armies at the time of the German surrender in World War II, or because an individual deliberately disobeyed an order to destroy a bridge.

As with any hobbyist, bridge enthusiasts are known to specialize. Instead of generally visiting random bridges of any type, they commonly focus their visits and photographs within limited subsets of the bridge world. While most casual tourists are probably visiting the large suspension bridges or the historic bridges in tourist centers, the specialists may be out collecting the different ways in which wooden beams are arranged to construct covered bridges. Or they may be studying the methods used to raise decks on movable bridges, finding all of the bridges remaining from a single iron bridge company from the 1880s, or cataloguing the different configurations of iron and steel bars that have been used to construct through-truss bridges. These specializations can often result in a tiny, apparently nondescript bridge, sitting out in the middle of nowhere, being recognized by the placement of numerous historical markers. These bridges may not be crawling with tourists all day like the Golden Gate, but you should not be surprised when you see people showing up to walk across, read the plaques, and take pictures.

STONE ARCH BRIDGES

The earliest bridges would have consisted of just a log, or a few big rocks, thrown into the creek to allow people to cross without getting their feet wet. However, these first "bridges" would have had limitations. One inconvenient characteristic of water, which arises whenever trying to engineer mechanisms to work with it, is that it always keeps flowing. It never stops. If obstructions, such as logs or rocks, are placed in the way of moving water, then the water from upstream will keep flowing, the water level will continue rising until it reaches the elevation of the blockage, and then the water will flow over or around the obstruction. Therefore, installing a solid structure made of logs or rocks does not solve the wet feet problem.

The flow of water over the top of the structure can be avoided by leaving empty spaces between the logs or rocks, allowing water to flow between them. This leaves the top of the structure dry, but now requires bridge-users to step across the empty spaces, from rock to rock. This may be fine and easy for people out for a stroll. However, if the people are carrying heavy objects, such as attempting to deliver products from their farm to a market, then the footing gets tricky. Even worse, this system will not work if they are trying to drive livestock across the stream. It also does not work for wheeled carts, which need a smooth surface to drive across.

For all of these reasons, the bridge needs to have a smooth, dry upper surface, known as the deck, supported by piers separated widely enough to allow water to keep flowing smoothly underneath the deck. The earliest form of an attempt to engineer a bridge in this manner is what is known as a "clapper bridge." Clapper bridges are stone structures in which the deck is constructed of thin layers of flat stone, similar to flagstones used to construct sidewalks or patios. The supports for the flat stones may be a series of individual stones set on their edges across the stream and embedded into the mud, or they may be piles of stones to form a pier. The primary characteristic of a clapper or stone slab bridge is that the walkway is composed only of stones laid flat, end to end, and resting on the upright stones or piers. It sounds and is primitive, but it was effective. Numerous medieval clapper bridges are still in place in England, and they attract tourists. One of the largest and most famous is the Tarr Steps near Dulverton in Exmoor National Park.

In a clapper bridge, the strength needed to support the bridge deck and the persons crossing it is contained within the structural integrity of the individual stones. However, the wider a stone is, the less structural integrity it has for holding weight. As a result, clapper bridges required very closely spaced piers.

The next generation of stone bridges, and the most common type, involved the stacking of stones into arches. In stone arch bridges, the structural integrity is derived from stones being held in place by the weight of the stones above, friction between the rough stone surfaces, and, in some cases, mortar or cement between the stones. Stone arch bridges may be as small and simple as a single arch a few feet long, capable of carrying only a single pedestrian, or as large and complex as the 1908 Bulkeley Bridge, which is still carrying cars and trucks on Interstate 84 across the Connecticut River in downtown Hartford today. There are hundreds of examples, some thousands of years old.

One early type of stone arch bridge is the packhorse bridge. Packhorse bridges are an excellent example of a subset of tourist bridges that attract hobbyists who specialize in visiting a very limited type of bridge. There are entire websites dedicated to packhorse bridges, and even a book, *A Guide to the Packhorse Bridges of England*, by Ernest Hinchliffe, published in 1994. Packhorse bridges were built from Roman times up through about 1800, and Mr. Hinchliffe's book documents more than 100 of them still existing in Britain. These bridges carried small-scale overland trade routes, and were used by individual horses carrying bags of goods across their backs.

Originally, these bridges would have been built in and near towns as well as in remote locations. Once packhorses were replaced in favor of carts and, later, railroads and trucks, the bridges ceased being used for commercial transport. Those in and near settlements quickly become obstacles to cart and truck transport, and were replaced with wider bridges. However, the little-used packhorse bridges in rural areas could be abandoned in place, because there was plenty of space to construct a wider bridge without needing to demolish the existing bridge. Therefore, the remaining packhorse bridges are generally found in remote, hard-to-reach locations. The largest, and one of the best-preserved, is Essex Bridge in Staffordshire, north of Birmingham. Based on the work of Hinchliffe, there appear to be concentrations of remaining packhorse bridges in North Yorkshire, Cumbria, and Somerset.

The more you study historic bridges, the more you begin to understand how integral they were to the origin of their community. We tend to think of cities as static. We know they change slowly over time—a building is constructed over here, one is demolished over there to make way for a new one, and so on. But the city and the people have always been there. The bridge is just another one of the structures that come and go, built to serve the people who live there at the time. It happens to be old but, if you took it away, you would still be left with a collection of other old structures.

In the historical development of many cities in the United States and Europe, this is not the case. The bridge was not built to ease traffic jams within an existing city, as they are today. Instead, the bridge was built because an overland trade route used to transport goods from Point A to Point B by horse or cart needed to cross a barrier, such as a river or harbor. Completely independent, the river or harbor was also a trade route, one on which goods were transported from Point C to Point D in boats and ships. As a result, bridges represented the intersection of a major overland trade route with a major water-based trade route.

Intersections of trade and transportation routes are magical places. The commercial functions of each of the two trade routes become synergistic because goods from one route are transferred to the other route. A commercial operation at Point A can now easily move goods not just to

Point B, but also to Points C and D, greatly expanding the markets that can be reached by that operation. In the case of bridges, this intersection became a place where goods were transferred from overland carts to boats and vice-versa. This transfer of goods required labor, spurring the creation of jobs and the need for housing for workers. At the same time, the flowing water in the river provided power to drive pumps and mills, thus generating more direct manufacturing jobs, as well as creating additional goods that needed to be transported by boat or cart.

Once the bridge was built, the community grew up around it to serve the bridge or, more accurately, to serve the commercial activity that was generated by the trade route intersection. In most cases, the original bridge is now gone, and has been replaced by a newer bridge. However, the original bridge location and the roadway patterns that converge on that location remain. If the bridge had not been there in the first place, the roadway patterns that now define the city and the structures that now line those roadways would never have been built.

The bridge also serves another function that attracts settlers. Because it provides the only way for people to cross the river to enter the community, it can also be used, if needed, to stop people from entering the community. The presence of a river and a properly designed bridge, one that is integrated into city walls and other defensive structures, makes it difficult for enemies to attack. These fortified locations attracted settlers for the obvious reason of the physical protection provided by the city walls, towers, and associated bridges. Historical paintings and etchings of many medieval European cities show small buildings huddled within stone walls, and clustered closely around the ends of a bridge.

When considered in this context, bridges can be categorized as either "primary" or "secondary." Primary bridges were constructed in previously undeveloped areas to improve trade routes or to serve as defensive structures. However, they were so successful at providing that service that the commercial and/or defensive activity increased to the point of requiring a substantial influx of labor. It is not that primary bridges were built in the middle of settlements, but that settlements grew up in concentric circles around the preexisting primary bridge.

Examples of primary bridges, or at least successor bridges at primary bridge locations, are found throughout Europe. It is likely that few of them, and maybe none of them, are the original primary bridge. Like any bridge, the primary bridge would be susceptible to rot, fire, decay, intentional destruction, or the need for expansion, but there would be subsequent generations of bridges rebuilt at the same location. In many cases, you will find an exhibition plaque or discussion in your tourist guidebook explaining exactly which bridge is the one and only primary bridge that created the community. Magdalene Bridge in Cambridge is a cast-iron bridge dating from 1823. However, it is also a successor bridge to the original primary bridge over the River Cam. Other probable primary bridge locations are London Bridge, Charles Bridge, Mittlerebrücke in Basel, and Romerbrücke in Trier. Even in the United States, where urban settlement and development happened differently than in Europe, the bustling city of Minneapolis was only made possible after the Stone Arch Bridge connected the wheat farms of the northern plains to grain markets on the East Coast.

Secondary bridges, then, are all other bridges constructed after a primary bridge settlement event has occurred. A primary bridge spurs commercial activity. Labor is needed, so people move from the countryside to be closer to the commercial activity occurring at the bridge. Labor needs housing, so a settlement is born. The laborers bring their families, so the population grows and other associated commercial activities develop, including localized agriculture, markets, blacksmiths, and governmental functions. These associated activities also use the primary bridge until, one day, the community finds that the primary commercial and defensive activities are being hindered because there are too many people using the bridge. To relieve the pressure, a secondary bridge is born. In this way, the primary bridges created the world we live in. The secondary bridges just make it easier for us to move around in it.

Once you view the primary bridge in this context, your whole understanding of the city you are visiting changes. It is no longer just a collection of old structures, one of which happens to be a bridge. It is now the inevitable outgrowth of the needs of individual humans, as constrained by their surrounding environment and as overcome by the state of their technology. The primary bridge is no longer just another way to cross the river, but is the very center of the commercial and social life of the community.

This sequence of events, with the primary bridge first and then settlement coming later, is demonstrated in the names of many of these communities. Instead of naming the later bridge after the existing town that it leads to, such as Brooklyn Bridge, there are dozens of places where the later town has been named after the earlier primary bridge. The simplest of these are towns that are named "Bridge." There is a village named Bridge southeast of Canterbury in England. Other examples are Brig in Switzerland, Bruges in Belgium, Most in Czechia, and Ponte in Italy. In other cases, the word "bridge" is combined with another descriptive word. A common form is to combine the word "bridge" with the name of the river it crosses. Thus we are given Cambridge on the banks of the River Cam in England, Banbridge on the River Bann in Northern Ireland, Innsbruck on the River Inn in Austria, and Saarbrücke on the Saar in Germany.

The word "bridge" is also found to be combined with other descriptive geographic features. This gives us multiple Bridgeports, Bridgetowns, and Bridgevilles. It works backward and forward. To complement several Bridgetons, we also have a Tonbridge and, nearby, Tunbridge Wells. The town of Pontypridd, in Wales, is named after the Bridge by the Earthen House. Drogheda, in Ireland, is a town named after the Bridge of the Ford. Drumnadrochit, a village on Loch Ness in Scotland, is named after the Ridge of the Bridge.

The age of the bridge is also a common descriptor added to the name of the town. We have both the town of Pontevedra in Spain, named after the old bridge, and the town of Droichead Nua, also named Newbridge, on the River Liffey in Ireland. The construction material for the bridge may also factor into the name of the community. A Stockbridge is a bridge made of logs. Several towns are named after their local Woodbridge, there are a few Stonebridges, and the most famous example is probably the village of Ironbridge in Shropshire.

In general, the historic bridges that became the focus of settlements in Europe, and which can still be visited today, are made of stone. Wooden bridges were built just as frequently, maybe even more frequently, than

stone bridges. However, old wooden bridges are rare for the obvious reason that they rot or burn, and are not nearly as resistant to floods as stone
bridges. The survivors are almost all stone bridges. These bridges can date
back two thousand years, with bridges built by the Roman Empire still
standing and open to tourists today. Medieval stone bridges, ranging in
date from the 1100s to the 1500s, are still carrying traffic hundreds of years
later in many old European city centers. In addition to the Crane Street
Bridge in Salisbury, another excellent example in England is the 1387 Old
Dee Bridge in Chester.

The earliest bridges in the United States are also made of stone, but
are much more recent than those in Europe. There are a few pre-1800
stone bridges in Massachusetts, Pennsylvania, and New Jersey, and visiting them and trying to figure out which are original and which are reconstructions can be part of the fun. Many of the bridges associated with the
National Road from Maryland to Illinois, including the gracefully curved
S-Bridges, were constructed before 1830. Parkton Stone Arch, the oldest
bridge in Maryland, was built in 1809, and still carries traffic to a bike trail
parking lot. For some obscure reason, there was a building boom of interesting stone arch bridges in Washington County, Maryland, in the 1820s
and 1830s. Almost 20 of these can still be visited today.

PONTE FABRICIO, ROME

Isola Tiberna, with Ponte Fabricio (on right), Rome

One requirement in Rome, which does not necessarily apply elsewhere, is that reading up on the history of the bridges before setting out to

visit them is highly recommended. You generally do not need to read the history of bridges that are exceptionally high, scenic, architecturally interesting, a substantial part of the urban environment, or nicely decorated to enjoy them. However, bridges that are smaller, more subtly decorated, or where the interest is primarily associated with their history require some preliminary study for you to appreciate what you are seeing.

This is definitely the case with the bridges of Rome, many of which have their roots in ancient Roman history. A highly recommended start would be a study by Rabun Taylor of Harvard University in 2002, titled "Tiber River Bridges and the Development of the Ancient City of Rome." This article discusses how the Tiber River crossings were developed to support the salt trade, and that the earliest Romans considered moving water to have some relationship with the boundary between the living and the dead, and therefore crossing of bridges was akin to a form of religious ritual.

The oldest documented bridges in Rome are no longer in existence. These were built of wood, were written about by the ancient Roman writers, and were then eventually destroyed by floods. Their locations seem to have been associated with the Isola Tiberna, a small island in the river located at the base of the Capitoline and Palatine Hills.

The locations of islands are obvious choices for early settlement for two major reasons. First, islands could easily be defended in case of attack, so they became the sites of fortresses and walled settlements in early cities. Second, islands make the construction of bridges easy because they reduce the width of river that needs to be crossed. The Palatine Hill is identified in legend as being the location of the founding of Rome and was, as the location of the imperial residences, the center of the Roman Empire. Therefore, the founding of Rome on a hill close to the island may suggest that the ability to construct early bridges at this location influenced the location of the settlement. The Isola Tiberna is the only island in the Tiber for miles in either direction, and the city was apparently founded on the hillside directly across the river.

The island is the site of the oldest bridge in Rome, the Ponte Fabricio. This is a small stone bridge that connects the Isola Tiberna to the east bank of the river, directly at the base of the Capitoline Hill. The bridge was constructed in 62 BCE. Only about 200 feet long, the pedestrian-only bridge consists of two stone arches, each resting one end on a central pier, and the other end on the bank. The bridge is about 15 feet wide, and the deck sits about 30 feet above river level. A small central third arch is decoratively inserted between the two main arches, and frames the central pier.

Although early, the bridge was more than just functional, as its builder used a combination of an inner core of dark gray tufa, light gray travertine highlighting of the arches, and then reddish brick on the spandrel between the arches to achieve a striking decorative effect. The deck is made of cobblestone, and there are historical plaques in Italian and English at either end describing the history of the bridge.

One of the more appealing features of the bridge is the inscription left by its builder, Lucius Fabricius, the curator of roads in Rome at the time. Most bridges have an inscription that identifies the designer, builder, and/or politicians who were in power when the bridge was built. Fabricius was no exception, and he placed an inscription that translates as "Fabricius, Son of Gaius, Superintendent of the road, took care and likewise approved that it be built."

This is a humble-sounding inscription. Except instead of placing it onto a small plaque in an inconspicuous place, he carved it into the travertine in gigantic, foot-high letters directly at the top of the arch. In case you missed it, he placed the same inscription over the other arch. And in case you were only looking from one side of the bridge, he placed it again over both arches on the other side of the bridge! The size, prominence, and repetition of the inscription are so over-the-top that you have to smile and give Fabricius credit for building a cute bridge, which has now lasted in original condition for more than 2,000 years.

The Ponte Fabricio is only one good reason to visit the Isola Tiberna. Only about 1,500 feet long and 400 feet wide, the island is reported to be the smallest inhabited island in the world. Most of this area is taken up by the Chiesa di San Bartolomeo all'Isola, a tenth century basilica that replaced an earlier Roman temple to Aesculapius, the god of healing. From stairs at the northern end of the island, you can walk down to a stone-paved esplanade that surrounds the island and provides a quiet riverfront walking area amidst the busiest part of the modern, urban city.

PONT NEUF, PARIS

Wrapped up in the beauty of Paris, it is easy to remain unconscious of most of its early history. Spending day after day chasing Napoleon, Marie Antoinette, the Mona Lisa, the Eiffel Tower, the Champs Elysèes, the Arc de Triomphe, and the boulevards of Baron Haussmann certainly seems like an immersion into history. However, in Paris, this is all recent stuff. This is only the very top and, therefore, most visible layer overlaid onto other layers dating back thousands of years. None of these top attractions hints at the origins of Paris or even begins to explain why Paris is here in the first place.

Only by peeling away the layers, not only vertically but concentrically, can you bore into the origins of Paris. When you do that, you eventually reach the center of the Paris of a thousand or more years ago, the Ile de la Citè. Forget about everything on the Left Bank, including the Eiffel Tower, the Invalides, and the Sorbonne. Forget about everything on the Right Bank, including the Louvre, Montmartre, the Opera, and the boulevards. Forget about Versailles, miles away. Do this, and you are left with a rather small island stretching out the banks of an even smaller river. An island covering about 50 acres, sitting in a river about 800 feet wide.

The Seine at this location had two major features that made this the ideal location for the early development of a major commercial and governmental center. First, the river is the perfect size for transporting commercial goods by water, the most efficient mode of transportation at that time. The Seine is connected to an enormous network of tributaries, thus allowing whoever controlled the river to control commerce throughout large sections of northern France.

The second feature is the island itself, with the river serving as a perfect natural moat to defend early occupants of the Ile de la Citè from attack. The river is not so wide that it cannot be bridged easily, even a thousand years ago. The bridges connecting the Ile de la Citè to the banks of the Seine are small bridges. However, the river is just wide enough that crossing it while someone was throwing or shooting things at you would have been unpleasant. So, for hundreds of years, Paris was the Ile de la Citè. There were outlying fields and communities on the river banks, but the settlement was able to be closed up when needed behind its walls, river, and bridges.

Being the oldest part of the city, the Ile de la Citè is where you will find the oldest of the Paris bridges, which is the Pont Neuf. Yes, the oldest bridge is named "New Bridge" because it is the most recent in a series of bridges at that location. Bridges have connected the Ile de la Citè to the banks of the Seine since at least AD 358 and probably earlier. By the time the Pont Neuf was constructed in 1607, the city had already expanded well past the Ile de la Citè. The royal residences were already in the Louvre, a short distance downstream of the Ile de la Citè on the Right Bank. However, the historic heart of the city, including Notre Dame Cathedral, was still on the Ile de la Citè.

The King of France at the time was Henri IV, perhaps best known for his massive rebuilding of the center of Paris during the Renaissance. That effort included the Pont Neuf, but it was much more than just the construction of a small bridge. It was really a reconstruction of the entire western end of the Ile de la Citè and some adjacent smaller islands into a city square, called Le Square du Vert Galant, which is the nickname for Henri IV.

The square as it exists today has multiple levels. The western end of the Ile de la Citè is fortified with a massive stone wall complex, more than 20 feet high. The walls serve to elevate the interior of the Ile de la Citè, to protect it from flooding and erosion. The walls also served a defensive function as fortress walls. The plaza enclosed within the walls then also happens to have, almost incidentally, small extensions that leap over the river and connect the square to the opposite banks. These extensions are the Pont Neuf.

The bridges of the Pont Neuf are constructed of light-gray stone blocks forming stone arches. The segment of the bridge leading to the Left Bank is about 400 feet long and consists of five stone arches. The highest arch is in the center, and the flanking arches are smaller. The segment leading to the Right Bank is a little longer at about 600 feet, crossing on seven arches. The stone parapets are not straight but have turret-shaped curve-outs at regular intervals, each with curved stone benches in them. Each of the turrets is also flanked by two decorative iron lampposts.

The appealing and somewhat amusing feature of the Pont Neuf, other than its age and history, is its decoration. The outer facing of the bridge, as well as the stone walls of the square, are lined with mascarons, which are carved stone grotesque faces. More than 300 of them, each about two feet high, are carved into the bases of the buttresses. Each face is unique and detailed, many with comical grimaces, masks, or other adornments. To observe the mascarons up close and from the best angle, you will have to take the stairway from the quay on either side of the river, descend to river level, and approach the bridge from below.

The Square du Vert Gallant is a popular gathering spot for tourists. The roadway carried by the bridge is bounded on the east by buildings of the Ile de la Citè. On the west side is the street-level part of the square, dominated by a massive bronze equestrian statue of Henri IV himself. The statue was originally placed here in about 1615, but that version was destroyed during the revolution. The current version is a replacement dating from 1818. The western, southern, and northern boundaries of the square are surrounded by heavily padlocked metal mesh fencing to protect tourists from plummeting down the 20 foot-high walls that define the plaza.

At the western end of this elevated part of the square, stairs lead down to river-level, which consists primarily of gardens surrounded by a riverfront promenade. Docks here are one of many places where you can board tour boats that ply the Seine. For those interested in city walking and city viewing, the short walk to the tip of the Ile de la Citè is mandatory. With the Seine at your feet, you have the riverfront buildings of the Left Bank on your left, the famous Pont des Arts just in front of you, and the massive Louvre to your right.

THE OLDEST BRIDGE IN THE UNITED STATES

There is some controversy and disagreement regarding the oldest bridge in the United States. You will find websites making this claim for the Frankford Avenue Bridge in Philadelphia, the Glen Mill Bridge in Rowley, Massachusetts, and the nearby Choate Bridge in Ipswich.

The listing on several websites of these three bridges as the oldest in the United States is problematic, and demonstrates two important principles in researching the history of bridges. One is that there are gray areas along the continuum—from the original construction to original plus additions, to reconstruction, to demolition/replacement. The second is how easily incorrect information can proliferate on the internet.

The small stone arch at Glen Mill, reported on some websites as having been constructed in 1643, is certainly an old and pretty little stone arch. Except for the outline of the arch itself, which is made up of roughly hewn rectangular blocks, the rest of the bridge is a higgledy-piggledy pile of round stones and boulders. The bridge is only about 20 feet long and still carries traffic today, if you can call being used as a driveway next to someone's house "traffic."

The reputed age of this bridge is apparently the result of its location on the same property as the Glen Mills Historic District, which is on US Route 1 outside of Rowley. This is documented as the first site of a fulling mill in the English Colonies, established in 1643. The area includes a cute, preserved mill building with historical plaques. Apparently, the presence of the bridge on this property resulted in people assuming that the structures on the property, including the bridge, were all original to the 1643 date.

However, the bridge is probably not original. An official Essex County Landscape Inventory report by the Massachusetts Heritage Landscape Inventory Program only states that the bridge is early and located on the Mill River "where there has been a crossing since 1642." The Massachusetts Department of Transportation historic bridge inventory website lists the date as "probably" 1860. If you wish to visit, please note that the bridge sits on private property. This is not obvious, because a sign at Glen Mill reads "Glen Mills Historic District," and the area looks like a small park. It turns out that one of the buildings is a house, and the site is privately owned.

The Choate Bridge, in Ipswich, is only about ten miles from Glen Mill. Choate Bridge is well documented as being original, dating from 1764, although it has since been expanded on one side. One stone on the parapet on the west side of the bridge has been inscribed "Choate Bridge, Built by

Town & County, 1764." The bridge crosses the Ipswich River on two arches and is about 100 feet long.

One story about the construction of the bridge is told in *Ipswich, Stories from the River's Mouth* by Sam Sherman. There was an opening ceremony in which the townspeople gathered to watch the wooden supports being removed from under the stone arches. For the ceremony, John Choate, the builder, apparently positioned himself on the northern side of the bridge so that he could make a clean getaway to Canada if the arches collapsed.

The Frankford Avenue Bridge in Philadelphia, dating from 1697, is probably the oldest bridge in the United States. The historical plaque at the bridge explains that the location was a trail crossing for the Lenape Indians and then was part of the King's Highway, one of the earliest roads in the United States. The bridge was already more than 80 years old when it was used in 1781 by American and French troops on the Rochambeau Route, during their march to Yorktown.

The bridge is both larger and more ornate than might be expected for so early a bridge. It crosses Pennypack Creek in Upper Holmesburg, an old commercial and residential working-class neighborhood ten miles north of downtown. What is amazing about the bridge, given its age, is that it is still used for traffic on Frankford Avenue, a busy urban street that is also US Route 13. Because it is a stone arch bridge supported from below, it has no superstructure. Aside from the unobtrusive historical plaque, which is almost certainly not read by most people crossing the bridge, passing drivers would never know that they are crossing any kind of an important bridge, let alone one that is more than 300 years old and may be the oldest bridge in the country.

Although you can see nothing of the bridge structure from the sidewalk, you can take paths from Frankford Avenue on both ends of the bridge down into Pennypack Park below, and from there you can get an unobstructed look at both sides of the bridge. It consists of three stone arches, each of a different size. All three arches are outlined with gray stones set in a radial pattern, and there is a high spandrel wall above the arches to the deck. The spandrel is composed of the same gray schist as the arches, but in irregular shapes and laid horizontally. The historical plaque reports that the downstream side of the bridge is a nineteenth century addition to widen the road, but the face on the upstream side is completely original. Pennypack Park below Frankford Avenue is configured so that you can walk directly up to the bridge walls on the upstream side to investigate the 300-year-old structure. The bridge can be accessed by parking on the street on Frankford Avenue or on any of the nearby side streets.

Although the Frankford Avenue Bridge does appear to be the oldest in the United States, even that is not without some question. The historical plaque at the bridge reads: "It is the oldest roadway bridge in continuous use in the nation." Not "the oldest bridge," but the oldest "roadway bridge." And "in continuous use." It is definitely not clear what these qualifiers mean. Are there older bridges that are not roadways? Are there older bridges that have not been in continuous use? If not, why was the language on the historical plaque so carefully worded?

A comparison between Choate Bridge and Frankford Avenue Bridge provides some additional clues regarding the definition of a "tourist" bridge. The Frankford Avenue Bridge is undoubtedly the older, by almost 70 years. Both bridges have plaques documenting their antiquity. The bridges are similar in size and appearance, neither of them so decorated nor of such unusual construction that they would attract more tourists than the other. However, Choate Bridge has plenty of tourists visiting, while Frankford Avenue Bridge only attracts the occasional historic bridge fanatic.

This difference in attraction is because Frankford Avenue Bridge did not become the focal point of an early settlement. It is just another bridge, constructed in a rural area that was eventually absorbed into the suburbs of a large city. However, Choate Bridge is a major downtown landmark in the middle of a busy tourist town. It still carries the traffic of Main Street on two lanes, with sidewalks on each side, just off the town green and historic shops and restaurants on Market Street. A particular recommendation is to visit near dinnertime and finish off your visit with a beer and burger in the Choate Bridge Pub on the corner of Main and Market.

COVERED BRIDGES

Wooden covered bridges have an attraction that is completely different from that of stone and steel bridges. They have spawned books, websites, movies, historic preservation and touring organizations, and iconic images in a way no other bridge type does. Once you have visited a variety of types of bridges, it becomes clear that covered bridges have been given special treatment in terms of making them accessible to tourists and bridge enthusiasts. A few stone and steel bridges have dedicated parking lots and historical plaques, which are useful for the bridge tourists, but many do not. In contrast, it seems that every single covered bridge, no matter how small or dilapidated, has a parking lot, historical plaque, and eight or ten people attacking it with cameras both inside and out.

In many places, the local covered bridges are the main tourist attraction, and are featured prominently on the home page of the town or county website. For most tourist bridges, you must find your own way, by car, from bridge to bridge. However, in some prominent covered bridge locales, tour companies are available to provide transportation and commentary. Some communities have even gone so far as to hold covered bridge festivals. In fact, the topic of covered bridges has been so completely explored that many modern authors and websites that cover a variety of bridge types, such as Historicbridges.org, specifically exclude covered bridges, considering them a topic separate from other bridge types.

Wooden bridges have been constructed for centuries. The earliest wooden bridges consisted of beams or planks laid horizontally across wood pilings or stone piers. Covers were installed on some of these early wooden bridges in Europe and China prior to the nineteenth century. This was done to protect the wooden deck and underlying support structure from the elements. Any wooden structure is only temporary, because wood will rot and degrade from rain, freeze/thaw cycles, bleaching by the sun, being food for insects, and a hundred other reasons. Although a waterproof cover cannot make a wooden deck and structure last forever, it can substantially extend their lifespan. Since wood is inexpensive and plentiful, the use of roofs was a low cost improvement to protect the major investment necessary to construct a bridge.

However, a true covered bridge is not simply a wooden bridge that has had walls and a roof constructed on top of it. A roof and walls that are not integrated into the structure of the bridge do protect the deck and substructure from weather, but they do nothing else. They do not assist in supporting the deck. In fact, they add extra weight to the deck and substructure, an effect that actually shortens the lifespan of the bridge. Another complication is that, by definition, the length of each span on these early bridges was limited to the length of the beams or planks available to construct it. Any wooden bridge of a substantial length would require multiple, closely-spaced pilings or piers, which is not practical for most waterways.

The thousands of wooden covered bridges constructed in the early years of the United States are a very special category of wooden bridges. They are not simply wooden decks with roofs placed on top of them. Instead, the development that took place in the United States starting in the late 1700s was the invention and evolution of wooden trusses.

A wooden truss is a four-sided box in which the arrangement of the individual wooden boards and beams creates a rigid, stand-alone, tubular structure. That structure can then be placed onto widely-spaced stone piers or abutments, crossing a wide water body without using multiple pylons that would block boat traffic. Place boards on the floor of the truss, and you have now created a bridge deck that can support foot traffic, livestock, and vehicles. Place boards across the top of the truss, and you have now created a roof that repels rain and extends the lifespan of the truss. Place boards along the side of the truss, and you have now provided additional protection for the interior. You have created a wooden covered bridge. And, because it is an engineered truss, the overall structure is far stronger than previous wooden bridges. You are now not only protecting the bridge from the elements, but also making it stronger to last longer and withstand floodwaters.

This difference between a pylon-supported wooden bridge versus a truss-supported wooden bridge can be seen on the two most famous "covered" bridges in the world, the Kapellbrücke and Spreuerbrücke in Lucerne, Switzerland. The Kapellbrücke is a pylon-supported bridge, and therefore has very short spans sitting on closely-spaced pylons. The roof and walls of the Kapellbrücke are non-structural additions placed on top of the wooden bridge, helpful to protect the wooden bridge from the elements, but not adding to its structural integrity.

The Spreuerbrücke is different, as you can see when walking across. It consists of two segments of different construction types, but neither of them was constructed by laying horizontal beams across closely-spaced pylons. Instead, the longest segment, on the south, uses diagonal beams anchored against stone piers to form a rudimentary arch. This allows the southern segment of the bridge to cross the river on only three stone piers, as opposed to the dozens of pylons needed to support the Kapellbrücke. The northern segment of the Spreuerbrücke is even more unusual in that it uses a laminated wooden arch to support the deck without needing any piers or pylons at all. It is not clear if the walls and roof are integral to the structure, creating a stand-alone wooden truss, but the use of diagonal and arched components result in the Spreuerbrücke more closely resembling a true "covered" bridge than the more famous Kapellbrücke.

Similar to iron and steel through-truss bridges, there are a myriad of different ways in which the individual components can be arranged to create a wooden truss. As a result, covered bridge design in the United States moved forward in trial-and-error fashion, with constant improvements. You might assume, with the limited communications and transportation available in the early 1800s, that covered bridge truss design was relatively random and localized. It is easy to imagine that a small town wants to construct a bridge, so an individual who has traveled, and maybe seen bridges in other locations, sketches out some ideas. Then, a few burly local men take the sketches out to the woods, chop down some trees, and construct a rudimentary bridge.

In fact, the system was much more sophisticated. Bridge design and architecture was already a profession, practiced by educated and experienced individuals. They tested their designs, and incorporated lessons learned into their future designs. More importantly, they patented their inventions and formed bridge construction companies. In most cases, towns did not design and construct a bridge on their own. Instead, they hired a company to construct a specific, patented type of truss, and paid a fee to the patent holder for the right to use their design. By the 1840s, some companies mass-produced their trusses in a fixed location such as a carpentry shop, placed them onto railroad cars, and transported them to their ultimate destination, making them very inexpensive.

One interesting feature of covered bridge tourism is that the visitors fall very cleanly into two camps—the outsiders and the insiders. The best known, and the most obvious, are the outsiders. These are the people attracted by the picturesque scenery provided by a freshly painted, well-maintained, quaint covered bridge crossing a babbling brook in the woods during peak fall leaf season. The lesser known are the insiders. These are the people lurking in the dark, inside the bridge, waiting until their eyes adjust to the absence of light so they can investigate and photograph the details of the structure. This includes identifying the overall type of truss used, as well as minor modifications made to the design by the local constructors, and any post-construction renovations or strengthening efforts.

On almost all wooden covered bridges, nothing can be seen of the construction details or the wooden truss type from the outside of the bridge. The inside is dimly lit, often dirty, and rarely freshly painted to make it attractive for photos. Also, while some iron and steel through-truss bridges, and even suspension bridges, can be decorative through the geometric arrangement of their components, this rarely happens with wooden covered bridges. On the through-truss and suspension bridges, these structures are framed against the background of a blue sky, adding to the appeal. On wooden covered bridges, it is not that the geometric arrangement of wooden trusses cannot be attractive, but that it is usually presented against the outer covering of planks.

Interestingly, the insiders and outsiders have two things in common. The first is that they are both attracted, at least in part, by an interest in history. The insiders are drawn mostly by an interest in early engineering, and how the wooden truss type fits within the overall history of wooden trusses in the region. The outsiders are more likely to be interested in the early date of the bridge and how it relates to other, non-bridge tourist sites in the region. The other commonality is that both types of visitors will be carrying cameras, often large, expensive cameras indicating that photography is a serious hobby. Again, there will be a noticeable difference because the outsiders will be trying to capture the setting of the bridge amongst the scenery, while the insiders will be running down their camera batteries due to excessive use of their flash. Of course, this outsider and insider analysis is simplified, and the insiders will usually do some photography of the outside, and vice-versa. However, after watching the visitors for a while, it is usually obvious where everyone's true interests lie.

There are approximately 900 old wooden covered bridges in the United States to visit, but a little research reveals that they exist in clusters. It is these clusters, where a tourist can hit five or ten picturesque covered bridges in a few hours, that are the focus of covered bridge tourism.

As expected, the epicenter of covered bridge locations, which almost defines the quaintness of the region, is in New England. However, another striking feature is that the bridges are clustered in the mountains, such as the Catskills, eastern Berkshires, and White and Green Mountains. There are fewer covered bridges in the coastal areas. This does not mean that no wooden covered bridges were built in the coastal areas. It is just that the coastal areas are much more heavily populated than the mountains, and more people means more traffic, and more traffic means that the quaint old bridges have to go, to make way for more efficient and less attractive cement girder bridges. In the rural areas, however, the covered bridges were allowed to remain. Then, as tourism in mountains to view scenery became popular, people realized that the cute, covered bridges were an important part of the scenery. Now they are protected and revered, with even new ones being built, completely inefficient for moving traffic but perfect as the background for selfies.

The second observation is that clusters occur in less obvious places. It is almost as if covered bridges travel in herds. There are a large number of covered bridges in Parke County, Indiana, north of Terre Haute. Nineteen covered bridges in Ashtabula County, Ohio, are enough to support an annual covered bridge festival every October. Lancaster County in Pennsylvania has more than 25 covered bridges, and companies lead tours of them on scooters. Only a few covered bridges are found in Iowa, but somehow all of them are clustered within a small area surrounding the town of Winterset, the focus of another annual covered bridge festival. Covered bridges are much rarer west of the Mississippi River, but more than 50 of them are clustered in the Willamette River Valley between Portland and Medford, Oregon.

Covered bridges are an enigma among tourist bridges. One of the most pleasurable features of visiting bridges is the outdoor experience—getting outside, hiking in the open air, taking in the views. By definition, these are not part of the covered bridge experience. Instead, the covered bridge visit can be likened to walking in a dimly lit barn, but with an occasional small window to peer out of. And the attraction of peering out of the windows may be dampened once you learn why these bridges have windows in the first place. It is not for the view, and it is not to let in light. It is so that the horse manure can be removed easily without having to shovel and carry it to the ends of the bridge.

The second challenge in visiting covered bridges is that they are generally not easily walkable. They do not have sidewalks. They tend to be narrow, especially the older ones, as they were designed to carry horses instead of modern cars. Many of them are in rural areas and get little traffic, allowing you to scamper across when it looks like no cars are coming. However, more often than not, you only get halfway across before a car approaches, and you have to squeeze yourself in between the timbers and wave sheepishly at the driver, apologizing for blocking traffic.

A third problem is that, with their large numbers and popularity as tourist attractions, there is such a thing as covered bridge overload. Unless you are a fanatic who enjoys studying the details of the arrangements of the timbers, the fact is that not all covered bridges are awesome. Many are short, unpainted, weathered, and just sitting on their own with no attractive scenery. Overall, only about half of the covered bridges in any given area are likely to be attractive and scenic. The others may be interesting because they are old, but after a while, they all begin to look the same—short, gray, poorly-maintained barns sitting in the middle of the woods.

Another unfortunate feature of some covered bridges is that they are effectively tourist gimmicks. Because they are such popular tourist attractions, new ones are constructed, or old ones are moved and reconstructed, in relatively unattractive settings. Moving or reconstructing an old, covered bridge is to be praised for its role in historic preservation. Few people would argue that 150 year-old bridges should be destroyed. However, just because a bridge is preserved does not mean that the reconstruction is an important attraction. Some reconstructed covered bridges, such as the 1870 Baltimore Covered Bridge in Springfield, Vermont, were reconstructed over ditches and do not even cross over flowing water.

A common theme is that very few covered bridges, even the most authentic of them, have escaped major reconstruction. At a minimum, many of them have had iron or steel strengthening members added to the interior framework. Examples include many of the Ashtabula County, Ohio, covered bridges, including Benetka Road constructed in the 1890s, and Doyle Road and Harpersfield from 1868. It is also very common for the hardware holding the individual members together to have been replaced. The earliest bridges would have had thick wooden dowels, or trunnels, driven to connect beams together. On many bridges, these have been replaced by modern nuts and bolts. The 1841 West Cornwall Covered Bridge in Connecticut has modern-looking steel brackets connecting its roof to the top chord of the truss.

Many of the bridges have been dismantled like Lincoln Logs and reassembled either in place, or in a different location. It is not uncommon to see hand-written numbering on the interior beams, showing that the specific location of each beam had been recorded before disassembly. This is found on the 1880 Martins Mill and 1840 Upper Falls bridges in Windsor County, Vermont.

You will often look underneath a covered bridge and note that it sits on cement abutments, a sure sign that the wooden truss has been removed, the original stone abutments replaced, and the truss reconstructed on top of the new, stronger abutments. Examples are the 1850 Utica Mills and 1860 Gilpins Falls bridges in Maryland. The 1870 Scott Covered Bridge had the longest wooden span of any bridge in Vermont, but the longer a span, the greater the weight, so it has had a cement pier constructed to support its center.

Taken to its extreme, some wooden bridges have been disassembled, a steel or concrete deck installed, and then the original wooden sides and roof reconstructed, but not the original wooden deck. In these cases, the original wooden truss no longer operates as a structural unit for support-ing the bridge deck, and the roof and walls are left for nostalgic decoration and historic preservation purposes. This occurred at the 1825 Hassenplug Covered Bridge in Pennsylvania.

CORNISH-WINDSOR COVERED BRIDGE, CORNISH, NH, AND WINDSOR, VT

Like suspension bridges, covered bridges are measured, ranked, and dis-cussed in superlative terms such as the oldest, longest total bridge, lon-gest single-span, oldest and longest of specific lattice type, and other char-acteristics. The longest covered bridge in the world is Hartland in New Brunswick, but it achieves this by linking together seven spans. Like sus-pension bridges, the engineering achievement for covered bridges is not total length but individual span length. Up until 2011, the longest single wooden covered span in the world was at Old Blenheim Bridge in New York, at 210 feet. Old Blenheim Bridge was destroyed by flooding in 2011, leaving the longest single-span in the world at Bridgeport, in California, at 208 feet. The Cornish-Windsor Covered Bridge crossing the Connecti-cut River is not the winner in most of these record categories, but it is close, making it one of the most iconic covered bridges in the nation, and an excellent example to visit.

Connecting the towns of Windsor, Vermont, and Cornish, New Hamp-shire, it is one of only three covered bridges in the US that crosses a border between two states. The bridge is the fourth at the site. Previous bridges constructed in 1796, 1824, and 1828 were destroyed by flooding. The cur-rent Cornish-Windsor Bridge was built in 1866, and is the longest total length covered bridge in the United States. It is more than 400 feet long, achieved with two spans of 204 feet each. It is wide for a covered bridge. Most covered bridges are only wide enough for a single car, but the Cor-nish-Windsor Bridge can accommodate two lanes of traffic. The sides of the bridge are unpainted, and the wooden roof was replaced with a sheet metal roof in 1924. The original tollhouse is still intact. It is the last build-ing on your left before you enter the bridge, as you approach from Bridge Street in Windsor.

The interior of a covered bridge is one of the main attractions for covered bridge enthusiasts, with as many different varieties of wood-beam truss configurations as there are for steel through-truss bridges. The structure of Cornish-Windsor is called a Town lattice, and is comprised of square wooden beams a foot wide on each side, rather than wood planks. The beams cross in a repeating X-pattern down the length of the inside of the bridge. In 1976, its structure was reported on its National Register of Historic Places nomination form to be mostly original, as opposed to many other old, covered bridges that have been reinforced with modern devices. However, it deteriorated to the extent that it had to be closed to traffic in 1987, and was largely reconstructed before reopening in 1989.

Like many covered bridges, Cornish-Windsor has a dedicated parking lot on one end for visitors, in this case on the New Hampshire end of the bridge. The parking lot has a metal historical plaque describing the construction and history of the bridge, and there are numerous other plaques on the ends of the bridge. These include a 100-year commemoration plaque placed in 1966 by the Covered Bridge Association of New Hampshire, designation as a National Historic Civil Engineering Landmark, an outstanding civil engineering achievement award for the 1989 rehabilitation project, and designation as New Hampshire Covered Bridge Number 20. The New Hampshire end of the bridge also has a sign warning that there is a two-dollar fine for not walking your horses.

One of the major attractions of many covered bridges is its place within the local scenery, which is to be enjoyed from the side of the bridge, and not from walking across it. The setting for Cornish-Windsor is gorgeous, with the White and Green Mountains rising on both sides of the flat, quiet river. Like most outdoor destinations in New England, the best time to visit is fall, when the leaves are turning.

The bridge is a little difficult to find, because it is not directly in the town center of either Windsor or Cornish. Traveling on US Route 5, the main north-south highway paralleling the Connecticut River in Vermont, there are signs for "covered bridge" indicating the way. Bridge Street is a nondescript residential road several blocks south of the central part of Windsor, which is a historic tourist attraction as the location where the Vermont Republic was declared independent of the British Empire in 1777.

On the New Hampshire end, it is not even clear where the town of Cornish is, as Bridge Street ends in a "T" and there is no sign pointing the direction to the town.

South of the parking lot, there is another nearby sign pointing toward the "covered bridge," and it leads to the Dingleton Hill Bridge about a mile south of Cornish-Windsor. This is a much smaller but still charming covered bridge. Its location so close to Cornish-Windsor demonstrates how easy it can be to get wrapped up in visiting covered bridges in this part of New England, with one seeming to pop up around each corner.

IRON AND STEEL ARCH BRIDGES

One common attraction of tourist bridges is the study and appreciation of early construction technologies and bridge types. After thousands of years of being limited to stone or wood, bridge technology exploded in the late-eighteenth and early-nineteenth centuries with the invention of cast-iron, wrought-iron, wire rope, concrete, and then steel.

The construction of metal arch bridges began in the late 1700s, became more common throughout the 1800s, and had completely replaced stone arch bridges by the early 1900s. Iron provided greater strength than stone, allowing wider arch spans to be constructed. This was important for bridging rivers that were used for commercial shipping. With their shorter spans, stone bridges required a series of piers across the width of the river, and these piers interfered with movement of boats and ships. By allowing the construction of wider spans, metal arch bridges could be built that spanned an entire river without any piers, thus allowing shipping to continue without any interference.

The earliest metal arch bridges were made of cast-iron, in which the individual structural components that made up the structure were cast in molds, not unlike bronze sculptures. This allowed the individual pieces to be formed into whatever decorative shape the designer wanted. Cast-iron bridges tend to be wildly decorated and, as a result, are attractions for photographers wherever they are found.

Examples of decorative iron arch bridges are found throughout England, Ireland, and France. The cast-iron Pont Au Double in Paris, which dates from 1847, crosses the Seine and leads directly to the front door of Notre Dame. The wrought-iron Westminster Bridge, built in 1862 at the foot of Big Ben and the Houses of Parliament in London, has spandrels cut through with geometric quatrefoil shapes, and these are mirrored in similar trefoil shapes in the railing. The quatrefoils, in turn, hold in their center the colorful, decorative coat-of-arms of Queen Victoria representing three golden lions for England, a red rampant lion for Scotland, and a harp for Ireland. In Bath, England, another early cast-iron bridge over the Kennett and Avon Canal was constructed in 1800, and its spandrel is almost entirely decorative, consisting of a series of diminishing circles. Dublin has three gorgeous iron bridges, the Sean Heuston Bridge, Rory O'More Bridge, and the Ha'Penny Bridge.

In the United States, the 1839 Dunlap's Creek Bridge on the National Road is the oldest cast-iron arch bridge, and was a famous engineering marvel at the time. Central Park is the location of five amazing cast-iron bridges that demonstrate perfectly how the casting of iron can be used to fabricate structural components into decorative shapes. These bridges all date from the early 1860s and include Pinebank Arch, Bow Bridge, and, their names serving as a demonstration of the large number of interesting, old bridges located in Central Park, three bridges known simply as Numbers 24, 27, and 28 (also known as Gothic Arch).

IRON BRIDGE, COALBROOKDALE, ENGLAND

The first use of cast-iron for a bridge was at a place now known as the village of Ironbridge, near Coalbrookdale in the Severn Gorge in Shropshire, England. Mass production and use of iron marks the beginning of the Industrial Revolution. Therefore, it is fitting that the first bridge constructed using this new material is located directly in the heart of a UNESCO World Heritage Site established to recognize the birthplace of the Industrial Revolution. Built in 1779, the Iron Bridge still stands and is a major tourist attraction. However, it is only one of many attractions that make up the collection of early Industrial Revolution sights in the Severn Gorge. Another important attraction is the Museum of the Gorge, located about a mile from the bridge.

One feature of iron arch bridges is that the greater strength and lower weight of iron, and then steel, allowed the arch to be built with much less material than a stone arch. In stone arches, it is possible to leave small holes open in the spandrel for decorative effect, as was done at Ponte Fabricio. More commonly, stone arch bridges had a closed spandrel. However, the use of metal freed up the designers to create completely open-spandrel structures, held up with only a few flimsy-looking metal bars crisscrossing geometrically through space.

It is tempting to assume that this happened gradually as designers and engineers became more comfortable with the strength of iron, and that metal arch spandrels might have started closed and become more open as experience with the technology was gained. As demonstrated at Iron Bridge, this did not happen, as this first-ever bridge made of iron is a completely open-spandrel arch structure. Similarly, it is tempting to assume that the designers of the world's first iron bridge would have been primarily concerned with the engineering of the new material and would leave decorative flourishes to later designers. This is also incorrect, as the individual structural pieces used to construct the Iron Bridge were shaped in pleasing circular, curved, and figure-eight patterns.

Ironbridge, Shropshire, England

Another interesting feature of Iron Bridge that attracts tourists is the unusual shape of the arch. The shape of most arches used to construct bridges is flattened, to allow the deck of the bridge to be as level as possible. The higher the arch, the more the deck of the bridge needs to be sloped. This, in turn, requires extra work on the part of horses and people to carry heavy loads up and over the bridge.

Being the first large-scale use of cast-iron, the easiest way to create the curved molds required for the arch of Iron Bridge was to use a pin and string, which generate a perfectly circular shape. Therefore, the deck of Iron Bridge is steeply sloped, which is noticeable when you walk over it. Of more importance to photograph-minded tourists is the reflection of the arch in the Severn River. Because the arch itself is a perfect half-circle, a photograph from the correct angle and time of day generates a beautiful complete circle. Among the many images of the bridge you will find printed on book covers, postcards, T-shirts, and coffee cups in the Ironbridge village shops, you will always find several taken specifically to demonstrate the circle.

The Iron Bridge was built not only to allow access across the Severn River, but also to advertise the exciting new product being made in the Severn Gorge, which was cast-iron. This advertisement was broadcast in gigantic letters on both sides of the bridge, and reads "This Bridge Was Cast at CoalBrook=Dale and Erected in the Year MDCCLXXIX." The marketing campaign was highly successful, and the Iron Bridge became a tourist attraction almost immediately upon completion.

The Iron Bridge is not easy to reach without a car, as trains do not go to Coalbrookdale, and you need to use a combination of trains and buses to get there. However, it is enough of a major tourist attraction that you will find plenty of people at the train station in nearby Telford to help you find the right bus.

STONE TOWER SUSPENSION BRIDGES

Another interesting type of historic bridge that attracts tourist crowds is nineteenth century suspension bridges on which the suspension towers are made of stone or brick, as opposed to iron or steel. Only a handful of these remain. In Britain, they include two of the earliest road suspension bridges ever built, the Menai and Conwy bridges in Wales, and the Clifton Suspension Bridge near Bristol. In the United States, the stone and brick tower suspension bridges are limited to Brooklyn, Waco, Wheeling, Delaware Aqueduct, and the Roebling Bridge in Cincinnati. One or both of the Roeblings, John and/or his son Washington, had a hand in each of these bridges. John designed the Aqueduct and the Roebling Bridge, and initiated the construction of the Brooklyn Bridge, which was completed by Washington. The Roebling Company supplied the wire rope used in the Waco Suspension Bridge, and Washington designed the diagonal auxiliary strengthening cables for the Wheeling Suspension Bridge in the 1870s.

These stone and brick tower suspension bridges represent a unique glimpse into the early use of steel at the beginning of the Industrial Revolution. Prior to the 1830s, suspension bridges were constructed using either rope or iron chains, suspended from either wood or stone anchors. In the 1830s, wire rope, the forerunner of steel cable, was invented in Germany, and John Roebling began producing wire rope in the United States in the 1840s. Having studied suspension bridges, Roebling realized the advantage of using wire rope and ultimately steel cable instead of rope or iron chains to suspend the decks of bridges. However, technology was not advanced far enough to understand the potential for use of iron or steel for the rest of the structure, so the towers holding the wire rope were still made of stone or brick.

Within the span of a few decades, later designers learned that steel could be used for the towers as well, resulting in the classic all-steel suspension bridges that we are accustomed to seeing today, such as the Benjamin Franklin, Mackinac, and Golden Gate. However, we are fortunate to be left with a handful of stone and brick tower bridges as a snapshot of the period when the possibilities of steel were just starting to be realized.

MENAI SUSPENSION BRIDGE, BANGOR, WALES

The first large-scale suspension bridge ever constructed was the Menai Suspension Bridge, completed in 1828.

In the late 1700s, political and commercial interaction between England and Ireland increased substantially. A London-Dublin Mail Coach service began in 1775 and involved two coaches per day by 1800. In 1801, the Act of Union created the United Kingdom of Great Britain and Ireland, dramatically increasing the need for improved transport between London and Dublin. The most direct route between London and Dublin used the road from London to Holyhead, a port directly across the Irish Sea from Dublin. However, Holyhead was situated on the Isle of Anglesey, separated from the Welsh mainland by the Menai Strait. The Menai Strait is not wide, but it has strong currents, making ferry crossings hazardous.

These developments and factors led to the need for a bridge across the Strait. Because the Strait was also an important passageway for tall ships, serving up to 4,000 ships per year, not just any bridge would suffice. The situation required a high bridge, one that could only be provided using high suspension towers. The bridge design was awarded to Thomas Telford, the most prominent British civil engineer at the time. The bridge is considered Telford's masterpiece.

The only original part of the bridge remaining is the stone suspension towers, which are quite distinctive. The towers are tapered, being bulkier at the bottom and narrowing at the top, so much so that they were referred to as the "pyramids" when they were being constructed. The stonework is decorative, with smooth-faced stones on the front and back of the towers and rough-faced stone on the sides and edges. Each tower is bisected at its base by two stone arches through which the roadway passes. Above each arch is a large, ornamental niche that looks as if it was designed to hold a statue but which is empty. At the base of each of the niches, just above the roadway, is a rectangular stone plaque, again looking as if it was designed to hold an inscription, but four of the eight of them are blank. Of the four inscribed plaques, one memorializes "Thomas Telford, Engineer," and gives the dates of his birth and death. The other three list the date of the bridge opening, the date that the bridge was freed from tolls, and the 1939 reconstruction of the deck.

One unusual feature of the towers is the low height and narrow width of the twin arches and, therefore, the roadway. This is expected, given the type of traffic that the bridge would have carried in 1828. Later stone-tower suspension bridges, including Clifton, Brooklyn, Roebling, and Wheeling, are much more open, with higher and wider arch openings. Those later bridges still carry traffic at normal speeds more than 150 years later. However, at the Menai Bridge, the small size of the arches restricts the nature and speed of modern traffic. Traffic does cross the bridge, but at a slow pace, as buses have only a few inches of clearance and must slow to a crawl to avoid scraping against the sides of the arch.

The suspension system is a double-eyebar chain that was originally wrought-iron but was later replaced by steel. There is an elaborate stone tollhouse on the southern end of the bridge. Two plaques, one in Welsh and one in English, installed on the side of the tollhouse in 2003 by the Institution of Civil Engineers and American Society of Civil Engineers, provide statistics for the bridge. The deck is 153 high over the water, the total length is 1,388 feet, and the length of the main span, the longest in the world at that time, is 580 feet. The suspended part of the deck is a complex steel-girder truss, with much of the structure extending several feet above the deck and separating the sidewalks on either side from the traffic lanes. This gives the bridge an early Industrial Age appearance.

The Menai Bridge is just one of four historically important bridges completing the link between London and Dublin via Holyhead, making this area of northern Wales a major attraction for bridgespotters. In addition to crossing the Menai Strait, geography demanded that the London to Holyhead roadway also cross the estuary of the River Conwy. The Conwy Suspension Bridge, much smaller than Menai, was also designed and constructed by Telford and opened in 1826 as part of the same effort to complete the roadway. In 1826 and 1828, these bridges revolutionized carriage travel between London and Dublin.

Limitations in the size of both bridges became evident shortly after they opened. By the 1830s, railroads linked London to Liverpool, replacing carriage travel and rendering the Menai Bridge with its too-narrow arches almost obsolete. In the mid-1840s, work began on two railroad bridges, one each at River Conwy and the Menai Strait. The Conwy Railway Bridge, sitting just a few feet away and parallel to the suspension bridge, was opened in 1849, and the Britannia Bridge, parallel to and about a mile from the Menai Bridge, was completed in 1850.

These bridges were the first two examples of wrought-iron box-girder bridge construction, and together they completed the railroad link between London and Holyhead via Chester. The Britannia Bridge burned in 1970, and has been reconstructed. The Conwy Railway Bridge, which still carries railway traffic, remains as the only surviving example of a box-girder bridge. The Telford Centre museum, in the town of Menai Bridge a short walk from the bridge, has exhibits on both the Menai and Britannia bridges.

Although the Menai Bridge and the other three historic bridges in northern Wales set numerous records for being the first and largest of various construction types, they are not as well-known as many other early suspension bridges, such as Clifton. This lack of fame is probably due to their semi-remote location in the northern corner of Wales, far from any major population or tourism centers. However, tourists do visit. The importance of the Menai Bridge is recognized by a small park on the northern end, where the bridge passes over the town of Porthaethwy (in Welsh) and Menai Bridge (in English). The park includes a bench overlooking the bridge, a plaque installed by the Institution of Civil Engineers to commemorate the 250th anniversary of the birth of Telford, and two large, detailed exhibition plaques installed by the Isle of Anglesey. The bridge even inspired a poem, quoted on one of the plaques:

High fortress above the sea—the world drives
Its vehicles over it.
You, all the ships of the ocean,
Go underneath its chains.

CLIFTON SUSPENSION BRIDGE, BRISTOL, ENGLAND

Although it is not the oldest, largest, most ornate, or most technologically advanced for its time, the Clifton Suspension Bridge is probably the best known and most photographed suspension bridge in Britain, and one of the most popular tourist bridges in the world.

The bridge is in Clifton, a suburb about five miles northwest of central Bristol. In the mid-1750s, Bristol was an important port city, but there was little other development near Clifton or, more importantly, in the more remote areas of England and Wales on the western side of the River Avon.

A low-level, stone arch bridge across the River Avon, the Bristol Bridge, already existed a few miles away. There simply did not seem to be a desperate need for a bridge to be constructed at Clifton, especially given the enormous length and height that would be required to cross the Avon Gorge at that location.

However, for reasons unknown, a single individual, William Vick, left a legacy of 1,000 pounds when he died in 1754, with the stipulation that it be invested and allowed to grow until it was enough to build a bridge across the Avon Gorge at Clifton. Over the following 50 years the money grew, and prospective bridge designers began dabbling with the challenge of bridging the gorge. The idea was delayed by the Napoleonic Wars, but revisited in the 1820s. Bristol had grown substantially, and Thomas Telford had helped to ignite Industrial Age fascination with his Menai and Conwy Suspension bridges. It was not even the need for a bridge at that location that drove the idea. It was because the nation had embarked on a building frenzy of canals, railroads, and bridges, and this particular bridge already had an established fund in place to finance the project.

By the late 1820s, a well-publicized design competition was held and judged by Telford himself. There followed the usual complications of finding that none of the designs could be built with the money available, disagreements and personality clashes among competitors, appeals to Parliament for additional funding, opposition from ferry operators, additional rounds of competition, social unrest, and economic highs and lows that made construction of the bridge appear more and then less and then more likely again. The design competition was eventually awarded to Isambard Kingdom Brunel, a famous engineer who would later construct the Great Western Railway.

Bridge construction began in 1831, immediately stopped, started again in 1836, and stopped again in 1843, leaving unfinished stone towers dominating the skyline views of the gorge. Work remained stopped until about 1860, when Hungerford Bridge in London was being dismantled and its eyebar chains, similar to those proposed for use in the Clifton Bridge, needed to be disposed of. This reinvigorated the Clifton project, which then moved forward quickly and was completed in 1864. These competitions and associated turmoil were widely publicized at the time, making the bridge a project of national importance and a tourist attraction even before it was completed.

The bridge is a symbol of the city of Bristol and has been prominently featured in railway and tourist advertisements from the start. However, it is not exactly clear why. The bridge is five miles away from central Bristol and must be reached by bus or car from the downtown area. Britain has several older suspension bridges. Even the United States has older suspension bridges. Not only was the bridge constructed using established technology, but it was constructed largely using the materials that were salvaged from the Hungerford Bridge, which had been built 20 years before. The bridge is high, with a height of 245 feet above river level in the Avon Gorge, but other bridges are higher. Finally, the design of the bridge's stone towers is plain, with no ornamentation except for a white cornice with an inscription at the top.

On paper, Clifton would certainly attract a few bridge enthusiasts but probably few other tourists. However, for some reason, this bridge is crawling with tourists, all gone well out of their way to get there, and taking thousands of pictures. It is not that the bridge is the oldest, highest, most technologically advanced, or prettiest. It is that the bridge is old, and high, and technologically interesting, and visually appealing, all at the same time.

The Avon Gorge is a major scenic attraction on its own, and the view of the 150 year-old bridge crossing high above it is incredibly impressive. There are several scenic viewing locations provided, and these are crowded with tourists trying to take the perfect picture of the fog lifting around the bridge in the morning, the bridge in full sunshine during the day, and then lit with a colorful light display at night.

One of the most popular events in Britain is the Bristol Balloon Fiesta, which occurs over three days in August every year. The balloons are launched from a field just west of the bridge, and the bridge visitor center sells the inevitable coffee cups and refrigerator magnets showing the image of the bridge being overflown by dozens of hot-air balloons.

EARLY IRON AND STEEL THROUGH-TRUSS BRIDGES

Another subset of bridges visited by hobbyists who specialize their efforts is early iron and steel through-truss bridges. There are dozens of different types, commonly named after their inventors such as Pratt, Whipple, Bollman, and Warren. In the United States, hundreds of cast-iron and wrought-iron through-truss bridges were built from about the 1870s through the 1930s, and many are still in place today. Large numbers of these still carry traffic, and many of those that have become obsolete are preserved in small parks and incorporated into recreational trails. These bridges frequently have a few gravel-and-dirt parking spaces available at their ends, and many of them display plaques to explain the history of the location, or to describe the technology used in the construction of the bridge.

Many of the specific types appear to be nothing more than a boring box built of steel girders, and only a bridge engineer or a fanatical bridge-spotter would be able to appreciate the beauty or ingenuity in their arrangement. However, some unusual types may be visited because they are rare, such as the Bollman Truss Bridge preserved at Savage, Maryland. In other cases, the geometric and symmetrical arrangement of the iron or steel components can present a photogenic appearance. These bridges are frequently preserved in small parks, and can attract even casual tourists.

A particularly attractive example is the lenticular truss, in which the truss consists of a series of lens-shaped structures. Possibly the most well-known and most visited lenticular-truss bridge is the 1883 Smithfield Street Bridge, which connects downtown Pittsburgh to a popular shopping and dining area on the opposite side of the Monongahela River. Another appealing type is the cantilever-truss bridge. When done on a small scale in central urban areas, these are amenable to riotous decoration. Examples include the Szabadsàg Bridge in Budapest, and the Northampton Street Bridge in Easton, Pennsylvania.

One of the special attractions of early through-truss bridges is that the horizontal crosspiece above the roadway, known as the portal bracing, is often decorated with a builder or date plaque, a decorative frieze, and/or embossed corner plates. These are usually ornate, and proudly announce the date of the bridge, the name of the construction company, and, often, the names of the local commissioners at the time of construction. In many cases similar plaques, also known as nameplates, can be found on bridges constructed by the same bridge company across a wide area, and collecting the remaining bridges associated with a single company can be the focus of a bridge collector.

One of the more prolific companies was the Wrought Iron Bridge Company of Canton, Ohio, which left its plaque over numerous early through-truss bridges in the late 1800s, including the Mineral Road Bridge in Massachusetts, the 1886 Nevius Street Bridge in New Jersey, and the Cuba Road and Sparks Road bridges in Baltimore County, Maryland. In most cases, these plaques only list the name of the builder, but not the date. However, the plaque on the 1898 Masemore Road Bridge, also in Baltimore County, lists the date, as well as the names of the county commissioners and the bridge superintendent.

Ornate date plaques, friezes, and corner plates are also found on the Exchange Street Bridge in Binghamton, constructed in 1902 by the Owego Bridge Company, and on the Rosemont-Raven Rock Bridge in New Jersey, built in 1876 by the Lambertville Iron Works. The 1882 Old Mill Road Bridge in Maryland has a lovely date plaque from the Pittsburg Bridge Company. The Penn Bridge Works left a nice plaque over the 1884 Fallston Bridge in New Brighton, Pennsylvania. Dean and Westbrook placed a decorative plaque on the 1889 Farley Bridge in Massachusetts and on the 1891 Lower Bridge in English Center, Pennsylvania. Unnamed builders placed interesting plaques on the 1890 Harpursville Bridge near Binghamton and the 1879 Carroll Road Bridge in Maryland.

One fun activity can be trying to solve historical mysteries resulting from your studies of the date plaques. Some bridges, such as the gorgeous Riverside Avenue Bridge in Greenwich, Connecticut, just have a decorative frieze and corner plates, without a date plaque. This raises the question of whether an original plaque was lost or if it never existed. In other cases, there may be multiple plaques with mismatched dates. This is the case with the Bollman Bridge in Savage, Maryland. As the only remaining iron Bollman Truss, this bridge is so historically important that it displays multiple plaques with multiple dates. The frieze over the bridge itself reports the dates of 1852 for the patent, 1866 for renewal of the patent, and 1869 for construction. The 1869 date is also displayed on a Maryland Historical Society plaque on the southern end of the bridge and on a National Historic Civil Engineering Landmark plaque on the northern end. However, another National Historic Civil Engineering Landmark plaque on the northern end lists a date of 1887. If you read carefully, this plaque actually states, "erected on this site circa 1887," and further research indicates that the bridge was built in 1869 and then dismantled, moved, and rebuilt in 1887.

Although it is not a through-truss bridge, the 1881 Tilton Island Park Bridge in New Hampshire has ten cast-iron builder plaques used as joint covers on the railing, and these display the patent date of 1856. These plaques are heavily rusted, but all ten of them also, quite legibly, display the construction information in letters cast into the iron. The construction information clearly reads "A.D. BRIGG & CO. UILDERS." Not "BUILDERS" but "UILDERS," capturing what appears to be a major typographical error and still displaying it for posterity almost 150 years later.

BERLIN IRON BRIDGE COMPANY LENTICULAR TRUSS BRIDGES, VARIOUS LOCATIONS IN EASTERN US

While there are dozens of early through-truss bridges to be visited, they are generally small in scale, and situated in relatively remote locations. You should certainly visit if you are in their area, and each of them receives some level of tourist visits, but it is difficult to pick one or two examples and recommend that you go out of your way to visit them. What some bridgespotters enjoy, however, is to attempt to collect a set of bridges with a common theme, such as all of the remaining examples of a certain type of truss, or the bridges remaining from a specific early builder, even though they may be in widely scattered locations.

One prominent early builder whose bridges seem to be preserved and celebrated more than those of other builders is the Berlin Iron Bridge Company of East Berlin, Connecticut. The company began business in 1870 as the Metallic Corrugated Shingle Company, and changed its name to the Corrugated Metal Company in 1873. In 1878, the company purchased the patent for the lenticular truss, and began building lenticular truss bridges. In 1885, the company name was changed to the Berlin Iron

Bridge Company, and it is under this name that most of its best-known bridges were constructed during the 1880s and 1890s.

Pineground Bridge, New Hampshire

Although it appears that no complete inventory of the company's bridges exists, they are known to number in the hundreds, and perhaps the thousands. Bridgehunter.com lists approximately 170 bridges attributed to the company, about half of which are lenticular pony trusses, which attract their own group of specialized bridgespotters. Another 70 bridges were lenticular through-truss bridges, of which 55 have been demolished, but approximately 15 of them can be visited. These remaining bridges are found between Vermont and New Hampshire in the north to Pennsylvania in the south. In research for the book, 11 of these special bridges were visited. These include South Washington Street in downtown Binghamton, New York, with Ouaquaga just a few miles away; Lover's Leap and Boardman's within a few miles of each other in Connecticut; Pineground near Chichester, New Hampshire; Bardwell's Ferry and Aiken Street in Massachusetts; Neshanic Station in New Jersey; and Pierceville, Pine Creek/Jersey Shore, and Waterville in Pennsylvania.

At first glance, it is not clear whether these bridges are special because they are so well preserved and presented, or whether they are so well preserved and presented because they are special. Either way, it does appear that Berlin Iron Bridge Company lenticular through-truss bridges are preserved, rehabilitated, and even serve as the centerpieces of parks more than almost any other type of historic bridge, except perhaps wooden covered bridges.

Visually, these are more appealing than normal through-truss bridges because they combine straight columns and beams with curved, arched components. This combination results in a very unusual and attractive geometric pattern. However, most importantly, the Berlin Iron Bridge Company took decoration of their bridges, especially the design of their date plaques, the grill along the portal bracing above the roadway at the bridge entrances, and even their railings, to a new level.

The most attractive feature, found on all but the two earliest bridges (Pierceville and Bardwell's Ferry), is an extremely ornate cast metal date plaque. The plaque takes the exact same form on each bridge. The construction date is presented in curved numbers at the very top and center of the plaque. The upper edge of the main plaque below the date is crenulated, with small, faux cornices representing the tops of columns. Below the date, following the same curve, the first line of text reads "BUILT BY". The second line of text reads "THE". Then, the third line of text is curved, and reads "BERLIN IRON BRIDGE CO." followed by the fourth line "EAST BERLIN CONN.". This much of the plaque is exactly the same for each bridge, except for the date. This is followed, on almost all of the plaques, by a line indicating that Douglas and Jarvis received patents on April 1, 1878 and April 7, 1885. The remainder, taking up about half of the space on each plaque, is a list of the commissioners responsible for the bridge. This undoubtedly served as an enticement for these commissioners to issue their contract to the Berlin Iron Bridge Company in order to have their names decoratively presented for posterity.

On six of the 11 bridges, the date plaque is flanked on both sides by a decorative, geometric grill along the portal bracing. A few of the bridges, including Neshanic Station in New Jersey, South Washington Street in Binghamton, Aiken Street in Massachusetts, and Lover's Leap in Connecticut, also have decorative railings using small, flower-shaped medallions as the joint covers.

Although it is subtle, the feature which makes these bridges stand out today is not something that was done in the 1880s, but something that was done more than 100 years later. Of the 11 bridges visited, all but one were rehabilitated and preserved, and are now freshly painted and proudly displayed by their communities. Only Boardman's, rusted and inaccessible behind chain-link fence, has been neglected. Four of the bridges (Neshanic Station, Bardwell's Ferry, Aiken Street, and Pine Creek/Jersey Shore) are still drivable, but even though it is drivable, Pine Creek/Jersey Shore does have a small historical park at one end. In addition to Pine Creek/Jersey Shore, six other bridges (South Washington Street, Ouaquaga, Lover's Leap, Pierceville, Pineground, and Waterville) have been incorporated into parks. These include multiple historical plaques, hiking trails, and access provided in parking lots.

To list just a few of the special highlights:

- In addition to being freshly painted, both Neshanic Station and Pine Creek/Jersey Shore are both bright white in color. This is a very bold color choice because, although it looks amazing, it easily shows rust or other discoloration if not maintained. In both cases, these bridges today are sparkling white in color.
- Similarly, Bardwell's Ferry, Aiken Street, Lover's Leap, and Pierceville are each bright red in color. This is another unusual and attractive color choice, far different from the usual gray or green color of steel bridges.
- Aiken Street is the largest, being five spans long. South Washington Street has three spans, Neshanic Station has two spans, and the others only one.
- Pierceville is the oldest of the group, dating from 1881. It does not have the classic Berlin Iron Bridge Company date plaque because it pre-dates the company name change, and instead it shows a Corrugated Metal Company plaque.
- While most rehabilitated bridges are reconstructed in place or moved, at most, a few miles, you will no longer find the Waterville Bridge anywhere near Waterville. This bridge was moved more than

100 miles in 1985 to carry the Appalachian Trail across Swatara Creek in Swatara State Park, east of Harrisburg. To capture two amazing bridges within a single hour, the Inwood Iron Bridge, dating from 1899 and rehabilitated in 2019, is only about a half-mile away.

RECORD-SETTING BRIDGES

As you visit historic bridges and read the plaques, your head will start to swim with all of the claims of various records once held by the bridge you are studying. Not just "the longest suspension bridge" but "the world's longest self-anchored suspension span," whatever that means. Not just "world's highest bridge" but "world's highest cement arch bridge." Not "world's longest truss bridge" but "world's longest continuous truss bridge span." To a layman, it seems that if you have to add several adjectives to claim a record, it cannot be much of a record. However, that does not stop owners of the bridges from making the claim on informational plaques and websites. It also does not stop bridge enthusiasts from visiting specific bridges just to see an important record holder.

Probably the most well-known category of record, and the one that is most frequently cited on historical plaques on bridges, is that of the world's longest suspension span. After all, a brief glance at the apparent flimsiness of any suspension bridge is enough to impress any casual observer with how difficult it must be to build longer ones. In fact, the history of the world's longest suspension spans is a microcosm of the Industrial Revolution itself, starting in Britain, and reflecting the post-World War change from Europe to the United States as the economic and industrial leader of the world. The record for longest suspension span in the world came from Menai Bridge in Wales to the United States in 1849, with the Wheeling Suspension Bridge at about 1,000 feet long. The record stayed in the United States, or jointly between the US and Canada, for more than 130 years before moving back to England with the Humber Bridge in 1981. Seventeen years later, the record moved to Japan, where it has stayed ever since. There are now six bridges with suspension spans longer than the Humber, and five of those are in either Japan, China, or South Korea.

GEORGE WASHINGTON BRIDGE, NEW YORK CITY

Although 12 bridges in the United States have held the record for the longest suspension span, perhaps the most impressive is the George Washington Bridge in New York City. It is subtle, but the primary appeal of the George Washington Bridge is related to the way that suspension bridges are measured.

To the viewer, driver, or bridge walker, what is generally noticed is the overall length of the bridge. Visually, the appearance of the bridge from shore to shore. Driving, the length of time it takes to go from the tollbooth on one side to the tollbooth on the other. Walking, the distance from the sidewalk entrance on one side to the sidewalk exit on the other.

In these measurements, the George Washington Bridge is not special. The shore to shore, or tollbooth to exit, or sidewalk to sidewalk distances on the George Washington Bridge are not any longer than other bridges. The total walk across the George Washington Bridge is less than a mile. The walk on the Brooklyn, Manhattan, Williamsburg, Benjamin Franklin, and Golden Gate bridges are all longer than a mile. Mackinac Bridge is almost five miles. For six years in the 1930s, the George Washington Bridge was the longest suspension bridge in the world, but so were many other US bridges, including four other bridges—Brooklyn, Williamsburg, Bear Mountain, and Verrazzano Narrows—in the New York area. With other enormous suspension bridges available to visit, including the Golden Gate and Mackinac, the George Washington Bridge seems like just another big, old bridge. It is big enough that it should be visited, but not clearly bigger than any of the others.

However, to the engineer and bridge designer, the length of the walk or drive is unimportant. In terms of the engineering challenge, the important measurement is the length of the main suspended span of the bridge between the towers. To understand the achievement of the George Washington Bridge, you have to look at the numbers. Between 1849 and 1981, 12 bridges in the US set a new record for the longest suspension bridge in the world. However, almost all of these record-breaking bridges set the new record by just a tiny bit. The Williamsburg Bridge claimed the record in 1903 by being five feet longer than the Brooklyn Bridge. Bear Mountain improved on this in 1924 by adding another 30 feet. Most of these bridges set new records in minor increments.

In 1931, when the George Washington Bridge opened, the longest suspension bridge main span in the world was Ambassador Bridge in Detroit, at 1,850 feet. It took more than 80 years for the record of the Wheeling Suspension Bridge to be almost doubled. Then, in one fell swoop, the George Washington Bridge set the new record at a length of 3,501 feet. That was more than 1,650 feet longer or almost double the length of what was, at that time, the longest bridge in the world.

The George Washington Bridge did not set the new record. It smashed the old one. It ushered in a new era of mega-bridges. It does not stand out as special to us today because there are now many other mega-bridges. In a country where we drive over, walk over, and see these large-scale suspension bridges throughout New York City, in Philadelphia, at both ends of the New Jersey Turnpike, over the Chesapeake Bay, and in a hundred other common places, the George Washington Bridge looks to be just another one of the crowd. The bridge seems normal. However, this is because the George Washington Bridge established what is now considered normal.

So why is this achievement unnoticeable during your visit? The main reason is that the George Washington Bridge has almost no approaches. Because the bridge extends from one elevated area to another, from the Palisades to Washington Heights, the bridge does not need extensive approaches to gradually gain elevation over the river. The bridge consists largely of the main span only and nothing else. In contrast, the Brooklyn, Manhattan, and Williamsburg bridges, all with much shorter main spans, have approaches that extend for a half-mile on either side. Most of your walk on those bridges is actually over neighborhoods, with only a small central part over the river. The George Washington Bridge walk is shorter, but it is almost all river. Another reason that this length does not seem special is because it has since been exceeded on other bridges. The main spans on both the Golden Gate and Mackinac are longer.

Finally, although this was the first of the mega-bridges, it is not appreciably older than the ones that followed. The 1931 George Washington Bridge was just one of several record-setting bridges all built at about the same time. Other record-setters or near record-setters built in this period included Bear Mountain (1924), Benjamin Franklin (1926), Mid-Hudson (1930), and Golden Gate (1937). While the historical importance of the bridge can be seen in the numbers, the point about this being the first of the mega-bridges is not obvious to you during your visit.

Even though it has since been eclipsed, it is still clearly a mega-bridge. Despite holding the length record for only six years, the George Washington Bridge is still, more than 80 years later, the twenty-third longest suspension bridge in the world, and the fourth longest in the US. Moreover, it is a mega-bridge not just in terms of length. The bridge carries more lanes of traffic, 14 total lanes, than any bridge in the US. It does this by carrying traffic on two separate decks. The bridge is enormously high, rising more than 200 feet above the Hudson River, about the same height as the Golden Gate. Although it is hated for its traffic jams, the George Washington Bridge is one of the most impressive technological achievements on a bridge anywhere.

BATTLE BRIDGES

Historic bridges may be interesting not just for their early use of a technology but because they were witness to, perhaps even the cause of, prominent historic events. The important attraction of these bridges is not that there was coincidentally a major historic event at the same location as a bridge. It is that a major historic event occurred here *because* there was a bridge. By funneling the mobility of armies, bridges became the sites of major battles, world-shaking events that changed the course of history merely because of the existence of a bridge. This can be seen in the names of many of the more famous battles in history, such as the Battle of the Milvian Bridge in Rome and the Battle of Stamford Bridge in England.

STIRLING BRIDGE, STIRLING, SCOTLAND

The setting of the town of Stirling and its famous castle are perfect examples of how easily small geographic features, which appear to be almost insignificant to us in the twenty-first century, shaped nation-scale events in medieval Europe. It is difficult to imagine, with our reliance on fuel-driven cars and trains gliding across steel and cement bridges, how substantial a barrier to travel was formed by just a little bit of water. However, the topography associated with the estuaries of the Rivers Clyde and Forth in Scotland formed an almost insurmountable barrier for centuries, isolating the residents on either side from each other, limiting trade, creating linguistic differences, and offering protection from armies. To look at the River Forth in Stirling today, it is mind-boggling to think that this specific location on this little river, only about 100 feet across and quite shallow, controlled the movement of armies for centuries.

At the location where the Clyde estuary cuts in from the west and the Forth estuary cuts in from the east, the island of Britain narrows from more than 100 miles to only about 20 miles wide, and much of that width was occupied by marshes. Early cartographers and chroniclers considered the Firth of Forth to be a sea and Scotland, the land beyond the estuary, to be almost an island separate from England. The only relatively easy crossing was at Stirling, but even that required construction of a bridge. A famous map of Britain by Mathew Paris, dating from 1247, shows one bridge in the entirety of Britain—the bridge at Stirling. Bridges have been situated here since Roman times. The crossing served as the gateway connecting England to Scotland, resulting in the importance of Stirling Castle in controlling the use of that gateway.

The most famous event at the bridge here was the Battle of Stirling Bridge in 1297. Like most events dating that early, the specific circumstances and locations are mired in a mixture of propaganda and legend. However, the battle is significant, not just in Scottish but in all of European history, as being the earliest incident in which an overwhelming force of heavily armed knights was defeated by a few commoners armed with nothing but spears, and the strategic use of the small wooden bridge by the outnumbered locals was a major factor in the outcome.

The forces of English King Edward I occupied the stronghold of Stirling Castle south of the bridge. The rebels under William Wallace occupied a hill overlooking the north end of the bridge, and blocked any attempt by the English Army to move north into the Scottish Highlands to subdue the population there. The English, relying on their advantage in numbers and arms, decided to cross the bridge to engage the Scots on the northern side. However, the bridge was only nine feet wide, and moving an army of 10,000 across was going to take a long time. The Scots waited until about half of the army had crossed and massed in the field to the north, and then they attacked. The English tried to retreat, but the bridge was destroyed, splitting the English army in two and cutting off retreat.

The manner of the bridge's destruction is the stuff of legend, with various reports of collapse from the weight of the knights and their horses, or deliberate destruction by the English to stop the Scots from pursuing them as they retreated. The popular legend in Scotland, reported on various historical plaques at the current bridge, is that Wallace gave the order to destroy the bridge to a carpenter named John Wright. At the critical moment, Wright pulled out a pin from a strategic location, allowing the bridge to collapse and trapping the remaining knights on the north bank, where they were slaughtered by the Scots. For the remainder of his life, Wright was known by the name of "Pin Wright," and the oldest Wright male was named "Pin" up into the twentieth century.

A famous image displayed on several exhibition plaques around town, wherever the history of the battle is presented, is the Seal of the Burgh of Stirling. The seal depicts two armies brandishing weapons against each other from opposite ends of a seven-arched bridge, with a crucified Christ in between them. The Latin motto on the seal roughly translates as "the Britons stand protected by force of arms, and the Scots by the cross." The image of the seal is depicted on an exhibition plaque overlooking the River Forth valley at Stirling Castle, in a relief inset into the cement in a plaza on the southern end of the current bridge, and in another relief plaque at the actual battlefield area on the northern end of the current bridge. The small seal itself, only a few inches across, is on display in the local Stirling Smith Art Gallery.

The coincidence of the imagery with the actual events of the Battle of Stirling Bridge implies that the image is a commemoration of the battle. However, the image is documented to have been used as the seal of the city as early as 1286, which is 11 years before the battle. In other words, the event depicted is not the famous Battle of Stirling Bridge fought by William Wallace, but an earlier encounter between the English and the Scots on the same bridge or on a nearby bridge. Although the William Wallace battle is the famous event we know about today, the military importance of the bridge and its role in serving as a border between the English and Scottish armies was already well-enough established for the image to be used as the town's seal prior to the battle.

The bridge that existed on the site was destroyed during the battle, but it was not the original bridge. It was likely just one of a series of wooden bridges constructed at this strategic crossing since Roman times. Several versions were built and destroyed in the years following the battle, as well. The current bridge is a stone arch bridge dating from the sixteenth century. The remnants of the battle bridge are reported to be found below water level just a couple hundred feet to the north of the current stone bridge.

Although the current bridge was constructed more than 200 years after the battle, it does serve as the focal point for tourists interested in the battle, William Wallace, and the Scottish Wars of Independence. There are historical plaques and observation areas on both ends, and monuments in a meadow on the northern end that is thought to be the actual battlefield area.

Aside from its association with the battle, the current bridge would be a tourist attraction just for being a gorgeous stone arch bridge dating from the sixteenth century. An inventory of early Scottish bridges documents only 30 bridges from the sixteenth century or earlier. The bridge is of a large scale for its small river, with four stone arches rising more than 20 feet high. By the early nineteenth century, the bridge was deemed too narrow, and proposals were considered to rebuild it. Eventually, another stone arch bridge was constructed about 100 yards downstream. In 1831, the bridge was closed to traffic. It was maintained as a pedestrian walkway, but also to act as a tourist attraction, a role it still fulfills almost 200 years later.

NORTH BRIDGE, CONCORD, MASSACHUSETTS

The North Bridge over the Concord River near the village of Concord, Massachusetts, was one of the smallest, most insignificant bridges you can imagine. It was so insignificant that, when they went to commemorate the 50th anniversary of the event, they had to place their monument on the wrong side of the river because there was no longer a bridge to get it across to the other side. There is a replica bridge there today that you can walk over. It is the sixth bridge constructed since the event, because tourists keep coming and expecting to see a bridge.

As small as the North Bridge was, the British Army placed guards on it on the morning of April 19, 1775. They did this so that a few hundred colonial farmers carrying guns, otherwise known as the Minutemen, who were gathered on a hill across the river, could not interfere with their search for arms in the village. There had already been trouble earlier that morning at Lexington, where eight colonists had been killed. With a bridge only a few feet wide and maybe 50 feet long, keeping the farmers away from Concord would not be too difficult. Unless something happened to make the farmers snap.

Back in the village, about a mile away, the British found some arms in the Inn, took them out front to the Green, and started a bonfire. The Minutemen saw the smoke and thought the British were burning the village. Outnumbering the British at the bridge by about 400 to 50, the Minutemen decided to cross the bridge to stop the arson. Shots were fired, killing three British soldiers on the spot. This was the first incident in the American Revolution where the colonists fired on the British army. It was the "Shot Heard 'Round the World."

The Minutemen chased the British back into Concord and then, with reinforcements arriving from other neighboring towns, all the way back to Boston along what became known as the Battle Road. All of this occurred because the bridge was the only way for the Minutemen to cross the river and get to the village to protect their homes, which is a big contribution to world history for one little wooden bridge.

So why should a sixth-generation replica of the tiny bridge be visited today? Well, partly because you can. And partly because, even though the little bridge is not authentic, the rest of the area is. The river, the Old Manse, the Colonial Inn in central Concord, the Battle Road. Even the graves of the three British soldiers. It is all there as part of Minuteman National Historic Park, operated by the National Park Service.

The absence of the original bridge is not important. It is the event itself that needs to be absorbed. And this does happen at the North Bridge, even knowing that the structure itself is a replica. This is because the magnitude of what happened here, and its effect on world history, is much larger than the little wooden bridge. Even though it is a replica, the bridge helps you to visualize and understand the event, doing its small part to make a visit to Concord complete. The best time to visit is during the Patriots' Day festivities, which commemorate the battle. Events, including parades and historical reenactments, occur over two weeks, climaxing on the third Monday every April.

CHAPTER 3

COMMUNITY BRIDGES

AN INTERESTING EFFECT RESULTS FROM a bridge being located in the center of a growing community and at the intersection of regionally important transportation systems. Back in the days when people were originally settling and passing through these bridge-centered communities, they were traveling on foot or horseback, at foot or horseback speed. And when people converge on a single location at slow speed, they interact. They talk to each other. The narrow end of the funnel, the bridge, became a community gathering place. Markets, shops, and chapels sprung up not just near the bridges, but on them. Bridges served a community function by being the location for the posting of proclamations, or the execution of criminals and rebels. Bridges were used for religious rituals and festivals. They provided defense mechanisms for communities on either end that were unfriendly toward each other, and served as the stage for good-natured rivalries among communities that were on friendly terms. Bridges were decorated, they served as memorials, and they became centers and symbols of their communities.

By World War II, these communal functions of bridges had evaporated. Traffic on the bridges no longer moved on foot or horseback. Now, in the twenty-first century, people pass through these pinch points at 60 miles an hour, windows closed, attention focused on their cell phones, and do not interact with their fellow barrier-crossers except for the occasional hand gesture. That is the best-case scenario. In the worst case, the pinch points become overcrowded, and we call this phenomenon a traffic jam. Instead of celebrating how these engineering marvels have brought distant communities together, we curse them whenever we have to tap the brakes.

Meanwhile, modern bridges carry elevated highways and have no pedestrian sidewalks. The bridges and highways themselves have become barriers, preventing people on one side of town from living, shopping, and schooling with those on the other, even blocking the visual connectivity of a community. Even while connecting a city 100 miles in one direction with another city 100 miles in the other, the elevated ramps to the bridge make it impossible for local residents to walk a few blocks to the supermarket.

Thankfully, this situation has been gradually changing since the 1990s. The slow-speed functions of bridges are becoming more important again, largely in response to government regulations requiring that large public works projects, such as bridge construction, be done in close collaboration with the local community. With increased public interest in both physical fitness and environmental protection, those communities have not been shy about demanding that the new bridges incorporate pedestrian and bike trails to enhance their recreation and park systems.

Because the bridges are funded by the government, the people and politicians are also insisting on using the bridge as a blank canvas on which to commemorate, celebrate, memorialize, advertise, adulate, and symbolize persons, groups, industries, and anything else they can think of which may be of importance to the community. Bridges are again being designed or modified to serve as a community gathering place, an object of public art, a recreational destination, and a location to preserve and honor our history.

Bridges are given affectionate nicknames known only to the locals such as Squinty, Tilting, Mighty Mac, Buffalo, B-M-W, Three Sisters, Thunder, Winking Eye, UFO, Blue, Green, M, and Q. The importance of a bridge to the local community can be reflected in a nickname derived from the cost of the toll. The charge for the Ha'Penny Bridge in Dublin was just that—a half penny. The amount of the toll also gave us the names of the Two Cent

Bridge in Maine and Pont Au Double in Paris. The 1895 Valley Drive Suspension Bridge, a gorgeous little eye-bar chain suspension bridge in Mill Creek Park in Youngstown, Ohio, is variously known as the Silver, Cinderella, Walt Disney, and Castle Bridge.

Much as old inns like to brag about their contribution to American history by claiming that "Washington Slept Here," communities do the same with the names of their bridges. Although the crossing of the Delaware River at Trenton is the most famous, it is only one of several places where a bridge has been named to commemorate one of Washington's short boat trips. Pittsburgh residents want to remind us that he also crossed the Alleghany, and Cumberland, Maryland, lays claim to a crossing of the Potomac.

Spaces underneath the arches of bridge approaches, known as the "down-under" space, have been turned into miniature neighborhoods. Restaurants and open-air markets flourish beneath the arches of the Manhattan end of Queensboro Bridge, the Brooklyn end of Manhattan Bridge, and the Southwark end of London Bridge.

These community functions of bridges cannot be observed, studied, or enjoyed at 60 miles per hour. The bridges must be visited on foot.

BRIDGE FESTIVALS AND EVENTS

The central location and prominence of bridges in many cities results in their playing a major role in community festivals, events, and celebrations. Bridges are used as the stage for performances, feature prominently in parades, and serve as a launching pad for fireworks displays.

In many cities, fireworks for the Fourth of July and other celebrations are set off directly from the bridge. Possibly the best known of these is the annual New Year's fireworks display on the Sydney Harbour Bridge, which is televised worldwide as the first arrival of the New Year. However, enormous fireworks displays are also presented on other large-scale bridges, especially on special anniversaries, including anniversaries of the bridge itself. In 2012, the Golden Gate Bridge served as the stage for fireworks during the Golden Gate Festival, a celebration of the bridge's 75th anniversary. In 2014, the Clifton Suspension Bridge hosted a massive fireworks display in celebration of its 150th anniversary.

In some cases, the bridge itself is the event. Many bridges are closed to traffic, either partially or completely, for running events. The most spectacular sight may be the Verrazzano Narrows Bridge during the New York City Marathon, while 50,000 runners are crossing it. Many other bridges are closed for race events, including the Talmadge Bridge in Savannah, and the Chesapeake Bay Bridge. For slower bridge enthusiasts, some bridges are closed to traffic once a year to allow pedestrians to take over the bridge. The New River Gorge Bridge in West Virginia opens its deck to bridge walkers on Bridge Day every October, attracting thousands of tourists to watch BASE jumpers hurl themselves off the bridge and into the gorge.

Some bridges are such prominent attractions in their community that they are the focus of bridge-related festivals on and near the bridge. Many cities have weekend festivals in their city parks in the summer to attract suburbanites to the downtown area. Where these city parks are located on and near prominent bridges, the bridge becomes the theme of the festival. Abandoned bridges are tied into the riverfront park systems, making the bridge the geographic center of the festival. For instance, the annual Stone Arch Bridge Festival in Minneapolis attracts thousands of people every June for music on multiple stages, local foods, and arts and crafts. In some smaller communities, such as Ashtabula County, Ohio, and Madison County, Iowa, covered bridges are their main tourist attraction, and so their festivals celebrate the bridges by offering tours.

As an antipode to the use of bridges as the stage, bridges are also used as seating for community events taking place within view of the bridge. The features of bridges that make them good places from which to view scenery and cityscapes, including the elevated platform and separation from trees and buildings, also make them good places from which to view special community events taking place in the water below or sky above. In many cities, fireworks are discharged from barges in the middle of the harbor or river. This provides a safety factor by separating the fireworks from the public. It also maximizes the amount of space for viewers by holding the fireworks display in an open setting away from trees and buildings.

It is common for cities to report traffic stopped on freeways and bridges during fireworks displays, although it is not just casual passersby who are stopping. Locals and tourists will deliberately go to the sidewalk, hauling lawn chairs and coolers, and will set up camp hours in advance to stake out the prime viewing spots.

When researching to find the best viewing locations for firework events, you will frequently find one or more of the local bridges specifically identified as the place to go. The website for the Fourth of July Fireworks on the National Mall in Washington, DC, suggests viewing from Key Bridge and Arlington Memorial Bridge, but warns that no lawn chairs are permitted. Websites providing information on fireworks in Minneapolis suggest viewing from the historic Stone Arch, and the website for viewing fireworks in Pittsburgh suggests the Roberto Clemente Bridge. The website describing the annual New Year's Day fireworks in London mentions Westminster, Tower, Southwark, Millennium, and Waterloo bridges as available viewing spots.

The best fireworks viewing bridge, by far, is the Jacques-Cartier Bridge in Montreal. Occurring on eight Wednesday and Saturday nights in July and August, L'International des Feux Loto-Quebec, or Montreal International Fireworks Competition, spotlights fireworks companies from various countries, with a choreographed display of fireworks and music for each country tied to a theme. As the premier fireworks competition in the world, these are the greatest fireworks you will ever see. The bridge, which is closed to traffic hours in advance to allow pedestrians to occupy the prime spots, is the best viewing location. This is partly because of the close proximity, but also because the bridge deck is elevated almost to the same level that the fireworks explode, giving a remarkable three-dimensional effect that you will never see from any other fireworks viewing location.

MACKINAC BRIDGE, MICHIGAN

Three hundred and sixty-four days a year, the Mackinac Bridge connecting the Upper and Lower Peninsulas of Michigan is an enormous, attractive bridge to drive over, or even to stop at one of the state parks on the shore to take in the view. It is not walkable on those three hundred sixty-four days but is worth stopping to view from a distance anyway.

Mackinac Bridge crosses the Mackinac Straits, the narrow water body that connects Lake Michigan and Lake Huron. It is not as if they need any help being bigger, but Lakes Michigan and Huron are really a gigantic single lake, with the same water elevation and no barriers preventing water flow between them through the Straits. However, the unusual shape and narrowing of the lake at the Straits has led them to be considered as two separate lakes.

The massive size of these lakes, part of the largest reservoir of fresh water in the world, resulted in the Upper and Lower Peninsulas of Michigan being effectively unconnected, for purposes of overland travel, for more than 120 years after Michigan statehood. It was only in 1957 that they were joined, a feat that required the construction of what was, at the time, the longest suspension bridge in the world. Although the length of the main span, or the distance between the towers, is shorter than many bridges, the total length of the suspended portion of the bridge is 8,614 feet long, the third-longest in the world. The total length of the bridge is more than 26,000 feet (5 miles), or about three times longer than the Golden Gate Bridge. The bridge is also enormously high, with the central section sitting more than 150 feet above the waters of the lake. This height allows passage of commercial ship traffic between the Lake Michigan ports, primarily Chicago, and the Atlantic Ocean.

The bridge is a classic suspension bridge design. On each end, where the bridge is only a few feet above water level, the deck sits on a series of closely-spaced concrete piers. Where the deck starts to rise toward the towers, it consists of an interlaced steel-girder substructure sitting on more widely spaced, increasingly higher piers. In the central section, the same substructure of the deck continues, but it is supported from above by steel cables. The two towers rise to a height of 550 feet above water level. The deck of the bridge is narrow, compared to other large-scale suspension bridges. The deck supports two lanes of traffic in each direction and has no sidewalks.

Although the bridge is not walkable, its beauty and importance have made it an iconic tourist attraction in northern Michigan. The image of the bridge is depicted on special state license plates and state park signs and is the logo for the Village of Mackinaw City. The southern end of the bridge leads directly into downtown Mackinaw City, a lovely lakeside re-sort town with hotels lining the shore. Mackinaw City sports several his-toric attractions associated with its prominent location on the Mackinac Straits. A fort, Colonial Michilimackinac, was located here from 1715 to 1781, and can still be visited through a tourist entrance located directly beneath the bridge. The shoreline east of the bridge in Mackinaw City is Michilimackinac State Park and includes the Mackinac Point Lighthouse, dating from 1890. This is a gorgeous house attached to a round light tower that is made of yellow brick that complements the beige color of the bridge towers.

The northern end of the bridge lands near the town of St. Ignace, al-though the bridge does not lead traffic directly into the town as it does in Mackinaw City. Signs just past the toll plaza indicate the direction to Bridge View Park, located just west of the bridge on the north shore of Lake Michigan. This park, constructed in 2002, serves as a visitor center for the bridge. The small building has displays on the history of the area and the construction of the bridge. A bronze statue is a memorial to the five workers killed during the construction of the bridge. A large bronze bell displayed in front of the building was the original fog warning from the south tower until it was replaced by a foghorn in 1961. The rest of the park is landscaped with gardens, walking paths, and picnic tables, all with an incredible view of the surrounding forested hills and the bridge.

Mackinac Bridge is a beautiful bridge three hundred sixty-four days each year. On the three hundred and sixty-fifth day, Labor Day every year since 1957, the Mackinac Bridge is no longer just a bridge. It is a statewide celebration.

At 5:00 a.m. on Labor Day, buses begin to transport people from Mack-inaw City to a staging area at the toll plaza in St. Ignace. After passing through a security check, the crowd gathers in the dark in front of a stage, trying to be closest to a gate in the fence. Despite the cold and dark, the atmosphere is festive. Many of the walkers have patches on their jackets indicating that they have participated in the bridge walk ten, fifteen, or twenty times. People have dressed for the event: funny hats, superhero costumes, beauty queens wearing their sashes, kilts, you name it. This will probably be one of your few chances to join an excited crowd, bundled up against the cold, passing around beach balls well before sunrise. Someone at a microphone occasionally informs the crowd of the time, and entertains them by recounting facts and stories about the bridge and the bridge walk event.

Mackinac Bridge, Michigan, on Labor Day

At around 6:30, you can see that the traffic on the northbound lanes of the bridge has been diverted so that there is only one lane in each direction on what are normally the two southbound lanes. At 6:45, with a glow in the eastern sky, the mayor of St. Ignace takes the stage and introduces the Governor of Michigan. A group of about 400 pre-selected runners is permitted to begin their run before the bridge walkers begin. After the Governor makes a few remarks, there is a countdown from ten, and then the gate is opened and the Governor leads the crowd in a walk across the bridge.

The walk traverses the entire five-mile length of the bridge, ending in downtown Mackinaw City. The faster walkers do the bridge walk in about an hour. Others cross at a more leisurely pace, taking photographs and enjoying the great view of the lakes, the bridge, and the spectacle of the event. Throughout your walk, buses, pickup trucks, and vans full of people pass just a few feet from you, heading north to the toll plaza to drop off another load of walkers.

The views from the bridge are amazing, with the shoreline hotels of Mackinaw City and the trees of Mackinac Island visible to the east. With a little luck, there will be one or more gigantic ships passing under the bridge, transporting grain or ore from one lake to the other. Although views to the west are obstructed by two lanes of traffic, you can get a good aerial view of the fort at Colonial Michilimackinac.

At the southern end of the bridge, the walkers are funneled through exits that are manned by volunteers. You will be given a numbered certificate documenting your completion of the bridge walk, and you can spend the rest of the day searching the downtown storefront windows to see if your number is displayed, resulting in winning a prize.

There are websites dedicated to the bridge walk that provide information, including http://www.mackinacbridge.org. Parking lots are set up throughout Mackinaw City and will cost you from five to ten dollars. There are "official" buses that leave from the bus loading area at the State Dock. Bus tickets cost five dollars, and sales at the State Dock begin at 5:30 a.m. However, there are "unofficial" buses leaving town from numerous other locations starting by 5:00 a.m. These buses can be found sitting at street corners and in hotel parking lots, just waiting until all empty seats are filled, at which point they leave for St. Ignace. The bus will drop you at the staging area, only a few hundred feet from the end of the bridge.

Once you have finished the walk, you will find yourself on the western end of downtown about a mile from the State Dock and hotel area on the eastern end, so you still have a substantial walk back to your hotel or car. Although the next obvious activity after ending your walk at 8:30 a.m. is breakfast, be warned that the downtown area restaurants become crowded, so be prepared to fight the massive crowds in Mackinaw City for the rest of the day.

Even better than pursuing a hobby on your own is pursuing it in a crowd with tens of thousands of other people who are there for the same reason. In 2013, 33,000 people participated in the Labor Day Mackinac Bridge Walk. Walkers are allowed to leave the toll plaza until 11:00 a.m., so you can get a late start if you want to sleep in. However, there is no doubt that the early walkers are a little more into it. As long as you are going this far to walk the bridge, you might as well join the early crowd and pass around the beach ball.

SHOPPING BRIDGES

One of the more popular tourist activities is shopping, which tourist bridges support by serving as a prominent subject for souvenirs. One measure of a bridge's tourist attraction is the portrayal of the bridge on refrigerator magnets, coffee cups, T-shirts, and boxes of chocolates. Where famous and iconic bridges attract tourists, hawkers of bridge-related souvenirs cannot be far behind.

In many cases, these items can be found in souvenir shops through the city, not just in shops near the bridge. However, there are many cases where the items are sold in gift shops situated within historic bridge structures, or in newly constructed gift shops near the ends of the bridge. Both the Tower Bridge and DuSable Bridge have museums operating within the old buildings that formerly housed machinery for operating their draw spans, and both museums have gift shops that sell bridge-related books and souvenirs. Similarly, the Legii Bridge in Prague has turned one of its former tollhouses, a lovely, ornate structure, into a tiny souvenir shop large enough for only one or two shoppers at a time. The Kapellbrücke in Lucerne has a souvenir shop halfway across, placed in prime position to catch the eye of the thousands of tourists walking by. Other bridges have placed gift shops into buildings that are near to, but not on, the bridge itself. Examples include the Golden Gate, New River Gorge in West Virginia, the Penobscot Narrows Bridge and Observatory in Maine, and the Clifton Bridge.

The more famous association of bridges with shops is found in a few European cities where shops were actually built on the stone bridge, lining one or both sides of the bridge. When you think about it from a marketing standpoint, this is brilliant. Commercial and retail firms, even today, strive to increase their visibility to passing traffic, whether it is on foot, by car, or on the internet. Before the days of railroads and cars, bridge-crossers were a captive audience. The bridges funneled traffic from miles in every direction to converge on the single spot where a river could be crossed, effectively forcing would-be shoppers into a limited area. Moreover, these travelers were moving no faster than foot or horse speed. No wonder merchants went out of their way to place shops directly onto the bridge itself. The most famous instance, of course, is the Ponte Vecchio in Florence. However, a few other examples exist that are equally impressive, even if lesser-known, and are prominent tourist attractions in their local area.

PULTENEY BRIDGE, BATH, ENGLAND

Bath is one of the more popular tourist towns in England. It is the site of Pulteney Bridge, which crosses the River Avon. Pulteney Bridge is a stone arch bridge about the same size as Ponte Vecchio, and having shops lining both sides, but the similarities end there. As historic as it is, having been built in 1774, Pulteney Bridge is still about four centuries newer than Ponte Vecchio.

This area of Bath was developed in the late 1700s and influenced by the Georgian style of architecture practiced by Robert Adam, the most important British architect at the time. An interesting feature of the bridge is the outward appearance of the shops from either side. The bridge marks the northern edge of the historic, central tourist area, which includes Bath Abbey, the Roman Baths, and the train station. The area north of the bridge is a later residential and commercial suburb, but probably relatively undeveloped at the time the bridge was built and not visited by many tourists today.

This situation influenced how the bridge was developed and is presented today. From the streets and riverwalks along the River Avon on its southern side, the outward appearance of the shops is clean, symmetrical, and aesthetically pleasing. This is the view that tourists see, and the view you will find in photographs of Bath. In contrast to the higgledy-piggledy arrangement on Ponte Vecchio, the shops on Pulteney Bridge are an orderly, symmetrical display of stately Georgian architecture that perfectly matches that of the shops and hotels on the surrounding streets. From the northern side, though, the appearance of the shops is much more similar to Ponte Vecchio. Some of the shops have been extended over the edge in modern times, presenting the appearance of being about to fall off, like the shops on Ponte Vecchio.

One difference between the architecture of the bridge and its surrounding buildings is the scale. While the shops and hotels on the adjacent streets had no limitations on their size and rose to four or more stories each, the shops on the bridge needed to be miniaturized to fit into the confined space. While the color, stone type, and outward ornamentation of the shops perfectly match the surrounding buildings, the shops are smaller in every dimension. The shops are only two stories high, and only ten or fifteen feet wide. At this scale, they obviously do not house major retailers, but instead are the locations of small specialty shops and a tiny snack bar.

Another difference between Ponte Vecchio and Pulteney Bridge is the location relative to the main tourist area. In Florence, Ponte Vecchio is in the middle of the action, and must be crossed to get from one prominent tourist sight to another. Pulteney Bridge is located a short walk from the tourist area, with no major tourist sights on its other end. It is also not visible from the Roman and medieval city center. As a result, it is likely that a large number of Bath tourists never see Pulteney Bridge and may not even know it is there. This may, at least partially, account for why Ponte Vecchio is so iconic, while Pulteney Bridge is relatively unknown, even though it is equally as interesting and attractive.

Curiously, the bridge somehow remains unmentioned in two of Jane Austen's novels. She lived in Bath from 1801 to 1805, only about 30 years after the bridge was constructed, and the settings of parts of her novels *Northanger Abbey* and *Persuasion* were in Bath. In these and her other novels, there is a great deal of socializing going on—calling for tea one day, picking up friends for an outing the next, and Austen gives a detailed, blow-by-blow account of the streets and neighborhoods in Bath. In one of the key scenes in Chapter 11 of *Northanger Abbey*, Mr. Thorpe and Catherine Morland take a carriage ride from Catherine's home in Pulteney Street into Laura Place, past Argyle Buildings, and ending in the Market. Argyle Street forms the eastern end of the bridge, and the Guildhall Market forms the western end. Therefore, it seems remarkable that Austen managed to provide a detailed description of this very short carriage ride, not more than a half-mile long, without directly mentioning that a crossing of the bridge, which must have been a very prominent landmark at the time, was also included.

CHAPEL BRIDGES

Travelers on bridges in medieval Europe did much more than shop. Another prominent community activity, then and now, is worship. Shopping is often done on a large scale, but can also be done on a tiny scale, in a tiny building shrunk to fit on a bridge. Worship is the same, sometimes occurring in enormous cathedrals, but also occurring in miniaturized settings placed onto bridges. Religious-themed decorations and components of bridges were commonly used by travelers to pray for a safe journey or, alternatively, to give thanks for having arrived in the town safely. However, some bridges went even further than religious-themed decorations by providing tiny, enclosed altars in a room only big enough for two or three persons.

There are two famous examples in Switzerland. A small chapel, called the Käppelijoch, is located in the middle of the Mittlerebrücke, in Basel. The original Mittlerebrücke, with its original Käppelijoch, was built in 1225. When this bridge was demolished and replaced in 1903, the builders provided a replacement Käppelijoch, although it is no longer used as a place of worship. The Käppelijoch in place today is a small red sandstone chapel with a gorgeous, multicolored, geometrically patterned roof. It is a prominent landmark in Basel, as evidenced by the hundreds of love padlocks attached to the grate covering the entrance.

The Spreuerbrücke, in Lucerne, also has a small altar contained within its structure. The altar, built in 1568, still serves as an active place of worship. It is enclosed within a carved wooden cabinet and is elaborate, complete with stained-glass windows and housing a small Madonna and Child statue.

Chapels on or near the ends of bridges are also common. A short walk from Spreuerbrücke in Lucerne, the Kapellbrücke is famous for the paintings held within its roof rafters. The name of the bridge is derived from the St. Peter's Chapel a few steps from its end. The Ägidienkirche in Erfurt is even closer to its bridge, the Krämerbrücke. Although the church technically sits on the river bank instead of the bridge structure, it straddles the roadway so that travelers must actually pass through an archway underneath the church to cross the bridge.

Finally, some cities built an actual chapel, large enough to fit dozens of parishioners, onto their bridges. This was usually done on bridges that crossed an island, where the island served as the foundation for a wider, central pier for the bridge. A major landmark of Avignon is the Pont Saint Benezet. Only four of its original 22 arches remain, but one of these houses the small Chapel of Saint Nicolas.

CHANTRY CHAPEL ON WAKEFIELD BRIDGE, WAKEFIELD, UK

An internet search on medieval bridge chapels identifies only seven prominent examples remaining in Europe. Of these, four are in England, at Bradford-on-Avon, St. Ives, Rotherham, and Wakefield. In Bradford-on-Avon, the Town Bridge dates from the thirteenth century, and a chapel was added in the seventeenth century. At Rotherham, St. Ives, and Wakefield, the chapel appears to be contemporaneous with the bridge, with dates of 1483 for the Chapel of Our Lady on the Bridge at Rotherham, 1426 for The Chapel on the Bridge at St. Ives, and 1342 for the Chapel of St. Mary Upon Wakefield Bridge, also known as Chantry Chapel.

The histories of these four bridge chapels are similar to each other. The Rotherham, St. Ives, and Wakefield chapels were closed as a result of either the dissolution of the monasteries in 1539 or the abolition of the chantries in 1547, and all three chapels were converted to other uses for several hundred years. These included an almshouse, a prison, residence, and then shop at Rotherham; a residence, pub, and tollhouse at St. Ives; and a warehouse, haberdashery, library, office, and tailor's shop at Wakefield. The chapel on Town Bridge in Bradford-on-Avon was also converted at some point, into a prison.

Each chapel also passed through some period of disuse in which they were almost reduced to ruins, but then each of the chapels was eventually "rediscovered" and restored. Three of them were reconverted to a chapel, with Wakefield being restored in 1848, Rotherham in 1924, and St. Ives in 1930. Bradford-on-Avon was restored to its condition as a jail and remains marketed to tourists as a historic prison today.

Another common feature is that each is tiny, as they must fit onto a bridge pier. However, the small size is part of the attraction to tourists. Each is open for tourist visits only on selected dates, published on their respective websites. Each is also relatively difficult to get to, being in smaller towns out of the tourist mainstream. However, within those towns, each is a prominent local landmark and attraction.

The bridge and chapel at Wakefield are the oldest of the group, both in terms of their original construction and in the restoration of the chapel. Only the crypt, a small empty room about 15 feet on each side, is original from the fourteenth century. The original chapel above the crypt had been in ruins, and was re-constructed as a chapel in 1848. The type of stone used for the 1848 reconstruction was of poor quality and degraded quickly in the corrosive atmosphere in this industrial part of Wakefield. The façade of the chapel was reconstructed again in 1939, using a more durable type of sandstone. The difference in stone types can be seen when descending the spiral stairs into the crypt, as the stone walls of the chapel are smooth-faced due to being cut by machine, while the stone walls of the crypt are rough-faced due to being shaped by hand tools.

Although small, the chapel is elaborately decorated. A carved stone statue of the Virgin, dating from 1848, is displayed next to the altar. The interior is well-lit, with a high carved wood ceiling. Three of the walls are filled with stained glass windows from 1848, and carved stone heads on either side of the East Window represent King Edward III and Queen Philippa, who reigned when the bridge and chapel were first built. The spiral staircase in the northeast corner leads down to the crypt and up to a small bell tower. The exterior façade is intricately carved, with two spires on the front and a single turret acting as the bell tower on the back.

Not to be forgotten is the bridge itself, more than 300 feet long and crossing the River Calder on nine stone arches. The bridge crosses an island in the river, allowing construction of a wider pier at that location, and the wider pier was used to support the chapel. The bridge was widened twice, in 1758 and 1797. It needed to be widened again in the 1930s, but widening would have required removing the chapel. Instead, a new bridge was constructed a few feet upstream, and the chapel bridge was closed to traffic and left open to pedestrians, as it remains today.

The bridge and chapel have been depicted in artworks throughout the centuries. An etching on display in the chapel shows the bridge back when Wakefield was an active port. The etching shows small boats on the upstream, town side of the bridge, and larger sailing ships anchored on the downstream, seaward side of the bridge. The bridge and chapel were also famously painted by J.M.W. Turner in 1797. The painting is owned by the British Museum, but is on loan and displayed at the Hepworth Gallery across the road from the bridge.

Even though it attracts far fewer tourists than more famous bridges, the Chantry Chapel on Wakefield Bridge is what bridge tourism is all about. It is easy for a bridge in a major tourist center such as New York or Paris to attract tourists, because the tourists are already there and looking for interesting places to visit. Also, it is easy for a new or converted bridge connected into bicycle trails to immediately attract local recreationists, because these people have already been riding in the area and have been chomping at the bit for their local trail system to be expanded.

Chantry Chapel is different. Wakefield is not a tourist city. You may well have not ever heard of it, let alone planned to visit. It is an outer suburb of Leeds, also not a prominent tourist city. It is not on the way from any prominent tourist sight to another. Even once in Wakefield, the chapel is not easily accessible. It is not located in the historic town center or in a quaint tourist area. Although the Chapel is just across the road from the Hepworth Art Gallery, the rest of the neighborhood is light industrial/commercial, not particularly attractive. The Chapel is not near the main train station, so must be accessed by car, bus, or taxi. On the town's website, the Chapel is featured with the same level of prominence as the local Mental Health Museum and the National Coal Mining Museum for England. The bridge itself is open to pedestrians at all times, but entry times for the Chapel are limited, so it is a wonder that it attracts any tourists at all.

Nevertheless, it does. The Friends of Wakefield Chantry Chapel operates an informative website, which provides the dates and times when the Chapel is open to tourists. When you arrive, you may well find that you are the only visitor. One or two docents, who are members of the Friends, will greet you and offer to answer questions. There will also be a variety of pamphlets, postcards, and posters on display and available for sale. Then, after a few minutes, another visitor will arrive, inspect the stained glass and the crypt, speak to the docents for ten minutes, sign the guestbook, and then leave. Then another two or three visitors will arrive, visiting from outside of England. These will leave, and then will be replaced by a few more.

There will never be the crush of tourists found on St. Bonifacius Bridge in Bruges, or Ponte Vecchio, or Brooklyn Bridge. However, you will slowly begin to realize that there is a small but steady stream of people, enough for you to see that their visits here are purposeful, and not accidental. These are not people walking through a highly trafficked tourist area and stopping in briefly at the old-looking building to see what is there. These are people deliberately going far out of their way, from other parts of England, from the United States, from Canada, from Russia, to visit this tiny bridge and Chapel.

BORDER BRIDGES

One major goal of tourists is to see specific sights, such as a museum, castle, or historic building. However, just as important to tourists is experiencing new places, cultures, histories, and languages. Moreover, whether we care to admit it or not, many of us keep score of our tourist travels by adding a new place to our life-list the moment we have set foot across the political boundary. There is a sign at the border stating that we have exited one place and have now entered another, a new place where great adventures await. It does not matter that political boundaries are usually arbitrary, and that there may be no difference between the cultures, histories, and languages on either side of the line. It does not matter that we have not yet gotten out of the car and interacted with the natives. Once we have crossed the line, it counts.

Because this experience is so momentous, it is not enough to make a mental note of it as we fly by at 70 miles per hour. The moment must be savored, and documented in photos. Drive along Interstate 70 across a featureless plain west from Kansas into Colorado, and you will see cars stopped on the shoulder, people risking their lives to have their photo taken in front of the sign. Even more enticing is the novelty of setting foot in two, three, or even four states or countries at once. These special boundaries attract tourists for no reason other than to allow us to increase our totals.

For a variety of reasons, rivers often serve to form these political borders. And when bridges cross these rivers, they do more than just cross the water. They now cross from one realm of possible experiences to another, and tourists who count these experiences will pause to walk across the bridge to savor the border.

Of course, travelers by car are aware that there are usually road signs announcing the border. However, they may not be aware that markings are provided for pedestrians, too. Borders are often marked on the sidewalk of bridges, to let pedestrians know exactly where they can stand in two states or countries at once. Rainbow Bridge has a bronze plaque with the seals of both Canada and the United States. The O'Callaghan-Tillman Bridge at Hoover Dam also uses a bronze plaque, this one to mark the exact Nevada-Arizona state border. The Bob Kerrey Bridge in Omaha has the Iowa-Nebraska border marked by a line in paint directly in the middle of the Missouri River.

This border function of bridges has not always been only for enter-tainment of tourists. As bridges may symbolically unite disparate peoples, rivers may symbolically divide similar peoples. This was the case with the Havel River separating Potsdam from West Berlin in Germany. The Glienicke Bridge crossing between East and West Germany became such a symbol during the Cold War. It was known as the Bridge of Spies, where prisoners such as Gary Powers, Anatoly Shcharansky, and others were traded directly at the border, in the middle of the bridge.

THREE COUNTRIES BRIDGE, NEAR BASEL, SWITZERLAND

The Three Countries Bridge near Basel, Switzerland, is in neither Basel nor Switzerland. The bridge crosses the Rhine, connecting the towns of Huningue in Alsace, France, and Weil-am-Rhein in Germany. Both Huningue and Weil-am-Rhein are suburbs of the much larger Basel and the three towns, as well as the three countries, meet at a point in the middle of the Rhine about two miles north of the Mittlerebrücke in cen-tral Basel. The bridge does not actually touch three countries. Instead, it crosses between France and Germany approximately 600 feet north of the triple-point.

There is a monument marking the triple point on the northern tip of the Westquaistrasse in Basel. The name of the pylon depends on which language you wish to speak. It is the Dreiländereck in German, the Pylone des Trois Frontieres in French, or the Three Countries Corner in English. According to waymarking.com, this location is the only three-country point in the world that is situated within a major city. The quay is located in an industrial port area but hosts the pylon, a dock for river cruise boats, and a restaurant. The aluminum-colored pylon was constructed in 1957 and is in the shape of a rocket, with three fins at the bottom. The flags of Germany, France, and Switzerland are shown on the fins, ostensibly showing visitors where they need to step to cross from one country to the next. However, because the actual triple point is in the middle of the river, the pylon is technically in Switzerland, approximately 500 feet south-east of the actual triple point, and the flags marking the borders are only symbolic.

Although the bridge does not really touch three countries, you can use it to walk through three countries within just a few minutes. From the pylon in Switzerland, walk back south to go around one of the channels of the port, and then cross back north along the quay from Switzerland into Germany. A few hundred feet later, cross the bridge from Germany into France. From the end of the bridge in France, you can walk back along the river about two miles into central Basel.

The bridge was constructed in 2007 and would be an important recreational and tourist bridge even if it were not associated with the international borders. The bridge is a modern, sculptural steel arch bridge, and at more than 750 feet long, it is the longest single-span bicycle and pedestrian bridge in the world. The international border is marked in the middle of the bridge with a plaque.

SYMBOLIC BRIDGES

One way to determine the importance of a bridge to the local community is to look around town for images of the bridge. If the bridge is just a way for residents to travel from one side of the city to the other, you will not see any images. However, the more central the bridge is to the identity of the city, the more likely you are to see its image used to symbolize the city itself.

There are many ways this is done. One subtle, but powerful, example is the background image used when an individual is interviewed on television news shows. This photograph always depicts a lovely view of the downtown skyline, or a prominent architectural feature of the city. This serves a function by communicating the location of the person being interviewed, but is also done for aesthetic reasons. It shows off the city looking its best. Different broadcasts may use different photographs, but there are certain cities for which the featured photograph almost always shows the bridge.

An obvious example is San Francisco, which is usually represented by the Golden Gate Bridge. Interestingly, it is unlikely that any of the subjects of these interviews are actually anywhere near the Golden Gate Bridge at the time of their interview. The bridge is not situated near downtown. In

fact, many of the Golden Gate images shown are not taken from downtown northwest toward the bridge. Instead, they are taken from a remote
location in the mountains north of the bridge and looking south. It is not
important that the photograph has any real relationship to the physical
location of the person being interviewed, only that it looks good and communicates the general region.

Other bridges frequently used as symbols of their cities in news interviews are the purple glow of the Zakim Bridge, lit at night, representing
downtown Boston, and the amber night lighting on the Stone Arch, representing Minneapolis. The obvious choice for a symbol of New York City
is the Brooklyn Bridge, so it is interesting to see that the city is also frequently represented by the distinctive profile of either Queensboro Bridge
or Manhattan Bridge.

Images of prominent local bridges are also used as symbols of their
cities on the city logo. A silhouette of the Liberty Bridge is displayed on
road signs indicating you have entered Greenville in South Carolina. The
Mackinac Bridge is not only depicted on the sides of city vehicles, including police cars, in downtown Mackinaw City, but it is also displayed on
Michigan state license plates. The state of West Virginia chose the image
of the New River Gorge Bridge to be shown on their state quarter as their
most prominent landmark. You can find Charles Bridge on the Czech 50
Korun coin, and Chain Bridge in Budapest on the Hungarian 200 Forint
coin.

A brief internet search of historic travel posters will reveal which cities relied on an image of their bridge to attract tourists. Prague obviously
used the silhouette of Charles Bridge in front of an image of Prague Castle, and Bristol used Clifton Bridge. Sometimes, the silhouette of a bridge
is so iconic that it becomes usurped as a symbol by a different town, one
with no apparent connection to the original. It is an understatement to
say that Rialto, in California, is nothing like its namesake in Italy. However, the city seal prominently displays the image of the famous Venetian
bridge.

In addition to serving as symbolic representations of their home cities, bridges may come to symbolize the aspirations of broader communities or nations. After the obvious "structure carrying a road across a river,"

which is the first definition of "bridge" found in the Oxford English Dictionary, there are several other definitions provided. The second definition is "something that is intended to reconcile or form a connection between two things," and bridge-building is defined as "promotion of friendly relations between groups." These symbolic meanings of the word "bridge" have not been lost on bridge designers and owners. Thus, many bridges have come to symbolize a desire to promote unity and peace among the communities on either end. As a result, we have the Peace Bridge linking the United States and Canada in Buffalo, and the Ambassador Bridge linking the United States and Canada between Detroit and Windsor.

TYNE BRIDGES, NEWCASTLE-UPON-TYNE, ENGLAND

Few cities are as closely identified with the image of their bridges as Newcastle. Its identity is not linked with a single bridge, but with an interesting grouping of five of them. What makes the image of bridges in Newcastle an undeniable symbol of that city is not that it shows more than one bridge. Certainly, most river-centric cities have multiple bridges. However, the situation of the bridges in Newcastle is quite unusual.

First, the River Tyne in downtown Newcastle flows through a steep-sided gorge. There are narrow quays at river level on both sides of the river, but then there are steep hillsides rising 50 or more feet high, also on both sides. This results in two completely different sets of bridges. High bridges extend from bluff-top to bluff-top more than 50 feet above river level. Then, a short walk away, low bridges just a few feet above river level connect from quay to quay. The second feature is that the river through downtown Newcastle is perfectly straight. There is no curve to it at all, for a distance of about a mile. A third feature is the variety in the ages, types, and colors of the bridges. The bridges are starkly different from each other in appearance, which makes them stand out from one another when seen together as a group.

Usually, when discussing a group of tourist bridges, the discussion is presented sequentially, starting at one end of the stretch of river, and progressing to the other end. This approach works nicely in Newcastle, if you want to walk across and study each bridge individually. The bridges are all historic, and unusual, with some high, and some low, and historical exhibition plaques explaining each one. However, when experiencing the iconic view of the landmark from the perfect place, what matters is not the sequence of bridges along the river, but that their different heights and construction styles create an unusual photo opportunity. As shown on the cover photo, when looking upriver at the scene, each successive bridge in the series is prominently visible through the blank spaces of the bridge in front of it.

The highest bridge in the vista is the Tyne Bridge, which is enormous. The roadway is high, extending from bluff to bluff, but its supporting steel double-arch is much higher. The plain, dark green bridge was constructed in 1928.

Within the open space directly beneath the deck of the Tyne Bridge, the decks of the High Level Bridge are visible. As the name implies, the beige-colored High Level Bridge also extends from bluff-top to bluff-top. The High Level Bridge is historically important. It was opened in 1849 by Queen Victoria and was an integral part of the first rail link between London and Edinburgh. The bridge is also unusual in appearance. It has four cast-iron arches sandwiched between a lower traffic deck and an upper railroad deck, both still in use.

Directly beneath the two decks of the High Level Bridge, the truss of the 1981 Queen Elizabeth II Metro Bridge can be seen. The Metro Bridge stands out in the image because it is baby blue, and has diagonal girders supporting its truss. This bridge carries light rail traffic.

Below the deck of the Metro Bridge, the 1906 King Edward VII Bridge, is visible. The King Edward VII Bridge is a rail bridge and is the only one of the five that is partially obscured and not completely visible.

Finally, lowest to the water and visible beneath the King Edward VII Bridge is Swing Bridge. This is so named because it can be rotated on a central pivot to allow the passage of ships. Constructed in 1876, Swing Bridge is the most visually appealing of the bridges. The movable section is a single white girder arch, connected to the deck by diagonal red girders and topped by a small, ornate white cupola.

This image of the five bridges, all aligned, is used as the symbolic photograph of the city of Newcastle. It is featured prominently, although without the newer Metro Bridge, on vintage travel posters. It is used as the background photo when individuals in Newcastle are interviewed on television. It was even used as the inspiration for a progressive rock composition, the *Five Bridges Suite*, by The Nice, in 1970.

To capture the iconic image, it is important to stand in one place. On a sunny day, you will find camera-bearing tourists micro-locating themselves, looking through their viewfinders, adjusting a few feet to the left or right, on the northern quay just off the end of the new Gateshead Millennium Bridge, to get the famous alignment just right. From that one location, you can see the image of the five unique bridges perfectly aligned, back-to-back-to-back, each clearly distinguishable, and pleasingly reflected in the river.

Interestingly, the most important tourist bridge in Newcastle, the amazing Gateshead Millennium Bridge, is not part of this vista. This is because the river curves, just slightly, between Tyne Bridge and Gateshead Millennium, to the extent that the axis of the vista formed by the five bridges does not continue through Gateshead Millennium. Instead, it falls onto the quay just to the north of Gateshead Millennium. Because the perfect photograph must be taken directly along the axis, it does not include Gateshead Millennium.

EDMUND PETTUS BRIDGE, SELMA, ALABAMA

A proper explanation of the symbolic importance of Pettus Bridge to the civil rights movement in the United States is impossible within the limited space in this book. Such a discussion would require multiple volumes to provide the historical, economic, and sociological context necessary to understand the series of events that elevated the status of this bridge from an inanimate collection of steel and concrete to that of a shrine.

In February 1965, Jimmie Lee Jackson was shot and killed after attending a voting rights meeting near Selma with his mother. During the procession from Jimmie Lee Jackson's funeral to burial, James Bevel suggested to John Lewis that they should carry the body all the way to Montgomery to confront the governor, George Wallace. This turned into the plan for a major protest march from Selma to Montgomery. Incidentally, because Selma was on the north side of the Alabama River and Montgomery was on the south side, the planned march route necessitated the crossing of a bridge.

The jumping-off point for the planned march was Brown Chapel AME Church, located a few blocks north of the bridge. The march was planned for Sunday, March 7, 1965, what would become known as Bloody Sunday. It would begin at Brown Chapel, proceed a few blocks south, cross the Pettus Bridge, and then continue on what was then the main route of US Route 80 more than 50 miles east to Montgomery. The march included about 600 marchers, crossing the bridge on its sidewalk two abreast, led by Hosea Williams and John Lewis.

The marchers never reached the other side. On the way from Brown Chapel to the bridge, they were surprised to see no sign of police or resistance. Then, as they crossed the crest of the bridge and were able to see what awaited them on the other side, they saw waves of blue-uniformed state troopers on Highway 80 at the base of the bridge. Also present were crowds of white men brandishing baseball bats and other weapons, and a different group comprised of reporters and photographers. After exchanging words with the leader of the state troopers, Lewis and Williams conferred on what to do and decided to kneel and pray. They never got the chance, as the order was given for the troopers to advance. They did, falling first upon Lewis with a billy-club and fracturing his skull, and then attacking the rest of the marchers with clubs, horses, and tear gas.

The mechanics of how the bridge was deliberately used to gain a positional advantage over the marchers was exactly similar to how other battle bridges have operated throughout history. Because the marchers were confined in a limited area between the edges of the bridge, a small number of troopers were able to effectively block the movement of, and cause major injury to, the much larger group. Once the lead marchers set foot on the Pettus Bridge, their fate was sealed. With 600 additional marchers advancing behind them, they could not move backward in retreat. Because the bridge was 100 feet high over the Alabama River, they could not move sideways. The only choice was to move forward toward confrontation with the state troopers at the base of the bridge. Even though the marchers greatly outnumbered the troopers, the leaders of the march were trapped, making violent confrontation by the troopers inevitable.

After the incident was televised nationwide in primetime newscasts that evening, horrified reaction began immediately and picked up steam. On Tuesday, March 9, two days after Bloody Sunday, Dr. Martin Luther King, Jr. led a short march from Brown Chapel to the bridge but did not attempt to confront the troopers. This event became known as Turnaround Tuesday and is part of the history of tension between the proponents of nonviolent civil rights protest and those demanding more aggressive action. On Sunday, March 21, after a federal judge had finally authorized the full march, the group left Brown Chapel again, this time more than 3,000 strong, including both King and Lewis. The marchers made it over the bridge and reached Montgomery five days later.

As we now know, these events did not change all hearts and minds and, 55 years later, much work remains to be done. However, it did change lots of hearts and minds immediately, including those of Lyndon Johnson and many members of Congress. Events in Washington, DC, moved swiftly, culminating in the signing of the Voting Rights Act by Lyndon Johnson on August 6, 1965, with King and Lewis looking on.

The importance of the bridge in the national consciousness has only grown since 1965. Of course, the bridge has sidewalks and can be visited by anyone at any time. However, there is also an Annual Bridge Crossing Jubilee on the first weekend in March, which is the largest annual civil rights celebration in the United States. Round-numbered anniversaries are highlights, often attracting national political leaders up to, and including, current and former presidents. The bridge has been designated as a National Historic Landmark. The City of Selma fully embraces the historical importance of the bridge. The city logo prominently displays the silhouette of the bridge and the city's website features, as its background, a gorgeous video of a helicopter flyover of the bridge. The US Olympic Torch was carried across the bridge in 1996 on its way to Atlanta. After his death in July 2020, John Lewis was carried across the bridge once more, on his way to lay in repose at the capitol in Montgomery.

In an enormous twist of irony, the namesake of this icon of the civil rights movement, Edmund Pettus, was a Confederate general and leader of the Alabama Ku Klux Klan. This may have made sense if the bridge had been constructed in, say, 1863. But it was constructed in 1940, revealing the sad circumstance that Selma could not come up with a better idea 75 years after the Civil War ended, and more than 30 years after Pettus had died. As of 2021, the Alabama state legislature is considering a name change. However, the one obvious person to be honored, John Lewis, opposed renaming the bridge because he felt that the name, no matter how ignominious, was an inseparable part of the history—not only of the bridge, but of the entire civil rights movement.

FACTORY BRIDGES

An unusual subcategory of bridges was built in the industrialized eastern and midwestern United States in the late 1800s and early 1900s, and many of these have since become local landmarks and tourist attractions. These are mill and factory bridges.

Mills and factories at that time relied on flowing water for motive power, as well as for the shipment of raw materials and manufactured products. Therefore, they were located directly on the banks of rivers. These industries were labor-intensive, so they employed thousands of workers. This was before the age of the automobile, so the workers lived in concentrated population centers in towns within walking distance of the mill. Sometimes the mill town was on the same side of the river as the mill, but in other cases it was located on the opposite side of the river. Where the mill town was on the opposite side of the river, bridges were built to provide access for the commuting workers. Because there were no automobiles, and these working-class laborers did not drive horses and carriages, the bridges did not need to be large or traffic-bearing. They only needed to be footbridges, on a small scale, and built as inexpensively as possible. As a result, a generation of these small, factory-specific foot-bridges was built. They were usually small-scale suspension bridges that, because they did not require stiffening trusses, became known as swinging bridges. In some cases, they were small-scale through-truss bridges.

More than 100 years later, most of those mills and factories have closed. Newer factories rely on electric power and railroads, so their locations are no longer tied to the riversides. Most of the former mill and factory buildings have been removed, although many remain in dilapidated condition. Even where the buildings remain, most of their swinging foot-bridges have similarly gone out of existence.

However, a few have been preserved or reconstructed, and can be visited by tourists today. Examples include the Hot Metal Bridge in Pittsburgh; a miniature through-truss bridge across the Turner Canal in Turners Falls, Massachusetts; another entering the front door of the former Fellows Gear Shaper Factory in Springfield, Vermont; the Patapsco Swinging Bridge, a 2006 reconstruction of the original Orange Grove Flour Mill Bridge in Patapsco State Park in Maryland; and the 1909 Brandywine Swinging Bridge in Brandywine State Park in Wilmington, Delaware. In Pontiac, Illinois, the city's two historic swinging bridges, one constructed in 1898 and the other in 1926, were such important attractions that, when a new pedestrian bridge was needed to connect access to city parks in 1978, the city constructed a third swinging bridge in the same style as the two earlier bridges.

TWO CENT BRIDGE, WATERVILLE, MAINE

The 1903 Two Cent Bridge is a factory bridge crossing the Kennebec River between downtown Waterville, Maine and a paper mill on the north side of the river. Formally named the Ticonic Footbridge, the Two Cent name is more commonly used, and reflects the cost of the toll charged to workers for crossing. The bridge is a small, six foot-wide all-steel suspension bridge, painted black, and with a wood plank deck. Although the bridge has stiffening trusses along its deck, it still swings quite a bit when being crossed. The bridge has impressive views of the swift-flowing Kennebec River, and the dominant sound comes from a waterfall on the river just a few hundred feet downstream of the bridge.

An unusual feature on the northern end of the bridge, surrounding the western leg of the suspension tower, is a red, open-sided hut about 20 feet square. There is no informational plaque describing this structure, but internet research suggests that it is a reconstruction of the original tollbooth. This is unusual because tollbooths are usually found at one end, not actually out on the bridge.

Although the factory on the north side of the river is still operating, the advent of automobile commuting eliminated the use of the footbridge for pedestrian workers by the middle of the twentieth century. In 1960, the bridge was turned over to the City of Waterville, and it has been used as part of the city park and trail systems ever since. The bridge is part of a regional trail system known as the Kennebec Messalonskee Trails. In addition to the parking lot and trail, the downtown entrance of the bridge has been developed into a small, brick-floored plaza. There are benches and a small kiosk for posting community information. Both are decorated with medallions of two Indian Head pennies dated 1903, a symbol of the bridge.

BRIDGES AND WATERWORKS

As discussed in Chapter 2, the factors that cause a specific location to be settled and to grow into a city are complex, but they often include the fact that the location is a good place to build a bridge. However, several other features of rivers also supported settlement and growth of communities, especially back in the day when the transport of goods by boat was the most efficient method, and when flowing water provided power for driving machinery. For supporting the transport of goods, the river either needed to be navigable, or it needed to be amenable to being engineered into becoming navigable. For providing motive power, the river needed to flow through a drop in elevation, the larger the better.

Each of these features, on its own, supported commercial activity that required workers, and therefore attracted community settlement and growth. However, the best locations for settlement and growth of communities were those where all of these features were present in a single place. For this reason, you will often find historic bridges near other early engineered waterworks such as dams, locks, canals, weirs, aqueducts, mills and mill races, levees, and water supply intakes.

Few freshwater rivers in Europe or the United States remain in their pristine, free-flowing condition. Most of them have been engineered to meet human needs to the extent that they would now be unrecognizable to the early settlers. The Charles River in Boston was a muddy tidal estuary until the Charles River Dam turned it into a placid freshwater lake in 1912. Cities were built at the outlet of many of the glacial lakes in Switzerland, including Zurich, Geneva, and Lucerne. However, once a city was settled at the outlet of a lake, natural fluctuation in the level of the lake became inconvenient for the settlers. In each case, weirs were constructed to maintain a constant lake level, provide a reliable freshwater supply, and drive mills and, eventually, turbines for electrical generation. In addition, everywhere you find a weir or a dam, you will find a system of locks in place to allow boats to navigate around it.

Historic mills and their associated mill races, which were small canals designed to deliver water to the waterwheels, are found on the Brandywine in Delaware, on the Ill in Strasbourg, and on the Danube in Regensburg. The Chicago River has been so drastically altered that its direction of flow has been reversed forever. In each of these cases, and in many more, the historic waterworks are found close to the historic bridges.

STONE ARCH BRIDGE, MINNEAPOLIS

Back in the days when the most efficient way to ship commercial goods was by boat, the head of navigation was the most important location on any river because it was the furthest inland location accessible by boat. The river above the head of navigation was unnavigable, so goods and materials from locations further inland had to be transported by horse and cart, the least efficient and most labor-intensive method, to the head of navigation. All of this trading and transferring of goods from carts to boats required labor, causing the head of navigation to become settled and to develop into a community.

Usually, the feature of a river that makes it navigable is its depth. Where shallow rivers flow over bedrock forming rapids or waterfalls, they are unnavigable. This is a large part of the reason that the head of navigation of a river often coincides with rapids. The river below the head of navigation is deep enough for shipping but also does not have any steep elevation drops that would attract the early construction of mills. However, as you travel upstream and reach the location of the first substantial elevation drop, you have now reached a single location that combines two separate reasons for the development of a community. The head of navigation marks a place where goods can be transferred from carts to boats, and also where there is a drop in elevation that can support operation of mills.

The situation of the head of navigation of the Mississippi River is somewhat unusual. The navigability of a river is often not simply a black-and-white question. There are shades of gray. A stretch of river may be navigable for one kind of boat, but not for others, or only during certain levels of flow, making it partially navigable. The usefulness of a river for driving mills is similarly gradational. Small-scale rapids in a stretch of river may be used for waterpower if there are no better options, but may not be used at all if there are larger-scale rapids or waterfalls available a few miles away. The volume of water in the river also plays a part. A large drop in elevation on a narrow river may drive one small mill, while a smaller drop on a large river may be put to multiple uses for a variety of industries.

These gradations occur in St. Paul and Minneapolis on the upper Mississippi River. The natural head of navigation for most types of boats was originally at St. Paul, although there were early attempts by business interests in Minneapolis to convince steamship companies that they could make it further upstream if they tried hard enough. There were also rapids beginning at St. Paul that could be used for mills, but they were small compared to St. Anthony's Falls, which are a few miles upstream. The result was that the natural head of navigation and the best location for mills did not coincide in a single location. There were excellent reasons to build port facilities at the location that became St. Paul, and there were excellent reasons to construct lumber and grain mills a few miles away at the location that became Minneapolis. This unusual configuration is what led to the existence of the Twin Cities that we know today.

There was still a problem, which was how to transport the products of the Minneapolis mills to the port at St. Paul, with several miles of largely unnavigable river in between. The solution was to construct a railway between the two. However, because the mills in Minneapolis were located on the west side of the river and St. Paul was located on the east side, the situation called for a railroad bridge across the Mississippi River. This is the Stone Arch Bridge in downtown Minneapolis.

The Stone Arch Bridge combines many of the different types of attractions that can result in the development of a good tourist bridge. If you enjoy historic bridges, it is old, having been constructed in 1883. It was also important in the historical development of the city of Minneapolis, providing a crucial link between the wheat fields of the upper Midwest and the rapidly growing population of bread-eaters in the eastern United States. If you appreciate the recent practice of converting abandoned bridges into pedestrian and bike trails that attract urban recreationists, then this is an excellent example. Rail traffic on the bridge stopped in 1978, but the bridge was renovated into an integral part of the downtown trail and park system in 1994. The bridge is also quite attractive. It is large, at more than 2,100 feet long, is gracefully curved and constructed mostly of rectangular granite and limestone blocks in varying shades of light gray to tan and beige. Because it is a prominent part of the downtown scenery and parks, the bridge is the focus of a Stone Arch Bridge Festival every June.

All of these are good reasons to visit the Stone Arch if you happen to be in Minneapolis. However, the striking feature of this bridge is its setting in the middle of an enormous complex of historic waterworks and river-centric industrial buildings in a way not found in any other city.

The drop in river elevation between Minneapolis and St. Paul is about 100 feet, and St. Anthony's Falls alone comprises about half that total or 49 feet. In addition to this substantial drop in elevation, the Mississippi River is wide, which means that there is a large amount of water there to be exploited. The result was not just a handful of small mills, but a large number of the biggest mills ever constructed anywhere, serving numerous different industries. These enormous mills, largely closed now and converted to condominiums, still line the top of the bluff on the western bank of the river. Also, the original mill races that fed water to them, as well as a complex of other water conveyance structures used to provide fresh water to residents and to carry away wastewater and stormwater from downtown, are preserved and visible at the base of the bluff in Mill Ruins Park, opened in 2001.

In addition to the mills, there was plenty of water power left over to construct the first central hydroelectric power plant in the United States, in 1882, on the eastern side of St. Anthony's Falls. Another hydroelectric plant, at the Lower Dam a little bit downstream of St. Anthony's Falls, was constructed in 1897, and rebuilt in the 1950s. Both of these plants are still in place, along with numerous transmission lines crossing the river.

The construction of all of this infrastructure to exploit St. Anthony's Falls depended on one major requirement, which was that the Falls stay in one place. Generally, waterfalls do not behave that way. Large-scale waterfalls in the northern United States, including Niagara and St. Anthony's, were created by retreating glaciers following the end of the last ice age approximately 12,000 years ago. These waterfalls have been eroding in a headward, upstream direction ever since.

This slow movement of waterfalls is fine, until people begin to construct permanent facilities to use the water. Once that happens, allowing the Falls to continue to erode headward becomes inconvenient. It requires that the dams, locks, and water intakes be moved to keep up with the erosion. In the case of St. Anthony's Falls, the natural rate of headward erosion was rapid, and the Falls had migrated upstream several miles since they were seen by the first European, Father Hennepin, in 1680. By the early 1870s, this situation was made worse by clumsy engineering efforts to capture the water, resulting in a partial collapse of the Falls. In 1871, the earliest of a series of protective aprons, first made of wood and currently made of concrete, were built to stabilize the Falls. For nature lovers, this completely destroyed the visual appeal of the Falls, and many visitors just assume that the unattractive concrete structure is the lower face of a dam.

Another important factor in the development of the area was that, while the Stone Arch was important in linking the mills in Minneapolis to shipping at St. Paul, the need to load and unload trains to transport the products of the Minneapolis mills to river shipping was still inconvenient. For the Minneapolis business community, the bridge was important, but they still preferred to skip the middleman and become the head of navigation themselves. As a result, the section of the river between St. Paul and Minneapolis was extensively engineered with locks, dams, and weirs, culminating in the construction of the enormous St. Anthony's Falls Upper Lock in 1963. The Upper Lock made the river navigable even above Minneapolis.

What does all of this have to do with the Stone Arch Bridge, and how do they contribute to the tourist attractions of the bridge? The answer is that all of these different engineered features are found at almost a single spot in the river, are all visible upstream, downstream, and directly underneath the Stone Arch, and are all interesting, visitable tourist attractions on their own. There are walking paths and informative historical exhibition plaques all over the place. The bridge is obviously an attraction that is open to the public. Directly beneath the base of the bridge, as it enters downtown, is Mill Race Park. The thundering water flowing over the cement apron of St. Anthony's Falls is located just a few hundred feet upstream of the Stone Arch. The original hydroelectric plant at St. Anthony's Falls is hidden behind the trees of an island, but the Lower Dam is visible, and the network of transmission lines passes overhead.

Most dominant of all is the Upper Lock, which is mostly upstream of the Stone Arch, but partially passes beneath it. In fact, a small stretch of the Stone Arch was demolished and replaced with a steel-girder truss to allow for the passage of ships through the lock beginning in 1963. The Upper Lock was closed to river traffic in 2015, due to declining use. The Corps of Engineers, which had operated the lock, transferred ownership to the National Park Service, which now operates the lock as a tourist attraction. Tours are available, and the facility was open to tourists during the Stone Arch Bridge Festival in 2018.

Unlike Niagara, Rhinefalls, or many other bridges associated with waterfalls, the tourist attraction of the Stone Arch is not derived from its natural scenery. Almost none of this, except maybe the view of the lit bridge piers at night, would be considered natural or scenic. Quite the opposite, in fact. The view is absolutely industrial and, with the mills closed and only now starting to be repurposed, could even be considered to be deteriorating. However, historic industrial structures do have an appeal to a certain segment of the tourist population, especially when they are accessible and well-presented, as are all of these structures in Minneapolis. The Stone Arch is just one piece of this puzzle, and is a perfect place to be able to see and study all of it.

AQUEDUCTS

Bridges are generally considered to be structures carrying traffic, trains, and/or pedestrians across a river or harbor. It makes no sense that bridges would be constructed to carry boats across a water body. If the owner of a boat wanted to move it from one side of the river to the other, why would he not simply put it in the water and float it across on its own?

The answer has to do with canals. At first glance, it may be difficult to understand why so much effort would be put into constructing a canal to carry boats directly next to a river that seems capable of carrying boats all on its own. However, the problem with rivers is that they are unreliable. The river may have some stretches that are more or less navigable. Also, even if they are completely navigable 99 percent of the time, the one percent misbehavior may not only limit the use of shipping during that time, but may also damage infrastructure needed to support the shipping industry, such as docks and wharves. A canal allows you to maintain a fully navigable waterway, and also to control the water flow rate in that waterway 100 percent of the time. It is an enormous undertaking to construct a canal, but to provide a constant and reliable water-based trade route, it is worth it.

The construction of a canal requires detailed study and consideration of possible routes. A canal is not a single waterway flowing downhill toward the sea. Instead, it is a series of flat, placid pools of water connected by locks. However, locks are inconvenient, slowing boat traffic and adding substantial time to the journey. Canal builders, therefore, spend a great deal of time and effort planning their routes to maximize the length of flat sections and to minimize the number and size of locks needed for the other sections. In some places, the optimal route may be on one side of the river, and in other places, it may be on the opposite side of the river. Because the elevation of the water in the canal is controlled by the locks, it has no relationship with the elevation of water in the river just a few feet away. At any given location, the elevation of the flat pool of water in the canal may be high above, or well below, the elevation in the adjacent river.

The result of these various design challenges is that the routes of canals sometimes need to cross rivers. Theoretically, this could be accomplished by lowering the water level in the canal to river level through a series of locks, letting the canal barges cross the river itself, and then raising the water level in the canal again on the other side through additional locks. However, this would create all kinds of problems. Barges and boats crossing from one side of the river to the other would risk collision with boats trying to move directly upstream or downstream within the river. It would be no different than a busy highway intersection, but without brakes and traffic lights. In addition, floods on the river itself would potentially damage the entrances to the locks. In general, because it is most desirable to keep the water elevation in the canal flat, the best solution would be to build a structure to carry the canal over the river at a flat elevation, so no interaction between the two is needed.

This structure is called an aqueduct. However, care is needed, because the word "aqueduct" has two different meanings. The most common usage is a structure intended to carry water, usually from one place where water is plentiful to another place where water is needed, such as for municipal or residential use, driving machinery, or irrigation. This can be done in a closed pipe, or in an open trough. Even a canal itself can serve as an aqueduct if it is used partially to carry water from a water supply to an end-user. For purposes of this book, the types of aqueducts that carry only water and do not carry boats, vehicles, or people are not considered bridges. Instead, this section focuses on a different definition of aqueduct, which is a structure that is only filled with water so that it can carry boats. Those are found where canals cross rivers.

The age of canal construction in western Europe, Britain, and the United States was intense, but also short-lived. In Britain, the phenomenon was known as canal mania, and lasted from the 1790s to the 1810s. Canals were constructed throughout England and Wales, primarily to transport coal for heat and slate for roofs. Canal mania also hit the United States shortly thereafter. The first canal to open in the United States was the Bellows Falls Canal on the Connecticut River between Vermont and New Hampshire in 1802. This was followed by the more famous Erie Canal in 1825, the Chesapeake and Ohio (C&O) Canal in 1831, and many others.

The reason that canal construction was incredibly intense was very simple. It was because canals worked. They were very labor intensive and expensive to construct but when completed, they improved the ability to move bulk goods such as coal, slate, building stone, and grain by orders of magnitude. One of the largest barriers to the development of these resources was the ability to cheaply transport them to their end-users. Canals made this possible and, once this was understood, everyone who had even a small mine or quarry wanted to build a canal to bring their product to market.

The reason that canal mania was so short-lived was also simple. It was because, shortly after canal mania began, railroads were invented. Canals were great for moving bulk goods, but railroads were better. Canal mania quickly gave way to railroad mania. As a result, most of the original canals constructed during canal mania ceased to be economical by the mid- to late 1800s, and most had closed by the early 1900s.

In general, when canals ceased to be used for shipping, they were abandoned. The stone walls and wooden structures associated with the lock systems caved in, as did the canal-side lock-keepers' houses, docks, and wharves. Once they were no longer maintained, canals sprung leaks, became dewatered, and quickly became overgrown. The arches of former aqueducts, such as the Aqueduct Bridge in Washington, DC, have collapsed, leaving only a few stones in place to tell the historical story. Many canals gradually filled in with silt and clay, and it is now difficult to tell where the old canal was even located.

This is the same story as that of many other abandoned historic structures, including bridges. However, also consistent with the stories of many abandoned historic structures, a few of the abandoned canals were appreciated and rescued just in time, before they disappeared completely. Abandoned, overgrown sections of old canals were rewatered, and now again float boats. They are pleasure and recreational boats now, instead of coal barges, but there are plenty of boats. The old locks and lock-keepers' houses have been restored, turned into museums, and now display exhibits celebrating the canal and its historical contribution to the settlement and development of the community. As the canals have been rescued, their aqueducts have been rescued along with them. Just a few, and not all of them rewatered and carrying boats, but some are major tourist and recreation attractions in their local areas.

DELAWARE AQUEDUCT, LACKAWAXEN, PENNSYLVANIA

The Delaware Aqueduct crossing the Delaware River from Minisink, New York to Lackawaxen, Pennsylvania, is a famous tourist bridge for a few reasons. Dating from 1848, it is the oldest suspension bridge in the United States, which should be reason enough. It is also one of three remaining bridges designed by John Roebling, and was one of the first-ever uses of wire rope suspension technology.

The aqueduct was one of four that Roebling built as part of the Delaware and Hudson (D&H) Canal system. The D&H Canal opened in 1828, and had four locations where boats on the canal needed to cross the river itself. As part of an expansion of the canal in 1848, Roebling constructed these four aqueducts, but not for pedestrian or horse traffic. Instead, each aqueduct was a water-tight trough, large enough to carry boats and suspended high enough above the river so that other boats could still pass underneath. It must have been an amazing sight at the time, seeing boats crossing over each other like cars cross over other cars on highway bridges today.

As with other canals in the United States, competition from railroads made the D&H Canal uneconomical, and it closed in 1898. The other three aqueducts were destroyed or dismantled, but the one at Lackawaxen was sold to a private company and converted to carry road traffic. This use continued until 1980, when the bridge was purchased by the National Park Service to preserve it for its historical significance.

Today, the bridge is the focus of a small park operated by the National Park Service as part of the Upper Delaware Scenic and Recreational River. The bridge is located directly on NY Route 97, and there are parking lots for visitors on both sides of the river. Signs in the parking lots direct drivers to tune their radio to a station that gives a narrative history of the bridge and canal. The Park Service has restored the bridge to its original trough configuration, using new wood but most of the original iron, stone, and wire parts. However, instead of refilling the trough with water and floating boats, it was left open on the ends, and cars today drive from one side of the river to the other on the floor of the suspended trough, with wooden walls rising high on either side. On top of the walls, on both sides, are sidewalks to allow visitors to walk across.

The configuration and construction of this bridge are not at all similar to what you are accustomed to seeing on modern suspension bridges. Whether this is because the trough design requires a different suspension technique, or because 1848 was such an early phase of suspension bridge design, is not clear. Instead of large suspension towers and cables hovering way above the road deck, the highest part of the suspension cables is only about three feet above sidewalk level. The cables are not supported by two large towers but are draped over the tops of a series of stone piers that just barely peek out above the sidewalk. In addition, the structure is a wall-lined trough, so it does not have a normal, flat deck. Instead of seeing a thin horizontal line from the side, you mostly just see the high wooden walls of the side of the trough.

The best way to investigate the structure is from the canal towpath that passes under the eastern end of the bridge. The mechanism is complex but, with some study, you can see how the suspension cable passes through iron U-bolts. The U-bolts are open downward, passing on either side of thick wooden beams. Beneath the beams, the U-bolts hold an iron plate that supports the beam. The Park Service has done an admirable job in helping to make the complex structure understandable. In the parking lot at the western end of the bridge, a full-size replica of one of the wood beam-U-bolt-cable structures is on display, allowing you to see up close how the cables hold up the trough. The small tollhouse on the New York end of the bridge has been converted to present historical exhibits of life on the canal. Outside of the tollhouse, the sides of the anchor structures are covered with glass or clear plastic, allowing you to see how the wire rope cable splays out and connects to the stone abutment.

You will probably end up walking across the bridge a few times, to investigate its parts and see the views from all sides. In addition to the sidewalks on top of the trough, the roadway on the bottom of the trough is wide enough that, with care, you can safely walk across at this lower level as well.

BRIDGES AT CASTLES AND FORTS

One category of enormously popular tourist sights, both in Europe and the United States, is historic defensive structures. Castles immediately come to mind, although many of these are popular tourist sights more for their function as a royal palace than as a defensive structure. However, other prominent examples include ancient city walls, towers, casemates, and fortresses.

Although technology in weaponry made such stone defensive works obsolete hundreds of years ago, you will still find them standing in many cities, and they are usually a major tourist attraction. The tourist industry of some cities, including York in England, Conwy in Wales, and Visby in Sweden, is partially reliant on the completeness of the walls. Many other cities, such as Prague, Lucerne, and Bruges, only have short segments of their walls, or the towers of the walls, remaining, but even these remnants are accessible to tourists and are major attractions. The entire city of Luxembourg exists because it is perched on top of formidable cliffs, and the honeycombed casemates directly beneath the city are one of its major tourist attractions. Even in the United States, historic forts are major tourist attractions in many cities, especially if they were the sites of major battles.

Because they supported transportation, many bridges also served a defensive function, in concert with the nearby castle, fort, or city walls. Bridges are built to facilitate moving people and materials across a barrier, which is great for commerce and the community. It is not so great when you are being attacked, and the bridge is making it easier for the attacker to get to you. Therefore, bridges were constructed with defensive purposes in mind.

A simple method of defense was incorporated into the Kapellbrücke and Spreuerbrücke in Lucerne. Both are wooden bridges that, unusually for bridges, are not straight. They have angles in them. Although this would slow down traffic and be inefficient for everyday commercial purposes, it also serves to slow down potential attackers. Another example is the Mittlerebrücke in Basel. The original bridge, torn down in 1903, was a hybrid bridge with stone and wooden sections. The purpose of leaving a portion of the bridge as a wooden construction was to facilitate easy destruction of the bridge, if needed, to protect the city of Basel.

Because these cities were located on rivers, the bridges were often incorporated into the fortifications. The river itself, bordering one side of the city, is a defensive feature, limiting the movement of armies, slowing them down, and making them vulnerable to attack. The remainder of the city that did not directly border the river was protected by high walls, guarded by archers. In cases where the fortified portion of the city was located entirely on one side of the river, the bridge was perpendicular to the walls, and the roadway carried by the bridge entered the walls through a gate. Gates are weak points. Armies would prefer to approach and enter cities across the bridge and through the gate. As a result, the bridges themselves became designed and fortified to stop that from happening. Many bridges still have their medieval defensive towers on their ends, even if the city walls themselves are long gone. A prominent example is Charles Bridge in Prague, where the bridge towers can still be climbed today.

Some cities occupied both sides of a river, making the incorporation of bridges into the fortifications even more complicated. In these cases, the bridge needed to be designed to allow water to pass into and out of the city but to still prevent attackers from entering. Examples are the 1390 Wenceslas Wall crossing the Alzette in Luxembourg, and the massive seventeenth century Barrage Vauban in Strasbourg. In both cases, the bridges have arches that allow water to pass through, but the arches could be closed by defenders inside the city. This had two defensive functions, the most obvious being that it prevented attackers from entering through the arches. But, once the arches were closed off, the bridges acted as dams. This caused water on the outside of the city to flood the areas where the attackers were encamped.

It is not just the older, historic bridges that have a link to tourism at historic castles, forts, and city walls. For reasons that are not obvious at first, there is a remarkable correlation of bridges, even new bridges—even bridges that never had any defensive function and were built long after the defensive structure ceased to operate—with castles, forts, and city walls. When tourists visit the castle or the fort, they tend to visit the bridge attached to it as well, even if the bridge is not contemporary.

One reason for the correlation of bridges with castles should not be a surprise. The castle was the center of government and economic life in medieval Europe, and the bridge was the center of the transportation system, so it makes sense that they would be found together. This is the case in both Prague and Budapest, where Charles Bridge and Chain Bridge, respectively, serve as prominent, even ceremonial, entranceways up to their respective castles. The situation at the Tower of London is slightly different, as the castle was built in the eleventh century and the bridge was built more than 800 years later. Although the bridge was not specifically located to serve activities at the castle, it does pay homage to its famous neighbor by taking its name and by being outfitted to look like a castle itself.

Even in the United States, bridges are often co-located with eighteenth and nineteenth century forts, the American equivalent of castles. The Golden Gate Bridge was built directly over Fort Point on its south end and close to Fort Baker on its north end. The Mackinac Bridge crosses directly over the historic fort at Colonial Michilimackinac. The George Washington Bridge is located at Fort Lee, the Penobscot Narrows Bridge and Observatory is accessed by parking at Fort Knox State Park, and Bear Mountain Bridge connects to two Revolutionary War-era forts, Fort Clinton and Fort Montgomery. In each of these cases, portions of the historic fort are still intact, are heavily visited tourist sights, and are within walking distance of the bridge. In Chicago, historic Fort Dearborn no longer exists, but its outline is highlighted on the sidewalk at the DuSable Bridge.

This co-location of bridges with castles and forts is not a coincidence. Bridges are built where the water body is narrowest because that is the easiest and least costly place to construct them. Forts were also situated where the water body is narrowest because this means that ships cannot pass without coming within range of the fort's guns. As a result, when visiting a historic fort in your area, you will frequently find a bridge nearby. In the cases of the Golden Gate and Mackinac, the bridges actually pass directly over portions of the old fort. In at least one prominent case, Fort McHenry in Baltimore, the fort was so historically important that it could not be desecrated by being overshadowed by a bridge. Instead of building the eight-lane, double-decked, high-clearance suspension bridge that was planned, the bridge was scrapped in favor of a tunnel, which carries traffic directly beneath the fort today.

One of the pleasures of visiting castles is to see the living and working spaces of their royal occupants, complete with sumptuous decorations, and this can be done at the Tower of London, Prague Castle, Buda Castle, and Neuschwanstein. However, visits to castle ruins are also popular, and Conwy Castle is one of the best. Built in the 1280s, during the reign of Edward I, as part of the border defenses after England conquered Wales, Conwy Castle was a large, complex structure situated on the northern Welsh coast. The castle ceased to be used as a functional defensive structure following the English Civil War in 1646 and gradually fell into ruin. Today, the castle walls and towers still stand but without a roof. The castle walls connect with the medieval walls of the town of Conwy, also built in the 1280s, which are some of the most intact town walls remaining in Britain today. In addition to the castle, the walls also enclose a lovely little medieval town with touristy shops and restaurants.

Many castles are built on hilltops, for various defensive and psychological reasons. Conwy Castle was built directly on the shoreline, and one of its features was that it had a dock on the west bank of the estuary of the River Conwy. The dock allowed ships to move supplies and people into and out of the castle even if enemy armies were camped outside of the castle and town walls. In addition, as with many castles and fortresses, it was built at the narrowest point of the waterway to keep passing ships within range of the defender's arrows. When it came time to build a bridge more than 500 years later, the bridge also needed to be built where the waterway was at its narrowest. As a result, parts of the castle, including the dock, were demolished to make room for the bridge. The bridge did not lead into the castle, though. At the end of the bridge, the roadway took a sharp turn to follow the outside of the castle walls into the town.

Not unlike the designers of Tower Bridge 60 years later, Telford used the proximity of the castle as inspiration in his design of the stone suspension towers. The bridge, constructed in 1826, is situated so close to Conwy Castle that the bridge's suspension chains are actually anchored into the walls of the castle. In an apparent attempt to make the nineteenth century bridge fit in with its thirteenth century neighbor, the stone suspension towers were built as miniature versions of the castle towers, complete with crenulated turrets.

The suspension bridge is owned and operated by the National Trust, so it can be visited and walked. The bridge is only open between March and November, and admission is charged. However, even when the bridge is closed, you can approach the gate and get close enough to inspect the towers and the eyebar chains anchored into the castle walls.

Unfortunately, it is impossible to get good photographs of the profile of the bridge from the side. The suspension bridge was closed to traffic in 1958, and the roadway diverted onto a modern arch bridge. The Conwy Road Bridge is directly adjacent to the suspension bridge, only about 100 feet away on the north side. There is also a railroad bridge, the Conwy Railway Bridge, only about 100 feet away on the south side. While historically important as the only remaining wrought-iron tubular bridge, built in 1849, the railroad bridge is not photogenic. Therefore, photographs showing an unobstructed side view of the old suspension bridge are not possible, and those you can get have the unattractive railroad bridge in the background. You can obtain a good aerial view of the bridge from an overlook area inside the castle which, of course, must be included in your visit. However, photographs taken from inside the castle mostly just show the interesting suspension bridge being squeezed in by its unattractive neighbors.

BRIDGES AND BASEBALL STADIUMS

Since bridges are specifically built to support transportation systems, it may seem unnecessary to discuss bridges used by spectators to gain access to community activities such as sporting events. That would be true, except that a few bridges are special, and valued by the community and visited by tourists, largely because of how they are used for that access.

One prominent example is the co-location of important tourist bridges with baseball stadiums. This may not be what you were expecting, and may possibly be coincidental, to the extent that they are not worth mentioning together. If there were only one or two of them, that might be the case. However, there are several of them, they are all historically important and/or nicely decorated, and tourists are walking on all of them.

Why are there baseball stadiums located near important bridges? First, in almost every case, the bridge is old, and the ballpark is new. The ballparks were built much later at the ends of historic bridges. Following 30 years of constructing cement-doughnut ballparks somewhere out on the interstate, the mold was broken with the construction of Camden Yards in downtown Baltimore in 1992. Integrating historic buildings, built with sweeping views of the downtown skyline, within walking distance of hotels and restaurants, it took only one look at Camden Yards before every city wanted a downtown ballpark as a prominent attraction for tourists and baseball lovers alike. Before Camden Yards, baseball stadiums were places to watch a game. After Camden Yards, baseball stadiums were the economic driver for the rejuvenation of neglected, industrial, downtown neighborhoods. Now, add in the fact that many of these cities are built on rivers, that riverfront property is among the most prominent and desirable real estate in these cities, and that riverfront property is often not far from a bridge, and there you have it—bridges at baseball stadiums, both minor league and major league.

There are several prominent examples. The Cincinnati Reds play just a long fly ball from the end of the Roebling Bridge. In Cleveland, the stadium was not only constructed at the end of the Lorain-Carnegie Bridge, but the team announced a name change in 2021 to honor the statues on the bridge. Several bridges lead to the stadium for the Iowa Cubs in Des Moines. Metro Bank Park, home of the Double A affiliate of the Washington Nationals, is located on City Island in the middle of the Susquehanna. City Island is connected to downtown Harrisburg by the wrought-iron Walnut Street Bridge, which lands directly outside of the entry gates. Philadelphia's Benjamin Franklin Bridge was, until 2015, the scenic backdrop for a baseball stadium, but not the one you are thinking of. Although the stadium for the Phillies is miles away, you could stand on the Benjamin Franklin Bridge sidewalk and have a close-up, elevated view of all of the action of the Camden Riversharks.

ROBERTO CLEMENTE BRIDGE, PITTSBURGH

The name of the Roberto Clemente Bridge has an important relationship with its location. The bridge carries Sixth Street, which borders the eastern edge of the PNC Park complex, home of the Pittsburgh Pirates. The northern landing of the bridge melds into a plaza on the outside of the baseball stadium, the most prominent feature of which is a large bronze statue of Clemente at bat.

During baseball games, the bridge is closed to traffic to allow pedestrians to walk the short distance from downtown to the ballgame. The ballpark is oriented so that the home plate area is opposite the bridge, and the outfield side of the stadium is open toward downtown, with the beautifully lit bridge prominent in the foreground of the view. Watch a Pittsburgh Pirates game on TV and, throughout the game, they will show gorgeous views of downtown Pittsburgh, with the bright yellow Clemente Bridge just out past the outfield. The prominent location has been marked with thousands of love padlocks on the bridge, some on the east side facing toward the Warhol Bridge, but most on the west side, facing the ballpark.

CHAPTER 4

DECORATED BRIDGES

DECORATIONS ON BRIDGES ARE SOMETHING we tend not to notice or think about in the twenty-first century, for one important reason. We are just going too fast. Prior to World War II, most traffic on bridges moved no faster than a person on foot or a horse pulling a wagon. As a result, decorations on bridges were seen, contemplated, studied, admired, and whatever else it is that we do with decorations. But who is looking at bridge decorations at 60 miles per hour?

The speed of the traffic is not the only issue. The world itself is moving too fast. After the war, urban populations grew rapidly, as did an automobile-owning middle class. Car ownership, and therefore the need for new highways and their associated bridges, exploded. Like most urban architecture at the same time, bridge design moved from the City Beautiful Movement of the early twentieth century to what became known as the "city practical" of the mid-century. For much of the mid- and late twentieth century, high-speed traffic bridges were generally built without decoration, and we had stopped thinking of bridges as community centers, public gathering places, and places for the display of art, decoration, and commemoration.

Fortunately, thousands of the old bridges are still around, and their decorations are still available for us to contemplate, study, and admire. Many of these bridges are now too small or weak for twenty-first century traffic, but their preservation-minded communities have connected them into their park systems and converted them into bike or walking trails, thus making them again accessible for the slow-speed public to enjoy. Even better, designers of new bridges are now frequently incorporating pedestrian sidewalks, bike lanes, benches, overlooks, fishing piers, historical exhibits, and other community-friendly features. By reintroducing slow-speed foot and bicycle traffic, we can now see and appreciate the historic decorations on the older bridges, and we are inspired to create decorations for the new ones.

One of the best-known types of decoration applied to bridges is statues. There are three typical locations for sculptures: on the bridge piers or spandrel at river level; mounted on top of the parapets in the middle of the bridge; and in an expanded plaza or park at the entrances of the bridge.

The placement of statues on the piers, hundreds of feet out in the middle of the river where they cannot be seen by people crossing the bridge or from the riverbanks, seems like an unusual location for decorations. However, remember that before the advent of railroads and trucks, rivers served as the superhighways for transporting people and commercial goods. When many historic bridges were built in the nineteenth and early twentieth centuries, river transportation was dominant. There were many more people viewing the sides of bridges from boats and ships than there are today, and bridges were decorated for these viewers.

Three prominent examples of the placement of statues on piers are the St. Servaasbrug in Maastricht, the Čechův Bridge in Prague, and the Vauxhall Bridge in west London. On the 1275 St. Servaasbrug, the oldest bridge in the Netherlands, a single carved limestone statue of St. Servaas blesses approaching boats with his outstretched hand. On the Čechův Bridge, built in the Art Nouveau style in 1908, boats from upriver are greeted by two larger-than-life bronze women, offering bronze fire in outstretched torches. On Vauxhall Bridge, dating from 1906, there are four piers, and each has a statue on both the upstream and downstream sides. The Vauxhall statues are also single, bronze, larger-than-life figures of both men and women, robed in classical style. One of the challenges in enjoying these types of decorations today is that they cannot be easily seen or photographed from the shore or the bridge deck. The figures were meant to be viewed from boats, so that is the only good way to see them.

More common is the placement of sculptures along the parapet of a bridge. Probably the most famous example of this, and possibly the most visited tourist bridge in the world, is Charles Bridge in Prague. With a statue atop each pier, and on both sides of the bridge, Charles Bridge displays dozens of larger-than-life sandstone sculptures of saints dating from the seventeenth and eighteenth centuries. Entire books have been written just on these sculptures, and trying to see and photograph each of them while being jostled by literally thousands of tourists is a substantial challenge.

The placement of a decoration is often not contemporaneous with the construction of the bridge itself. Because they are ancillary, nonstructural components of the bridge, decorations are commonly added or removed long after a bridge was constructed. In the United States, the practice of rehabilitating obsolete, historic bridges has resulted in the creation of new spaces for decoration that did not previously exist. When old bridges are closed to traffic and converted to pedestrian use, the open space at each end of the bridge ceases to be needed for traffic purposes. The common practice is to convert this unused space into an open plaza or park, which is usually graced with historical exhibition plaques, benches, Veterans' memorials, and/or sculptures. An example is the South Washington Street Bridge in Binghamton, New York, which has memorial statues in parks at both ends.

In contrast to the ubiquitous statues, there are few examples of paintings being used to decorate a bridge. This is because paintings are more fragile than sculptures, especially over the centuries-long time frames involved. For paintings to endure in an outdoor setting such as a bridge, they need to be located in a protected space, which means underneath a roof. Few bridges have roofs, and those that do are dimly lit inside, making it difficult to see paintings. Therefore, only a handful of bridges were decorated with paintings to begin with, and many of those that were have not survived. In fact, decoration of bridges by paintings is so rare that it would not even merit a discussion in a book on tourist bridges except for one fact—one of the most overrun tourist bridges in the world, in Lucerne, Switzerland, is overrun mostly for one reason, which is for its paintings.

Smaller-scale decorations such as emblems, coats-of-arms, medallions, or depictions of human or animal figures in relief, are also common. Any part of the bridge structure is fair game, especially those at eye level for pedestrians, where they can be seen and read. Geometric patterns created by decorative stonework or iron work are found on railings, balustrades, parapets, and lampposts. They are also found on the spandrels of arch bridges. A bridge superstructure, such as a truss or suspension tower, is always an empty canvas begging to be decorated. We tend to think of these as undecorated, but that is because we are accustomed to seeing the large-scale towers on bridges over large rivers, on which decoration would be too far away to see. However, the historic, smaller-scale suspension and truss bridges in urban centers were almost always elaborately decorated.

MUNICIPAL BRIDGES

Bridge decorations serve the obvious purpose of helping the structural, utilitarian features of bridges appear aesthetically pleasing. However, they usually also have another important purpose. Sometimes obvious, sometimes subtle, sometimes forgotten, and sometimes even completely bewildering, the decorations are usually meant to convey a message of some importance within the community.

With few exceptions, bridges are public structures. They are meant to be used by everyone in the community, and are therefore usually constructed by the government. Early bridges were often privately built, as a profit-making venture, but even these enterprises were chartered by the government. Most of those privately-built bridges have long since been acquired by, and are now operated by, the government. Because of this communal role in building and operating bridges, it should come as no surprise that the most common message sent by bridge decorations is, in some manner, supporting or celebrating that community and its government.

The decorations may document the history of the community through the commemoration of a single important event or through a more general display of images celebrating multiple events. They are commonly used to dedicate the bridge to a single individual, such as a local government official, or to groups, such as war veterans. They may even be used to promote products or industries of local importance. In many cases, such as Paper Mill Road Bridge north of Baltimore or Hammersmith Bridge in London, the decoration is the seal of the city or governmental body that constructed the bridge.

KAPELLBRÜCKE AND SPREUERBRÜCKE, LUCERNE, SWITZERLAND

Lucerne is situated at the outlet of the Vierwaldstättersee, a large glacial lake on the northern side of the Alps. Translated into English, Vierwaldstättersee means "the Lake of the Four Forest Cantons." Although this official Swiss name is highly romantic, it has also proved difficult for non-Swiss tourists to pronounce, so the lake has become known as Lake Lucerne to visitors.

The town of Lucerne, the roads leading to its bridges, and the lake itself are central to both the history and the mythology of the founding of the Swiss Confederation in the 1200s. The Alps leading up to Gotthard Pass flank the sides of the lake. The pass was used for hundreds of years as one of the main overland connections between Germany and Italy. In addition to its importance for trade, Gotthard Pass also had substantial military and political significance. This overland connection was used by kings and emperors north of the Alps to maintain communications with Rome to ensure Papal support for their various wars, dynastic maneuverings, and marital endeavors. Because of its large size, more than 20 miles long, and its irregular shape, the lake provided a substantial barrier to this overland traffic. The only place to go around the barrier was at its narrowest point, at the northern end of the lake where the water spills out as the Reuss River and flows north over the lowlands toward the Rhine. This strategic location became the city of Lucerne.

The importance of Gotthard Pass, and the lake as the most effective means of transport to the pass, led to Lucerne and the other cantons surrounding the lake being coveted by the Holy Roman emperors and other various kings and counts. Prominent among these in the 1200s were the Hapsburgs. Desiring to maintain their independence from the Hapsburgs, the cantons of Uri, Schwyz, Nidwalden, and Obwalden—the four cantons that give their name to the Vierwaldstättersee—formed a pact of confederation at Rütli meadow, overlooking the lake, in 1291. Lucerne joined the confederation shortly thereafter, and the subsequent history includes battles, as well as the heroic actions of William Tell, all leading to Swiss independence.

The most visible landmark presenting itself to tourists arriving at the train station in Lucerne is the octagonal Wasserturm, or Water Tower. The Wasserturm is a stone tower that was constructed in the middle of the Reuss River around 1300. Originally constructed to serve as part of the city's fortifications, the Wasserturm later served as a city treasury, a prison, and an archive. About 30 years after the Wasserturm was built, the Kapellbrücke, or Chapel Bridge, was constructed to link the Wasserturm to both banks of the river. The image of the wooden bridge and the adjacent Wasserturm is emblazoned on coffee mugs, T-shirts, and chocolate bar wrappers in every gift shop in Switzerland. Some guidebooks report the bridge and tower to be the most photographed sight in Switzerland, which is quite a feat if you think about it.

However, the most amazing feature of the bridge is not the view of the outside. It is the view inside of what was once more than 150 paintings on triangular-shaped panels displayed within the ceiling rafters of the bridge. These panels were painted in the seventeenth century by Hans Heinrich Wägman. They depict the history of Lucerne, including scenes from the lives of St. Leodegar and St. Maurice, the patron saints of the city.

The Kapellbrücke was famous for centuries for being the oldest covered bridge in Europe, as well as for its paintings. More recently, it is famous for having been almost completely destroyed by fire in August 1993. The Lucerners lost no time in replacing the bridge and restoring those parts that could be salvaged, with the current bridge having been opened in April 1994.

After the fire, the city has obviously had to make some hard decisions regarding what to rebuild, and how to preserve what remained. Most of the painted panels were destroyed in the fire, a great loss to the city. Only 30 panels were saved and restored, and these are displayed along with several reproductions. The sections of the bridge near the banks are still original, but the entire central portion has been replaced. The city has chosen to leave in place the charred beams and, in many cases, half-burned panels as a reminder of the events of 1993. Because the charred beams are in the ceiling structure and are therefore not well lit, you could miss seeing them except for your attention being drawn, after more than 25 years, by the smoky smell of the charred wood. While disappointing to not see the original structure and paintings, the portions that remain are amazing enough that a walk through the bridge is still a requirement for any bridge tourist.

Interestingly, Lucerne also has a second wooden bridge with painted ceiling panels, the Spreuerbrücke, built in 1408. Although it is only a ten-minute walk from the Kapellbrücke, many of the hordes of tourists do not even know about the Spreuerbrücke. Situated close to the lake, the Kapellbrücke and Wasserturm are visible from throughout the lakefront area, and are almost the first thing you will see when you walk out the front door of the train station. As a result, the Kapellbrücke is world-famous, and overrun with tourists. The Spreuerbrücke is not as old as the Kapellbrücke. Having been built in 1408, the Spreuerbrücke is 75 years newer than the Kapellbrücke.

In all other respects, though, Spreuerbrücke is just as amazing as Kapellbrücke. The bridges are very similar in construction, being made of wood, having unusual angles in the middle of the river, and being covered with a wooden roof. The Spreuerbrücke also has incredible paintings among the ceiling rafters, about 60 triangular panels dating from the 1600s and 1700s. While the Kapellbrücke has a large souvenir stand built into the middle of the bridge to serve the hordes of tourists, the Spreuerbrücke has a small chapel built in 1566, displaying a small Madonna-and-Child statue. And while Kapellbrücke connects the busy sections of the Alt Stadt where tourists go to buy Swiss Army knives and watches, the Spreuerbrücke connects sections of the Alt Stadt that are just as charming but much quieter.

The special feature of the Spreuerbrücke is the paintings. The information available in guidebooks varies, with the number of paintings reported to be from 56 to 67. They are usually listed as having been completed in the early seventeenth century by Kaspar Meglinger, although many have dates from the 1700s painted on them. In addition, the theme is not consistent across the bridge, so it appears that there may have been paintings added by more than one artist over time.

The main mass of the paintings is a series titled the Dance of Death, and they are, at the same time, disturbing and wonderful. Painted during a time when plagues occasionally swept across Europe, death was a common theme in many artistic works. In this series, the artist has depicted a large number of normal, daily genre scenes such as a game with children, or people at a banquet, which at first seems uninteresting. However, you then notice, in each, one or more skeletal figures of death popping up in unexpected places. Each painting likely has a specific meaning, but the overall theme appears intended to serve as a reminder of how death can come unexpectedly, even when things are at their most normal.

Viewing the paintings high up in the rafters is not convenient, but there is obviously a charm to seeing them in their original locations, where the artist intended them to be seen. Although it is counterintuitive, the best way to view them may be by visiting the bridge at night. During the daytime, your eyes adjust to the bright sunshine of the view outside the bridge, and the glare from the open sides of the bridge makes it hard to see the paintings in the shadows up among the rafters. At night, the paintings are brightly lit, and there is no visual competition with glare from the sides.

DYNASTIC BRIDGES

Because bridges are generally constructed by the government, the government usually decides what decorations to apply, and which persons should be memorialized. Therefore, the type of government in place at the time of decoration, and even the short-term political situation, are often reflected in the decoration. In most of Europe before World War I, the governments were dynastic in nature, ruled by hereditary monarchies and empires. Therefore, it should be no surprise that decorations used to glorify the local ruling families are a common theme on bridges of the time. These decorations are often statues of prominent family members, such as on the Hohenzollern Bridge in Cologne. The name of the bridge derives from the Hohenzollern dynasty, which provided the Kings of Prussia and, after 1870, the German emperors. The bridge has large bronze equestrian statues of major Hohenzollerns on each of its four corners.

Dynastic decorations also include monograms, seals, coats of arms, and crowns applied to parts of a bridge, including suspension towers, anchor blocks, spandrels, and railings. Many bridge spandrels, especially on bridges in prominent governmental centers, are wildly decorated with garlands, coats of arms, crowns, and allegorical figures. Even the lampposts on Westminster Bridge celebrate the British monarchy with their entwined V&A monogram.

Because governments change, there are many prominent examples where a bridge has been undecorated, redecorated, or renamed. What is now the Sean Heuston Bridge, in Dublin, was originally King's Bridge, constructed to celebrate the visit of King George IV to the city in 1821. As with many bridges built to commemorate a ruler, it is overrun with monarchy-themed decorations. These include ornate crown-topped lampposts, gilded flower-shaped decorations on the railings, and gold curlicues encircling a crown on the white spandrel. In 1923, the name of King's Bridge in Dublin was no longer politically correct. The bridge was renamed for Patrick Sarsfield, a seventeenth century Irish rebel. Then, in 1941, the bridge was again renamed, this time for Sean Heuston, who was executed for his part in the 1916 Easter Rising. Despite the displacement of the king from the name, the bridge is still overrun with crowns and other monarchical symbols.

Another example is the Pont Napoleon, in Lille. When the Germans occupied Lille in 1918, they did not simply rename this bridge. They destroyed it, and scratched out the names of many of Napoleon's battles inscribed on its stone monuments. The gorgeous covered footbridge was rebuilt in 2014, but the monuments still show the damage done to the inscriptions 100 years ago.

For obvious reasons, dynastic decorations are extremely rare in the United States. However, they do exist. A confusing use of coats of arms is on the 1883 Smithfield Street Bridge in Pittsburgh. Why heraldic symbols are used on a bridge in the United States is definitely not obvious.

HAPSBURG BRIDGES, BUDAPEST

Budapest is an interesting study in dynastic decorations on bridges. It is an enormously old, historic city, having been the center of kingdoms for hundreds of years. However, for some reason, no permanent bridge was built in Budapest until the middle of the 1800s.

The Danube is not a particularly large river. At Budapest, the river is only about 1,100 feet wide, or less than a quarter-mile. Many less important cities in Europe, even in the United States, built permanent bridges across much larger rivers earlier than the mid-1800s. The reason may be that the opposite sides of the river were separate towns, even rivals, for most of their history. It was only in 1873 that royal Buda, the castle on top of the hill to the west, was joined with working-class Pest, stretching out on the plains to the east, to form Budapest.

Whatever the reason, there were no bridges at all until 1849, and much of the history of Budapest since 1849 has not entirely embraced dynastic government. Instead, much of the history of Budapest between 1849 and 1918 involved resistance to dynastic government, namely, domination by the Hapsburg-led Austrian Empire. In addition, all four bridges that existed in central Budapest before World War II were destroyed in that war. The bridges were reconstructed, but in a much different atmosphere of domination by the Soviet Union. This was not exactly an atmosphere friendly to the remembrance and celebration of pre-war dynastic governments. Given this history, it is remarkable not only to find dynastic decorations and dedications in Budapest, but also to find them on all four of the bridges, and running amok on three of them.

The first permanent bridge in Budapest was the one that has become world-famous, Chain Bridge, known in Hungarian as Szèchenyi Lanchid after its major proponent, Count Istvan Szèchenyi. Chain Bridge was constructed in 1849. Most tourist guides and history books provide interesting stories about the construction of the bridge, which occurred during a crucial period in the history of Budapest and Hungary. The dominant political force in Hungary, and throughout Europe, at the time was Nationalism, with the local people who had a common language and culture rebelling against their foreign, imperial rulers hundreds of miles away. This Nationalism had two effects, the most obvious of which was political unrest and civil war that broke out in Hungary in 1848. The other effect was a flowering of nationalistic culture, architecture, and economic development independent from that of the imperial center in Vienna.

This was the atmosphere in which the Chain Bridge was constructed. Count Szèchenyi was a Hungarian noble who had traveled extensively throughout Europe, including Britain, noting the major differences in economic and infrastructure development between those countries and his native Hungary. He returned to Budapest determined to promote similar economic developments. The bridge was based on the design of the Thames River bridge at Marlow, which Szèchenyi had observed while in England. The traffic circle at the bridge's western end is still named after the English engineer responsible for overseeing construction, Adam Clark. The bridge narrowly escaped destruction in the War of Independence in 1848 and 1849 but was not so lucky at the end of World War II. The original bridge was destroyed to thwart the advance of the Soviet Army in 1945 but was immediately rebuilt according to the same design and using many of the same materials, reopening in 1949.

The walk across the bridge is a terrific experience. The cement sidewalks are about eight feet wide, and flanked by the early industrial-looking deck truss and eyebar chains on one side and a cast-iron railing with floral patterns on the other. The cast-iron motif continues in the large, ornate Victorian-style lampposts at intervals along the deck truss. The stone carving on the arches can be investigated up close from the sidewalk and is amazing. The bottom portion of each arch is rough-faced stone, with the edges of the individual blocks recessed to make each block stand out. The upper part of each arch is a smooth-faced stone except for the radially-placed highlights around the arch ring. The arches are topped with a lion head, crest, and Crown of St. Stephen, recognizable by its bent cross on the top. The same crest and crown can be found in cast-iron on the bases of the lampposts. The entrances to the bridge are also decorated, with a gigantic, larger than life-sized lion resting on a large pedestal at each of the four corners of the bridge.

Finally, the views from the sidewalk are world-famous. The bridge was built at the base of the castle complex in Buda, with the roadway crossing off the bridge into the Clark Adam Tèr traffic circle, and then immediately plunging into another ornate archway framing a tunnel underneath the castle. The stunning Hungarian Parliament Building dominates the riverfront on the north side. The bridge attracts a large number of tourists. Many of these are just traveling between the sights on the Buda and Pest sides of the river, but many are there to see the bridge itself. The lamppost struts on the north side, facing the Parliament Building, are heavily padlocked, demonstrating the prominence of the view from this location.

The bridge is centrally located among the must-see sights in Budapest. Just across the Clark Adam Tèr traffic circle, on the left side of the tunnel entrance, are the stairway and funicular leading to the top of Castle Hill with its famous Fisherman's Bastion, Matthias Church, and Royal Palace. The eastern end of the bridge leads directly just a few blocks to St. Stephen's Basilica, the most important church in the city. The bridge was constructed in 1849, and most of the major sights in Pest, including the Parliament Building and St. Stephen's, were built much later in the 1800s, after Pest and Buda had been joined.

Visible in the distance from the north side of Chain Bridge, just past the Parliament Building, is the Margit Bridge that connects the urban park on Margit Island with both banks of the river. The Parliament Building is as far north as most tourists are likely to venture, so most of them probably do not get close enough to Margit Bridge to see it, which is a shame. They can see a distant view of it from Chain Bridge, from the riverside promenade, and from the elevated viewing locations at Buda Castle, a striking golden line crossing the river.

Up close, Margit Bridge can be seen as an interesting structure that is very elaborately decorated. The bridge was originally built in 1876, but was destroyed in World War II and subsequently rebuilt. The railings are composed of steel panels with elongated oval openings and floral medallions. The entire bridge, including arches and railings, is painted bright yellow, making it appear like gold from a distance. The lampposts are elaborate, 20-foot tall Victorian-style iron posts, each carrying three frosted glass globes on curled iron arms. Even the posts in the center of the bridge carrying the power cables for the electric trams are designed with intricately curled iron arms.

Although the bridge carries traffic from one side of the Danube to the other, it is also the only way for pedestrians and bicyclists to access the urban park on Margit Island. In keeping with this role in providing access to the park, the sidewalk on the bridge is wide, with designated bicycle lanes. Margit Island is a quiet oasis in the middle of this major city. The island is car-free, but has restaurants, running and biking paths, playing fields, benches, a theater, historic sights, concession stands, and public art. The bridge is not straight, but has an angle in its middle where it crosses the southern tip of the island. The bridge carries light rail trams across the river, and the trams stop to pick up and discharge passengers in the middle of the bridge where it crosses the island. A transverse extension of the bridge here, open only to pedestrians, leads down into the park from the main part of the bridge. On the southern side of the bridge, next to the tram stop, is a small plaza with carved stone obelisks, wrought-iron lampposts, and a gigantic carved Crown of St. Stephen resting on a stone pillow. The small plaza also has amazing views of the entire city to the south, including Parliament, Chain Bridge, and Buda Castle.

Erzsebet Bridge, just downstream of Chain Bridge, is the only one of the four central Budapest bridges that was not reconstructed in its original form after being destroyed in World War II. The bridge was not reconstructed until the 1960s, and is a normal, classically shaped steel suspension bridge. With our Western view of architecture in Eastern Europe during the Communist era, we tend to assume that this means that the bridge was designed to be strictly functional, with no consideration of aesthetic features. This is partially true. In contrast to the other Budapest bridges, the Erzsebet Bridge has absolutely no additional decoration, monuments, memorials, geometrically-patterned supports, sculpture, stonework, painting, or plaques on it. The bridge is plain white, and the color and structure contrast with the historic church and other buildings on the Pest end. The only slight nod to decoration is a subtle fluting on the sides of the white steel towers. This description sounds like it is a plain, unattractive bridge, but nothing could be further from the truth. The fact is, the form and structure of the bridge are incredibly clean, simple, and elegant, and are best left unadorned, making the bridge much more decorative than decorated.

Despite the lack of decoration on the bridge itself, Erzsebet Bridge is still a dynastic bridge. A small park in the curve of the on-ramp on the western end has a large bronze memorial statue of Erzsebet Kiralyne, for whom the bridge was named, and who is better known to Westerners as Elizabeth or Sisi, the Queen of Hungary and Empress of Austria. Elizabeth is revered in Hungary for having supported Hungarian causes within the Austro-Hungarian Empire.

The final bridge that must not be missed is the Szabadsàg Bridge or, in English, Liberty Bridge. Located south of Erzsebet Bridge, Szabadsàg Bridge is partially hidden from view from the main tourist areas of Chain Bridge and Buda Castle. However, it is not that far of a walk, only about a mile from Chain Bridge and less than a half-mile from Erzsebet Bridge, and it is absolutely worth the walk. Again, this is a post-war reconstruction of an earlier bridge from the 1890s. The structure was only partially damaged and required minimal reconstruction, so the current bridge was the first of the Budapest bridges to be reopened after the war, in 1946.

Szabadsàg Bridge, Budapest

The bridge is interesting both for its unusual structure, as well as for its elaborate decorations. The decorative metalwork on the Szabadsàg Bridge is amazing. The two central towers are made of steel, and each is covered with decorations from top to bottom. The sides of the towers are not flat girders, but are, instead, a stacked series of panels, each with a quatrefoil pattern cut out of its center, rising from each sidewalk, and then curving into an arch over the roadway. This filigree-like arch is then topped with geometric girders fronted with medallions covering the crosspiece in the center. The girders are then topped by an even more intricate metalwork screen. In the center of the screen, over the middle of the roadway, is a painted Hungarian coat-of-arms, topped with a golden Crown of St. Stephen. The sides of the towers continue upward in elongated, open-lattice pyramids, and they are topped by golden birds sitting on golden orbs, with outstretched wings. These are turul birds, from Hungarian mythology. The railings and lampposts continue this theme, with a riot of curlicues and geometric patterns.

The entire bridge, including towers, supports, railings, lampposts, and all decorations is freshly painted a deep, dark green. The only parts of the bridge that are not green are the two large customs houses on the Pest end. These are elaborate, three-story stone structures topped with ornate metal roofs, displaying engraved dedication plaques in Hungarian that indicate that the bridge was originally named for Franz Joseph, King of Hungary at the time it was built.

MONUMENTAL BRIDGES

No community would be complete without monuments and memorials dedicated to its prominent citizens, or otherwise celebrating local culture and industry. Many bridges are designated as memorials in some way, either through the name of the bridge, or through plaques, statues, monuments, or other physical reminders placed on or near the bridge.

One of the most common dedications is to veterans, either of a specific war or generically, as a group. Examples include the Vietnam Veterans Memorial at the end of Hanover Street Bridge in Baltimore and another on the Chicago Riverwalk, the Spanish-American War Memorial at the end of the South Washington Street Bridge in Binghamton, and the World War II Memorial at the end of the Naval Academy Bridge in Annapolis. Dedications to veterans of a single war present a problem in that they optimistically assume that there will be no veterans of future wars who will need similar dedications. There are many old bridges and monuments out there, constructed between 1918 and the late 1930s, and dedicated to veterans of "the World War" without the foresight that more specificity would someday be needed. Some of these bridges have later plaques adding a dedication to veterans of World War II and later wars attached in places where they look as if they were tacked on as an afterthought.

Other bridges take a broader approach, memorializing multiple groups or themes. Bridges have four corners, after all, so there is space for monuments to at least four groups. These other themes commonly include the early settlers, industry and commerce, and the arts. Market Street Bridge in Wilkes-Barre even includes schools and teachers among the dedications inscribed onto its four enormous, monumental arches.

The physical manifestations of memorials on bridges can take several forms. The most common is a dedication inscribed on bronze or stone plaques, usually on the parapet on one or both ends of the bridge. Other bridges go further in that they have large granite monuments or archways along the sidewalk. There was a boom in the construction of these bridges in the eastern United States during the interwar period in the 1920s and 1930s, and one common feature is that the inscriptions combine decorative styles such as neo-classicism and Art Deco. Decorations can also celebrate the history of a city and its industries. One of the more amusing of these is the plaza at the downtown end of the Waco Suspension Bridge, which is populated with life-sized statues of steers being driven on the Chisholm Trail.

It is important to note that the effectiveness of any physical reminder such as a plaque, statue, or monument depends on the ability of the public to see it. Before the 1920s, this was not a problem, as bridges were primarily designed to be used by slow-speed horses and pedestrians. Because the intended audience was on foot, these bridges had small-scale plaques, statues, and monuments that could be read and appreciated by pedestrians standing just a few feet from them. An interesting situation exists at Bulkeley Bridge in Hartford, which was constructed in 1908 and has an elaborate dedication plaque to former Connecticut Governor Morgan Bulkeley. The plaque was readable in 1908, when the bridge carried horses.

However, the bridge was later converted to carry an interstate highway, and the dedication plaque is now on the parapet literally three feet from 60-mile-per hour traffic. It can now only be read by peering at it through a telephoto lens from the sidewalk on the other side of six lanes of traffic.

Now that traffic is moving much faster and small-scale decorations are no longer visible, bridge designers are using a variety of other approaches. The simplest is to name the bridge after an individual as a memorial, but then have no physical manifestation of the dedication. Thus, many bridges are not walkable but are still named after someone. Even some walkable bridges have a name without any physical dedication plaque. You can walk across the George Washington Bridge over the Hudson, or the Benjamin Franklin Bridge in Philadelphia, and never see any decorations intended to memorialize those individuals.

Other bridges include a physical monument, but make it gigantic so that it can be seen at 60 miles per hour. This was the choice made at the Woodrow Wilson Bridge over the Potomac, where an enormous medallion with a profile of Wilson sits above two foot-high gold letters on a 30 foot-high granite monument.

Another option is to construct a physical monument separate from the bridge. Millions of people drive across the Delaware Memorial Bridge without knowing what it memorializes. However, military veterans and a few locals know that there is also an elaborate war memorial owned and operated by the Delaware River and Bay Authority, the same agency that owns and operates the bridge. The Veterans Memorial Park covers several acres about a mile away from the Delaware end of the bridge and is accessible by taking the New Castle exit.

ARLINGTON MEMORIAL BRIDGE, WASHINGTON, DC

Of the numerous bridges that cross the Potomac River in downtown Washington, Arlington Memorial Bridge is the only one that attempts to serve a community function other than moving cars or trains across the river. All of the other bridges support major roads or highways, with the sole purpose of moving commuters into and out of the city each day. However, in its position linking the Lincoln Memorial at the western end of the National Mall with Arlington National Cemetery in Virginia, the

Arlington Memorial Bridge also serves a substantial ceremonial and memorial purpose in the US capital.

The bridge was completed in 1932 and consists of eight cement arches, four on each side of a central steel drawbridge arch. The cement arches are faced with white granite and are decorated with large medallions depicting eagles, giving the bridge a bright, sparkling white appearance that complements the marble memorials on the National Mall and at the cemetery. The bridge is low over the water, sitting only about 20 feet high so that it does not obstruct any views. The bridge is about 2,200 feet long, crossing the Potomac just to the north of the Tidal Basin. Although originally built with a drawspan to allow commercial shipping to reach Georgetown, later bridges on the Potomac blocked off this access, so the drawspan on the Arlington Memorial Bridge has not been opened since the early 1960s.

Although the bridge does carry traffic, the roadway is not an extension of any major highway or road and was not primarily intended to support the road network. Instead, the bridge is part of a large complex of memorials, parks, traffic circles, parkways, and displays of public art that make up the tourist center of Washington. It does not just connect parts of the complex on either side of the river. With its decorative statues at the entrances and carved white granite balustrades and benches along its sides, it is completely integrated into the motif of the surrounding memorial and ceremonial structures, and is as important a memorial as any of the others.

The story of the federal government's approval and construction of the bridge reads like a quintessential Washington tale. The bridge was originally proposed by Congress in 1887 as a memorial to Ulysses S. Grant. As can be imagined, this proposal was not unanimous, and led to squabbling over whether Grant was worthy of memorializing or whether others were more worthy. Committees were established, and proposals for various orientations and heights of the bridge were argued over for more than 40 years. Decisions were made, but no action occurred because funding was curtailed as a result of World War I. President Warren G. Harding pushed for funding for a new commission to study the bridge in 1922, after he got caught in a three-hour traffic jam on another bridge trying to cross the river to attend the dedication of the Tomb of the Unknown Soldier at the cemetery. Congressional squabbling over funding continued for several years until construction was finally authorized in 1925.

After all of this squabbling, it is still not obvious what the Arlington Memorial Bridge is memorializing. There are no plaques on the bridge describing its memorial purpose. Its location leading into Arlington National Cemetery implies that it serves as a memorial to fallen military heroes. However, the four gigantic, bronze statues at the eastern end of the bridge display an international, friendship-among-nations theme. The statues were placed on the bridge in 1950, as a gift from the people of Italy to the United States. The two equestrian bronzes directly on the end of the bridge represent Sacrifice and Valor, as the Arts of War. The two Pegasus bronzes on the nearby entrance to Rock Creek Parkway represent the Arts of Peace.

As can be imagined, the views from the bridge are terrific. The terrain in the area is flat, so the views are not of impressive landscapes. Also, Washington, DC, has no tall buildings, so there are no major city skylines in the view. Instead, the bridge is perfectly situated so that it provides good views of almost all of the prominent Washington landmarks and memorials. The Arlington Memorial Bridge may possibly set the record for the highest number of monuments and memorials that can be viewed from a single bridge.

To the east, on the Washington bank of the river, the view is dominated by the bulk of the Lincoln Memorial, situated just a few feet from the end of the bridge. To the right of the Lincoln Memorial, slightly further distant, the Washington Monument looms over the trees. Depending on the time of year and whether the trees are filled out, you can also catch glimpses of the Capitol dome and the Jefferson Memorial from the bridge. The view directly west is dominated by the Custis-Lee Mansion, also known as Arlington House, which was the former home of Robert E. Lee. The mansion was appropriated by the Union during the Civil War, and still serves as the focal point for Arlington National Cemetery. It is surrounded by rows of white gravestones on the slope of the hill overlooking the river.

Just north of the cemetery is the urban skyline of Rosslyn. Various other landmarks on the Virginia shore are visible to varying degrees depending on the season and include the Pentagon, the Air Force Memorial, and the Iwo Jima Memorial. The view to the north is dominated by Theodore Roosevelt Island, Roosevelt Bridge leading from Virginia into the District, the Kennedy Center for the Performing Arts, and the adjacent Watergate hotel and apartment complex. Perched on a hill in the distance is the Washington Cathedral.

Although there were arguments over what was to be memorialized, there is no escaping the symbolism of the placement of the Arlington Memorial Bridge. It provides a direct link between the Lincoln Memorial, situated on the north shore in what was the capital of the Union during the Civil War, and the Custis-Lee Mansion, the home of Confederate General Robert E. Lee, in what was part of the Confederacy. This location also completes a ceremonial corridor leading from the US Capitol to Arlington National Cemetery. This corridor is occasionally closed to accommodate funeral processions for prominent politicians and soldiers who have lain in state at the Capitol before being taken to Arlington for burial.

SPRINGFIELD MEMORIAL BRIDGE, SPRINGFIELD, MASSACHUSETTS

Springfield Memorial Bridge crosses the Connecticut River in downtown Springfield, Massachusetts. You may not have planned to visit Springfield, especially to see a bridge. If you are visiting the area, you may just be passing through on your way to or from Hartford, which is about 30 miles away. However, if you pass through Springfield on Interstate 91, and you have the slightest interest in bridge decorations, you will probably want to stop for a walk.

The eye-catching feature of this bridge is not a prominent superstructure. In fact, the bridge is not a suspension or through-truss bridge. It is an arch-and-pillar bridge, and therefore has no superstructure above the deck. The seven arches and two central piers are outlined in decoratively shaped cement, and the top of the central arch is decorated with medallions of eagles, but you will not see these when walking across the bridge. What will grab your attention are the four enormous monuments rising from the deck in the center of the bridge. Since the bridge is only a few feet from Interstate 91, you cannot miss them when you are driving through.

The bridge dates from 1922, right after World War I, and the beginning of an era when bridges memorializing veterans of the war were being constructed in cities throughout the United States. Interestingly, plaques on the bridge indicate that planning and design began in 1915, which was before the United States entered the war. Therefore, it is not clear whether it was originally intended as a memorial, or if that dedication was added during the later stages of bridge planning.

There are numerous monuments, plaques, and other decorations on the bridge, both at the end and along the sidewalks and railing. The most prominent are four massive columns rising about 50 feet above the deck. The lower portion of each column, at sidewalk level, is a small octagonal stone base, about 15 feet on each side and about 20 feet high. This small base has a door facing the river, probably to allow access to electrical systems for the lighted globes on top. The sides of the bases facing the roadway, on all four of the columns, display a large bronze dedication plaque. The top of each base is decorated in what appear to be carved stone garlands, although they are probably cast cement. The bases are then topped by a round column 30 feet high and about ten feet in diameter. The top of each column is capped by a square cornice, on which rests a large lighted orb that is several feet in diameter. These orbs are frosted glass held in a spherical metal frame.

The orb-topped columns are not the only decorative structures. The columns sit at the four corners of the main central arch. Sited symmetrically two arches further out from the center are four large tapered structures that resemble obelisks, but instead of being topped by a pyramid, they are topped with another orb, this one all bronze, and radiating metal spikes. The obelisks are about half the size of the columns, or about 25 feet high. Finally, the sidewalks are lined with rows of lampposts with ornate tops and almost as high as the obelisks. The entire length of the bridge bristles with these vertical decorations protruding high above the deck.

The symbolic or allegorical significance of the large monuments and spiky orbs is not clear, but the bridge includes numerous plaques describing its dedications. The large bronze plaques on the columns provide dedications to "The Pioneer and Colonial Period", the "Period of the Revolutionary War," the "War to Preserve the Union," and "The Later Wars on Foreign Soil." Each plaque includes several paragraphs of text discussing the dedication in detail. The plaque in memory of "The Later Wars on Foreign Soil" has references to both the war with Spain and the World War.

A much more recent plaque, attached to the parapet in the middle of the central arch, demonstrates the problem with dedicating bridges to honor military veterans of a specific conflict. Attached more than 50 years following the original dedication of the bridge, it appears that the bridge was trying to catch up to current events by including brief references to veterans of World War II, Korea, and Vietnam. Then, it seems like they threw up their hands and gave up. Somewhat depressingly, instead of trying to continue adding dedications to new veterans of new wars with new plaques, they made a preemptive strike on the need for future plaques by continuing the dedication to veterans of "subsequent conflicts and military missions around the world."

POLITICAL BRIDGES

There is a fine line between memorial bridges and political bridges. Sometimes, it is difficult to know when commemoration for community unity ends and propaganda to perpetuate political power begins. A plaque honoring veterans of a recent war or battle seems innocuous enough until you remember that there are always those in the community who opposed the war or battle, or were even actively rooting for the other side. For those, the dedication may seem to have ulterior motives. Dedications to politicians are common and even more suspect. In general, politicians dedicating things to other politicians seems a bit unseemly, and reading the history of these bridges usually reveals some controversy having occurred at the time of the dedication.

Even dedications to cultural leaders, such as authors and artists, may seem innocent enough until you learn more about the role of that author or artist in the political life of the community. The individuals who are memorialized certainly tell you something about the community. For example, there are 15 bridges over the River Liffey in Dublin, and many of them are named after prominent Irish patriots, rebels, and cultural leaders. However, across the Irish Sea in London, there are a similar number of bridges over the Thames, and not a single one of them is named for an individual. Why this difference? In the same situation in central Paris, only two of the numerous bridges are dedicated to an individual—one to a former President of Senegal and the other to a Russian Czar. It may not be clear to visitors what these dedications are telling us, but they are trying to tell us something.

PONT ALEXANDRE III, PARIS

One of the mysteries of the Pont Alexandre III, not obvious to us in the twenty-first century more than 100 years after it was built, is why a bridge constructed in the French Republic was dedicated to an autocratic Russian Czar opposed to representative government, and why its decoration is so flamboyant. France in 1900 was finally and completely a republic, finished with its experiments with revolutions, restorations, dictatorships, empires, communes, and more restorations that dominated the nineteenth century. Why, then, would the leaders of a republic wish to dedicate an extravagant new landmark not only to a monarch, but to a foreign one at that? Czar Nicholas II himself came from Russia to lay the cornerstone of the bridge in honor of his father.

The answer is simple, if not entirely satisfactory. After getting soundly thumped by the Germans in the 1870 Franco-Prussian War, France spent the following decades feeling threatened by the newly proclaimed German Empire. They finally concluded a defensive alliance with Czar Alexander III of Russia in 1893, an alliance that effectively threatened the German Empire on both sides. This was an advantageous alliance for France, one that was celebrated a few years later by dedicating the new bridge to their ally. This alliance was one of many dominoes that began to topple in Sarajevo in 1914.

One of the surprising features of the bridges of Paris is that they are generally small, simple bridges with few ceremonial and decorative elements. Aside from the mascarons on the Pont Neuf, and a few obelisks and statues here and there on the ends of some other bridges, the Seine bridges are remarkable for their clean elegance and restraint in decoration.

However, they made up for it all on Pont Alexandre III. To celebrate the dedication, the Pont Alexandre III has been riotously decorated with allegorical stone statues, gilt bronzes, and carved stone garlands. Each of the four corners of the bridge has an enormous 50 foot-high stone pedestal topped by a gigantic gilded statue of a winged horse and other figures. The pedestals are each formed of four pillars, and encased from top to bottom in carved stone decorations. The base of each pedestal has a 25 foot-high stone statue of an enthroned figure representing the France of Charlemagne, the Renaissance, Louis XIV, and the contemporary era. The equestrian figures on top of the pedestals are also allegorical, representing the Fame of Arts, Sciences, Commerce, and Industry.

The front of the arch facing upstream is decorated with figures representing the Nymphs of the Seine and the coats of arms of Paris. The side of the arch facing downstream is similarly decorated with the Nymphs of the Neva and the coats of arms of Russia. The crazy decoration continues along the curve of the arches and on the balustrades. The curve of the arches is decorated with a stone-carved, geometric, nautical-themed pattern. Along the base of the deck, carved garlands are draped from the deck across the open spandrel below, with carved faces spaced along the deck at the top of every second pillar of the open spandrel. The balustrade is a series of urn-shaped stone pillars spaced between small monuments that support lampposts. The color scheme of the entire structure is a light gray with bright gold gilded highlights, and topped by the black cast-iron and frosted glass of the ornate lampposts. The bases of the lampposts are all decorated with cast-iron figure sculptures with a nautical theme, including nymphs surrounded by fishes, frogs, and crabs.

The structure of the bridge below this layer-cake icing is a single cast-iron arch holding up narrow vertical beams to support the deck. The bridge was one of the first prefabricated structures ever built, with the pieces of the arches cast at another location, transported to Paris by barge, and then lifted into place by crane.

RELIGIOUS BRIDGES

Separate from the construction of fully functional chapels on bridges, more restrained placement of decorations with a religious theme was also common in Europe before the twentieth century. Again, the best example is Charles Bridge, which is lined with statues of saints. However, there are many other forms of religious decoration, ranging from applied crosses and other religious symbols to single sculptures, small chapels, and all the way up to full-blown churches.

The iconography of these decorations may be a general symbol of the religion, such as a crucifixion of Christ on the Romerbrücke in Trier, Germany, or the bronze Virgin and Child, complete with dozens of love padlocks, on the aptly-named Marienbrücke in Vienna. In other cases, it may represent a specific religious personage important to the community, such as the statue of Archbishop Baldwin of Luxembourg on the Balduinbrücke in Koblenz. Decorations may also depict a miraculous event that occurred on the bridge—Charles Bridge again being the best example, with its depictions of St. John of Nepomuk. An enormous St. John of Nepomuk, complete with his halo of five stars, can also be found on the J. Nepomucensbrug in the tourist center of Bruges.

PONTE SANT'ANGELO, ROME

Located about a mile from Ponte Fabricio, the Ponte Sant'Angelo is probably the closest thing Rome has to a famous, monumental bridge. This fame is largely not associated with the bridge but with its location leading to the more famous Castel Sant'Angelo. The name of the Castel Sant'Angelo may not sound familiar, but a view or picture of this round fortress will likely be recognized as a Rome landmark, if not from tourist guidebooks, then at least from fans of 1950s movies.

The Castel was built in the second century as a mausoleum for Emperor Hadrian and the bridge was constructed shortly after, in the year AD 134, to provide a grand approach to the mausoleum. The Castel was the site of a miracle in the seventh century, when Pope Gregory I witnessed an angel appearing on the roof to announce the end of a plague that was ravaging Rome. Following that incident, the name of "Sant'Angelo" was given to the Castel and bridge. The Castel was eventually developed into a fortress, being incorporated into the protective walls surrounding the Vatican, and was used as a protective sanctuary by many popes throughout Rome's turbulent history.

The Ponte Fabricio is located near the Palatine Hill and Imperial Forums and is, therefore, usually associated with the ancient history of the Roman Empire. The Ponte Sant'Angelo is more centrally located near the Vatican. Therefore, the bridge's history is associated more with events surrounding the Vatican, including access for pilgrims to St. Peter's Basilica, and visits of various medieval and Renaissance emperors and kings to the popes. The bridge was the site of a tragedy in 1450, when an enormous crowd of pilgrims trying to reach St. Peter's for a celebration caused the parapets to collapse, killing hundreds of people. The bridge also helped the popes maintain their political control of the city by serving as a prominent location to display the bodies of executed criminals.

Although the bridge is historically interesting, it would mostly be visually unappealing except for two factors. The first is that the bridge has been amply decorated with amazing statues. The earliest statues, those of St. Peter and St. Paul, were funded by tolls on the bridge and were installed in 1535. In 1669, ten statues of angels designed by Bernini were added. In these statues, each angel holds an instrument of the Passion, such as the Holy Lance or the Crown of Thorns. The statues now present are a mix of some originals and some replacements, with the other originals located in museums in the city. Now reserved for pedestrian traffic only, the bridge is thronged with tourists and hawkers of souvenirs, and definitely worth visiting to see the angels.

The second visual treat is how the bridge frames the approach to the Castel, and how both the Castel and bridge, in turn, frame the approach to St. Peter's. The initial feeling upon seeing the Castel across the bridge is that it is much smaller than you imagined, from the pictures and films you have seen. However, it is still very interesting, being completely round and surrounded by medieval-looking battlements. The bridge is centered directly on the front entrance of the Castel, which is located just a few steps away from the end of the bridge. The effect is particularly powerful at night, when the Castel is lit up and dominates the view on the north side of the river. The promenade between the northern end of the bridge and the Castel is directly lined up with the Via della Conciliazione, the road leading directly into St. Peter's Square. Thus, stepping off the end of the bridge and looking west provides a direct view through the square to St. Peter's Basilica about a mile away. Conversely, the Castel is the prominent visible landmark when looking out of the square from the steps of the basilica.

ZOOLOGICAL BRIDGES

A common decoration on bridges both in Europe and the United States is sculptures of animals and, where they are found, they attract photographers. In most cases, the animal is relatively small, hidden, or incidental to the main theme of the bridge decoration. For example, horses are common, but only because equestrian statues of rulers and mythological heroes are common. Equestrian statues are found on Hohenzollern Bridge in Cologne, and mythological horses are found on Arlington Memorial Bridge in Washington, DC.

Eagles are also not difficult to find, especially in the United States, as they are a symbol of the nation. Other animals are obvious symbols of protection. Lion sculptures guard the approaches to many bridges, including Westminster Bridge, Chain Bridge in Budapest, and the Bridge of Lions in St. Augustine, Florida.

Because the Pont Alexandre III in Paris celebrates the symbolic link between cities on two rivers, the Seine and the Neva, it has aquatic creatures of all kinds, including fishes, frogs, and lobsters sitting at the feet of its bronze nymphs. The inclusion of nautical-themed bronzes, including waves, seashells, frogs, and turtles on Pont Fragnée in Liege is more confusing because Liege is nowhere near the sea.

Dogs are sometimes found hiding on the edges of figure groups, such as on Charles Bridge in Prague. However, the most well-known dog on Charles Bridge is a bronze relief plaque of a suited knight petting his seated dog. Legend has it that touching the bronze image of St. John of Nepomuk on the opposite plaque will bring good fortune. Apparently, petting the dog is more popular, because its patina has been rubbed off even more than that of St. John.

Several deer can be found on the Rich Street Bridge in Columbus, Ohio. They are not grazing, or being stalked by hunters. They are just deer standing on their two back legs, leaning on the railing and gazing out at the view toward downtown.

WILLIAM HOWARD TAFT BRIDGE, WASHINGTON, DC

Rock Creek Valley is narrow and deep, and slashes like a knife through Northwest Washington, DC, disrupting the normal spoke-and-wheel street pattern laid out by L'Enfant. Because the valley is so deep, the streets do not go down one side and back up the other. Instead, the city constructed a series of high surface-level bridges connecting the top of the valley on one side to the top of the valley on the other side. Thus, Washington has a series of historic and decorated bridges hidden in the residential neighborhoods of Northwest DC, known only to locals and bridgespotters. These are all high substructure arch bridges, so the car traffic does not even notice that they are crossing more than 100 feet above a semi-isolated wilderness in Rock Creek Park below.

William Howard Taft Bridge, carrying Connecticut Avenue across the valley, is 136 feet high. Because it crosses close to and at an angle to the Duke Ellington Bridge, pedestrians can see how enormous these arch bridges really are. On the Taft Bridge, there are no reinforcing iron bars within the concrete arches, making this the largest unreinforced concrete bridge in the world. The bridge was constructed in 1907 and acquired its name following the death of the former president in 1931. Taft lived nearby when he was chief justice of the United States Supreme Court and used to walk across the bridge every day.

Taft Bridge is well-known for its four gigantic lions, one on each corner, sculpted out of concrete. Roland Hinton Perry was one of the major sculptors in the US during the early twentieth century, a time when addition of large-scale, classically inspired, and allegorical sculptures and reliefs to public architecture was rampant. Perry designed the large allegorical statue of Commonwealth on top of the Pennsylvania capitol dome in Harrisburg, as well as the statues of nymphs and Neptune at the Court of Neptune Fountain at the Library of Congress.

The four lions at the Taft Bridge are seven feet high and 13 feet long. The original lions were removed for renovation in 1993, but it was found that they were too degraded to be restored. Replacements were provided in 2000, and a quarter-size replica from the replacement project is currently displayed in the lobby of the US Commission of Fine Arts. The fate of the original lions became something of a mystery until a *Washington Post* reporter tracked them down in 2019. They are stored in a side-chamber of the tunnel carrying Interstate 395 underneath 3rd Street NW through downtown Washington.

In addition to the lions, the Taft Bridge displays 24 fierce, bronze bald eagle statues, perched, with wings fully spread, on top of each lamppost. Each green, bronze lamppost is 22 feet high, and consists of a pedestal with draped garlands of bronze fruits, a large fluted column topped by a cornice, glass globe lights hanging from each side of the cornice, and then the enormous eagles on top. The eagles were designed by Ernest Bairstow, who was also responsible for sculpting the exterior details on the Lincoln Memorial, as well as the lettering for the Gettysburg Address and Second Inaugural Address on the interior.

THEMATIC BRIDGES

When confronted with a depiction or dedication to a real, historic person, it is easy to understand what is going on. Even if you are not familiar with the specific history of the person, you can make a reasonable guess that this is someone who was important in the city's or nation's history. Similarly, anyone raised and educated in the United States or Europe can readily recognize the iconography of Western religions. Again, even if you do not know the exact biblical story depicted, you can generally recognize when a bridge decoration is religious in nature.

However, there is a third, miscellaneous category of decorations, those whose meaning is more obscure. These could be called "allegorical" or "thematic," but what they have in common is that their meanings are probably not well-known. They may be figurative sculptures of one or more people, but something tells you that they are not intended to represent specific individuals. It may be in the way the figures are clothed, or in how they are posed, but you know that this is not a simple memorial to a former mayor.

These figures are often mythological and convey information about the legends surrounding the founding of the city or nation. An example is a bronze of Boadicea, the female leader of a revolt of the Britons against the Romans, on the north landing of Westminster Bridge across the street from the Houses of Parliament. During her long reign, Queen Victoria was symbolically equated with this British folk-hero, and the statue was installed in 1902, the year after Victoria died.

They may also be allegorical in nature, meant to represent progress, industries, or virtues valued by the community. The Calvert Street Bridge across Rock Creek in Washington, DC, now named for Duke Ellington, has allegorical reliefs on its four corners depicting the four modes of transportation, by car, plane, train, and ship, which represented modern progress when the bridge was constructed in 1935.

Sometimes zoological sculptures on bridges are just decorative, but in other cases, the animal depicted has an allegorical meaning. Turul birds, part of the mythology of the founding of the Hungarian nation, are found on top of the towers on the Szabadsàg Bridge in Budapest. Other depictions of animals are clearly mythological. On Grattan Bridge in Dublin, the bases of the lampposts present an odd creature that appears to be a hybrid between a normal land-based horse and a seahorse. A similarly odd combination of a horse with a fish is carved into the parapet of Clare College Bridge in Cambridge.

LORAIN-CARNEGIE BRIDGE, CLEVELAND

The Lorain-Carnegie Bridge crosses the Cuyahoga River on the south side of downtown Cleveland. The bridge dates from the 1930s, when bridges throughout the United States were being decorated with large-scale, carved stone monuments and allegorical artworks. In the case of the Lorain-Carnegie Bridge, these decorations take the form of a thinly-veiled allegory titled "The Guardians of Traffic."

Guardian of Traffic on Lorain-Carnegie Bridge, Cleveland

The Guardians of Traffic consist of four large monuments carved out of sandstone. The Guardians are remarkable and worth traveling a long distance to see, for a few reasons. The first is their size, which is simply enormous. Each of the monument structures is about 30 feet high, 15 feet wide, and 25 feet long along the sidewalk. On each side, facing the oncoming traffic, is a carved, full-length human figure standing almost the entire height of the structure, or about 25 feet tall. The second attractive feature is the beauty of the Art Deco-style carving of the figures.

The largest part of the eight figures and monuments, including the bottom three-quarters of the figures, are identical. Each of the figures is enclosed in decorative robes, with the folds stylistically carved into the sandstone in geometric patterns. However, the upper quarter, from about the navel level on the figures to the top of their helmets, have differences among the figures. There are two different styles of face, four of each. One of the face styles is shorter, with narrow eyes, while the other is much longer, with round eyes. Then, there are two styles of helmets worn by the figures. Both styles have Mercury-type wings on the sides. However, one type has a medallion or badge across the forehead, while the other has laurel leaves across the forehead. Again, there are four of each type, but they are mixed on the different face types. Some large-faced figures have a laurel leaf helmet, while other large-faced figures have a medallion-type helmet.

The biggest difference among the figures, and the reason for this being one of the easiest-to-decipher allegories you will ever see, is that each of the figures is holding a unique item in its hands. A gigantic statue holding an item cradled in its hands is an obvious symbol of protection, thus the figures are clearly guardians. What are they guardians of? Well, their name is the Guardians of Traffic, suggesting that they are holding . . . traffic.

That is exactly what they are holding! Each figure is protecting a different type of vehicle that would have been crossing the bridge when it was new in 1932. These include a horse-drawn carriage, two different types of box-sided local delivery trucks, a cement truck, a hay wagon, a Conestoga-type covered wagon, a coal delivery truck, and a luxury automobile. Each of the vehicles is carved out of the sandstone and, because they are held in the hands of such gigantic figures, each vehicle is quite large, probably up to about two feet long. One does not see gigantic, carved figures protectively holding large, sandstone, 1930s-era cars and trucks every day. As a result, these statues are likely to bring a smile to your face, especially if you have some interest in transportation history.

These figures have become a well-known local landmark. A mural inside the Cleveland airport, which shows Cleveland landmarks, includes a depiction of one of the Guardians. One is also shown on a large mural on the side of an office building in the downtown area. The eastern end of the Lorain-Carnegie Bridge lands directly at the base of the baseball stadium for the major league team formerly known as the Indians. In 2021, the team announced that they were changing their name to the Cleveland Guardians, which was already the name of the city's roller derby team. It is likely that few people outside of Cleveland, except for possibly a few maniacal bridgespotters, understood that the new team name paid homage to the statues on the bridge.

Even though the bridge is located in the downtown area, and has recently been renovated to provide a wide pedestrian sidewalk and bike trail lane, the figures are probably not seen by many people. When it was built in the 1930s, the bridge was probably the primary entrance into downtown from the western side of the river, carrying a major, four-lane street from the western suburb of Lorain into downtown. However, even then, the bridge was somewhat on the southern fringes of downtown. Later highway expansion resulted in more bridges being built, including the interstate highway bridges used today. The Lorain-Carnegie Bridge ceased to be the major entrance into downtown and now carries mostly local traffic, baseball fans, and a few bridge tourists, there to see the guardians.

CHAPTER 5

DECORATIVE BRIDGES

IN ADDITION TO BEING DECORATED, bridges can be *decorative*, intended to serve more as an object of public art than as transportation infrastructure. There are many ways that a bridge, or any piece of architecture, can be decorative. The most obvious is through its geometric shape. Once modern materials and engineering techniques made possible the construction of buildings and bridges in any shape imaginable, it became only a matter of time before communities began to build bridges in the form of large-scale, abstract sculptures to enhance their skylines. This effect may be amplified by lighting the sculpture at night or by allowing parts of the sculpture to move.

The ability of a bridge to be decorative and to enhance the aesthetics of its location depends on the scale of the bridge relative to its surroundings. In a downtown setting or crossing a wide water body, large-scale office buildings and landscape features demand large-scale public art and, therefore, large-scale sculptural bridges. More intimate settings, such as narrow streams or ponds in parks, require small-scale bridges. These may be decorative either by being sculptural, like the Liberty Bridge in Greenville, South Carolina, or by being miniature versions of larger bridges, like the tiny, faux suspension bridge in Boston's Public Garden.

Another of the most important considerations in the aesthetic appearance of a bridge is that it must be concordant with its surroundings, and this means its form and color must be complementary to the adjacent buildings and landscape. The extent to which this needs to be done depends on the angles and distances from which the bridge will be viewed, as well as the other structures or landscape features visible in the foreground or background view. This can be done using a color to match the surrounding landscape or an architectural style that matches that of nearby buildings.

Choice of color is always a controversial decision for a bridge. The higher and, therefore, the more visible the superstructure, the more vocally opinions are expressed about its color. Steel gray and light shades of blue or green are common choices because they mimic the color of the sky above and the water below. They may not be particularly attractive choices on their own, but they do help the bridge to fit into its surroundings and to be concordant with them. Examples are the light blue Benjamin Franklin Bridge in Philadelphia, the steel gray of Mid-Hudson and Bear Mountain bridges over the Hudson, and the light green of Jacques-Cartier Bridge in Montreal. Probably the most famous bridge color chosen specifically to complement its surroundings is the Golden Gate. The bridge was painted with a rust-red primer to protect it from the elements while its ultimate color was debated. In the end, the rust-red color was judged to make the bridge stand out, while at the same time, its earth tones subtly complemented the rocks making up the nearby Marin Hills.

Most suspension bridges are painted a single color because the bridges are just too big, and the painted surfaces too distant, for the effect of different colors to be seen. One successful exception, though, is the Mackinac Bridge, dating from 1957, which connects the Upper and Lower Peninsulas of Michigan. In a book on the construction of the bridge, Lawrence Rubin, the executive secretary of the Mackinac Bridge Authority, related how one of the bridge construction subcontractors approached the Authority during bridge construction. They were planning on using the image of the bridge in their advertisements for their services and contacted the Authority to find out what color it would be. The Authority's response? They had not decided yet. The subcontractor went forward with an advertisement showing an artist's rendition with their own selection of colors. When the Authority saw the beautiful combination of dark green for the deck truss and light tan for the towers used in the advertisement, they immediately decided that it would be used for the bridge itself.

Color is an important factor for large-scale bridges where the sky, water, and hillsides make up the largest part of the viewscape. On smaller-scale bridges, especially those nestled up against one or more prominent buildings, the form, construction material, and outer decoration of the bridge becomes important, so that it will complement the appearance of the adjacent buildings. The most famous example of this is Tower Bridge, which was given an outer covering to make it appear almost as an extension of the adjacent Tower of London. Similarly, Conwy Bridge was designed with simulated crenulated turrets to match the actual turrets of the adjacent Conwy Castle.

SCULPTURAL BRIDGES

The most important feature of a bridge that affects its visual prominence to nearby viewers is whether it does, or does not, have a superstructure. Does the deck of the bridge pass over the top of an arch, truss, or girder structure, or does it pass through suspension cables or a truss extending above the roadway? In general, substructure arch bridges lacking a superstructure are not used for decorative effect for one basic reason, which is that the people crossing in cars never actually see anything of the bridge except for the sidewalk and maybe some lampposts. There is no point in decorating an arch or truss if only a handful of residents and visitors will ever see it.

In contrast, the visual appearance of bridges with a superstructure is enormously important. Obviously, the cables and girders are the most prominent visual feature to people using the bridge, because they are literally driving through the middle of the structure. However, these bridges can also rise hundreds of feet above the waterway, making them prominent landmarks for the surrounding community. The bridge must, therefore, enhance rather than detract from the view. The importance of aesthetics on these bridges is amplified by the fact that rivers and harbors are scenic places. Plans to construct these bridges frequently turn confrontational between forces touting the economic development advantages of a higher bridge versus forces in favor of a lower bridge that preserves the viewscape.

Until recent years, bridge designers were limited in how far they could go in incorporating aesthetics into these bridges. On conventional suspension bridges, two main cables are strung from tower to tower, like a power line between transmission towers. Suspender cables connect to these main cables, and drop vertically to support the bridge deck. By relying entirely on the vertical force, there is only one place the towers and cables can be, and that is directly in line with the deck, with perfectly vertical suspender cables. As a result, suspension bridges all start looking similar to each other. There are always minor differences in the style and color of the towers, but the general scheme of the main cable attached at the top of the towers, dropping down through a catenary arc between the towers, and connected to vertical cables holding a straight, flat deck is always the same.

After about 100 years of building these "normal" suspension bridges, the trend for large-scale bridges in recent years has been to use cable-stay technology. Just in the United States, recent large-scale cable-stayed highway bridges have been constructed in Savannah, Minneapolis, Boston, San Francisco, Charleston, St. Louis, and many smaller cities. Cable-stay technology has also been used for smaller-scale pedestrian bridges in dozens of urban centers, such as the Hoge Brug in Maastricht.

To the layman bridge-tourist, the reason for this recent trend is not clear, and it likely has something to do with improvements in technology, allowing these bridges to be more economical. However, it is almost certainly also a style choice because cable-stayed bridges look incredibly cool and modern. By using angled cables, the array of shapes available to cable-stayed bridges is unlimited. The cables can connect to one or more central towers, towers at the ends of the bridge, towers to the sides of the bridge, or high, broad arches. The cables can be connected to the towers at a single point, creating a fan shape, or they can be connected at different elevations, allowing the cables to be parallel like on a harp.

The twin angled towers on the Skydance Bridge in Oklahoma City were designed to mimic the forked tail of the scissor-tailed flycatcher, the Oklahoma state bird. The single angled tower on the Calatrava-designed

Sundial Bridge in Redding, California, actually functions as a gigantic gnomon, allowing the bridge to be used as a functional sundial to tell the time of day. The bridge deck on a cable-stayed bridge can even be curved, such as at the Bob Kerrey Bridge in Omaha, which is not possible on a conventional suspension bridge. There can also be multiple decks, such as on the Center Street Bridge in Des Moines. By comparison, conventional suspension bridges seem dated in appearance.

Aesthetics are also important on small-scale bridges in tourist and recreational areas, where they will be seen by large numbers of visitors on foot. Transportation planning in urban centers often requires striking a balance between moving residents and commuters quickly from place to place versus creating a pleasant walking experience for tourists and urban dwellers. In addition to moving traffic with new bridges, cities are either converting their historic old bridges to pedestrian-only use or constructing new pedestrian bridges specifically designed to accommodate those who prefer to enjoy the city at a slower speed. Although these smaller-scale bridges may not be visible from large distances, they are visible to large numbers of people who live and work nearby, so great attention is paid to aesthetics.

Using the freedom in the shapes of the towers, cables, and deck provided by cable-stay technology, more and more of these bridges are being considered works of public art as much as they are transportation infrastructure. Cities pay ultra-premium prices to procure the services of the hottest new bridge architect, just as they have for the designers of their art museums and concert halls. The aesthetic function of bridges can become so important in some cases that the transportation function is secondary, or even nonexistent. Cities are constructing these public artworks in parks, or in prominent downtown tourist areas where they have high visibility, even when there are plenty of other bridges nearby providing the necessary transportation function.

CLYDE ARC, GLASGOW, SCOTLAND

The configuration and ages of the River Clyde bridges tell a story about the historical development of Glasgow, a story that is similar to that of Dublin, Newcastle-upon-Tyne, and many other port cities. These cities were founded at the location where their respective rivers turned from free-flowing to tidal because this was the furthest inland point at which the rivers were navigable for ocean-going ships. In each case, the river is fairly straight, and it evenly splits the Old Town area in half as it moves from a narrow, freshwater river to widen out into an estuary that served as the harbor for centuries. As a result, each of these cities has multiple interesting, historic bridges connecting the two halves of their Old Town areas. In Glasgow, these include many old stone arch bridges, as well as the gorgeous stone-tower South Portland Street Suspension Bridge from 1853.

Another feature that these old port cities have in common is that bridges were not built over the wider, deeper, tidal portion of their rivers. This was because the tidal portion of the river served as the harbor, and bridges would have interfered with the movement of ships. This tidal part of the river became lined with docks and warehouses supporting the wool trade, coal exports, and shipbuilding.

The use of the river and these associated port facilities changed in the twentieth century. Ocean-going ships became much larger and, as a result, dock and port facilities in each city were moved to other locations where the water was deeper. In addition, the invention of railroads and trucking reduced the importance of shipping to move goods to inland locations. When goods were moved to and from ships by inefficient and slow-moving horse-and-carts, it was desirable to have the ships come as far inland as possible to reduce the distance of overland travel needed. However, once goods could be moved more quickly by rail and truck, it was no longer necessary for ships to carry their cargo as far inland as possible, and ports much closer to the open ocean could be developed. As a result, commercial ships stopped using the tidal part of the river adjacent to the centuries-old docks and warehouses.

As the shipping activity declined, so did the dock and port facilities. By the 1990s, the former dock and warehouse areas had ceased to be used for these purposes and, after years of decay, eventually became redeveloped as high-end office, commercial, and residential areas. This involved a combination of new development and redevelopment. Old, decrepit wood and brick buildings were demolished and replaced by gleaming, glass-sided towers. In many cases, the brick mills and warehouses were stripped to their bare walls, and their interiors were redeveloped as high-end lofts.

The redevelopment in these cities was not limited to the buildings. Because the tidal area was no longer used for shipping, there were no longer any limitations on the construction of bridges. By the 1990s, new bridges were being constructed in these redeveloped areas. Because these areas were close to downtown and supported well-heeled residential and commercial development, the bridges were designed as public art using sculptural, cable-stayed designs. In Glasgow, Newcastle, and Dublin, the new sculptural bridges are mostly found on the seaward end of town, in the former dock area.

Glasgow has been prominent in the modern bridge movement, with four modernistic bridges constructed in the former dock areas. These are Millennium, Bells, Tradeston, and Clyde Arc.

Millennium Bridge, constructed in 2002, is the farthest seaward of the new bridges, on the western edge of the walkable tourist area. It is also the least elaborate of the sculptural bridges. It was constructed to provide pedestrian access between the modern Science Center and the Glasgow Gateway Complex. The bridge is an open tubular steel structure rising in an inverted "V" shape above the river. The central section is movable and can be opened to allow passage of larger boats.

Bells Bridge, constructed in 1988, is also a pedestrian-only bridge linking new commercial developments in what were former dock areas. Bells Bridge is one of the earlier sculptural, cable-stayed bridges. It is also movable, but differently than Millennium Bridge. On Millennium Bridge, the central span rises on a hinge in the way we think of a typical drawbridge. Bells Bridge is constructed with a single, central suspension tower to which the fan-shaped cables are attached. This tower sits on a rotatable pylon, so the entire bridge deck can be rotated to create an open channel on both sides of the central pylon. The bridge links to the modernistic Clyde Auditorium known locally as the "Armadillo" due to the curved, overlapping shell-like structure of its roof. Bells Bridge is also unusual in that it has a roof, and so is a modernistic covered bridge. The roof is constructed of curved glass panels that mimic the curved white roof of the Clyde Auditorium.

Tradeston Bridge, from 2009, is another pedestrian-only bridge that also serves as modernistic public sculpture. The deck of Tradeston Bridge is not supported by piers or cables, but by gigantic, triangular-shaped white steel pylons. These pylons are curved, thus allowing the bridge deck itself to be curved in an "S" shape, making it a three-dimensional experience to visit.

One of the most well-known examples of a cable-stayed bridge in Europe is the Clyde Arc. The supporting structure of the Clyde Arc is just as it is named, a single, sweeping white curving arch from bank to bank. Beneath this arch, crisscrossing diagonal cables form a honeycomb to support the deck. Of all of the bridges in Glasgow, the Clyde Arc has the highest and, therefore, most visible superstructure, making it a prominent landmark of the city. The Clyde Arc also demonstrates a common feature of the new generation of sculptural bridges, which is the use of modern lighting techniques to make the structure an attractive, prominent part of the cityscape at night.

JAMES JOYCE, SEÁN O'CASEY, AND SAMUEL BECKETT BRIDGES, DUBLIN

There was a spurt of modernistic bridge construction in Dublin in the decade from 1999 and 2009, with four new bridges built, including two pedestrian-only bridges and two pedestrian-friendly traffic bridges. Because the Liffey is a small river and can be easily crossed by a single arch, there is no technical reason to construct large-scale suspension or cable-stayed bridges with a high superstructure. Of the 15 bridges in central Dublin, all but two are low profile bridges that, because they do not have a superstructure, are not prominently visible from a distance. But in this new era of complex cable-stayed bridges intended to act as public art object as much as bridge, low profile bridges with limited public visibility are not sufficient. Therefore, Dublin sought the services of one of the most prominent modern bridge architects in the world, Spaniard Santiago Calatrava. Dublin has not one, but two Calatrava-designed bridges, both sparkling white cable-stayed bridges with a highly visible superstructure.

The first of these is the James Joyce Bridge, constructed in 2003 on the western end of the city. The structure of the James Joyce Bridge consists of two white steel arches rising about 20 feet above deck level. From the side, the structure looks like a common suspension bridge, with vertical cables descending from these arches to the deck. From the ends, you can see that the structure is much more complex. The arches are curved not just vertically, but also horizontally, and they lean out from the deck of the bridge. In addition, the cables are not vertical, but angled inwards toward the center of the deck. The bridge also has not one deck, but three, as the traffic deck in the center and the sidewalk decks on either side are actually separate from each other. The sidewalks are wide, curved, and expand to include a mid-river plaza, complete with benches, halfway across the bridge. The angle of the cables actually creates this open space underneath the arch.

A description of the structure of the Seán O'Casey Pedestrian Bridge does not fit neatly into any of the bridge types seen anywhere else. Two piers in the river hold large-gauge, V-shaped structures parallel to the bridge deck. The ends of these structures rise about ten feet above the deck, and hold angled suspending rods. These rods extend outwards and connect to the deck, resulting in a zig-zagged suspension appearance. The deck is a wide, metallic pedestrian pathway with a metal mesh railing perfect for application of padlocks.

Possibly the most visible and well-known of the modern bridges in Dublin is the Calatrava-designed Samuel Beckett Bridge. The bridge was constructed in 2009, and its design was inspired by the Irish national symbol of the harp. It is a cable-stayed bridge in which the cables are held by a gigantic pylon anchored at the southern end of the bridge, and then curving over the bridge as it rises toward the middle. The cables then extend in parallel lines from the pylon down to the deck. The bridge was famously pre-fabricated, and pictures can be found of its iconic structure towering high above the deck of a barge as it was shipped to Dublin and then lifted into place by crane.

KINETIC SCULPTURAL BRIDGES

Sculptural bridges with moving parts may seem to be just a subset of other sculptural bridges. However, to the bridgespotter community, the movement adds more than just visual interest to the bridge sculpture. As discussed in Chapter 2, bridge enthusiasts have been known to specialize, and to concentrate their bridge collection efforts on specific types of bridges. Wooden covered bridges are an obvious example. Less obvious are specific subsets of types of iron trusses, bridges constructed by a specific company, or styles of decorative date plaques. However, one powerful subset that attracts a focused group of enthusiasts is movable bridges.

A more generic term than the commonly heard "drawbridge," a movable bridge is just that—a bridge that can be moved out of the way to let boats pass. Every bridge involves a compromise between supporting the ground traffic crossing over the bridge while not interfering with the shipping traffic crossing under it. There are two choices. You can build a high bridge, high enough to allow ships to pass under, or you can build a movable bridge. Both types have drawbacks. A high bridge requires approaches, which are ramped sections of highway that gradually gain elevation toward the center of the bridge. The higher the bridge, the longer the approaches must be and, in some urban settings, there is not enough space to build approaches. In addition, high bridges are prominently visible, and some communities in historic and scenic locations object to the visual intrusion. Movable bridges, on the other hand, require that traffic be stopped to allow ships to pass under, and this is inconvenient. Movable bridges also present engineering challenges depending on the space, technology, and power source available.

The engineering challenges associated with movable bridges have inspired as many different solutions as there are bridge designers. Some types, such as a simple double-leaf bascule, known as a "drawbridge," are common. Others are rare, represented by only one or two remaining examples, and others are just unusual or clever. It is this latter category of rare and unusual movable bridges that attracts its own subset of bridge enthusiasts.

Now, let us combine three of the various attractions that have been discussed to this point. First, we have a group of bridgespotters interested in unusual or clever engineering, specifically associated with the operation of movable bridges. Then, we have the evolution of cable-stayed technology and its increasing dominance of bridge design since about 1990.

Finally, we have bridges being designed as public art sculptures. If you go into any modern art museum, you will see that modern sculptures no longer stand still. Known as kinetic art, they move. Moreover, just as a small-scale sculpture can be made to move, a large-scale sculpture can be made to move. Most importantly, it can be done in a manner that also serves the function of a movable bridge. The movement serves two purposes—that of operating the movable bridge to allow ships to pass underneath and that of a kinetic sculpture.

ROLLING BRIDGE AND FAN BRIDGE, LONDON, ENGLAND

Two of the more prominent examples of bridges as kinetic sculptures are the Rolling Bridge and Fan Bridge in the Paddington Basin in London.

On any website proclaiming to show the world's wackiest bridges, you will see a picture of the Rolling Bridge in action. The bridge is tiny in scale, only about 25 feet long, but its operation is unique. To move and clear the waterway underneath, the bridge neatly curls up into an octagon, about ten feet in diameter, which sits on the sidewalk. This is achieved by the bridge deck consisting of eight separate sections connected to each other by hinges and shaped to fit together like a puzzle, being moved by hydraulic power.

An interesting feature of the Rolling Bridge is that, although it does move, it does not function to allow the passage of boats. The Paddington Basin, also known as Little Venice, was once a busy port as an arm of the Grand Union Canal linking London and Birmingham. Although it no longer supports commercial shipping, it has been rehabilitated into a historic tourist attraction and is used by tour and pleasure boats. The Paddington Canal ends near Paddington Rail Station, in what is now a booming area of new glass-sided office buildings. Although the canal is busy with small boats, Rolling Bridge does not need to move to allow passage of these boats, because it does not cross the canal itself. Instead of crossing perpendicular to the canal, the bridge is parallel to it, and crosses a tiny arm of the canal that connects about 20 feet away to a small pool and fountain. Boats do not use this tiny arm, because there is nowhere to go. The bridge does not move, and has never moved, to make way for boats. It was never more than an interesting kinetic sculpture used as decoration in an office complex.

Despite the lack of any actual function, the bridge does open on occasion, just for the novelty. According to a sign on display in 2018, the bridge is opened at midday on Wednesdays and Fridays, and at 2:00 p.m. on Saturdays.

The opening has two completely disparate effects: it annoys one group of people, and pleases a different group. The annoyed group is comprised of office workers who just happen to be out at lunchtime and need to use the sidewalk at that time. As with any movable bridge, the traffic crossing it must be stopped until the bridge is restored to its normal position, and this is always aggravating to those who have to wait. At Rolling Bridge, the movement of the bridge does not completely block the hungry office workers from using the sidewalk. When the bridge is open, the pedestrians can just take a slight detour around the fountain to the other side, a distance of maybe 50 feet total. In addition, the opening of the bridge lasts only for a few minutes. However, these facts do not stop some subset of the office workers from grumbling or dashing past the operators to try to get across before the opening begins.

The pleased group consists of tourists who come specifically to watch the show. The opening times are regular and publicized, and the bridge is actually, for its small size and semi-remote location away from any prominent tourist areas, quite famous for its unusual operation. On a warm sunny day, about 15 minutes in advance of the opening, you will see more than a few people scouting out the best vantage points for photographs.

The Rolling Bridge was such a hit when it was constructed (perhaps "installed" is a better word for so small a bridge) in 2004, that Merchant Square installed a second kinetic sculpture bridge in 2014. This is the Fan Bridge, located just a few hundred feet further inland, at the end of the canal. The opening of Fan Bridge is similarly unique. At first glance, the bridge appears mundane, just a short, aluminum-colored steel-girder deck. However, the deck consists of five separate segments, side-by-side in a longitudinal manner, and each independently hinged at one end. On the opposite side of the hinge are fan-shaped counterweights, used to raise each of the five longitudinal sections. The mechanism is designed so that each of the five sections rises independently, one after another, as in the opening of a fan. The Fan Bridge is larger than Rolling Bridge, and actually does cross the canal. It crosses the canal at its end and, again, the opening a few times each week is just a gimmick, for five or ten minutes, to entertain the lunching office workers and a few tourists.

LIGHT SHOW BRIDGES

Almost all bridges are lit at night, and the same lighting principles and techniques used for enhancing the visual appeal of a stage play can be used to enhance the visual appeal of a bridge.

The earliest method was to floodlight the structure with white light from a distance, so that it can be seen at night much like it is during the day. A variation on this method is to place the light sources within the structure, so that it highlights either the structural framework or the decorative elements of the bridge from unusual angles. White lights within the towers of the George Washington Bridge highlight its industrial, erector-set structure. On the 1768 Bristol Bridge over the River Avon in central Bristol, England, a yellow light is hidden behind columns facing the beige sandstone of the spandrel, resulting in a golden halo effect that complements the deep royal blue color of the deck girder. Another stunning example is the lighting within the ornate, pastel-colored columns of the Albert Bridge, in London. The effect is so striking that the lit bridge was given a cameo appearance in a night scene in the movie *Love Actually*. A third method, commonly done on suspension bridges, is to highlight the curved suspension cables by lining them with small, outward-facing lights. In this case, the purpose is not to illuminate the bridge structure itself, but to highlight the form by outlining it.

In each of these early cases, the lighting is white or pale yellow. However, a fourth method, starting to become increasingly common, is the use of deeply colored lighting. Like white lighting, colored lighting can be applied as a wash from the outside of the structure, hidden within, or faced outward from the cables and towers. The early examples involved a broad wash of a single color to illuminate modern, sculptural cable-stayed bridges at night. The purple angled cables of the Zakim Bridge are now a prominent landmark in downtown Boston, and the blue wash on the cables of the Indian River Inlet Bridge in Delaware can be seen for miles in every direction. In general, the color can only be seen if the towers and cables themselves are light in color, which is one reason the towers and cables of many recent sculptural bridges are white.

Even cement pier bridges, which have no towers or cables, can be lit at night. Cement, which is generally white or beige in color, is a perfect blank canvas for colored lighting. A recent example is the Route 52 Bridge in Ocean City, New Jersey. At two miles long, and with many curves and elevation changes, the play of lights on this serpentine structure is visible for miles around. The Kenneth F. Burns Bridge in Worcester, Massachusetts, uses the same technique of colored lighting on the white cement piers but also splashes colored lighting onto large modernistic sculptures designed to resemble sailboat sails. The lighting on the I-35W Bridge in Minneapolis is especially bright and vivid. It is usually blue but changes to different colors on holidays and for special events.

The most important development in bridge lighting has come with advances in LED lighting technology, in which light sources that have color-changing capability can be used. Like white lights, colored lights can be placed outside and projected inward onto the towers, cables, and piers, bathing the white bridge structure in a colored wash which can be changed. Two prominent examples in Britain are the Clyde Arc in Glasgow, and Gateshead Millennium in Newcastle. Colors can be mixed, with red and blue LED lights turned on to wash the bridge in purple. In general, color changes are done slowly, sometimes so slowly that a blue bridge may have turned yellow during the few minutes while you looked away. The color schemes can be seasonal, such as slowly interchanging red and green lights on the piers of the Route 52 Bridge during Christmas time, or red, white, and blue for the Fourth of July. In other cases, the color changes can be fast, with light displays dancing across the structure. The Lowry Avenue Bridge in Minneapolis is about two miles from downtown, but worth a side trip to see the display.

Even more dramatic than the use of a color wash is the more recent use of small, colored LED lights focused outward from the bridge. Instead of projecting color onto components of the bridge, the structure is now just a framework on which to hang strings of lights that can be used to create elaborate colored light shows. This is where the concept of colored lighting of bridges has taken off in recent years. An elaborate light show was installed to celebrate the 75th anniversary of the San Francisco Bay Bridge in 2013. Designed by artist Leo Villareal, the Bay Lights used more than 25,000 individual lights, programmed by computer to form ever-changing, colored, geometric patterns. Intended to be temporary, the display was removed in 2015. However, it was so popular that money was raised to make it permanent, beginning again in 2016.

Following this success, almost every major city with a prominent bridge is now scrambling to hang strings of color-changing LED lights on it. In New York City in 2017, the opening of the new Kosciuszko Bridge included a citywide display involving not only the new cable-stayed bridge but several other city bridges, as well as the Empire State Building. The light show was choreographed to music transmitted over several radio stations. As with the San Francisco Bay Bridge, the event was so popular that a permanent display, involving all prominent city bridges, is being planned. Not to be outdone by New York City, London is also planning a coordinated display across multiple bridges.

Although the phenomenon began on the modern, sculptural bridges, it is rapidly spreading to older, conventional bridges. Similar displays are now found on the 1895 Big Four Bridge in Louisville, on multiple bridges in downtown Tampa, on Harbor Bridge in Corpus Christi, and on Peace Bridge between Buffalo and Fort Erie. Even small, non-tourist towns are getting into the game. An internet search shows complex light shows in Atchison in Kansas, Johnstown in Pennsylvania, and Little Rock in Arkansas.

There are both challenges and solutions associated with researching and visiting light show bridges. On the solution side, they can be researched in advance by viewing YouTube videos. Anytime there is a short event to be experienced, you can be sure that someone is recording and posting it instead of actually experiencing it, which is their loss but our gain. There are many amazing videos of bridge light shows available. Among the most impressive are Big Four, Lowry Avenue, San Francisco Bay Bridge, and Queensferry Crossing in Edinburgh.

On the challenge side, bridge light shows only occur after dark, meaning you have to plan to visit at a specific time of day to enjoy them. A bigger problem is that, because they are an event, they usually do not occur every night. Many of the shows available on YouTube were temporary displays or a one-time event. The incredible show on Queensferry Crossing was done for the opening of the bridge in 2017, but there are no plans to repeat it. Other shows occur only on specific days of the year or only on weekends. Both Lowry Avenue and I-35W have a schedule of lighting events posted on their websites. Both bridges, as well as the Skydance Bridge in Oklahoma City, also allow groups to request special displays in advance. For other bridges, it may be more difficult to determine, in advance, whether there is a show to make it worth going out of your way.

JACQUES-CARTIER BRIDGE, MONTREAL, QUEBEC, CANADA

While the use of colored lighting began on modern, sculptural bridges, many cities are now retrofitting colored lighting onto their old bridges. In many cases, the effect is discordant. Colored lights on stone or on an otherwise unattractive industrial-looking bridge may just serve to emphasize the fact that the bridge was not very attractive to begin with. However, the use of colored lighting within the enormous, interfingered girders of the 1930 Jacques-Cartier Bridge in Montreal is phenomenal.

Although the Jacques-Cartier Bridge is considered an important historic and architectural Montreal landmark by its residents, it probably does not attract many tourists to walk across. It is a high cantilever-truss bridge crossing the St. Lawrence River between Montreal and the Ile St. Helene. However, it is not particularly historic or attractive. Located a few miles from downtown, it would certainly not attract any tourists from that area. It does have sidewalks on both sides, and the one on the eastern side has a great view of downtown, but it is unlikely that any tourists would walk several miles onto the bridge just to get this view. It does not have any special decorative elements that need to be seen up close, by tourists on foot. During the day, the Jacques-Cartier is just a big, aging, industrial-looking bridge that only the local residents could love.

At night, every night, every hour on the hour, the bridge is different. Instead of a big, industrial-looking bridge, the structure becomes the stage for a massive colored light show. The show combines two types of lighting. The first is colored flood lighting on the interior girders, from light sources placed within the inside of the truss structure, with no floodlighting of the outside of the truss. This design makes it seem as if the bridge is glowing from within. Then, the show also features small, outward facing lights that highlight the truss structure. The pace of the movement of these lights can be changed, so they sometimes move slowly, but other times move so quickly that the bridge sparkles. The bad news about Jacques-Cartier Bridge is that it is too distant from downtown to attract pedestrian tourists. The good news is that it is the perfect size and distance from downtown to make it the ideal platform on which to present this display.

The display is supported by an informative website, http://www.jacquescartierchamplain.ca/en/. The website discusses the history of the display, and provides a map recommending the best viewing locations. The bridge website also discusses how the lighting program on any given night is specifically designed to capture the "mood of the city," as interpreted from the daily traffic, weather, and social media postings. If the mood for the day is focused on the environment, the primary color used in the lighting that evening is green. Other colors used to capture the mood are aqua for technology, yellow for business, pink for religious and municipal institutions, purple for the arts, and red for health, education, and lifestyle issues. The website also has a black-and-white webcam so you can view the movement, if not the colors, from home, in real-time. Given that this is a relatively unattractive 1930s bridge, the lighting of it is surprising and stunning.

WEIGHTLESS BRIDGES

Structural stability is, of course, the most important factor in designing a bridge, and this is usually done by making the foundations for piers and towers as thick and heavy as possible. Our normal observation of buildings and towers is that they are wide, sometimes even clunky at the base, and then they taper as they rise upwards. In addition to being a structurally stable form, this technique also makes structures appear taller and, therefore, more prominent than they really are. You will see this technique on every cathedral on your European trip.

What happens when the opposite is done? One variation on the sculptural theme is for the bridge engineer to show off his or her talents by making the bridge appear to be sitting on little or no support. The effect can be disconcerting, once you see that the enormous weight of the bridge just barely touches the ground. One example is the Erzsebet Bridge in Budapest, which has an almost unnoticeable feature that, once seen, will attract your eye. The suspension towers on this large-scale bridge taper down to a rounded, circular base that sits, making almost no contact, on top of a rounded, circular support. Where one circle touches another circle, they touch only at a single point, and that is what holds this entire bridge up. The effect is subtle, and cannot be seen or appreciated from a distance. However, the designers made sure to pass the riverfront sidewalks just a few feet from these bases on both sides of the river, so you can see them from up close.

CHARLES DE GAULLE BRIDGE, PARIS

There are dozens of important tourist bridges crossing the Seine in the central tourist area of Paris, between Notre Dame and the Eiffel Tower. However, venture outside of the central tourist area, either to the east or west, and you will find . . . even more gorgeous tourist bridges crossing the Seine. Just because these areas do not attract foreign tourists does not mean that their bridges are not special. They tend to be newer than those in the central tourist area, and include several modern traffic bridges built in the 1990s and 2000s.

Located about two miles east of Notre Dame, the Pont Charles De Gaulle is a perfectly sleek, flat, unadorned modern traffic bridge built in 1994. The visual theme appears to have been "understatement." Not only does the bridge not have any visual texture to its structure, but it was also deliberately designed to hide the structure. Any normal steel bridge has visible girders. On Pont Charles De Gaulle, the steel girders have been covered by a silver-colored sheet metal sheathing that gives the bridge a completely smooth, slightly curved surface, not unlike what you would expect to find on a flying saucer. The obliteration of texture even applies to the railings and to the traffic crossing the bridge. The sheathing covers the entire underside of the bridge, then curves upwards on its sides to form the railings, which are solid and so high that they obscure the view of most of the vehicles crossing the bridge. From most vantage points, the bridge just looks like a perfectly flat, straight silver line crossing the river.

Of course, this silver line must sit on piers, and it does. However, normal piers—especially piers that reinforce the normal "heavier on the bottom, slimmer toward the top" construction we are accustomed to seeing—would just destroy the entire purpose of the visual theme. The piers are there, and the sleek silver line does sit on them, but only just barely.

The silver base of the bridge deck sits about eight feet above the tops of the two concrete piers. The connection between the pier and the bridge within this eight-foot space is made by four upturned, open-sided cones, two on each pier. Each cone consists of 12 rods, arranged so that they all meet at the base on the pier and angle upward to support the smooth underbelly of the bridge. Because the rods spread in a cone, they create open space between them as they rise toward the bridge. From the perspective of total volume, each cone appears to consist of about 5 percent metal and 95 percent open space. To add to the weightless effect, the rods are painted white, making them all but invisible. From a distance, the effect is to make the silver line of the bridge appear daintily perched on a few narrow metal fingers.

This daytime appearance of the bridge is impressive. However, the effect really jumps out at night. During the daytime, the smooth, curved sheet metal sheathing is just that—aluminum-colored sheet metal sheathing. However, the shape of the edges of the bridge is cleverly curved to hide lighting fixtures and to capture and reflect light from those fixtures. At night, the sheet metal sheathing turns into a perfectly straight, narrow band of white light. Then, there are also lights hidden within the cones on the piers which light their interiors. So, at night, the straight white line of light is supported not on piers, but on four beams of light. The effect is spectacular, and worth making the trek from the tourist area.

MINIATURE BRIDGES

Often, something will be aesthetically attractive and will brighten your day just because it is a cute, miniature version of something we usually see at a much larger scale. Bridges are no exception. We are accustomed to seeing them cross rivers and harbors. For them to be functional, they must be large enough to carry cars and trucks. A miniature bridge would, by definition, be too small to function. At best, it would support pedestrians only, or maybe be wide enough for one traffic lane. So why build it at all? The answer, of course, is just to be decorative. Aesthetic considerations are important factors in the construction of large-scale bridges, which are seen by multitudes of people. However, even though miniature bridges will be seen by far fewer people, they will be seen up close, by people on foot. Therefore, aesthetics are also driving bridge design in parks, and for pedestrian bridges in urban areas.

We tend to consider parks nothing more than preserved green space. Land is purchased, walls or fences are built around it, and the county or city decrees that no city streets or buildings shall be allowed within. Trees are allowed to grow unhindered, and people are permitted to wander inside and escape the city.

In fact, there is a lot more to a park than simply fencing off an area and preserving the green space within. Once people are permitted to access the park for recreation, the infrastructure to facilitate that access becomes a necessity. This includes roads and trails and, where roads and trails are found, bridges are needed. In many locations, the development of the park goes further than a few roads and trails. There are also gardens, hedges, artificial ponds and waterfalls, and other aesthetic improvements. Thus developed the profession of landscape architecture, of which small, decorative bridges are a prominent component.

Not only are these bridges needed for access purposes, but they also must be pleasingly designed to contribute to an enjoyable recreational experience for park visitors. As a result, many urban parks have one or more bridges, and they are often far more decorative than functional. However, because they are generally pedestrian-only bridges, they are usually on a small scale. They often lead nowhere at all—for instance, just from one side of a small pond to the other side, a trek that could also be completed in a few minutes by just walking around the pond. They may not even cross water bodies, but may exist just to carry one set of park trails across another set. While this is still being done today, with small-scale cable-stayed bridges being constructed in parks, it is not just a new trend. It has been happening ever since parks started being developed. As a result, you will find many examples of bridges that are, for want of a better word, cute, because they are copies of larger-scale arch or suspension bridges, but on a miniature scale.

PALLADIAN BRIDGE, BATH, ENGLAND

We are so familiar with parks being public places owned and managed by our municipal, state, and federal governments that we have forgotten how they originated. Before about 1800, governments did not provide landscaped, open spaces for public recreation. There were, however, wealthy people who owned large estates, manor houses, and palaces, and it was a common practice to design gardens for the enjoyment of the inhabitants and their guests. This is how public parks and the profession of landscape architecture began. Much as today's governments use small bridges to decorate urban parks, wealthy landowners in the eighteenth century did the same.

One of the architectural tools used for these gardens and parks was the Palladian style, named for Venetian architect Andrea Palladio, whose designs were based on ancient Roman and Greek structures. The Palladian style was frequently used by Capability Brown, one of the giants of landscape architecture during this period. Brown designed more than 150 parks and gardens throughout Britain, including Prior Park in Bath.

Prior Park was the estate of Ralph Allen, who was, among other pursuits, a quarry owner who built the house at Prior Park to advertise the qualities of his Bath stone for construction. His efforts were successful, as Bath stone was eventually used for the construction of most of the Georgian architecture in Bath, throughout the Cotswolds and Bristol, and even, through transport via the Kennet and Avon Canal, in London. The house at Prior Park was constructed of Bath stone in the Palladian style, at the top of the hill south of the city. So that the house could both see and be seen from the city, Allen hired Alexander Pope and Capability Brown to clear the trees from the hillside below the house, and landscape the area into a park.

Palladian Bridge, Bath, England

The most famous feature of the park, constructed in 1755, is the cute Palladian Bridge crossing between two small ponds in a bowl at the base of the hill. The bridge at Prior Park is one of four bridges constructed in the Palladian style still existing. The earliest is a major attraction at

Wilton House near Salisbury, and the bridge at Prior Park is a copy. There are also copies at Stowe, in England, and in St. Petersburg, Russia. The importance of Prior Park and its bridge are recognized by their inclusion on the Grade 1 list on the National Register of Historic Parks and Gardens.

From a distance, the most attractive feature of the bridge is its setting in the park. The mansion now houses Prior Park College and is not open to the public. However, the Park was acquired in 1993 by the National Trust, is open, and the view from the house at the top of the hill is spectacular. The slope of the hill from the house at the top to the ponds at the bottom is a meadow grazed by picturesque cattle. The area in the far distance beyond the ponds is the pale yellow of the Bath stone buildings in the city, about two miles away. Nestled in between, seeming tiny within this enormous landscape, the bridge, which is the only man-made structure in the park, can be seen crossing between the two ponds.

The bridge is probably higher than it is long. It consists of steps leading up across a stone arch on one end, a central section crossing three stone arches, and then another set of steps leading to the other bank. The bridge would be an attractive and old stone bridge, but the special feature is the roof. Sitting on top of the deck, the roof is supported on stone archways at the ends and colonnades in the middle. Constructed of soft stone, the bridge has been subjected to carved graffiti, some of it dating back to the eighteenth century.

WACO SUSPENSION BRIDGE, WACO, TEXAS

At 475 feet long, it is not a large bridge, but that is part of the charm of the Waco Suspension Bridge over the Brazos River in Texas.

Most well-known suspension bridges cross wide harbors and estuaries, requiring high bridges on a grand scale—the Golden Gate, the Delaware Memorial Bridge, the Brooklyn Bridge. Suspension bridges tend to be built in those places where the size of piers would have to be enormous.

Smaller water bodies like the Brazos tend to be crossed by bridges on piers. The Brazos at Waco is only a few hundred feet wide, so it would only require a few piers to complete a span. The natural depth of the river in 1870, when the bridge was built, was probably less than about ten feet deep. This shallow depth is certainly not an impediment to the construction of piers. Another reason that a bridge on piers would be expected here in Waco is the availability of materials. Humans have been building stone bridges by the pier and arch method for thousands of years. There is no shortage of stone in the Waco area. However, suspension bridges require wire rope or steel cable. Although readily available today, these were not so easy to find in central Texas in 1870.

The reason, then, for spanning the tiny Brazos River in Waco by a new-fangled suspension bridge is unclear. The builders acquired cable for the bridge from the Roebling Company in Trenton, New Jersey. Transport to Waco proved difficult because railways had not yet been built to Waco. Instead, the cable and other materials were transported by rail to the nearest depot 100 miles away. Other materials were shipped by steamer from Galveston, more than 200 miles away, to the town of Bryan. At Bryan, the Brazos was no longer navigable, so the materials were hauled the rest of the way in wagons, by oxen. The towers themselves were made of almost three million locally-produced bricks. This enormous effort needed to construct the suspension bridge in what was, in 1870, an extremely remote place, is part of its charm. Given that this location appears to be ideal for the construction of a bridge on piers, it is curious that the builders chose this substantial extra effort to build a complex suspension bridge destined to be crossed, mostly, by cows.

One possible reason for expending the extra effort and expense to build a suspension bridge may be that suspension bridges have an aesthetic attraction not available in pier-supported bridges. Pier-supported bridges sit low over the water, with the entire supporting structure below the bridge deck and, in some cases, even under water. Because they have a low profile, pier-supported bridges are not visible from large distances, and the low profile means that there is not much space on which to place decorations.

Suspension bridges, on the other hand, are prominently visible because the supporting superstructure sits above the deck. The high visibility requires that they also be aesthetically appealing. In addition, it is obvious to the casual observer that suspension bridges require a different level of engineering ingenuity, adding to the appeal. As a result, suspension bridges tend to be more interesting and pleasing to view than pier-supported bridges.

The Waco Suspension Bridge is no exception, and whoever decided to spend the extra cost and effort to use the suspension technique did a great favor to more than 140 years of Waco residents, because the bridge is delightful. The two towers each consist of a stacked double-arch, built of brick, in a Spanish-Colonial style reminiscent of the Alamo, which is not that far away. The towers are about 50 feet high, and are faced with unadorned, flat walls. The railings are steel girders, and the deck is made of wood planks. The cables are anchored at either end of the bridge within matching brick structures, again in a Spanish-Colonial style, approximately 30 feet high. The structures have doors indicating that they housed indoor space at one time, presumably for toll collectors. Both the cable anchor buildings and the above-deck portion of the towers are faced with white stucco or adobe. Therefore, the entire structure appears simple, clean, and glowing white. The portions of the towers below the deck, which are visible from the river-level sidewalk, are not faced, allowing you to see the original red bricks.

The visual appeal of the bridge, though, is not just in its being a nicely designed suspension bridge. Because we are accustomed to seeing suspension bridges on a grand scale, seeing one on such a small scale is amusing. It is almost like a cute, miniature toy model of a real grown-up bridge. You cannot look at it without smiling, and wanting to take the ten minutes necessary to walk across. A visit is extremely convenient if you happen to be in Waco for business. It is located directly across the street from downtown hotels and restaurants, making it an irresistible place for an after-dinner stroll. The towers, railings, and cables are beautifully lit at night. The attraction of the lighting combines with the Waco daytime heat to make a visit after dark a particularly favored recommendation.

In 1870, the bridge was built largely to allow herds of cattle to be driven into the city from the Chisholm Trail. The bridge continued to be open to traffic through 1971, by which time several larger, newer bridges had been built over the Brazos. At that time, the bridge was closed to traffic and converted for pedestrian use only. The road that had formerly passed through the bridge was closed, and riverfront parks were constructed at either end of the bridge.

These parks today are Indian Springs Park on the southwest end of the bridge near downtown, and Martin Luther King Jr. Park on the northeast end. These parks are part of a system of riverfront parks that include a riverwalk extending about seven miles from downtown to Baylor University. When the bridge was finally closed and incorporated into a park more than a hundred years after its construction, the historic link to the Chisholm Trail was celebrated with the placement of a herd of life-sized, bronze longhorn steers being driven over the bridge by a life-sized, bronze cowboy on a horse.

NOSTALGIC BRIDGES

One choice that is sometimes made for the aesthetic appearance of a newly constructed bridge is to use a retro design. In some cases, this is done to honor the historical importance of a location, but it can also be done for its visual and sentimental appeal. The architectural style can be real, such as the specific use of an older construction technique deliberately for its appearance, or it can be fake, such as cloaking a steel and cement bridge structure in an outer cladding designed to achieve a decorative effect.

An example of the former is the Hennepin Avenue Bridge in Minneapolis. The bridge was constructed in 1990, so a modernistic design could have been chosen. Instead, the designers chose to commemorate that the bridge is situated at the location of the first bridge constructed across the Mississippi River, in 1855. Instead of a sculptural cable-stayed bridge, the Hennepin Avenue Bridge is an old-style suspension bridge, with a form and decoration intended to reflect the long history of suspension bridges at this special location.

Tower Bridge in London is the most prominent example of the latter, with its steel girders hidden under a veneer of stone designed to look like a castle. The George Washington Bridge in New York narrowly escaped this fate because there were insufficient funds to complete its faux stone cladding. Saved from the indignity of fake stone suspension towers, most

New Yorkers are proud of the industrial, erector set-type appearance that seems more appropriate for the Industrial Age.

MIDDLE COVERED BRIDGE, WOODSTOCK, VT AND QUECHEE COVERED BRIDGE, QUECHEE, VT

As discussed in Chapter 2, covered bridges can be such popular tourist attractions, as well as so numerous within a fairly limited geographic area, that they may constitute a substantial proportion of the overall tourist industry in the region. Within these areas, one might assume that there are enough original, authentic, and historic covered bridges to satisfy any level of tourist demand. It would seem that new covered bridges that are not original, authentic, or historic would not only not be needed, but might be scoffed at and avoided by the more serious of the covered bridge tourists.

Southeastern Vermont is certainly such an area where the covered bridges are one of the region's primary tourist attractions, and where there is no shortage of original, authentic, and historic examples. In a short drive on back roads between Brattleboro and White River Junction, there are plenty of original covered bridges, some of them among the most historically important and picturesque in the country. The Cornish-Windsor Covered Bridge, one of the longest wooden bridges in the United States, is here. So is Taftsville Covered Bridge, constructed in 1836, whose bright red paint job makes it one of the most photographable bridges you will see. Creamery Covered Bridge, dating from 1879, is preserved close to downtown Brattleboro, in a small park with picnic tables. Dummerston, from 1872, is also photogenic and located close to Brattleboro. These are just the highlights, and there are dozens more original covered bridges in the region.

In addition to all of these original covered bridges in southeastern Vermont, there are also a handful of non-original covered bridges mixed in, with varying degrees of success. One of the unfortunate side-effects of popularity is imitation, for the sole purpose of attracting additional tourists. The non-original bridges include a mixture that are new, fake, reconstructed, and/or relocated.

While the Kissing Bridge in Rockingham is historic, it was purchased and reconstructed in 1967 to serve as a tourist attraction in a faux "Victorian Village," which was never built, and is today sitting in a parking lot. The Baltimore Bridge in Springfield was also dismantled and reconstructed in a roadside rest stop, not even pretending to cross water. The McWilliam Covered Bridge in Grafton was newly constructed in 1967 to serve as an attraction in the parking lot of the Grafton Cheese Company, which is a shame because the cheese is more than enough reason to visit Grafton. The bridge at Bartonsville was constructed in 2012 as a replacement for the original, destroyed in the Hurricane Irene flood in 2011. One of the famous pair of twin covered bridges in North Hartland dates to 1871, but the other was constructed in 2001.

Scattered in among the original bridges and these others of more limited appeal are two popular reconstructions, both crossing the Ottauquechee River. The location of the Middle Covered Bridge in Woodstock was originally crossed by an iron bridge dating from 1877. In 1966, the bridge was condemned and required replacement. By that time, there had been no completely wooden, covered traffic bridges constructed in either Vermont or New Hampshire since 1895. Most replica-covered bridges, whether they are new, reconstructions, or even just renovations of older bridges, use metal components to some extent, whether as supporting structural members or in the form of steel nuts and bolts holding the wooden timbers together. At Woodstock, the decision was made to replace the original iron bridge with a completely wooden bridge, using no structural steel components at all. Instead, the timbers are held together by more than 1,400 wooden trunnels.

Interestingly, a historical exhibit posted inside the bridge claims that the decision for wood over steel was a financial one, with a wooden replacement being less costly to construct than a concrete and steel bridge. This is true only when construction costs are the only costs that are considered. However, construction cost is not why wooden bridges ceased being built. Wooden bridges will always be cheaper to build than concrete and steel. However, concrete and steel bridges will be more stable, require less maintenance, will last longer, and will, in the long run, be much more cost-effective than wood. The town of Woodstock learned this the hard way when its new wooden bridge burned in 1974 and required costly repairs. The combined cost of the wooden bridge, and then the repairs of the fire damage a few years later, substantially exceeded the cost of a concrete and steel bridge which, of course, would not have burned.

Clearly, this story claiming that cost was the reason for constructing a wooden bridge does not fool anybody. The wooden covered bridge was constructed in Woodstock because, by the 1960s, covered bridges and quaint town greens had become important drivers of the tourist industry in New England. Woodstock not only has one of the most picture-perfect town greens in New England, but the bridge is situated right on the edge of The Green, directly across from the historic Woodstock Inn. It seems obvious that the major driving force behind the decision to replace the old iron bridge with a wooden bridge was to capitalize on the growing popularity of covered bridge tourism. While some bridgespotters may object to constructing a replica just to attract tourists, the fact is that a modern concrete and steel bridge situated almost directly on The Green would have been entirely discordant with the otherwise perfectly preserved Victorian architecture of the buildings. In fact, even a faithful reconstruction of the iron bridge which, by its construction date was also legitimately "Victorian," would have detracted from the aesthetics. Based on the twenty-first century vision of what tourists seek in the quintessential New England village, no bridge other than a replica wooden covered bridge would suffice.

Woodstock is not the only community in the area that has deliberately constructed a replica wooden covered bridge to preserve the appearance of the town and, incidentally, successfully serve as a stand-alone tourist attraction. A few miles from Woodstock, the village of Quechee has done this twice.

The village is centered on the scenic Ottauquechee Gorge, the site of a historic textile mill complex, the Quechee Mill, which began operations in 1825. Adjacent to the mill, a series of bridges were constructed over the gorge beginning in 1769. Wooden replacements were built in 1803 and 1885, but the era of wooden covered bridges at this location appeared to have ended in 1933, when a concrete and steel replacement was built.

The mill closed in 1952, leading to a repurposing of town buildings as a historic and tourist attraction, including the bridge. The mill was eventually converted into the Simon Pearce Glassblowing Factory, with an associated restaurant with outdoor seating perched high above the rushing waters of the gorge.

No longer fitting into the historic scenery, the existing 1933 bridge structure had a wooden roof and sides installed on it in 1969, completing its conversion back to a replica of the 1885 covered bridge. The 1933/1969 bridge was then damaged in the same Hurricane Irene flood as Bartonsville, in 2011, and was reconstructed again as a wooden covered bridge in 2012. Today, the bridge is a central tourist attraction of the village and, like Woodstock, no bridge construction type other than a wooden covered bridge would be acceptable in this scenic New England location.

CHAPTER 6

CULTURAL BRIDGES

EVEN THOUGH YOU MAY NOT notice them, images of bridges in media and artworks are all around you, every day. They are depicted in paintings; they serve as the setting for car commercials on television; they are used as metaphors in novels; they inspire poems and songs. And if a bridge is prominently depicted in artworks that are popular enough, it may begin to attract tourists, not for the bridge itself, but for the connection of the bridge to the popular artwork.

Another connection to popular culture may be found in the names of bridges. There are thousands of bridges named after an individual, but they generally do not attract tourists just because of a name. After all, names are easy to apply and easy to remove, and they usually have no actual connection to their namesake. In Frankfurt, the Holbeinsteg is a modern sculptural pedestrian bridge that connects the Alt Stadt area to the Städel Art Museum. However, it is not clear why Holbein, who was from Augsburg and worked mostly in Basel and England, is commemorated in Frankfurt. In other cases, there is an obvious connection, especially if the bridge is located near other attractions associated with the person, such as a former home or museum. Where this occurs, tourists attracted to the home or museum will visit the bridge as well, even if the bridge was constructed hundreds of years later.

These concepts sound tenuous, possibly even imaginary, until you begin the research, start visiting the examples, and witness the tourists coming and going.

PAINTED BRIDGES

Visit your local art museum, and it will not take you long to find a bridge in it. Maybe not a painting in which a bridge is the main subject, but certainly a landscape with a bridge subtly placed in the background. This should come as no surprise, as many bridges are in scenic locations and thus serve as visually attractive subjects for these artworks. Many of the bridges in these paintings are invented, not representative of an actual bridge. Alternatively, they may be an actual bridge that no longer exists. However, sometimes they do depict an actual bridge that is still in place and can be visited today. And if the artist or the artwork is popular enough, then the bridge itself begins to attract visitors. These are not bridges that were painted because they were famous. They are bridges that became famous because they were painted.

One prominent example is Ponte Sant'Angelo in Rome. In this case, the famous paintings are not actually focused on the bridge itself. Instead, the bridge is just part of the overall scene. Probably no painter in history has ever gone to Ponte Sant'Angelo and said to himself "This bridge must be painted." However, what did need to be painted, over and over, was the massive, round hulk of the Castel Sant'Angelo. Because the only way to get a complete view of the Castel is from across the river, and because the bridge leads across the river almost into the front door of the Castel, it is almost impossible to paint the Castel without also painting the bridge. The French painter Corot painted the Castel and bridge many times.

MONET'S BRIDGES, LONDON AND GIVERNY

The most famous painter of bridges, and possibly the most popular painter to twenty-first century fans of art, may be Claude Monet. One important bridge painted by Monet comes to mind, but he actually painted several other famous bridges. Monet visited London frequently and painted several series of paintings from his window at the Savoy Hotel on the banks of the Thames. These paintings include dozens of famous views of Waterloo Bridge and Charing Cross Bridge, now more commonly called Hungerford Bridge.

As famous as these bridges and the paintings of them are, you will probably find few people walking on them, as tourists, just because they have been inspired by the paintings. The Waterloo and Charing Cross bridges that you see today are mostly not the same ones that Monet painted more than 100 years ago. Monet's Waterloo Bridge was demolished and replaced in the 1940s. The Charing Cross Bridge he painted is still in place, but it has been substantially modified, including the attachment of modern, cable-stay sidewalks, to the point where it would be unrecognizable to him. In addition, these bridges were both painted from a distance, from Monet's hotel room. As a result, tourists do not go there today to walk across them, but they do go to stay at the Savoy Hotel, ask for the right room, and then enjoy Monet's view. The hotel has taken full advantage of its relationship with the famous paintings and markets the experience as "The Savoy Suite, An Artist's Residence."

Monet's treatment of Westminster Bridge also deserves some mention, because it is perplexing. Monet painted Westminster Bridge once, in the 1870s. In the Waterloo and Charing Cross period between 1899 and about 1904, Monet painted dozens of views of Waterloo and Charing Cross bridges. He was visiting London frequently and concentrating a great deal of his time on painting bridges. Westminster Bridge, which he had painted 20 years before, was just a short walk from Charing Cross Bridge. It is a picturesque bridge, in a picturesque setting. During the early part of this Waterloo and Charing Cross period, Monet also painted a series of at least 19 views of the Houses of Parliament. Westminster Bridge practically lands at the front door of the Houses of Parliament. It would be almost impossible to paint a view of the Houses of Parliament from across the river without including Westminster Bridge in the view. Yet, somehow, Monet managed to do just that. The Houses of Parliament series cleverly, and apparently with intention, crops the bridge just out of the right-hand side of all the paintings. Somehow, during the same period that Monet was concentrating enormous energies on Waterloo and

Charing Cross bridges, he was deliberately going out of his way to avoid depicting Westminster, the bridge next door.

One of the most famously painted bridges of all time is also one of the smallest. The subject of another one of his "series" paintings, Monet had the Japanese Footbridge built in his gardens in Giverny in the 1890s. He painted a series of 12 paintings of the bridge beginning in 1899 and exhibited them together in 1900. The paintings show a relatively realistic view of the bridge, from a distance, mostly in shades of green and blue, with the famous waterlily pond spreading out in the foreground. In the following years, Monet concentrated more on the water lilies in the pond at the base of the bridge. When he returned to painting the bridge later in his life, he created much more abstract impressions of the bridge, from a much closer vantage point, with no extraneous views of the waterlily pond or trees. He was still painting the footbridge in 1923, at the age of 83.

After Monet died, his son owned the house until 1966 but never lived there, allowing the gardens to fall into disrepair. The house and gardens were willed to the Acadèmie de Beaux-Arts and were restored to their original condition, along with the bridge, beginning in 1977. In 1980, they were placed under the control of the Foundation Claude Monet, which operates the area as a popular tourist attraction today.

One of the crowd control problems at Giverny is visitors bringing canvases and paints with them. Not satisfied with being able to see the spot, they arrive hoping to be able to paint the bridge, garden, and water lilies as Monet did. The website specifically informs visitors that they may bring a sketchbook and draw, as long as they are not bothering other visitors. However, walking in the front gate and sitting down to paint is strictly forbidden. At the same time, though, the website states that an art school affiliated with the gardens offers classes that have access to the bridge.

MUSICAL BRIDGES

Several possibilities come to mind when contemplating the concept of musical bridges. The first would be bridges commemorating a prominent musician or composer, and these do exist. As expected, Salzburg does have its Mozartsteg, built in 1903. Washington, DC, a city you would think would have enough politicians to provide bridge names for the foreseeable future, has two bridges dedicated to local musicians—John Philip Sousa and Duke Ellington.

Another possibility would be songs about bridges, or bridges that inspired musical compositions. These exist as well. The website lyrics. com provides more than 10,000 hits of song lyrics containing the word "bridge." Most of these are generic, but a few refer to a specific bridge. With the number of popular songwriters and singers who have passed through New York, it would be surprising if there were no Brooklyn Bridge song. There is, made famous by Frank Sinatra. Simon and Garfunkel provided a specific bridge song, but not the one you are thinking of. Although the *Bridge Over Troubled Water* is just a metaphor, the official name of the song best known as *Feelin' Groovy* is actually the *59th Street Bridge Song*. Interestingly, the song lyrics fail to mention anything suggesting that the song is about a bridge.

Another example is the *Five Bridges Suite* by The Nice, in 1970, inspired by the iconic bridges of Newcastle. This work is not only specific to the bridges, but waxes poetic about them, saying that some go north and some go south, but each one seems to cry.

An interesting case is *Three Manhattan Bridges*, a concerto for piano and orchestra written by Michael Torke in 2015. The three movements are inspired by the George Washington, Queensboro, and Brooklyn bridges. However, the work was commissioned by the Albany Symphony. Because downtown Albany is situated directly on the Hudson River, you might think the Albany Symphony would prefer to commission works celebrating their own bridges, and not those of their intrastate rival at the other end of the Hudson. However, a little research shows that Albany only has two bridges crossing the Hudson, neither of them historic or attractive.

Famously, Sonny Rollins spent most of a three-year sabbatical, reportedly 15 or more hours per day in all types of weather, practicing his saxophone on the Williamsburg Bridge, apparently because the noise bothered his neighbors. The result, once his sabbatical ended, was his album *The Bridge*, now considered a jazz classic.

Although these relationships between bridges and music do exist, they are too easy. They probably do not inspire many visitors to go out of their way to see a bridge because it was named after a musician, mentioned in a song, or served as rehearsal space. However, one relationship between a bridge and music does attract visitors. It is when a bridge has been turned into a musical instrument.

MID-HUDSON BRIDGE, POUGHKEEPSIE, NY

The Mid-Hudson Bridge is a major highway bridge constructed in 1931. The bridge was named Mid-Hudson because, at the time it was built, it became the only highway bridge in the 120 mile stretch of river between the Bear Mountain Bridge and Troy. The Mid-Hudson is one of several major suspension bridges built in the US in the 1920s and 1930s, a period when the world's record for longest suspension bridge was broken every few years by the Bear Mountain (1924), Benjamin Franklin (1926), Ambassador (1929), George Washington (1931), and Golden Gate (1937) bridges. The Mid-Hudson Bridge is longer than Bear Mountain but was never the holder of the record because it is not quite as long as the Benjamin Franklin Bridge constructed five years earlier.

The Mid-Hudson Bridge is very high, resulting in amazing views of the surrounding hillsides. As a large-scale suspension bridge from the 1930s, the bridge has gorgeous suspension towers as appealing as those on the Golden Gate. The crosspieces of the towers are arranged in an elegant, curved X-pattern. The anchor tower on the eastern end of the sidewalk displays dedications to Franklin and Eleanor Roosevelt, who were governor and first lady of New York at the time the bridge was constructed, and who were present at its opening.

If the history and the architecture were the only attractions, Mid-Hudson would still be a nice bridge to walk across if you happened to be in Poughkeepsie. However, the most appealing feature of the bridge is completely unexpected and unusual. In 2009, a major enhancement was added to attract visitors and make the bridge walk entertaining for locals and tourists.

In the parking lot on the western end of the bridge, signs direct you to tune your radio into station FM 95.3 to listen to Joseph Bertolozzi's *Bridge Music*. Tune in, and you will hear what seems to be rhythmic drumming and synthesized percussion melodies. It is definitely not obvious what this has to do with the bridge.

However, out on the sidewalk, it becomes clear. At the locations where the sidewalk expands to go around the two suspension towers, explanatory panels describe the *Bridge Music*. It is not drums. It is percussive music made by the composer beating on various parts of the bridge with hammers and dropping ball bearings down shafts within the towers, among other noisemaking methods. There are speakers at both towers, and you can push buttons on the panels to choose to listen to the various tracks. The panels describe the tracks, including an explanation of the source of the sounds used for each one. It is amazing, and yet another way in which part of a bridge has been taken over by the local community to make it a place where you want to go and hang out, 200 feet above the Hudson. Even if you cannot visit the bridge, you can purchase the music online.

LITERARY BRIDGES

Similar to musical bridges, you might expect that literary bridges include those named after an author or poet, and there are many examples. Sometimes, this naming appears to be random. For example, Shakespeare is memorialized by a bridge in Los Angeles, which seems to be a bit of a stretch. More commonly, bridges are named to commemorate an author who actually lived or worked in the city. Walt Whitman spent the final years of his life in Camden, where a bridge over the Delaware River now bears his name.

Samuel Beckett, Seán O'Casey, and James Joyce are all memorialized in Dublin. Beckett's bridge includes a plaque with a quote from his story, *The End*, referring to the unchanged appearance of the river flowing between its quays, and giving the impression of flowing in the wrong direction. O'Casey's bridge includes a plaque with a quote from his play, *Red Roses for Me*, referring to the city's hidden splendor.

The James Joyce Bridge has an even more substantial connection to the author. The bridge was constructed at a location that leads directly into the quayside house of Joyce's great-aunts. The house is famous among Joyce fanatics as the setting for the annual dinner party depicted in his iconic short-story *The Dead*, written in 1914, and included in the short-story collection *Dubliners*. Now known as the House of the Dead, it is a magnet for Joyce enthusiasts visiting Dublin. The house can be rented for events and is occasionally used for re-creations of the famous dinner. Even though the modernistic, sculptural bridge was built more than 60 years after his death, it is certainly visited by more than a few Joyce enthusiasts.

Bridges can also feature in the title of a work of literature. Like song lyrics, there are numerous instances where the reference to a bridge in the title of a work is generic, not meant to refer to a specific bridge, and therefore does not induce bridge tourism on any particular bridge. A common thread in literary works named after a bridge is that the referenced bridge usually collapsed as the climax to the story. Willa Cather's *Alexander's Bridge*—collapsed. Thornton Wilder's *Bridge of San Luis Rey*—collapsed. Pierre Boulle's *Bridge on the River Kwai*—collapsed. The implication seems to be that a bridge only merits stardom in a literary work if it does something dramatic, like fall apart.

Bridges can be characters in literary works as well, if you use a little imagination. Check out *The Little Red Lighthouse and the Great Gray Bridge* by Hildegarde Swift and Lynd Ward. Yes, it is a children's book, and the George Washington Bridge is the antagonist, the big bully threatening the existence of the heroic Little Red Lighthouse, at least until the end. But the important thing is that the popularity of the book still brings tourists to the actual Little Red Lighthouse at the base of the George Washington Bridge today, 75 years after it was published.

POOHSTICKS BRIDGE, NEAR HARTFIELD VILLAGE, ENGLAND

Much like a group of enthusiasts with a common interest in bridges, there is definitely a robust Winnie-the-Pooh culture, with certain locations that must be visited by dedicated Pooh fans. These include the Disney parks, where children and adults alike can go to explore a re-creation of the Hundred Acre Wood, purchase Pooh-related paraphernalia, and meet and greet the Pooh characters in person. However, many Pooh purists scoff at the Disney-Pooh connection, which only exists because Disney purchased the rights long after Pooh had already become an icon.

True Pooh enthusiasts are not satisfied with bought-and-paid-for re-creations. They want the real thing, such as A.A. Milne's original manuscripts for *Winnie-the-Pooh* and *The House at Pooh Corner* at the Wren Library at Trinity College, Cambridge. In addition, you can see most of Christopher Robin's original stuffed toys, including Kanga, Tigger, Piglet, Eeyore, and Pooh himself on display at the New York Public Library.

Alternatively, if you have the wherewithal, you can purchase one of the original drawings made by E.H. Shepard for the Pooh books in the 1920s. In July 2018, Shepard's famous map of the Hundred Acre Wood, which served as the frontispiece for the original book, sold at Sotheby's for more than a half-million dollars. This beat the existing world record for the highest price ever paid at auction for a book illustration, which was set in 2014 for the original drawing of Christopher Robin, Pooh, and Piglet playing Poohsticks on the Poohsticks Bridge. A 1929 redrawing of the Poohsticks scene by Shepard was also sold in the 2018 auction, bringing in more than $230,000.

Poohsticks Bridge, East Sussex, England

Another of the Pooh tourist sights known to attract Pooh enthusiasts is the real Hundred Acre Wood. More commonly known as the Ashdown Forest, the Hundred Acre Wood is in East Sussex, about 40 miles southeast of London. This is where the Milne family lived in the early 1920s, and where Christopher Robin's adventures with his stuffed toys were written into the iconic Pooh books. And, for Pooh enthusiasts and bridgespotters alike, the most important attraction is the original Poohsticks Bridge near Hartfield Village, where the seven year-old Christopher Robin invented the game introduced to the world in *The House at Pooh Corner*, and depicted in dozens of Pooh videos since.

What is Poohsticks? A brief description of the rules is that you and your opponent stand on the upstream side of the bridge, drop sticks at the same time, and then run to the downstream side of the bridge to see whose stick emerges first. There are many websites, and even a few books, such as Mark Evans' *The Poohsticks Handbook*, that elaborate on these rules. However, there is no point in even considering going to the bridge without reading the original description in *The House at Pooh Corner* because no mechanical recitation of the rules can capture the essential Pooh-ness of the game.

Physically, the Poohsticks Bridge may be the least impressive bridge discussed in this book. Originally called Posingford Bridge, it is made of rough-hewn wooden slats. It is about 25 feet long, and maybe eight feet high above the water. It is about ten feet wide. It is not historic or even authentic. The original bridge was constructed in 1907 to support a small logging operation. That bridge was rotting by the 1970s, and it was replaced in 1979. For those Pooh-purists who scoff at the latter-day Disney takeover of Pooh, it is heart-warming to learn that the reconstruction of the bridge was largely paid for by Disney.

An important note is that multiple bridges attract Poohsticks players. The game can be and is played on lots of different bridges, and there are organized Poohsticks competitions held at many locations. In fact, one of the locations where there is not an organized competition is at the original Poohsticks Bridge at Hartfield. While the original bridge at Hartfield is clearly the most important to be visited, its location and setting are not amenable to the large numbers of competitors and spectators who are attracted to the organized competitions like a small bear to honey.

The website www.visitEngland.com recommends 12 different bridges across Britain as prominent Poohsticks bridges. The most famous competition is the World Poohsticks Championships, which have been held since 1984. The original venue had been Day's Lock at Little Wittenham, near Didcot, but the event ultimately grew too large for the venue. In 2015, the event was moved to a small bridge across the River Windrush near Witney, in Oxfordshire. The event drew 500 participants and thousands of spectators in 2018, the 35th annual championships. In addition to the individual and team Poohsticks competitions, there are other festivities, a Fancy Dress Competition, and, of course, people costumed as their favorite Pooh character, all for charity.

A good Poohsticks Bridge requires the perfect combination of bridge width and water velocity to match the attention span of the participants. The objective here is to give you plenty of time to get to the other side of the bridge, watch for your stick, and create just the right amount of anticipation anxiety before it emerges. If the stick takes too long to emerge, the participants will lose interest and look away. If the stick emerges too quickly, there is no time to build the suspense needed for a satisfying finish. However, if the width of the bridge and the velocity of the water are just right, then the perfect Pooh moment is achieved.

This effect will differ depending on the age of the participants. Children may lose interest quickly if their stick does not appear. Therefore, a good Poohsticks bridge for children requires a narrow deck and/or fast-moving water. Adults, at least some of them, may enjoy the suspense and be able to wait a little longer. This requires a wider bridge, and/or slow-moving water. At the original Poohsticks Bridge, the game was invented by a small boy who had, one could assume, the attention span of a small boy. As a result, it is a narrow bridge, and the length of time needed for your stick to emerge is not long enough to really build the anticipation needed for exciting competitions for adults. However, it is probably the exact right amount of time for a seven year-old boy.

There are two important observations regarding the prominence of the Poohsticks Bridge as a tourist bridge. The first is its remote location.

If visiting London without a car, you need to take a train to Royal Tun-bridge Wells and a bus to Hartfield Village, then find the Pooh Corner shop in town to buy a laminated map. While at Pooh Corner, you can also purchase other Pooh items, get information on other nearby Pooh sights, and have a miniature tea party at child-sized tables. Then, you must hike approximately 45 minutes to the bridge, following signposts indicating the direction to the Pooh Bridge in both English and Japanese because, apparently, Japanese-speaking tourists love Pooh. All-in-all, it is about a three-hour trip, one-way, from London.

Driving is a little better, with a Pooh car park situated south of Hart-field Village, but still requiring an approximately 20-minute walk from the car park to the bridge. The nearest town with any tourist interest at all is Royal Tunbridge Wells, about eight miles away. The point is, it takes a great deal of effort to visit the bridge, with nothing much else to see on the way. Only maniacal Pooh enthusiasts and some bridgespotters who have been unwittingly caught up in the fun are going to make this trip.

The second observation regards the size of stick required to play Poohsticks at this particular bridge. It turns out that stick size must be taken seriously, lest your stick gets stuck. The creek is shallow, with many obstructions, and if the sticks you and your opponents choose to drop are too large, the water is not deep enough to carry them away, and they will get stuck. And what happens, then, to the next stick? It gets stuck behind the initial stick. And what happens if, say, a thousand people have visited and dropped a thousand sticks? This would create a logjam of small sticks, a stick-jam, if you will, on the downstream side of the bridge. Which is ex-actly what you will see when you visit the Poohsticks Bridge.

On the one hand, after traveling three hours to get here, nothing could be more pleasant than to drop your stick on the upstream side, run to the downstream side, wait with building anticipation for your stick to emerge, and then watch it slowly disappear downstream as you imagine it entering the sea sometime next week. However, watching it float only about 15 feet downstream before it becomes lodged in a stick-jam is a seri-ous disappointment.

That is until you realize that to have built the stick-jam, thousands of people have journeyed to this relatively isolated location and dropped sticks, just like you have. True story—the day your author visited the Poohsticks Bridge was an overcast, chilly Wednesday in September. Not many people out. During the 20 minutes he spent photographing the bridge and, yes, dropping many sticks that immediately got stuck, the bridge was visited by nine other people. Of these nine people, the number who stopped and photographed each other dropping a stick was—nine!

Maybe not a large number, but a 100-percent participation rate is impressive, and says something important about this bridge. Even locals out for a hike or to walk the dog, who have crossed the bridge a thousand times, cannot resist the urge to play Poohsticks just once more. It would be more enjoyable to watch your stick float away. However, it is also enjoyable to realize that you are one of the thousands of people who leave their sofas to go out in the world and do extraordinary things, like play Poohsticks at the one-and-only original Poohsticks Bridge.

CINEMATIC BRIDGES

As with artistic, literary, and musical bridges, tourists may visit cinematic bridges because they are a fan of a particular movie in which a specific bridge played a prominent part in the story. There are plenty of those, but a different category of cinematic bridges, one that does not have a corollary among artistic, musical, and literary bridges, also deserves mention. This includes bridges that only make a brief cameo appearance instead of playing a prominent role in the story.

This is done in three common ways. One method is a brief close-up of a bridge, backed by mood music, inserted in between scenes of your favorite TV show or movie, to subtly inform you of the location of the next scene. This only works if the vast majority of the audience will recognize the bridge and draw a subliminal association with the location, so it is usually only done with well-known or iconic bridges. A three-second close-up of the Brooklyn Bridge, and the scene of the action shifts to New York City. Or Golden Gate for San Francisco, or Tower Bridge for London.

A second method is to shoot a scene of the actors conversing while standing or walking on a bridge or with a bridge in the background. In this case, the purpose is not to inform the viewer of the location, because the bridge may not be recognizable to them. Instead, the purpose is primarily decorative, to set the scene and mood. It is sufficient just to have the background of the scene look good if attractive scenery is appropriate to the mood of the scene.

Bridge locations are often picturesque, especially when they are inhabited by a decorative bridge. For a romantic comedy, a cute decorative bridge in the background will convey a comfortable, visually attractive setting for the comfortable, visually attractive actors. Once you have taken just one day to visit and photograph the pretty bridges in Central Park, you will never be able to un-see them because you will recognize them in movies and television shows for the rest of your life.

The concept works in reverse, as well. For a gritty crime drama, film noir thriller, or tragedy, an undecorated, industrial-looking bridge down by the docks may impart a sense of danger. Actors fall in love while strolling across Bow Bridge, or while dancing on a barge in the shadow of the Ponte Sant'Angelo, or while picnicking in the Public Garden. But prostitutes commit suicide by jumping under the wheels of an army convoy on foggy Waterloo Bridge, and the office of Sam Spade, private detective, is set against the gritty backdrop of the San Francisco Bay Bridge.

The third method is a combination of the two. In this case, the featured characters are shown traveling across the bridge, to communicate to audiences that they are moving to or from a particular location. It may be an aerial shot of their car crossing the bridge or a view of the bridge outside of the window of the car.

This method presents a risk, because bridge-savvy viewers will take note and frown if the direction of travel is incorrect, or if the bridge itself is just obviously the wrong bridge. In Hitchcock's *Strangers on a Train*, Bruno Antony travels from his home in Virginia to Union Station in a cab across Arlington Memorial Bridge, with the Lincoln Memorial receding into the background. This is visually pleasing. It also communicates "Washington, DC" to audiences. However, it is also wrong, showing him traveling west away from Union Station, instead of east toward it.

Similarly, the scene of Benjamin Braddock driving across the San Francisco Bay Bridge in his Alfa Romeo to find Elaine Robinson in Berkeley in *The Graduate* is iconic. The experience, in person, of passing through the dark tunnel on Yerba Buena Island and then popping out into a blaze of sunshine directly underneath the suspension tower of the Bay Bridge is so memorable that it was captured, quite successfully, to add to the immediacy of the scene in the movie. However, that experience only occurs when traveling west on Interstate 80 into downtown San Francisco, not when traveling east toward Berkeley.

A very confusing situation occurs near the end of *Human Desire*. The final scene of the movie shows the main character driving a train, with a bridge in the background. Because the setting of the movie is in California, the movie studio could have chosen a bridge in California. They could have chosen a generic bridge that was unlikely to be identifiable. They could have chosen an identifiable bridge, and hoped that most of the audience would not recognize it. Instead, they chose the Lower Trenton Bridge in New Jersey, the one and only bridge in the United States that has the name of its location, Trenton, emblazoned on its side in gigantic letters. As for hoping that nobody would notice, the enormous lettering on the Lower Trenton Bridge is an iconic symbol of Trenton, and would have been recognized by any members of the audience that had ever driven, or taken the train, between Philadelphia and New York City

These cameo appearances are unlikely to attract tourists to bridges because the bridges are just part of the setting rather than playing an active role in the plot. However, there are cinematic bridges that have become famous, and which are visited, because of the role they played in a movie. Note that there is a great deal of overlap between literary and cinematic bridges, for the obvious reason that many books are adapted into movies. In some cases, it may be difficult to tell if tourists are visiting the bridge because they were fans of the book or fans of the movie.

Actors traveling across bridges can also be used to communicate subliminal or symbolic meanings to the audience. In ancient Rome, bridges were considered to represent a passageway between life and death. In *The Mystery of Edwin Drood*, Dickens described the dark bridges spanning the shadows of London "as death spans life."

This theme of bridges transporting people between the worlds of good and evil is taken up in *Picnic*, where the bridge represents the choice young people must make between a life of conventionality and duty versus one of passion and adventure. A small pedestrian swinging bridge figures prominently in the Labor Day picnic scenes. Madge, the newly crowned Queen of Neewollah, played by Kim Novak, is forced to leave her young friends to dance with the frumpy, elderly members of the picnic committee on one side of the river. While nobody is paying attention, she works her way to the middle of the bridge to watch the wild, offbeat dancing of Hal, played by William Holden, and several others, all fueled by a bottle of whiskey. Madge eventually crosses the bridge to join Hal in a sensuous dance, making the bridge a symbolic means of transport between a life of boring respectability and duty on one side and one of romantic adventure on the other. The 1938 bridge is still found crossing the Little Arkansas River in Halstead, Kansas, today, and has become a prominent local landmark due to its role in the famous movie.

Bridges are also used in movies as magical devices. In *The Music Man*, Professor Harold Hill successfully uses the footbridge in Madison Park to woo Marian the Librarian. In *Brigadoon*, the stone bridge on the outskirts of the town protects the magical spell that allows the town to remain frozen in time. In a climactic scene, the lovelorn Harry races the townspeople in an attempt to cross the bridge, an act that would make the town disappear forever.

There is a least one important bridge that was robbed of its chance at Hollywood stardom by being left out of a critical scene, in a famous movie, in which it had every right to demand a major role. Although little historical information is known about the thirteenth century figure William Wallace, there does not appear to be any question that the Battle of Stirling Bridge actually took place at or near the bridge, or that collapse of the bridge played a role in the outcome of the battle. However, in the depiction of the battle in the movie *Braveheart*, there is no bridge to be found, and the outcome of the battle is imagined to be based on other tactics.

BRIDGES OF MADISON COUNTY, IOWA

As discussed previously, there are more than a thousand wooden, covered bridges in the United States. Wherever they are found, they attract visitors because of their quaint appearance and scenic setting. They usually have a parking lot and historical plaque to facilitate tourism. They tend to occur in clusters, allowing enthusiasts to visit five, ten, or more bridges in a single trip. You can go to almost any covered bridge in the United States during daylight hours, and chances are good that someone else will drive up and get out of the car to photograph it within ten minutes.

The Bridges of Madison County, however, take covered bridge tourism to the next level. As covered bridges, the Bridges of Madison County are about the same as any other covered bridges, maybe a little less so. The number of them is from three to seven, depending on how you want to count them. Three of them, Roseman, Hogback, and Holliwell, are wooden covered bridges, still in their original locations and located within eight to ten miles of Winterset, the county seat of Madison County. Cedar Bridge was also a wooden covered bridge located near Winterset, but was burned down in 2002, rebuilt in 2004, and re-burned in 2017. Cutler-Donahoe Bridge is a wooden covered bridge that was moved from its original location to Winterset City Park in 1970. Stone Bridge, also located in Winterset City Park, is just that, not a covered bridge. Imes Covered Bridge is a wooden covered bridge still in its original location, but it is located about 15 miles from Winterset.

The bridges are generally shorter than the covered bridges found in New England. They are fairly uniform in appearance—red-sided, with no windows. They are historic, having construction dates ranging from 1870 to 1884. They are located a convenient distance of less than 30 miles from Des Moines, not a major tourist destination, but at least a substantial-sized city. In addition, because they are situated in a cluster, they can all be visited within a single afternoon.

All of these features suggest that these bridges should receive some level of tourist attention. However, the level of interest far exceeds that which would be warranted without the book in 1992, and the movie in 1995. In 2021, these are not just the most prominent covered bridge attractions in the United States. These are probably among the most visited bridges, of any kind, in the United States. In the middle of Iowa.

On a random summer afternoon, you can visit them and expect to see carloads of tourists coming and going. Not hundreds of people, like you will see on the Golden Gate or Brooklyn bridges. There will be a few people, all taking photographs, when you first arrive. They will not stay long, because the bridges are small and there is not much to see. However, as they leave, more arrive. Never more than about six, eight, or ten at a time, but always being replaced by more, all day long. In case you are thinking these are local people, look at the license plates in the parking lots—Texas, Missouri, New York, Minnesota, Wisconsin, California, and New Jersey. Then look at the graffiti inscriptions on the wood-plank sides inside the bridges—quotes from the book, testimonials to lost love, poems from Spain and Germany, and messages written in Asian languages.

It is not clear whether the book and movie would have been so successful if they had been based on a fictional set of bridges, but the fact that they are based on real bridges has definitely had a long-lasting effect on the community. These bridges are not a local tourist attraction. They are not even a nationwide attraction. They are an international phenomenon, more than 20 years after the book and movie.

Tourists at Holliwell Covered Bridge, Iowa

There are some differences between the book and the movie regarding which bridges were visited by Robert and Francesca. The most prominent bridge in both versions is Roseman Bridge, the one that Robert and Francesca first visited together, where Francesca left a note for Robert to find the next day, and where Francesca's ashes were scattered.

In the book, they meet again the next evening at Cedar Bridge, but in the movie, this meeting takes place at Holliwell Bridge. The reason for this switch is not apparent. Roseman and Holliwell are the only covered bridges actually shown in the movie. However, a bridge not found in the book, the Stone Bridge, is also used as a shooting location in the movie. Robert and Francesca go on an outing at an old pedestrian stone bridge, which Robert photographs before they lie on a grassy hillside and talk. Although their outing is ostensibly outside of Winterset, for fear of being caught by locals who know Francesca, the actual bridge used for the scene is the scenic Stone Bridge adjacent to the Cutler-Donahoe Covered Bridge in the City Park in Winterset. Despite not being a covered bridge and not being part of the setting of the book, even the Stone Bridge and the grassy hillside above it are visited by fans of the movie.

Tourist visits to the bridges today are promoted and facilitated by the county. All of them are closed to traffic, but have parking lots on their ends and display brass historical plaques. Many, maybe even most, covered bridges have parking available, but it is usually enough space for three or four cars. In Madison County, the parking lots are big enough for 20 to 30 cars. The county advertises the bridges on its website, along with its other big local attraction, the birthplace of John Wayne in Winterset. The website provides directions for self-directed tours, but guided tours are also available. There is a covered bridge festival in October every year which began in 1970, long before the book and movie. Roseman Bridge, the most important of the bridges, even has a gift shop selling bridge souvenirs, with a copy of the movie playing on DVD on a television in the corner, all day long. Other indications that Roseman Bridge is considered the most important of the group are that the road to the bridge has been renamed Francesca Avenue, and that love padlocks can be found attached to steel reinforcing rods at the bridge.

Interestingly, the book and movie really have nothing to do with bridges at all. The bridges are just the backdrop for the love story, and it is the love story that became popular. Robert could just as easily have arrived in Winterset to photograph the lovely, historic Madison County Courthouse. Alternatively, the story could have been set amongst grain silos in Kansas or historic gas stations on Route 66. The only requirement is that there be something remotely photogenic situated in an otherwise un-photographable location, to contrast the exciting, adventurous lifestyle of Robert with the dreary, everyday existence of Francesca. The tourists do not come here to see bridges. They come here to find Robert and Francesca. Judging by the graffiti, many of the visitors found them.

SCIENTIFIC BRIDGES

Just as some people enjoy art as a hobby, or reading, or music, or movies, many people enjoy science as a hobby. If a bridge has some relationship with a famous scientist or a well-known scientific principle, or is just scientifically interesting, then it will attract bridge tourists. Although it is a common theme in this book, it bears repeating that the concept seems tenuous, until you see that there are multiple prominent examples. For instance, the Bridge Between Continents in Iceland was constructed and named specifically as a tourist magnet, because of its unusual location across a boundary between the earth's tectonic plates. This makes it a must-see attraction for anyone interested in geology.

MATHEMATICAL BRIDGE, CAMBRIDGE, ENGLAND

There are several examples of clever, innovative bridge designs at major universities, where students and masters stimulate and show off their skills for each other. The most famous is probably the Mathematical Bridge at Queens' College, Cambridge.

The scientific connections associated with Mathematical Bridge are apparent even in its name. It was originally built in 1749, and is an unusual arch bridge constructed of nothing but straight pieces of wood. From a distance, the bridge looks like any other curved arch bridge. However, up close, you can see that the arch is composed of perfectly straight boards, cleverly arranged so that they tangentially outline a curved structure.

Just as interesting as the real bridge are the legends surrounding the bridge, including the belief that Isaac Newton himself designed it. This is not true, as Newton died more than 20 years before the bridge was built. Another myth is that the bridge was originally built without nuts and bolts, and that mischievous college students had disassembled it but could not figure out how to put it back together. In fact, the original bridge had been built with pins inserted from the outside that could not be seen by people crossing the bridge. Later versions of the bridge, including the current one built in 1905, have bolts passing through the entire width of the boards.

The bridge connects the President's Lodge of Queens' College with The Backs on the opposite side of the River Cam. You can access the bridge to walk across and view it up close by paying the entrance fee and going into Queens' College. You can also get a good view and photographs from Silver Street Bridge without entering the college.

HARVARD BRIDGE, CAMBRIDGE, MASSACHUSETTS

The name of the Harvard Bridge can be a little confusing, as it is not associated with the famous university. Both the bridge and university were named for John Harvard, but the bridge is located a couple miles to the east of the campus and leads directly into the center of the campus of a different university, MIT.

The bridge is famous among engineering and science geeks for its introduction of a new unit of measure, the "Smoot," to the engineering world. A Smoot is a unit of measure equivalent to the 5'7" height of Oliver Smoot in 1958 when, as an MIT student, he was laid end-to-end 364.4 times to mark out distances along the bridge as part of a fraternity prank. More than 60 years later, the Smoot units are still marked and numbered on the bridge in yellow, and are repainted by the fraternity pledge class every year.

CHAPTER 7

RECREATIONAL BRIDGES

ALTHOUGH MANY OF THE WAYS that bridges served their communities throughout history no longer apply, new uses have come into being. Primary among these is their use as a place for recreation and pursuit of hobbies.

The use of bridges for recreation is a recent phenomenon, one that would probably not have occurred to most bridge designers until the latter half of the twentieth century. However, in the twenty-first century, designing a major bridge without considering additional features to accommodate recreational uses, or even to attract tourists, is unthinkable. In general, outdoor recreational activities such as hiking, jogging, biking, and walking dogs are a recent phenomenon. They became widespread starting in the 1960s and 70s, coincident with an increase in appreciation of environmental conservation. It is no surprise that those participating in outdoor activities prefer to do so in a natural setting surrounded by trees, grass, and water. These are places where bridges are also found.

Bridges are constructed where a barrier exists, and barriers are usually formed by either water bodies, steep terrain, or both. Water bodies and steep terrain, in turn, both make for excellent scenery. In addition, bridges, by being elevated above the surrounding trees and buildings, are an excellent place from which to view it. Consequently, the incorporation of features that enhance outdoor recreation has become a major consideration in the repurposing of older bridges, and in the design of new ones.

To serve a recreational purpose, a bridge obviously needs to provide a safe space to protect the slow-speed recreationists from the high-speed traffic. This either means that a bridge must be closed to traffic and repurposed only for pedestrians, or that it includes a sidewalk. For much of the twentieth century, many bridges were built entirely without sidewalks.

However, recreation-friendly features mean much more than just adding a sidewalk. There is a big difference between a narrow sidewalk designed only to allow people to cross to the other side and a recreation-friendly sidewalk. Recreation-friendly features require, at a minimum, a sidewalk wide enough for bicycles, joggers, hikers, roller bladers, and dog walkers, all at the same time. It is also important that this wide sidewalk lead somewhere that people want to go, such as connecting into a network of parks and trails on either end of the bridge.

Allowing lots of people to pursue different activities on the bridge all at the same time is only the first step. It is not sufficient to just let a large number of people cross at the same time. A true community-centric bridge also provides reasons for the people to stop in the middle. Because once people stop, they begin to talk to each other. The bridge has now become a community gathering place.

In many cases, the reason for people to stop on the bridge is organic, with no assistance from the bridge designer. Many early bridges were constructed in scenic places, and people were going to stop to look at the view regardless, even on a narrow sidewalk. However, the effect can be amplified through the decisions of the bridge designer. Widen the sidewalk, install a few benches, put up a plaque, and employ dozens of other subtle but effective design choices to encourage pedestrians to stop in the middle of the bridge and to allow the community interaction to begin. The placement of benches is becoming common on newer bridges. These may be accompanied by historical plaques and exhibits, telescopic viewers, and even speakers playing music. A more subtle feature is a widening of the sidewalk into a small plaza, usually accompanied by benches and exhibits.

On older suspension bridges, it is interesting to see how the sidewalk interacts with the suspension and anchor towers, which are usually an obstruction. On some bridges, such as the Golden Gate, the sidewalk gets constricted at the towers, creating unpleasant pedestrian and bicycle traffic jams. On other bridges, like the Brooklyn, Benjamin Franklin, and Ravenel bridges, the intersection of the sidewalk with the towers was used as an opportunity to expand the sidewalk into a small plaza. By widening out, the plaza invites the pedestrians to stop to look at the view without blocking other pedestrian traffic. The wall of the tower right next to the plaza is a perfect location for historical and dedication plaques. Many newer bridges, such as the StadtPark Steg in Vienna, have small widened plazas in the middle even though there is no part of the superstructure blocking the pathway.

The desirability of using bridges for recreation is so strong that it has even been extended to communities whose bridges do not have sidewalks. Mackinaw City in Michigan and New River Gorge in West Virginia have bridges that are prominent attractions due to their history, size, views, and architecture, but both lack sidewalks. These communities are left with no way to incorporate the popular bridge into their recreation systems. What to do? Well, if people cannot walk over the bridge, lead tours and let them walk under it. Or just shut it down now and then, and let the bridge-walkers and BASE jumpers take it over.

TRAIL BRIDGES

The most obvious use of bridges for recreation is to connect biking and hiking trails on either side of the river. By definition, any trail system more than a few miles long is ultimately going to encounter some kind of a barrier that needs to be crossed, leaving the choice of having several short, independent trail systems, or building a few bridges to connect them. The connection can be accomplished by expanding the sidewalk on an existing bridge, by repurposing an abandoned road or railway bridge, or by constructing a new pedestrian and bike-only bridge.

However it is done, the use of bridges to connect trail systems can be extremely powerful. Although having a sidewalk is a seemingly innocuous feature of a bridge, it can magically turn an inanimate piece of transportation infrastructure into a prime destination for tourists and recreationists.

Consider a river that has 20 miles of riverfront trails on one side and 20 miles of trails on the other side. A slight widening of a sidewalk on just one of the bridges in that stretch of river, only a few hundred feet long, turns a 20 mile-bike ride into a 40 mile-bike ride. This is a major expansion of the local recreation network, at the price of a few hundred feet of wider sidewalk.

You may also think about it in reverse, working from the trail down to the bridges. Take the Appalachian Trail, more than 2,000 miles long from Maine to Georgia. At some point, the Appalachian Trail is going to have to cross the Hudson River. It cannot go around. It does that on the sidewalk on the Bear Mountain Bridge. It will also have to cross the Connecticut River, the Delaware River, the Susquehanna River, the Potomac River, and dozens of smaller rivers in between. These crossings are on the Ledyard Bridge in Hanover, New Hampshire (Connecticut), Interstate 80 Bridge at the Delaware Water Gap (Delaware), the Clarks Ferry Bridge in Duncannon, Pennsylvania (Susquehanna), and the Harper's Ferry Bridge (Potomac).

Many of the bridges discussed in this book that are tourist destinations for other reasons also, coincidentally, connect to trails. The major attraction of Ravenel Bridge is probably its modernistic architecture, but it is also integral to the regional bike trail system in Charleston. Thousands of San Francisco residents could not care less about the iconic Art Deco architecture of the Golden Gate Bridge, but are happy to use it to access bike trails in Marin County. In other cases, connecting trails was the entire reason for the construction of a bridge, or for the repurposing of a historic bridge into a trail bridge.

BOB KERREY BRIDGE, OMAHA, NEBRASKA

Although support for recreational activities is one of the attractions of walkable bridges, the recreational function is usually a secondary consideration. Highway bridges are built to serve a transportation function, and the designers throw in a wide sidewalk as a bonus. Old bridges are preserved as part of the community history but, since they cannot carry traffic any longer, they are turned into pedestrian bridges and connected to bike trails. Pedestrian-only bridges are built, but most of the foot traffic consists of tourists or commuters moving from a destination on one side of the river to a destination on the other. When recreation-focused bridges are built, they tend to be small ones in urban parks and, even then, much of the foot traffic is commuters.

The Bob Kerrey Bridge, crossing the Missouri River between Omaha and Council Bluffs, breaks this mold. Completed in 2008, the Kerrey Bridge is a large-scale bridge crossing a major river. However, the bridge does not carry traffic. It is not a historic bridge that is being preserved. It does not connect urban or tourist areas that would create incidental foot traffic. Instead, the bridge is entirely about recreation.

The bridge is part of the new generation of cable-stayed bridges. The structure consists of two slender, needle-like towers holding cables at their tops. The cables then fan out at increasingly shallower angles to support the deck. In an unusual and appealing twist, the deck is wildly curved, weaving in and out of either side of the towers. The bridge is very high, with the deck sitting more than 50 feet above the river and the towers reaching 200 feet. The river is about 1,000 feet wide, but the lengthy, curved approaches on either end of the bridge increase the total length to about 3,000 feet. The structure is all steel, painted white, and the cement deck is about 20 feet wide. The bridge was apparently designed to sway and, if you visit on a windy day, you will find that it sways a lot. The movement is not noticeable while you are walking, but when you stop and sit in the middle, it is clear that the deck is moving several feet in each direction.

The deck is expanded at each of the towers, and also in the middle of the bridge, to encourage people to stop and admire the view of the river. The central area also has benches and historical plaques, and the Iowa-Nebraska state line is marked in paint on the deck. Although the river is not particularly picturesque, it is historic. It is a bit of a thrill to sit on the benches in the middle of the river and consider that Lewis and Clark navigated this section of the Missouri River with their keelboat both outbound on their way to the Pacific and on their return to St. Louis, more than 200 years ago.

The bridge exists almost solely to connect trails on the Nebraska side of the river to those on the Iowa side. On the Nebraska side, the bridge entrance is located in a plaza at the National Park Service Midwest Regional

Office. This building also houses the Lewis and Clark National Historic Trail Visitors Center. Trails that follow the riverfront past the Park Service building include: the Lewis and Clark Interpretive Trail, which links 16 historic and memorial Lewis and Clark sites in the Omaha area; the 3,700 mile-long Lewis and Clark National Historic Trail, which passes through Omaha on its journey between Illinois and Oregon; and the Omaha Riverfront Bike Trail, which connects to other bike trails throughout the Omaha area.

Kerrey Bridge, Omaha

On the Iowa side, the bridge leads to a parking lot in Tom Hanafan River's Edge Park. There, the bridge connects to the Iowa Riverfront Bike Trail, which, in turn, connects to a variety of bike and nature trails in and around Council Bluffs. Prior to 2008, there was no easy link for pedestrians or bikers to cross the river and connect from one of these systems to the other. The only bridges in or near downtown Omaha or Council Bluffs were either interstate highways or railroads, none of them with pedestrian access. The Kerrey Bridge, once it was constructed, became the only connection.

One interesting feature of the Kerrey Bridge is its location. Omaha is not the only city to renovate or build a landmark bridge to provide a link between regional bike trail systems. This is especially the case with bridges that are as much public artworks as they are bridges, such as the Kerrey Bridge. However, most cities do this at prominent downtown locations, as part of major redevelopment projects.

Although the Kerrey Bridge is not far from downtown Omaha, it is not in it. Instead, it is in a neighborhood called North Downtown, or NoDo, which is separated from downtown by Interstate 480. The bridge is only about a mile away from downtown, but it seems isolated because Interstate 480 crosses the Missouri River on a high bridge, and there is also a massive arena complex called CenturyLink Center blocking the view from downtown to the bridge. In general, this tall, landmark-scale bridge is not even visible from downtown unless you are on one of the higher floors of the office buildings. You may not even know it exists unless you happen to drive north of downtown along Abbott Drive to the airport.

Moreover, it is not like there is much happening in the immediate area of the bridge. There are the trails, of course. There are several new buildings scattered around, including the Park Service building and plaza on the south side of the bridge, a few new condominium buildings on the north side, and the CenturyLink Center that blocks the view of downtown. However, at the time of the author's visit in 2014, the rest of the area, including the banks of the river, was undeveloped with lots of open space.

On the Iowa end of the bridge, the River's Edge Park appears to be new. Except for having signs naming it as a park and having a parking lot, there is not much else you would normally associate with the phrase "park." No benches, no trees, no playing fields. Just grass and tall lampposts. The remainder of the area north and east of River's Edge Park consists of small residential houses just a few steps off the end of the bridge.

Given its separation from downtown and lack of nearby development, the choice to build a landmark bridge in a relatively isolated location is curious. Omaha has a fully developed park system, called Heartland of

America Park, directly on the downtown riverfront. The Omaha and Iowa Riverfront Bike Trails are directly opposite each other in this area, which is much more directly linked into downtown. A landmark bridge here would be prominently visible from anywhere in downtown. It would become a major part of the downtown cityscape. Why not build this new landmark bridge, connecting the bike trails, directly in downtown, instead of in a semi-remote location where it will not be seen?

The answer is not obvious but appears to be that the bridge is part of a proactive redevelopment of the formerly industrial NoDo area. The bridge was apparently located here not to fill an existing demand for pedestrian access across the river, but as a magnet to attract new development. Given that the bridge was completed in 2008, right about the time of an economic downturn, it is understandable this new development was still a work in progress in 2014. It is not that the area is a bad neighborhood. It is actually nicely done. It just does not have riverfront hotels or restaurants yet, and while a few condos have been built, more are probably planned.

The bridge would probably have more people on it if it had been located on the downtown side of Interstate 480, instead of to the north. However, it does appear to be attracting visitors. There are quite a few people out on the bridge at any given time. There are kids on roller blades, taking advantage of the steep, sloping curve of the approaches. Organized Scout groups stopping in the middle to discuss Lewis and Clark passing directly underneath this spot. Even several people simply out for a hike, taking their time to admire the bridge and the view. It would have been understandable if, in building a bridge in an isolated location in an attempt to attract development, the city had built the bridge on a much smaller scale and following a more conventional design. But they went all-in, building a large-scale landmark work of public art, and the resulting bridge is definitely worth a visit.

PARKS ON BRIDGES

Bridges have been placed in parks for centuries, but parks placed onto bridges are a recent development. As government regulations have allowed the public to comment on bridge designs, sidewalks connected to trails are only one of the recreational enhancements being requested. In response to public demand, park features being placed onto bridges include benches, informational plaques, historical exhibits, telescopes for viewing scenery, tubes for holding fishing poles, tables for cleaning fish, public artworks and exhibits, bike racks, and other items.

The most common place for adding these features is on repurposed bridges, those that have been closed to traffic but claimed by the community for historic preservation and recreational purposes. These are addressed in Chapter 8. However, the practice is becoming common on new bridges, as well.

Most new bridges are being designed with a sidewalk to either provide recreational opportunities, facilitate movement of pedestrians, or both. Once the decision to add a sidewalk has been made, the next logical step is to make the sidewalk wide enough to allow passing bicycles, and then to add a few small features to support other types of recreation. In Washington, DC, the piers of the old 11th Street Bridge over the Anacostia River are being redeveloped into 11th Street Bridge Park, which will be a complete, stand-alone park in the middle of the river. Following the opening of the new 11th Street Bridge in 2009, the city considered options for the old bridge. The deck was removed but two of the piers, which were only about ten feet from the sidewalk of the new bridge, were left in place. The city then constructed two small pedestrian observation platforms on the piers. The platforms were accessible by either foot or bicycle by using the sidewalk on the new bridge. As of 2021, planning is underway for the Bridge Park, which will replace the small platforms with a multilevel deck that will provide landscaped green spaces, multiuse buildings, benches, a water-feature, a performance space, and more.

FOUNDERS BRIDGE, HARTFORD

Founders Bridge, which crosses the Connecticut River in downtown Hartford, is an excellent example of one of the post-World War II bridges designed for the sole purpose of moving traffic from Point A to Point B. Built in 1958, its only purpose was to move automobiles quickly, with no consideration of aesthetics or support of recreational opportunities for the local community.

The bridge is not an unusual type, historically interesting, or particularly attractive. It is a steel-girder bridge, sitting on cement piers, carrying a major highway into downtown, one of thousands of functional, cookie-cutter bridges offering no reason for anyone to take a second look. There was no need for the bridge to be attractive because its surrounding area was not that attractive. Interstate 91, constructed in the 1950s and 1960s, certainly supported economic development. However, it was also placed directly between the Connecticut River and downtown Hartford, effectively cutting this historic city off from the river that was its original reason for existence. There was no reason for the bridge to support the relationship between the city and the river because that relationship had already been severed by the highway.

In 1980, this situation in Hartford was changed by the formation of Riverfront.org, an organization that mounted an enormous joint public and private effort with the inspirational name of Riverfront Recapture. At the same time, the Connecticut Department of Transportation was planning a major reconstruction of the I-91 corridor in downtown Hartford. Both organizations and many others used the opportunity to do exactly what the title of the project said—recapture the riverfront as an important component of the downtown community. The project was enormous and is still in progress 40 years after it began. But several of its major features have been completed, the most important being, for the purposes of this book, the reconstruction of the Founders Bridge as a major urban pedestrian and bicycle destination.

The Founders Bridge reconstruction was completed in 1998. The bridge still carries a major highway into downtown Hartford, but three major changes have been made. First, Founders Bridge originally crossed into a mess of elevated highways and on- and off-ramps to I-91 between the river and downtown, and these blocked any visual connection between the bridge and downtown. This interchange was removed, I-91 was reconstructed at ground level, and Founders Bridge today has a clear, unobstructed view toward the glass-sided office towers and historic buildings in downtown.

The second major change is that the riverfront has been redeveloped into a series of four separate parks, which are today operated by Riverfront.

org. The parks include miles of hiking and biking trails, benches, over-looks, public art, and outdoor performance spaces on both sides of the river. The reconstruction of Founders Bridge included stairs and ramps down into the park areas on both ends, allowing the bridge to be used as part of the trail system. Finally, the reconstruction of the bridge included expansion of its width, leaving a wide, landscaped promenade that is an elevated urban park on the south side of the bridge. The surface of the promenade is decorated with blocks of different colors arranged into geometric designs, and it is lined with public art, flagpoles, and decorative lampposts and railings. The promenade is separated from the traffic by a high, solid railing and is wide enough that the bridge is not dominated by traffic noise. The effect is powerful, turning a major negative into a major positive contribution to the urban community.

THRILLING BRIDGES

A major recreation-related attraction of tourist bridges is the exhilaration associated with climbing to a great height and then standing on the edge looking into the abyss. It is difficult to define this attraction, and it certainly varies from person to person. However, it is also undeniable. It is part of the reason why we climbed trees as kids. It is a large part of the reason why we build towers and then wait in lines with hundreds of other people to get to the top. Sometimes, we climb to the top of something and lean over the edge just for the thrill.

It seems logical that the primary characteristic of bridges contributing to this adventure is height. The higher the bridge, the more enticing is the experience of walking out to the middle and peering out over the edge. However, once you have walked across dozens of bridges, you will see that there are numerous other factors involved. In fact, bridge designers can consciously make design choices, other than height, that enhance or detract from this part of the tourist bridge experience.

One of the more subtle features having an effect on this experience is the placement of the sidewalk in relation to the superstructure of the bridge. On most suspension and cable-stayed bridges, including the Golden Gate and George Washington bridges, the suspending cables are on the outside of the deck, and the sidewalk is therefore on the inside of the structure. On these bridges, even when standing on the edge, the supporting cables are still within your peripheral vision. On others, such as the Benjamin Franklin, the suspending cables are connected along the roadway and the sidewalk is outside of the cables. Intellectually, you know that one type of structure is just as stable as the other—the sidewalk is not going to fall off the bridge. However, the experience of being on the edge, with the suspender cables invisible somewhere behind you, leaves you seemingly dangling above the water with no visible means of support. The effect can be disconcerting.

The effect is also influenced by the visibility of the substructure as you look straight down from the sidewalk. On many bridges, again including the Golden Gate, you do not look straight down into the water. Instead, you see parts of the deck truss extending out laterally from beneath the sidewalk. Some are even more extreme. The Bob Kerrey Bridge in Omaha has its substructure steel girders sticking out at least three to five feet on either side of the sidewalk, so that the sidewalk is not on the edge of the bridge structure at all. On the Brooklyn Bridge, the sidewalk is not even outside of the traffic lanes. It runs down the middle between the traffic lanes, so there is no experience of standing on the very edge. Conversely, some bridges have no visible substructure extending out from the sidewalk, so when you are on the edge and looking straight down, there is nothing between you and the water.

Another way in which this effect can be modified by the designer is through the type of railings on the bridge. Many bridges these days have a sidewalk lined with a high, unattractive chain link fence, completely obliterating the thrill of being on the edge. Some have railings that are solid stone or cement parapets, or are heavy gauge steel I-beams. However, others have railings of light gauge metal wire that seems like you could break through it if you are not careful. Even the color of the railings affects the experience. Railings that are painted dark colors give a feeling of solidity, while white railings are less visible and seem lighter.

Finally, the effect is also different depending on the motion of the bridge. Substructure arch bridges, such as the O'Callaghan-Tillman Bridge at Hoover Dam, can be enormously high. However, they do not move much in wind, or when trucks or trains cross them. Suspension and cable-stayed bridges do move, sometimes a great deal, and standing right on the edge and looking straight down while this is happening can be disturbing. Again, the design can deliberately decrease or increase the amount of movement that will occur on a bridge. It is common for small-scale, pedestrian suspension bridges, both old and new, to become famous for having a substantial amount of sway, and people are known to seek out these swinging bridges to experience them.

While it seems unusual to suggest that bridge designers would deliberately consider such things as height-induced exhilaration in their design, some bridges combine all of these factors into their sidewalk, and the only logical conclusion is that the effect is intentional.

ROYAL GORGE BRIDGE, CAÑON CITY, COLORADO

It is difficult to know how to categorize Royal Gorge Bridge in a book on tourist bridges. Is it historic? Does it provide incredible views? Was it a record-setting height, attracting thrill-seekers to lean over the edge of the abyss? The answer is yes, to all of these. However, none of them captures the essential tourist character of the bridge. Almost every bridge discussed in this book was constructed with a purpose, to move people to the other side of an obstacle. In almost every case, the tourists came later, a secondary result of the bridge already being there.

Royal Gorge is different. It was built for one reason only and that was to serve as an attraction for tourists. It did this quite effectively, to the extent that today, 90 years later, tourists line up each day for their chance to pay a substantial entry fee to walk across the bridge.

The bridge is located in Cañon City, Colorado, about one hour south of Colorado Springs. It crosses the Arkansas River, one of the longest rivers in the United States. However, what the bridge really crosses is not the river itself, but the incredibly deep, narrow chasm that the river has cut down through solid granite over millions of years. It was this gorge, with its bright pink, vertical walls, deeper than it is wide, that begged for someone to throw a suspension bridge across, just to show that they could.

A bridge was not needed here. The Arkansas River is not particularly wide and can be bridged much more easily, without crossing a 900 foot-deep gorge, a few miles upstream and downstream. In addition, in 1929, there was nothing much to get to on either side. The roadway carried by most bridges grew organically, from a human recognition that this was the easiest place to cross the river. That recognition led to the development of early trade routes leading to and from that special location. In many cases, early bridge engineers did not need to perform site surveys and calculations to scientifically determine the best place to build their bridge. Instead, they simply paved over the foot-and-horse path that had already existed for centuries, and built a bridge where it crossed the river. The bridge was just an improvement on what was already an active crossing.

Royal Gorge Bridge, Colorado

This was not the case at Royal Gorge. This was not the easiest location to bridge the Arkansas River, but the most difficult, by far. Natives and early settlers would never have crossed at this location. They would have walked to the edge, admired the view, and thrown down a rock to see how long it would take before they heard it hit bottom. Then they would have moved up or downstream to find a place where crossing did not involve scaling 900 foot-high vertical cliffs.

Even today, the bridge does not carry a public road. It is wide and strong enough to carry cars and pickup trucks but, 90 years later, there is still nothing on either side that requires a road at this location. The bridge can be reached by a winding, climbing two-lane road from US Route 50, which passes through the area four miles to the north. The only development, even on this major highway, is a few bridge- and tourist-related gift shops and restaurants located at the turnoff.

Although the bridge was the first structure built here to attract tourists, many others have been added. A narrow-gauge inclined railway descending to the bottom of the gorge was added in 1931. The attraction was so successful that it eventually led to an entire amusement park. In addition to the bridge and inclined railway, an aerial tramway across the gorge parallel to the bridge was added, as well as normal amusement park rides, a zip line attraction, and a visitor center.

The bridge is still the main attraction. It is a small suspension bridge, with steel cables and a wood plank deck. It is not decorated and, in fact, quite plain and industrial-looking in appearance. It is small, less than 20 feet wide, and about a quarter-mile long, no longer or more technologically advanced than any other suspension bridge built in the 1920s. The difference, though, is the height. At a time when other suspension bridges were being built a hundred feet or so above their river to allow passage of ships, Royal Gorge Bridge was thrown 900 feet high across the river.

A look at the list of the highest bridges in the world, with their construction dates, is revealing. At the time of the author's visit in 2016, Royal Gorge was only the 19th highest bridge in the world. However, of the 29 highest in the world, Royal Gorge was built in 1929; New River Gorge in West Virginia, number 24 on the list, was built in 1977; and the other 27 were all built after 2000. No bridge came even close to challenging the Royal Gorge height record for more than 70 years. Now, 90 years later, it is still the highest bridge in the United States.

As can be expected, the view from the bridge is the highlight. The broad valley through which the gorge is cut is surrounded by mountains in the distance, but this view is similar to that which can be seen from almost anywhere in western Colorado. The gorge itself is so steep-sided and narrow that it cannot be seen until you are almost right on top of it. There are viewing platforms on the edges of the gorge, but none provides the 360-degree view and vertigo-inducing thrill of being out in the middle of the bridge. The view can also be enjoyed by cable car along the aerial tramway, except that experience is enclosed and moving. The view can also be enjoyed, at high speed and un-enclosed, by braving the zip line. However, the bridge is the only place where you can stand, take your time, enjoy the view in all directions, lean out over 900 feet of empty space, and listen to the roar of the rapids beneath your feet.

The railroad along the river, famous for being the focus of the Railroad Wars among competing companies trying to dominate trade with the mining community of Leadville in the 1870s, clings to the barren rocks along the river. The river is so closed in by its canyon walls that one segment of the railway, the famous hanging bridge built in 1879, is cantilevered out over the river. The railroad today is a popular tourist attraction, operating out of Cañon City as the Royal Gorge Route. The river itself is also an attraction as a world-famous site for white-water rafting. You can hear the screams of the rafters above the roar of the river as they pass in their yellow rafts almost 1,000 feet beneath your feet.

Much of the park was destroyed in a massive wildfire in 2013. The steel structure of the bridge was not affected, but many of the wooden planks of the bridge deck burned. The inclined railway was destroyed, along with the visitor center and many of the other attractions. Rebuilding began immediately. The bridge deck was repaired and was reopened on a limited basis in late 2013. The area is still recovering, but as of 2016, the new visitor center, aerial tramway, zip line, concert venue, and children's rides were open.

The bridge can only be accessed by purchasing a ticket to enter the park. Although the park attractions and rides, including the visitor center, are only open for part of the day, the bridge can be accessed outside of normal park hours, starting at 7:00 a.m., and continuing into the evening. Visitors can even rent golf carts to drive the trails through the park, including across the bridge. Most visitors, though, cross the bridge on foot, taking their time to enjoy the view.

RAVENEL BRIDGE, CHARLESTON, SOUTH CAROLINA

The Arthur Ravenel Bridge in Charleston, South Carolina, is one of the newer generation of large-scale cable-stayed bridges. The bridge crosses the Cooper River, an estuary that is part of Charleston Harbor. The bridge was constructed in 2005 to replace the old Grace and Pearman bridges, which were steel truss construction. The Grace Bridge had been in this location since 1929, and both bridges were dismantled in place after the Ravenel Bridge opened.

The bridge is enormous. It is more than two miles long, and more than 185 feet high above river level. The towers, each almost 600 feet high, are centered in the middle of the bridge. In a cable-stayed fan design, the cables meet at a single point at the top, while in a harp design the cables parallel each other. The Ravenel Bridge is a hybrid in which the cables are strung across different elevations on the towers as in a harp design, but the cables then spread out in a fan shape towards their anchors on the deck.

The most important feature for bridge tourists is that, thanks to a great deal of community encouragement, the bridge includes a pedestrian sidewalk on its eastern side facing Charleston Harbor and downtown. At more than two miles long, the sidewalk is a prominent feature of the local trail system for bikers and runners. It is also a tourist attraction in itself. Although obviously not as iconic as the Golden Gate yet, the pedestrian sidewalk was designed to be used not only by local bikers and runners, but also by tourists visiting the Charleston area. The bridge is several miles from downtown so cannot be easily accessed on foot by visitors walking from the touristy downtown area. However, several of the Charleston tourist attractions, including the USS Yorktown aircraft carrier and some military museums, are located in an area called Patriot's Point on the north shore of the Cooper River. The bridge and the access for the sidewalk have been designed to function along with these other attractions at Patriot's Point. The area has been substantially redeveloped, and now houses new apartments and condos overlooking the river and bridge, as well as numerous parks and museums.

A major part of the experience on the Ravenel Bridge is the vertigo. The bridge is lovely and the views are nice, but do not look down. Also, do not look up. Also, you might want to not look to the side. It might be best to just keep your eyes on the sidewalk straight ahead, and squeeze yourself along the rail next to the traffic lanes. This is because the bridge is enormously high, and the towers are even higher.

At first, it is not clear why the vertigo is so high on this bridge. After all, the Golden Gate Bridge, as an example, is much higher over the water, and the towers are much higher over the deck. However, Ravenel incorporates all of the features that can be used to magnify the sense of vertigo for pedestrians. The sidewalk is on the outside of the cables, not inside. In addition, the railing is a very open weave of light-gauge steel bars. The bars are painted white, so do not seem heavy enough to stop you from crashing through. Moreover, the deck does not extend out past the railing at all. The result is that, when you stand on the edge of this bridge, you are on the very edge. When you are walking on the sidewalk looking out at the view, there is almost nothing between you and oblivion. In fact, it appears that the sidewalk was deliberately designed to appear and feel as weightless as possible. The effect is very disconcerting.

INTERIOR SPACES ON BRIDGES

One of the more unusual attractions of bridges is specialized access to parts of the bridge other than the deck and the sidewalk. Have you ever walked past a locked steel door at the base of a tower on a suspension bridge and thought to yourself, "I wonder what is in there"? Or seen the catwalks from a distance and considered that it might be fun to explore them? Or thought about what a great view the bridge workers must have from the tops of the towers?

There are few bridges that allow access or give tours of these unusual spaces, but those that do are popular and often charge high prices. Some of the existing bridges that provide access to interior spaces have already been mentioned. Tower Bridge offers tours up through the interior to the top of its northern suspension tower, across the catwalk between towers, down through the interior of its southern suspension tower, and then into the Engine Rooms. DuSable Bridge in Chicago has turned one of its tender houses into a museum, complete with views of the operating motors for the drawbridge.

The attraction and the revenue potential of allowing access to interior spaces on older bridges are so evident that these spaces are being intentionally incorporated into newer bridge designs. Many cities have built towers with observation decks and elevated restaurants as tourist attractions. The similarity between a stand-alone tower such as the CN Tower in Toronto, or the Space Needle in Seattle, and the suspension tower of a bridge is undeniable, and it did not take long for someone to combine them. The 1972 Bridge of the Slovak National Uprising, also known as the Most SNP, also known as the UFO Bridge, crosses the Danube in Bratislava and houses an observation deck and restaurant, accessible by an elevator up through the leg on one side of its single suspension tower.

NEW RIVER GORGE BRIDGE, LANSING, WEST VIRGINIA

The New River Gorge Bridge is wildly popular and iconic among those who know about it. Unfortunately, that number is small and mostly limited to West Virginians, extreme sports fanatics, and a few bridge enthusiasts. A major reason that this bridge is relatively unknown is due to its remote location in southern West Virginia, a sparsely populated area.

Still, even though people may not know the name or location, the profile of the bridge can be found now and then. It has appeared frequently in television commercials. When you enter West Virginia by car, the giant letters spelling out "West Virginia" on the welcome signs are shaped in the arched form of the bridge. And you may have a portrait of the bridge in your change jar at home, as it was chosen to represent the state on the West Virginia state quarter issued by the US Mint in 2005.

Why has the state chosen to make this remote bridge, miles from nowhere, into a prominent symbol of their state? The answer is because it is so enormous. And beautiful. And because they have turned it into a major tourist destination through the world-famous "Bridge Day" and by offering walking tours along the catwalk down amidst the bridge's substructure.

Although the New River is a small river, the gorge it flows through is wide and deep. For hundreds of years, there was no way to cross except by boat. In 1889, the Fayetteville Station Bridge was built at the bottom of the gorge to cross the river, but even reaching the bridge at the base of the steep-sided gorge was an arduous task. To solve this regional problem, the New River Gorge Bridge was constructed in 1977 to carry US Route 19. And instead of being built across the river, it was built across the entire gorge.

At the time it was constructed, the New River Gorge Bridge was the world's highest vehicle bridge, the world's highest arch bridge, and the world's longest steel single-span arch bridge. It has since been surpassed in all of these categories, but not by much. It is still the third-highest in the United States, standing 876 feet above the New River. Most of the higher bridges in the world are suspension bridges—only the new O'Callaghan-Tillman Bridge at Hoover Dam and two bridges in China are higher arches. It has also been surpassed as the world's longest steel arch bridge. But at 1,699 feet long, the arch span is still the world's third longest, and a highway sign at each end of the bridge proudly proclaims the bridge as still being the longest arch bridge in the Western Hemisphere.

These dimensions would make this bridge interesting in any location. However, what is most impressive is how the community has embraced the bridge, not just to speed cars across the gorge in 30 seconds, but as a recreational destination. The entire New River Gorge area is a complex of parks, resorts, and outdoor recreation facilities. Previously designated as a National River, the area was redesignated as New River Gorge National Park and Preserve in 2021. In addition to the bridge itself, there are hiking, viewing, and other recreational sites operated by the National Park Service, and as part of nearby Hawks Nest State Park. The river is a world-class whitewater rafting site, attracting rafters from around the world.

The bridge itself is fully integrated into these activities, which is an impressive feat considering that the bridge is almost invisible to most area visitors, and is also not walkable. Being composed of a steel arch, the bridge has no visible superstructure. It is easy to drive over at 65 miles per hour and not even notice that you are on a bridge, let alone elevated almost 900 feet above the river. It also has no sidewalks. Signs at the ends warn that no pedestrians are allowed, and they mean it. If you try, you will be seen on cameras and stopped by the police before you get very far. Not that you want to be walking narrow road shoulders with cars passing at 65 miles per hour anyway.

So how does the bridge play into the regional recreation system if you cannot see it or walk it? The answer is because the local community has gone out of its way to make sure you get to enjoy it. They have done this in a few ways.

The first is that they have provided several options for you to get down into the gorge to get a good view of it. The National Park Service visitor center at the northeastern end of the bridge has viewing platforms at the rim of the gorge and at the base of a set of stairs some 200 feet down into the gorge. Both platforms have a great view of the bridge from the side. Another option is a boat tour on the lake in Hawks Nest State Park. While most of the lake is out of view of the bridge, the boat tours include a visit to the eastern end of the lake, from which the bridge is visible.

Another way to get a great view is to drive down into the gorge on the old Fayetteville road. There are several small parking lots and viewing areas along this winding road. At the bottom of the gorge, the old Fayetteville Station Bridge, now rededicated and named the Tunney-Hunsaker Bridge, is in a great position to view the arch bridge almost 900 feet above. Apparently, this small bridge became known as a great viewing location even as the larger bridge was being built, and the tourists crowding the tiny one-lane bridge started to create a traffic hazard. To accommodate all of this attention, the Tunney-Hunsaker Bridge has had sidewalks, complete with historical plaques, added to it. You have to work a little to get to one of these locations to view the larger bridge, but it is definitely worth it because it is a stunningly gorgeous structure.

The local community has also partially resolved the lack of walkability by offering Bridge Day. Similar to Labor Day at Mackinac Bridge, Bridge Day, occurring on the third Saturday in October every year, involves closing the bridge to traffic to allow people to walk across. However, the similarity ends there. At Mackinac on Labor Day, one half of the bridge is closed to traffic, but the other half remains open. In addition, while the Mackinac Bridge is open for walking on that day, it is open in only one direction, and walking is the only activity allowed on the bridge. The New River Gorge Bridge Day is not famous for allowing walking. It is famous because, for one day, the entire bridge is closed and used for BASE jumping and rappelling. Most of the 200,000 visitors are not there to walk the bridge—they are there to watch the BASE jumpers.

Finally, unlike Mackinac, you do not have to visit on the one day each year to enjoy the bridge on foot. True, you cannot walk across the top. However, you can do much better. This is because they offer tours that allow you to walk across the bridge—underneath the deck, along a catwalk, between the girders that make up the deck structure. This tour, led by an organization called Bridge Walk, LLC, is not cheap. At the time your author visited in 2013, it cost almost $75 for a tour that lasts about two hours. In addition, you need to have reservations in advance, and they fill up. But it is absolutely worth it to get this unique view of the inside of this gorgeous bridge.

Although you might expect the substructure to be cramped and dirty, it is clean, spare, and spacious. The catwalk is perfectly level and straight, passing smoothly through the middle of a geometric triangle of girders. The steel used in the bridge is called Cor-ten steel, a type that is intended to rust into a surficial coating that protects the metal beneath. As a result, the girders are not painted but are left a pleasing rust-brown color.

When considering doing this walk, you may have some worries. The first is probably about safety. They take this very seriously. The tours are done in groups of about 15 people and are led by a guide. Each walker is suited up into a harness that is then clipped onto a cable above the catwalk. The narrow width of the catwalk, only about three feet wide, and the fact that you are clipped in mean that the walk is regimented. You cannot wander around at leisure or interact with people except for the ones directly in front of or behind you. If you stop to stare at the scenery, you may be holding up the rest of the group who may want to move forward. In addition, there is no cutting your visit short once you have had enough. Since you cannot pass each other on the catwalk, you go where the group decides to go, when they decide to go there.

Even though the catwalk has solid footing and railings, it is a great comfort to know that you are strapped in, because the vertigo factor on this bridge is enormous. On any other bridge, no matter how high you are, you are on a solid bridge deck that is at least 20 feet wide. If you get dizzy, you can back away from the edge. At the New River Gorge Bridge, there is no backing away from the edge. Your right hand is holding onto one edge on one side, and your left hand is holding onto the other edge on the other side. Both sides drop 876 feet down to the rocks, trees, and river.

Catwalk under New River Gorge Bridge

Another concern is that being located within the girder structure interferes with the great views you expect from a bridge of this magnitude.

The girders do interfere, but not much. In fact, it is not that the view is better or worse, just that it is different. It is difficult to see every part of the gorge in one elevated view. On the other hand, you get an unparalleled view of the bridge structure itself, which is just as interesting. The girder system is actually quite open, so if there is something you want to see, you can usually just walk another ten feet down the catwalk and get a view, or great pictures.

The view is mostly of the river and the trees on the slopes of the gorge. However, you can make out many details in the gorge far below. A railroad follows the river right below, and you can see both ends of mile-long coal trains as they pass by. The Tunney-Hunsaker Bridge looks like a toy model bridge, and those tiny things are people standing on it and waving up at you. And keep your eye out on the bridge structure, as falcons nest on it and can often be seen sitting on the girders a few feet away, staring at you.

One of the greatest pleasures of the catwalk tour is getting to see how the bridge is constructed. It is not as obvious and simple as you would think. It looks like a bunch of steel girders attached to each other. It is not. The arch and the vertical beams that extend above it are a bunch of steel girders attached to each other. The horizontal truss, of which the deck is a part, is also a bunch of steel girders attached to each other. However, the deck truss is not attached to the arch structure. It sits on it, but there is no physical attachment. If you had a large enough helicopter, you could lift it right off, without so much as unscrewing a nut. It is a little disconcerting when you realize that the deck is not physically attached to its supports, but the fact that you can study and understand the system up close is amazing.

The best part of the catwalk tour is the camaraderie that develops among strangers in the small tour group. Like you, these people have made reservations in advance, traveled long distances, and paid a lot of money to be linked to strangers for two hours in a steel-girder cage suspended hundreds of feet above certain death. There is obviously some commonality of interest between you and your fellow walkers, and it does not take long before you are trading bridge stories.

Finally, the tour guides are amazing. They are not there just to show you the way to go, or to make sure you are safe, or even to provide little historical anecdotes. They are there to make sure that everyone in the group gets out of the tour what they want to get out of it. They provide information, answer questions, and offer to take pictures of you. Even though they may be doing it for the thousandth time, they are clearly as fascinated with the bridge as you are. They are fellow bridge tourists, only they happen to have more of the inside information than you do.

The catwalk tours leave from the Bridge Walk building in Lansing, across the road from the National Park Service visitor center. They will outfit you, load you onto a bus, and drop you at the catwalk entrance on the other side of the river. The tour will go all the way to the other end of the bridge and then come back, where you will be picked up by the bus.

PENOBSCOT NARROWS BRIDGE AND OBSERVATORY, MAINE

The Penobscot Narrows Bridge and Observatory, in Maine, may be one of the most loved, and at the same time most hated bridges you will see. It is loved because it is gorgeous and there is an observatory incorporated on top of one of the suspension towers, turning it into a major tourist destination. However, some bridgespotters hate it because it replaced a historically important bridge, the Waldo-Hancock Bridge, which was demolished once the observatory was opened.

The bridge carries US Route 1 across the Penobscot River estuary near Bucksport, about 30 minutes south of Bangor. At this location, Verona Island sits in the middle of the estuary, squeezing the river into a narrow channel on either side. To the south, the river widens out into Penobscot Bay, so the narrowed channels on either side of Verona Island are the logical place to construct the furthest downstream crossings of the river. The channel on the eastern side of Verona Island is spanned by a low-lying girder bridge on piers. To maintain shipping access to Bucksport, Bangor, and other cities inland to the north, the western channel needed to be spanned by a high bridge that allowed clearance for large ships.

This was done, starting in 1931, with the Waldo-Hancock Suspension Bridge. However, in June 2003, an inspection revealed that corrosion had caused breaks in wires that comprised the suspension cables. Immediately, a decision was made to replace the Waldo-Hancock Bridge. It was reinforced to allow it to continue to be used during the construction of the new bridge. Ground was broken on the new bridge in December 2003, and it opened in December 2006.

Given that there was only a six-month period between identification of structural problems on the old bridge and groundbreaking on the new one, it might be assumed that the new bridge would just be an uninteresting workaday bridge designed to be constructed as quickly and cheaply as possible. Nothing could be further from the truth, because the Penobscot Narrows Bridge is stunning in its beauty, in its incorporation of community-friendly features, and in its celebration of the national importance of the local granite-quarrying industry.

The bridge uses a cable-stayed design, with diagonal cables angled from two high towers situated on either bank of the estuary. With all cable-stayed bridges, the options for the locations and angles of the cables are almost unlimited. In most cases, the cables are anchored near the top of a tower within the axis of the bridge, and they splay outwards toward the sides, connecting near the edge of the deck. The Penobscot Narrows Bridge does the opposite. The towers are centered within the axis of the roadway, but the cables are not situated within the center of the towers. Instead, the cables are situated on the outside edges of the towers, and they splay inwards toward the center of the deck. This design results in the modernistic, geometric pattern usually seen on cable-stayed bridges from a distance. However, it is unusual in that it means that the roadways are open to the sides of the bridge. This allows travelers in cars to admire the view of the estuary and surrounding hills without the view being interrupted by the intervening flash of white cables every few seconds.

Cable-stayed bridges are also noted for having no limitations in the shape, color, or texture of the towers. In the case of the Penobscot Narrows Bridge, the designers chose to honor the role of the local granite industry in supplying building stone for many of the nation's most important monuments, including the Washington Monument in Washington, DC. The entranceway and plaza surrounding the base of the western tower, as well as some of the publicly accessible areas inside the tower, are constructed of different types of granite from various locations in Maine. The towers are obelisks, the same shape as the Washington Monument, although slightly reduced in size from 555 feet in Washington to 447 feet at the bridge. Finally, similar to the Washington Monument, the western tower was constructed with an elevator in the middle, leading 420 feet up to a glass-walled observation platform at the top.

The views from the top of the tower are amazing. Large stretches of the Penobscot River and Bay are visible, as well as aerial views of historic Fort Knox less than a mile away and the town of Bucksport across the estuary. A large industrial complex on the north side of Bucksport dampens the view a little bit. Plaques in the observatory area provide the names of the surrounding hills and mountains visible in the distance.

Just as impressive as the view is the way the bridge designers provide it to you. A common feature of observatories and elevated viewing platforms around the world is that the elevators or stairs providing access are situated within the core of the observation area. You can usually obtain views in all directions by walking entirely around this core, but its presence in the middle of the platform means you can only see out one direction at a time. The designers of the Penobscot Narrows Bridge went to great lengths to maximize the viewing experience at the top. The elevator in the core of the tower does not go all the way to the top. Instead, it stops two floors below. The observatory level is then reached by stairs, meaning that there is no obstruction in the center. As a result, you can stand and see a 360-degree view from the center. A small, secondary elevator is present to provide disabled access to the top, but it is off to the side, only about three feet high, and unobtrusive.

It is also common for enclosed towers and observatories to have tiny windows. The Penobscot Observatory has floor-to-ceiling glass windows, allowing you to feel like you are standing on the very edge. An interesting feature is the ceiling of the observatory. From the outside, you can see that both towers are topped by an aluminum-colored pyramidal cap. You might expect that the observatory room would have a flat, false ceiling, meaning that the aluminum-colored pyramid is somewhere up there, hidden from view. Instead, the ceiling of the observatory is left open so that you are effectively within the pyramidal cap, about 15 feet above your head. It definitely adds to the vertigo effect to look up and realize the top is not in some undefined, invisible space. The top is right there, on the other side of that thin sheet of metal.

The observatory is accessed by following the signs to Fort Knox State Park, and the entrance is actually inside of the park. You need to pay the fee for entrance to the park, with different rates depending on if you are visiting just the fort or the observatory as well, and whether you are a Maine resident. The fort, which has a gift shop that sells bridge-related items, is accessed from the upper parking lot, which you will come to first. The observatory is accessed from the lower parking lot, about a quarter-mile back toward the bridge. The lower parking lot has restrooms, a picnic area, and a large section of the deck of the bridge on display.

A walking path from the lower parking lot leads down to a plaza surrounding the base of the western tower, and the entranceway is through an elaborate granite portico. Note that the opening hours of the fort and the observatory vary throughout the year, and that the observatory is only open from May 1 to October 31. In addition, to control the number of people at the top, tickets to the observatory are timed, so you cannot enter before the time on your ticket.

Once you are done with the observatory, Fort Knox is also a major landmark and tourist sight on its own. Built in fits and starts throughout the 1800s, the fort was never completely finished and never became fully operational. It is built of enormous blocks of Maine granite, and has been restored with reconstruction of the casemates and placement of cannons.

SCENIC BRIDGES

Bridges are excellent places for the viewing of scenic attractions in their local area. Views of wooded hills, bedrock cliffs, and flowing rivers can only be obtained by either rising above the visual obstructions of the surrounding hills and trees or by stepping away from them. Bridges provide the opportunity to do both. Most tend to be elevated above the surrounding landscape, either because they are connecting bluffs on either side of a valley, or because they are deliberately elevated to allow the passage of boats underneath. This lifts them above the surrounding hills and trees, providing an unobstructed view in all directions. Even if the bridge deck is not elevated, the absence of trees or buildings in the middle of the river or harbor opens up the view. It helps that rivers, creeks, and harbors are scenic places to begin with. However, they are best seen from an elevated spot away from the trees, like the sidewalk of a bridge.

This feature results in some bridges becoming famous tourist attractions largely because of the view available from the sidewalk. A perfect example is the Golden Gate. As much interest as there may be in its history and Art Deco-style decoration, the views of San Francisco Bay, the surrounding mountains, and the skyscrapers of downtown San Francisco are the highlight of any visit. Tourists may come for the iconic structure, but they linger for the view.

Even in less scenic places, providing a view is a consideration for bridge designers. Many bridges have only one sidewalk or, having two, only keep one of them open for public access. In addition to the Golden Gate, examples include Wilson Bridge in Washington, DC, Benjamin Franklin Bridge in Philadelphia, George Washington Bridge in New York, and Ravenel Bridge in Charleston. In each case, the single sidewalk available for public access is on the side that provides a view of the downtown skyline. This is not a coincidence but is instead a subtle, thoughtful gift from the bridge designer to the community.

While we tend to think only of hills and trees and water when discussing scenic views, the same concept applies to the use of bridges to view cityscapes and skylines in urban locations. We may spend days wandering around our favorite European city, but never get the full sense of the layout of the city because we cannot see any further than the buildings that line the street. However, step out on the bridge, away from the buildings, and the city opens up at your feet. Prague is famous for its narrow, winding medieval streets, which are charming. But walk out onto Charles Bridge and you have the full view of the buildings of Mala Strana climbing up to the Castle, wooded Petrin Hill and its famous tower, the flowing Vltava on both sides, the fortress of Vyšehrad in the distance, and the spires of the Old Town Square churches behind you, all from one viewing position.

The same effect happens when walking out on the Pont Alexandre III and Pont Neuf in Paris, London or Westminster bridges in London, or Ponte Sant'Angelo in Rome. There is only one place in the world where you can stand and see the whole of the Willis Tower in Chicago, from street level to the top, and that is from the sidewalk of the Van Buren Street Bridge.

The view available from the deck of a bridge in an urban setting is far more than just aesthetic. What you will see there is not just pretty, only to be photographed and enjoyed for the view. It is actually the key to unlocking the entire history of the city, because the river you see was the reason a community was founded in this spot. The buildings lining the riverbanks may no longer be the original mills, warehouses, docks, and homes of the settlement, but they are, at least, situated on the same spots as the original buildings, and, in many cases, they actually are the original buildings. Important historic events may have occurred in other buildings in other locations in the city at a later time. However, those were secondary historic events, occurring among people who already lived here. The view from the bridge shows the primary historic event, which is the settlement of the location by people. It may not be as exciting as later events, but it reveals the reason people came here in the first place, and what they did to earn a living.

FRENCH KING BRIDGE, GILL, MASSACHUSETTS

Even though we think of New England as a beautifully scenic area completely covered by the Appalachian Mountains, there is actually one major part of the region that is relatively flat and scenically uninteresting. This is the Central Lowland area of central Massachusetts and Connecticut.

The Central Lowland remains as the result of a rift valley known as the Deerfield Basin, formed in the Triassic geologic period 220 million years ago when North America separated from its attachment with Africa during the breakup of Pangaea. Because it is at a lower elevation than the surrounding Appalachian Mountains, rivers and streams in New England are largely funneled into this Central Lowland. The main river in New England, the Connecticut, slices neatly on a straight north-south line through its middle. Meanwhile, smaller rivers and streams oriented in an east-west direction flow into the Central Lowland from the hills and mountains on either side. The bridges over the southern half of the Connecticut River and its tributaries in the Central Lowland have some interest due to their history but, because their surrounding area is flat, none of them are particularly scenic.

The northern half of the Connecticut River Valley, the part flowing between the Green Mountains in Vermont and the White Mountains in New Hampshire and on into northern Massachusetts, is a much different story. In this section of the river upstream of the Central Lowland, the Connecticut River Valley is stunning, with the river surrounded by mountains on both sides. The area near the towns of Deerfield and Turners Falls in northern Massachusetts, right before the river enters the Deerfield Basin, is a particularly interesting area for bridges because the river flows over granite bedrock rapids and falls and through steep-sided gorges. The river in this area is also joined by a variety of smaller, scenic tributaries tumbling down out of the mountains, including the Deerfield River and Millers River. And there are interesting, historic bridges at every turn.

The most well-known of the Connecticut River bridges is French King, so named because it is located near a rock in the middle of the river, French King Rock, which was identified as a useful landmark during early exploration of the area by a French officer. Located less than ten miles south of the Massachusetts border with Vermont and New Hampshire, this area is known as the Connecticut River Gorge, a particularly narrow and steep-sided part of the river.

As in other areas with steep, elevated riverbanks such as the New River Gorge or Niagara Gorge, the early bridge builders had two choices. One was to build narrow winding roads down the slope of the gorge to the river level at the bottom, build a short, low-lying bridge over the river, and then build more narrow winding roads back to the top of the other side. The other choice was to throw an enormously high arch over the entire gorge, from the top on one side to the top on the other. One choice gives you a small bridge, hard to reach, hemmed in by trees and rocks on all sides, with little to see. The other choice gives you an elevated platform from which you can see for miles.

The French King Bridge is just such a bridge, carrying the two-lane Mohawk Trail (Massachusetts State Route 2, also known as French King Highway) 140 feet above the river. The bridge is about 800 feet long and was constructed in 1932. As the only major bridge in New England elevated above a gorge in this way, the bridge has become a prominent local landmark and tourist attraction. A plaque on the western end of the bridge indicates that the view of the gorge has been designated as a "Special Place" by the Massachusetts Executive Office of Environmental Affairs.

There are small parking lots at both ends of the bridge, with room for 20 or 30 cars, and the sidewalk always has at least a few tourists out on it taking pictures. Lots of bridges have parking lots. In addition, lots of them have elevated views of impressive landscapes. However, French King is different, especially when the fall leaves are turning colors, and especially on weekends.

In peak tourist season, traffic on Route 2 almost comes to a standstill due to the enormous volume of tourists wanting to walk across the bridge and take a few pictures. It is almost a carnival atmosphere. Cars slow as they approach the bridge to find an open parking space. Not finding one, they slow even more, try to pull off on the narrow shoulders of the road, stop in the middle to wait for another car to vacate a spot, do U-turns to attack an open spot, and generally block the normal flow of traffic.

Meanwhile, the photographers on foot cross the road back and forth between the two sidewalks, oblivious to the fact that the bridge carries a narrow, two-lane, 50 mile-per-hour highway. Because it was built in a rural area in 1932, the bridge designers did not plan for the twenty-first century view-seekers. The sidewalks on the bridge are extremely narrow, with only a low rail a few inches high separating the hundreds of elbow-throwing tourists from the impatient drivers who could not care less about the view and just want to get across. However, the view is so amazing that it is worth it to wait patiently for your parking space, squeeze in amongst the crowd, and try to stay out of the views of other people's selfies.

Because the deck of the French King Bridge is supported by an arch, there is no bridge superstructure to be seen while driving or walking across. The designers have included decorations in the form of large white stone monuments on each of the four corners, supporting decorative iron lampposts topped by cast metal eagles. The railings are also decorative, with white balustrades connected to the monuments on the ends and black iron railings across the middle between the monuments.

Of course, it is never satisfactory to just walk across an arch bridge. You need to get to the side or under it to see the structure. It is likely that few of the people who visit to look at the view will also venture down into the gorge to see the structure itself, but they are missing a treat. The bridge is a combination cantilever-arch, with a single steel arch crossing from side-to-side over the river and cantilever sections anchored into the bedrock walls of the gorge, linking the central arch to the roadway on tops of the banks. The arch is made of steel and is a completely open web of black steel girders. To get down into the gorge, follow Route 2 east of the bridge for about a half-mile, and take your first right turn onto Dorsey Road. Follow this narrow, winding road down into the gorge, and it will eventually pass under the bridge.

Before you get to the bridge, though, you will find an unexpected bonus bridge hidden almost underneath the French King Bridge. French King is located just where a small tributary, Millers River, enters the Connecticut River from the east. At the junction of the two rivers is a small, rustic campsite with signs indicating that it is called Cabot Camp. This location was the site of a dam and sawmill as early as 1799. The site still includes a couple of stone buildings and stone walls, a parking lot, and signs indicating that the road entering the site, East Mineral Road, is part of the Franklin County Bikeway bike trail. Lawn areas at the camp provide a stunning view of the French King Bridge.

Crossing Millers River in the middle of Cabot Camp is an old wrought-iron through-truss bridge called the Mineral Road Bridge. This bridge dates from about 1888 and has a plaque indicating that it was built by the Wrought Iron Bridge Company of Canton, Ohio. The bridge is closed to traffic but has been rehabilitated with a new wood deck and railings and is open to pedestrian and bicycle traffic.

The general area of these bridges is rural, located about two hours from Boston. There are no substantial tourist sights nearby, except for the many outdoor recreational opportunities associated with the nearby Berkshires, Green Mountains, and White Mountains. The area is laced with hiking trails, parks, bike trails, wineries, historic sights, and other attractions we associate with quaint, rural New England. Since the main attraction is the scenery, the best time of year to enjoy the area is fall, when the leaves are changing, and when you will have to wait for a parking spot to open up so that you can walk out on French King.

RAINBOW BRIDGE, NIAGARA FALLS

The Rainbow Bridge at Niagara Falls is a historic bridge at a historic location. The steep, rocky slopes, the violent nature of the water in Niagara Gorge, and the harsh winter weather have challenged bridge designers since the early 1800s. Early arch and suspension bridges were constructed by many of the prominent early bridge designers of the nineteenth century, including John Roebling. Bridges have crossed at this specific location since 1867. Honeymoon Bridge, the immediate predecessor to Rainbow Bridge, was constructed in the 1890s but collapsed as a result of ice buildup in 1938.

Rainbow Bridge, the replacement, was completed and opened in 1941, with the site having been dedicated by King George VI during his 1939 tour of Canada. The famous Niagara Falls carillon tower dominates the northwestern landing of the bridge in Canada. The bridge is an open steel arch with vertical girders supporting the deck from below. The bridge is enormous, with its single arch spanning almost 1,000 feet wide and almost 170 feet high over the Niagara Gorge.

Of course, none of this is the reason you are visiting Rainbow Bridge. You are visiting because of the falls. You can have a great day viewing them without crossing Rainbow Bridge, or any of the other smaller bridges in the area. However, there are many good reasons to go ahead and walk across them anyway.

The view of the falls from Rainbow Bridge is amazing. That actually is not saying much—a view of Niagara Falls from almost anywhere is amazing. In fact, the view of the falls from the bridge is a little distant, and partially obstructed, and there are several places in the area with much better views. The bridge is only about a quarter-mile from American Falls, but the view of American Falls is partially blocked by a viewing tower constructed on the edge of the falls. The bridge is even farther from Horseshoe Falls, almost three-quarters of a mile. However, even with that large distance, the falls are so large and impressive that it is certainly worth crossing the bridge for the view. There are several other places you need to go during your day in the area to get even better views, but the bridge should be included.

Another good reason to walk the bridge is for convenience in having a complete, comprehensive visit to Niagara Falls. Unless you live in Buffalo or Toronto, you have probably come a long distance to see Niagara Falls. As long as you are here, you should make sure to see everything, from all of the best viewing locations. Some of the best viewing locations are on the American side, and some are on the Canadian side. For a complete visit, you are going to have to visit both sides. You can do this by driving to the American side, parking (which you must pay for), walking to the falls, and seeing the sights on the American side. Then you will need to walk back to your car, drive across the international border, wait in a long line of cars for immigration and customs, find parking again on the Canadian side (paying for it again), and then walk a large distance back to the falls. Once you are done with the sights on the Canadian side, you need to return to your car and wait again in a long line of cars for immigration and customs on the American side.

Any crossing of the US border by car these days is a pain in the neck. You can avoid the hassle by crossing Rainbow Bridge on a bridge walk. You only need to park and pay once. There are no major lines for processing pedestrians through immigration or customs in either direction. In addition, because you are reading a book on tourist bridges, you are obviously interested in that aspect, and Rainbow would be a great walkable bridge even without the views.

Although walking Rainbow Bridge does require going out of your way a little, it is still thoroughly in the middle of the tourist area. On the American side, the bridge is located directly adjacent to one of the available parking areas in Niagara Falls State Park. It is only a short walk, less than a quarter-mile, from the bridge to the edge of American Falls. On the Canadian side, the bridge leads directly to the promenade on the northwestern shore of Niagara Gorge. This promenade is directly opposite the falls, so it provides the best views of the falls from across the river. The promenade is lined with viewing platforms, gardens, outdoor restaurants with amazing views, and other attractions, and extends for almost a mile to the Welcome Center at the edge of Horseshoe Falls. In fact, the view of the falls from this area is so good that the proximity of the falls causes other problems. While you are close in, you will be immediately soaked by mist unless you have an umbrella or raincoat.

A word of caution before venturing out to walk the bridge. It is an international border, and you will be required to have a passport to go from one side to the other. The border itself is marked by a plaque in the middle of the bridge. However, you will need to pass through turnstiles at the American end to enter the bridge sidewalk, which is on the southwest side of the bridge, facing the falls. There are signs at the turnstiles warning you that you need travel documents to proceed, but there is no person there to check your documents and stop you from leaving the country without proper documentation.

Once you are through the turnstiles and out on the bridge, you are legally not in either country. If you want to return to the US, you need to present your passport at immigration at the southeastern end of the bridge. If you wish to proceed into Canada, you need to present your passport on the northwestern end of the bridge. However, in the middle, you have legally left one of the countries and have not yet entered the other. It is possible to pass through the turnstiles without your passport and find yourself in between countries with no way to enter either one. In addition, although there is no toll to walk from the US to Canada, there is a 50 cent-toll to walk from Canada to the US. The turnstile at the Canadian end requires you to insert 50 cents, in the form of two quarters (US or Canadian) to exit out onto the bridge. Change is not made, so you will need to make sure you have the quarters—otherwise, you will need to walk back out into the town to find change.

The source of the name for Rainbow Bridge is not as obvious as you would assume. One obvious association is with the shape of the steel arch of the bridge, which is definitely rainbow-shaped. You might also be under the impression that the mist from the falls forms rainbows under certain conditions, and that the bridge is named for these. This is partially true, but it is a major understatement. The mist from the falls creates rainbows all over the place, all day, under all kinds of conditions. We tend to think of rainbows as a special event, to be seen a few times a year. At Niagara

Falls, they are everywhere—amazingly bright, multiples, even 360-degree rainbows that arch over your head while reconnecting at your feet.

The rainbows are so ubiquitous that the area became associated with the passage about rainbows from Chapter 9 of Genesis, in which God told Noah that the bow in the cloud was a token of the covenant between him and the earth, and that it would serve to remind him of his promise that waters would never again become a flood to destroy every living creature upon the earth. This passage is carved into the stone on the front of the carillon at the Canadian end of Rainbow Bridge. In this biblical sense, the chosen rainbow shape and the name of Rainbow Bridge symbolize that the Niagara area is a place where God's covenant with man is widely displayed.

HAUNTED BRIDGES

You may not be aware that haunted bridges exist. However, while researching a bridge you plan to see on vacation, it is not unusual to see a short footnote at the end which mentions, almost as an aside, that this bridge is reputed to be haunted. Once you find two or three of these and decide to perform a search to see if there are other haunted bridges, you will find yourself overwhelmed by the number and variety of them. It is amazing to learn not only how many bridges are haunted, but how many different types of hauntings can occur.

There are some common features of these bridges and their associated paranormal activities. The legends usually involve someone who died on, or near, or because of, the bridge. This includes car accidents, suicides, lynchings, murders, and the association of bridges with battlefields. Haunting also usually applies to older bridges, presumably because they have had more time for unfortunate incidents to have occurred on or near them. The phenomena experienced include actual sightings of spirits, hearing of voices or cries, unexplained movements of cars, the appearance of mysterious handprints, the presence of supernatural beasts, and the sighting of unexplained lights. On some bridges, all you need to do is sit at the bridge and wait to see or hear the spirits. On others, you need to perform certain actions or recite specific phrases to summon them.

Without actually going into the towns to interview witnesses, the readily available sources of information include books and websites. A book titled *Haunted Bridges,* by Rich Newman, was published in 2016, and describes ghostly happenings at more than 300 bridges in the United States. These, and many more, can also be investigated using online sources. And there are a few interesting observations that result from having researched haunted bridges.

The first observation is the prevalence of the different categories of haunted bridges, because the result may not be what you expect. Of the numerous different types of hauntings that could occur, you might think that the reports are either fairly evenly distributed among them, or that the simple sighting of spooks would be the most common observation. This is not the case.

In fact, a large number of the reports are of an unexpected type, which is the phenomenon of crybaby bridges. Yes, there are ghosts, there are unexplained lights, and there are handprints. However, it appears that the most frequently reported supernatural event is the sound of a crying baby. This is usually identified as one who was killed in an accident at the bridge, or one who was thrown to its death from the bridge by its friendless mother. It only takes a few moments of researching haunted bridges on the internet to come across crybaby bridges. There is a dedicated Wikipedia site for crybaby bridges. Even Rich Newman, in the introduction of his book, singles out crybaby bridges as being a familiar story, with them being found in almost every state.

The second unexpected observation is the geographic distribution of the bridges. You might expect that the haunted bridges would be evenly distributed across the nation, or maybe concentrated in states where there is also a concentration of older bridges, and you would again be wrong. A cursory internet investigation actually shows a concentration of haunted bridges in Ohio, Maryland, and South Carolina. The crybaby bridge Wikipedia site also lists bridges in Virginia, Illinois, Indiana, Oklahoma, Texas, and Utah, but shows the largest concentration in Ohio and Maryland. A website dedicated to haunted locations in Ohio lists 56 bridges. Even though Rich Newman identifies haunted bridges in all 50 states, he identifies Maryland as "the land of crybaby bridges."

The reason for this unusual geographic distribution, as well as the prevalence of crybaby bridges among the types of haunted bridges, may be related to the way information proliferates on the internet. Several websites discuss how a Maryland folklorist, Jesse Glass, investigated crybaby bridges as an example of how fake folklore is created and distributed on the internet. He found that a large number of similar stories regarding crybaby bridges in Maryland and Ohio appeared on the internet in 1999, even though there was no record of these stories prior to 1999. He was even able to trace the stories to a specific paranormal website. This appears to show that someone invented the legend from scratch as a hoax. They distributed it on the internet in 1999, and it became believed. This would explain why internet searches on haunted bridges lead so quickly to crybaby bridges, and why the phenomenon appears to be focused in Maryland and Ohio.

Regardless of how the stories originated and proliferated, and certainly regardless of whether they are true or not, it cannot be denied that the stories and legends attract supernatural hobbyists to these bridges, particularly at night.

There are numerous challenges associated with trying to provide a description of one or more prominent haunted bridges. The first is the sheer number of bridges that are purported to be haunted, with none of them appearing to be more prominent than any other. There does not appear to be a single haunted bridge that attracts visitors from large distances. Instead, each of them appears to draw visitors from the local area only.

A second problem is the ephemeral nature of the hauntings. Many of the bridges visited to support the profiles in this book have an associated legend involving hauntings yet, unfortunately, none of these hauntings were actually witnessed by your author. This leaves the Rich Newman book and internet sources as the only available information to support the profiles.

Finally, the actual haunted bridge is, in some cases, not agreed upon. For instance, the original crybaby bridge investigated by Jesse Glass is located in Westminster, Maryland, but different websites disagree on which bridge is involved. The Rich Newman book and multiple websites report it to be a cement road bridge situated at Roops Mill Road and Adams Mill

Road. Other websites report that it is a late nineteenth century iron suspension bridge on the property of Roops Mill, a small bridge "just down on the right" past the Adams Mill Road bridge or bridges on Rockland Road or Uniontown Road.

Given these challenges, a couple of examples from Maryland, the home of the author, have been selected.

JERICHO COVERED BRIDGE, KINGSVILLE, MARYLAND

Jericho Covered Bridge crosses Little Gunpowder Falls approximately 12 miles northeast of Baltimore, and is one of only six covered bridges remaining in the state of Maryland. The bridge was constructed in 1865 and was most recently reconstructed in 2016. One common haunting theme associated with bridges in the eastern US from the 1860s involves the Civil War and its aftermath. In the case of Jericho Bridge, the legend is that Southern sympathizers, disappointed with the outcome of the war, used the rafters inside the bridge to hang former slaves. The bodies of these slaves are still seen by some visitors. There is also a spirit of a woman dressed in 1880s clothing, carrying a basket of flowers, who ignores people who see and try to speak to her. In addition, a young girl with a badly burned face approaches visitors and asks for their help. There are also reports of car engines stopping directly in the middle of the bridge and then taking several minutes to restart.

Jericho Bridge is logistically challenging to visit. Unlike most covered bridges that have dedicated parking lots, Jericho Bridge has none. In addition, the bridge is only one lane wide, and there is no place to pull off Jericho Road for some distance on either end of the bridge. The only access to visit requires parking at Jerusalem Mill, a part of Gunpowder Falls State Park, and then walking down either park trails or narrow roads to the bridge. Since you need to visit at night to investigate the paranormal activities, this access may be closed, and certainly would be dangerous.

GOVERNOR'S BRIDGE, BOWIE, MARYLAND

Governor's Bridge is a steel through-truss bridge dating from 1907. The bridge was so named because the first bridge on this site was constructed to provide a route for the colonial Governor of Maryland to cross the Patuxent River between Annapolis and his plantation in Collington.

Governor's Bridge is famous locally as a crybaby bridge. An apparition of a young woman has been seen in the middle of the road at the bridge and is reputed to have caused at least one driver to swerve and hit the side of the bridge with his car. This woman is reported to have killed her out-of-wedlock baby and then herself, or both of them were hit by a car which may or may not have been driven by her husband, or they were killed at the bridge by the Ku Klux Klan. Regardless of the cause, there are numerous reports that the baby has been heard crying.

Interestingly, the bridge has been opened and closed multiple times since 2013. It was closed in 2013, ostensibly due to an inspection that revealed deterioration of the deck girders. It was repaired, reopened in 2014, but then closed again after another inspection in 2015. It has been reported that the bridge would be undergoing a substantial reconstruction but, as of 2021, it is still closed. Meanwhile, visits to the bridge are discouraged by the county. Governor's Bridge Road is closed off by jersey barriers a substantial distance from each end of the bridge, requiring a lengthy hike to visit the bridge. These facts are consistent with the need to repair the bridge, but could they also be consistent with a cover-up of supernatural events at the bridge?

ROMANTIC BRIDGES

What location frequented by tourists is more romantic than a bridge? It is undeniable that many bridges have an established reputation for stirring romantic feelings among their visitors.

The most obvious romantic association with bridges in the twenty-first century is the love padlock craze. At its beginnings, padlocks were placed on bridges that were already prominent tourist destinations or community centers. However, in many places, the padlocks have become so elaborate and overwhelming that they have themselves become the attraction.

It appears that there are many factors involved in shaping the extent to which a community has embellished a bridge, or a city full of bridges, with love padlocks. The major criterion, apparently, is that the bridge is in a romantic or sentimental locale frequented by young lovers, preferably with views of iconic landmarks. Another major factor is logistical since the bridge must have railings or other pieces of its structure that are narrow enough to be padlocked. Stone bridges, bridges with stone parapets, and bridges with metal balustrades with thick components tend to not become padlocked because there is simply no place to physically attach the locks.

In some cases, the padlockers become clever and refuse to take "no" for an answer. On Charles Bridge in Prague, Brooklyn Bridge in New York, and Chain Bridge in Budapest, there are no padlockable railings available, so the vandals have moved on either to less romantic components or to other nearby structures such as fences. On these three bridges, the padlocks have been attached to the narrow metal supports that hold lighting fixtures.

Another workaround involves wrapping a chain around a railing or post. Although the railing or post may be too large to attach padlocks, the locks can be attached to the links within the chain. Then, once one padlock is attached, a new padlock can be attached to the first padlock. In this way the padlocks become parasitic, with no limits on their proliferation. This practice is common on railings at the ends of stone bridges in Paris.

A third major factor, of course, is official sanction. Love padlocks have been known to create load issues on some bridges, collapsing railings and lampposts, causing authorities to remove them. In other locales, the padlocks are considered just another form of vandalism or graffiti, so their attachment is prohibited and punishable by a fine. The owners of these bridges can choose to discourage the practice by replacing padlockable railings or light fixtures with a different type of structure such as plain plexiglas, much like they place spikes and nets on public statues to discourage pigeons. Conversely, some cities appear to be encouraging the practice by deliberately installing fences and railings with narrow metal components.

Although they are the most well-known, padlocks are not the only items that lovers attach to bridges. In addition to love padlocks, at least one of the lighting fixtures on the Brooklyn Bridge in 2016 was covered with a variety of miscellaneous items, including elastic hair scrunchies, bandages, religious-themed photographs, strings of beads, and earphone wires. During a visit to the Waco Suspension Bridge in 2013, there was a single padlock, and we know why it was there. However, that lock was attached amid hundreds of other objects attached to the bridge rails, girders, and cables. And those objects were . . . empty plastic bread and tortilla bags. Most of them were at deck level, but some were tied to cables very high up, indicating that someone had shimmied up a cable just to tie a bag. There were enough of them to indicate that this is not just an act of vandalism by kids overnight, but a longer-term cultural phenomenon that apparently has some mysterious meaning.

Many other bridges have had an association with lovers since long before the padlock craze began. Bridges are perfect for romance. Many are secluded from noisy city traffic and prying eyes, separated from the surrounding buildings and trees that block views of the full moon, and often provide idyllic views of scenic locations. Conversely, covered bridges are frequently referred to as "kissing bridges," and many specific covered bridges are locally nicknamed as "the Kissing Bridge." This includes the West Montrose Covered Bridge in Ontario, the bridge at Rockingham in Vermont, and bridges in Ticonderoga, New York, and Oxford, Alabama. This association occurs because romantic activities that may occur within the wooden walls of the bridge are hidden from view.

On some bridges, the romantic effects have become legendary. The Fall Creek Gorge Suspension Bridge on the Cornell University campus is reported to be in danger of falling if someone refuses a midnight kiss on the bridge. More than 100 years later, and the bridge still stands. Love goes the other way, as well. One of the more romantic things lovers do when love has gone wrong is jump from high places. Therefore, there are more than a few "Lover's Leap" bridges out there. A famous one in Connecticut is the location where a lover of Princess Lillinonah, daughter of Chief Waramaug, jumped from the cliffs in a futile attempt to save his love from the rapids.

HOHENZOLLERN BRIDGE, COLOGNE, GERMANY

The Rhine River can be something of a disappointment for bridge tourists. When considering the historical and cultural significance of water bodies throughout the US and Europe, it is hard to think of one more important than the Rhine, especially the Middle and Lower Rhine flowing near the German-French border. The Rhine has been one of the most important commercial transport corridors in the Western world for more than 2,000 years. The Rhine Gorge, also known as the Romantic Rhine, has been celebrated in literature, art, and song. This should be a great place to visit historic bridges. However, as of March 1945, the 600-mile stretch of the Rhine downstream of Basel had a grand total of zero bridges on it.

All bridges that exist today in this ancient land are younger than 70 years old. Even the Mittlerebrücke at Basel, the oldest continuously used Rhine crossing, is only about 100 years old. Therefore, bridge tourists seeking the Romantic Rhine by exploring a large number of old bridges are going to be disappointed. Of course, this does not mean that there are no satisfactory bridges on the Rhine and, for several reasons, it is worth going out of your way to visit the Hohenzollern Bridge in Cologne.

The Hohenzollern Bridge was originally built in about 1910 as a railroad and road bridge, and it was one of the most important bridges supporting the German war effort in World War II. For this reason it was targeted by the Allies during the war, but it was never substantially damaged until it was deliberately destroyed by the German army during its retreat across the Rhine in early 1945. The bridge was almost immediately rebuilt following the war, but as a railroad and pedestrian bridge only. The bridge connects the historic Alt Stadt of Cologne with the suburban Köln-Messe neighborhood on the east bank of the river.

On both sides of the bridge, a pedestrian sidewalk extends outside of the steel truss superstructure. Because the bridge is located in the center of this major city, the primary purpose of the walkways is to help commuters, both on foot and on bicycle, to access the city from its eastern suburbs. However, the walkways have been turned into a major attraction for another reason because, as of the time of the author's visit in 2013, Hohenzollern Bridge may have had more love padlocks on it than any other bridge in the world.

The steel I-beam supports of the superstructure separate the walkways from the trains passing on the rails just a few feet away. For safety reasons, the supports have been lined with a steel mesh fence, so that pedestrians cannot reach past the I-beams and be hurt by the passing trains. It just so happens that the size of the wire that makes up this steel mesh fence is absolutely the perfect size for the attachment of padlocks.

If you have not seen padlocks on other bridges, the scene is hard to describe. We are not just talking about a railing with a few padlocks attached. Here is a rough calculation, for entertainment purposes. The bridge is 1,300 feet long, and the fence extends almost the entire length, about five feet high. If a padlock takes up about four square inches, and they are packed in as tightly as possible, then there is room for almost 250,000 padlocks on each side. This is space for a half-million padlocks, total. Now, at Hohenzollern, the locks are not packed in as tight as can be. Most of them are on the south side, and the north side has not been infested nearly as much. Also, the locks are extremely tightly packed near the end of the bridge at the Alt Stadt and Dom, less tightly packed past the halfway point, but then packed tightly again near the Köln-Messe end of the bridge. But you get the idea. This is not a few hundred, or even a few thousand padlocks. It is probably well over 100,000 padlocks.

Thanks to the inscriptions and other personal touches, the padlocks are captivating. Most of the locks are a basic, brass-colored padlock with a written or engraved inscription. Other locks are custom-made specifically to be used as love padlocks, with decorative locks of bright blue and red colors being common. In some cases, hundreds of locks of a similar type, color, or inscription are grouped together, apparently as a result of some purchase of locks by subscription and placement by a large group of people in a common effort.

The fastened object is not always a normal, modern padlock. Among the items present at the Hohenzollern Bridge are combination locks, although this would seem to disregard the symbolic permanence associated with throwing the key into the river. Perhaps lovers who place combination locks want to leave their options open. There are also chains, bicycle locks, old-style locks with gigantic keyholes on their fronts, engraved sheet metal in the shape of a heart, and small plaques. It is an impressive sight to behold.

The setting of the bridge, just a few steps from the train station and the historic and touristic sights in Cologne, makes a short visit to this bridge convenient. The south side of the bridge, on the western bank, is integrated into a riverside plaza as part of the Alt Stadt. There are boat landings, outdoor restaurants in front of medieval-looking buildings, the Philharmonic Hall, the Roman-German Museum, and the amazing Cologne Dom, one of the largest cathedrals in the world. The view from the south side of the bridge is quite romantic and only a few steps from some of the most visited tourist sights in Germany, explaining why the concentration of padlocks is highest near the southwest corner of the bridge. If visiting Cologne, or even stopping for a short layover at the train station, there is no excuse for not taking ten minutes to walk out onto the bridge to see the padlocks.

WIJNGAARD AND ST. BONIFACIUS BRIDGES, BRUGES

Sometimes, love can addle the mind and result in confusion. Bruges, one of the more scenic tourist destinations in Belgium, is famous for having a magical "Lover's Bridge." One kiss on the bridge, and you are now bound for eternity. The problem is that nobody can seem to figure out exactly which bridge it is that does the trick.

Historical plaques at the Minnewater, located south of the tourist center, refer to the small pond here as the Lake of Love. This would seem to suggest that the scenic Wijngaard Bridge is the place. It certainly looks the part. It is a lovely stone arch bridge dating from 1740, overlooking swans floating in the Minnewater. However, the Minnewater is a little remote from the crowded tourist center of town. It is likely that few tourists go there, especially at night.

Fortunately, Bruges has another bridge, situated directly in the middle of the tourist frenzy, which is assumed by some to play the role of the Lover's Bridge. This is the St. Bonifacius Bridge, a tiny single stone arch bridge dating from 1910. Some of the available tourist guidebooks and websites refer to the St. Bonifacius Bridge as the Lover's Bridge, and this is apparently accepted by lovers too lazy to walk a mile or so to the Minnewater. The St. Bonifacius Bridge may hold the record for being the most densely packed tourist bridge in existence. The bridge achieves this in two ways—partly by having a large number of people visiting and stopping for selfies, and partly by being only about 15 feet long and five feet wide to begin with. It is common to have to stop for a few minutes to allow traffic jams to clear before crossing the bridge.

Both bridges have drawbacks that might detract from their purported magical powers of love. The Wijngaard Bridge leads directly into the Begijnhof, which served for centuries as a semi-monastic, religious community for women who had been widowed as a result of the Crusades, and that still serves today as a convent for Benedictine nuns. While scenic, the front entranceway to a convent may not be your first choice for a romantic rendezvous. St. Bonifacius Bridge, on the other hand, has the perfect setting. However, it is a little too perfect, drawing in too many tourists and leading to a lack of the privacy that might be needed for its romantic effects to take hold.

CHAPTER 8

REPURPOSED BRIDGES

STUDYING THE MANNER IN WHICH historic bridges were born is useful in helping to understand the history of a city or region. For some areas, studying how they died is similarly illuminating. Many old bridges continue to be used today, hundreds of years later. However, some were destroyed through structural failures, extreme weather events, or demolition during a war, capping a dramatic historical event in the city. Others are subjected to a routine safety inspection in the morning and are then closed forever by lunchtime. And some die with a whimper, rather than a bang. Having been designed for the horse and buggy, they are now bypassed by bridges designed to carry six lanes of interstate highway. Or, having been designed to provide transport related to an important local industry, they fall into disuse when that industry declines or moves to a different place. When that happens, the owner simply decides that the cost of maintenance and renovation is too high, the trains or cars stop moving, and the bridge begins to rust. The bridge immediately, overnight, ceases to be an asset and becomes a rotting liability, and it is just a matter of time before it begins to drop chunks of concrete or iron onto persons and property below.

Many of these forgotten bridges are now finding a second life. Once the bridge has been abandoned and become a liability, the community, working with the owner, must decide what to do with it. The choices depend on a variety of factors, including the condition of the bridge, how accessible it is, whether it is connected to local or regional trail systems, the cost required to make structural repairs and recreational improvements, and whether the space it occupies is needed to construct a replacement bridge.

Among these, two options do not result in the creation of a tourist bridge. These are complete demolition and abandonment in place. Sometimes, abandoned bridges are too decrepit or remote to make it worth converting them to recreational uses. However, even demolition costs money, so some are just left to the elements. While they may be preserved for historic-preservation purposes, these are heavily rusted, with weeds and trees growing out of their decks, decorative features falling off, and ends closed off by unattractive chain-link fencing. Examples include the 1888 Boardman's Bridge in Connecticut and the 1890 Center Village Bridge in New York. In both cases, there is another historic bridge preserved and turned into a park only a few miles away. The Boardman's Bridge is close to the Lover's Leap Bridge, and the Center Village Bridge is within a few miles of the Ouaquaga Bridge. Lover's Leap and Ouaquaga are both unusual lenticular-truss bridges, so it is understandable why these communities have chosen to preserve these, rather than the less interesting Boardman's and Center Village bridges. In other cases, such as the Phoenix Road and Oaks Creek bridges in Cooperstown, New York, there are no other nearby bridges that have been preserved, and these beautiful old bridges are just rusting away.

There are three other options that do result in the creation of a tourist bridge. These include leaving the entire bridge in place and converting it to recreational use, reusing pieces of the bridge, and moving the bridge to a new location. Repurposing of old bridges is a hybrid between historic preservation (discussed in Chapter 2) and recreation (discussed in Chapter 7), and there is a great deal of overlap in tourist interest in these bridges. Some people may visit the bridge only to investigate its history, while others may just want to ride their bike across.

Whatever the reason for preserving a historic bridge, an important resource is Mike Mort's *A Bridge Worth Saving, A Community Guide to Historic Bridge Preservation*, which serves as a how-to manual for the process. Mort's book covers all of the necessary steps, from winning support in the community and raising the necessary funds to strictly technical functions such as rust removal and repainting, and even to disassembling and reassembling the bridge somewhere else.

CONVERTED BRIDGES

There is only so much you can do with an old bridge, and recreation is the obvious choice. If the bridge is located near regional trails or city parks, it is commonly used to link hiking and biking trails together. The bridge preservation movement routinely joins forces with the bicycle-driven rails-to-trails movement, renovating abandoned railroad bridges and converting them to bike and pedestrian trails. A good example is the Norwottuck Rail Trail in Northampton, Massachusetts, an 11 mile-long bike trail on the bed of the former Boston and Maine Railroad. The trail crosses the Connecticut River on the Northampton Lattice Truss Bridge, an eight-span truss bridge built in 1887 and converted to pedestrian and bike use in 1992. The 1929 Chain-of-Rocks Bridge north of St. Louis once carried traffic on Route 66 from Chicago to San Bernardino, but was closed to traffic in 1968 and converted to serve as a connection between bike trails on both banks of the Mississippi River in 1999.

Many abandoned bridges are out in the middle of nowhere, with no ability to be connected to city sidewalks, parks, or hiking and biking trails. However, this does not stop the community from developing a new park, focused solely on the presence of a historically interesting bridge. These usually have a small parking lot, large enough for a handful of cars to allow historic bridge enthusiasts to stop, walk across, and take a few pictures. The park may consist of just the bridge with a few informational plaques, like the Paper Mill Road Bridge north of Baltimore and the Bollman Truss Bridge south of Baltimore. On the Susquehanna River in Ouaquaga, New York, the 1888 lenticular-truss bridge is accessed by a small parking lot at one end, and can be walked, but there are no other park amenities. At Lover's Leap State Park in Connecticut, the 1895 lenticular-truss bridge is preserved in a small park with trails and other attractions besides the bridge.

In some cases, the bridges are located in small towns and may serve to provide pedestrian access to connect communities on either side of the river. In these cases, there are often historical plaques, statues, and benches installed, either at the ends of the bridge or on the bridge itself. This has been done at the 1886 Nevius Street Bridge in Raritan, New Jersey, the lenticular South Washington Street Bridge in Binghamton, New York, and the Belfast Memorial Bridge in Maine.

If the bridge is in an urban setting, it may be converted into a pedestrian-only bridge linked into the city sidewalks, like the Green Bridge and the Union Pacific Railroad Bridge in Des Moines. Or, depending on the size of the bridge and the attractiveness of the view, the deck of the bridge may be turned into an urban park, elevated above the city, complete with benches and other parklike features. These bridges are often incorporated into extensive downtown redevelopment projects and are integrated into the new riverfront promenades, parks, memorials, and historic buildings that have been converted into condos, shops, and restaurants.

BIG FOUR BRIDGE, LOUISVILLE, KENTUCKY

The Big Four Railroad Bridge in Louisville, Kentucky, opened in 1895, is located about a half-mile east of downtown Louisville. The bridge crosses the Ohio River from Louisville to Jeffersonville, in Indiana. The bridge is more than 2,500 feet long and is elevated more than 50 feet above water level to allow uninterrupted shipping traffic. The bridge is a steel through-truss, consisting of a series of six round-topped steel truss spans sitting on tapered white stone piers. The name of the bridge derives from its being owned and operated by the Cleveland, Cincinnati, Chicago, and St. Louis Railroad, also known as the Big Four Railroad.

By the mid-1960s, changes in railroad ownership and freight requirements resulted in the owner at that time, the Penn Central Railroad, deciding that the bridge was too expensive to repair and maintain. The bridge ceased being used in 1969, and the lengthy approaches to the bridge on both banks of the river were removed and sold for scrap metal. The rest of the bridge sat neglected, a visual blot on the Louisville skyline, for almost 40 years. During that time, ownership of the bridge changed hands a few times, with schemes to dismantle the bridge, or possibly reconstruct it in another location.

Big Four Bridge, Louisville, Kentucky

Fortunately for the bridge tourist community, as well as for greater Louisville, the decision was eventually made to rehabilitate the bridge and integrate it into the city trail and park system. This has also been done in Chattanooga, Harrisburg, Poughkeepsie, Binghamton, and other locations, but Louisville did it with a subtle but important difference. In those other cities, the approaches linking the bridges to the riverbanks were still intact. In general, their conversion only required repair, painting, and some landscaping to turn the ends of the bridge into small parks. At Big Four, the removal of the approaches and the large height of the bridge required the development of new approaches in a major construction project.

To do this, the city completely redeveloped the landing area on the southern bank of the river into an extensive riverwalk and urban park system. Unlike the converted bridges in other cities, the Big Four Bridge is not just a nice way to access the park, nor is it just another part of the development. At Big Four, the bridge is the highlight, the centerpiece of the park. Instead of just adding some landscaping, historical plaques, and military memorials scattered around the landing of the bridge, the park covers more than 13 acres and is connected to riverwalks that extend both east and west of the main park. The park system includes hiking paths, overlook areas, water sculptures, riverside restaurants, lawn and playing field areas, bicycle repair stations, pedal car rentals, boat docks, and extremely comfortable swinging benches.

The new approach ramp leading up to the bridge deck is a highlight of the development. To get joggers and bikers from river level to bridge level in the smallest space possible, the ramp was constructed of steel and cement in an enormous, sleek spiral that is visible from downtown and from the other Ohio River bridges. Signs at the end of the bridge indicate that it is open 24 hours a day and encourage kids and couples on romantic dates to walk across and enjoy the bridge. The entrance of the spiral ramp to the bridge is a large brick plaza. The bridge deck is cement, with bike lanes designated in the middle. The railings are lined with benches and historical exhibits. The center portion of the bridge even has speakers with piped-in music to encourage people to hang out.

WALKWAY OVER THE HUDSON, POUGHKEEPSIE, NEW YORK

The earliest crossing of the Hudson River was the Poughkeepsie Bridge, a steel cantilever structure that opened in 1889 and transformed the entire transportation system between New England and the areas south and west of the Hudson. The bridge has had several names, including Poughkeepsie Railroad Bridge, Poughkeepsie-Highland Bridge, and the current Walkway over the Hudson. This bridge was noted for being integral to the US war effort in World War I, as it was the only bridge allowing transport of millions of soldiers from the mainland US to their debarkation points in New York City and New England. At its peak, the bridge carried more than 3,500 train cars per day.

By the 1960s, rail traffic on the bridge decreased as railroad companies were consolidated and other crossings were used. The owner at that time, the Penn Central, ran fewer and fewer trains, and let the bridge fall into disrepair. In 1974, the bridge caught on fire, damaging the tracks. Instead of being repaired, the bridge changed hands several times, with each owner choosing to not invest the money needed to repair it. The bridge started to fall apart, causing a hazard to roadways below. In 1992, the Walkway over the Hudson group was formed to rehabilitate the bridge and integrate it into the regional bike-and-hike trail system. The group assumed ownership of the bridge in 1995, reconstruction began in 2007, and the Walkway over the Hudson opened in 2009.

Turning abandoned rail beds into bike trails is not new and is being done all over the United States. The practice is commonly combined with historic-preservation efforts to rehabilitate the old bridges associated with the rail line. The fact that they have done this in Poughkeepsie may not seem that special. However, it is. If you get to visit only one bridge converted to a bike trail, this is the one that you want to visit, because the bridge is enormous.

This part of the Hudson was known as the Long Reach, a straight section of the estuary where sailing ships would not have to adjust their sails for a while. The estuary is about a mile wide at this location, and the banks on both sides of the river in this area are high and steep. This large size meant that the resulting bridge had to be both one of the longest ever built and, at the same time, one of the highest. The bridge is 212 feet high over the river, and well over a mile long. It is the longest elevated pedestrian bridge in the world. The extreme height of the bridge means that the views of the surrounding Hudson Valley are amazing. The city of Poughkeepsie on the eastern shore of the river does not have a major skyline, so the view on that end of the bridge is limited. However, the remainder of the valley is flanked by wooded hillsides and is especially scenic during the fall color season.

The deck of the bridge has been completely rebuilt, with a cement surface and walls. The history of the bridge and the town of Poughkeepsie is shown on historical plaques along the walls, and there are benches and telescopic viewers at intervals. The walkway is more than 30 feet wide, easily accommodating crowds of bikers, hikers, and strollers. If there is any complaint about the Walkway, it is that it is almost too long for a short, pleasant hike. At almost three miles for a round trip, you need to plan at least an hour for the hike, and much more if you want to take the time to enjoy it. A better idea may be to ride across by bike, as the bridge connects the Hudson Valley Rail Trail on the west side of the river to the Dutchess Rail Trail on the east.

The walkway can be accessed from a small parking lot and park on its western end. It costs five dollars to park there, or you can park free at the entrance to the Mid-Hudson Bridge and walk a half-mile to the Walkway. The park has picnic tables, a concession stand, and more historical plaques, and is right on the western end of the bridge. Access from the eastern end is a little more difficult because the hillside is not as steep, and the bridge has a lengthy approach of approximately a half-mile over the town. There are three ways to enter or exit the Walkway on the eastern end. Where the bridge crosses the shoreline, there is a 21-story high elevator. Further to the east, the Walkway has a stairway down to a commercial and residential neighborhood on Washington Street. Finally, there is a dedicated parking lot for the Dutchess Rail Trail a little further on.

The Mid-Hudson Bridge, described in the subsection on musical bridges in Chapter 6, is located only about a half–mile south of the Walkway, so they can, and should, be visited together in a single hike or bike ride. As a tourist attraction, the Walkway is better known and better advertised, and casual visitors may not even know that there is easy pedestrian access to Mid-Hudson. However, it would be a shame to get this close and not experience both bridges.

HIGH LINE, NEW YORK CITY

The High Line is a little unusual as a repurposed bridge because, unlike all other bridges featured in this book, it does not cross over any water bodies. The Hudson River Railroad, later the New York Central Railroad, originally began in 1847, connecting docks on the Hudson with industries and food distributors along 10th Avenue south to the Meatpacking District. The street-level railroad had more than 100 road crossings, leading to the need to have men on horses, called West Side Cowboys, ride in front of trains to clear pedestrians and traffic. In 1929, the decision was made to elevate the railway to eliminate the road crossings, resulting in the construction of a bridge, 30 feet high and more than a mile long, which was opened in 1934.

The lifespan of the High Line was short. By the 1960s, industry in Manhattan was declining, and goods were shipped into the city by trucks using the new interstate highway system. The last train ran in 1980, and the bridge was abandoned and allowed to overgrow.

As with any abandoned bridge, options were considered. The southern segments, comprising 14 city blocks, were demolished. Demolition of the rest of the bridge was favored by the city, but even demolition costs money. In addition, allowing a rusting bridge to fall to pieces and, eventually, collapse onto traffic in the middle of 10th Avenue was not an option. In 1999, the Friends of the High Line was formed to advocate for the conversion of the bridge to recreational use. In 2005, CSX donated the southern portion of the High Line to the city, followed by the donation of the northern portion in 2012. The southern portion of the new park was opened in 2009, and the remainder was opened in 2011 and 2014.

The conversion of the High Line involved much more than laying a walking surface and building a couple of staircases for pedestrian access. As with other converted bridges, there are places to sit, overlooks, public art, access stairs and elevators at regular intervals, and restrooms. However, there are some interesting differences. Other converted bridges are generally renovated to turn the previous road or railbed into a walking trail, usually connected to park trails, or at least sidewalks, on either end. The former rails and ties are removed, and the former railbed is replaced with a wooden or asphalt deck that spans the entire width of the bridge deck, from edge to edge. Some parklike amenities are always added, but the main objective is to convert a traffic or railroad surface to a pedestrian-friendly surface. It is an improved bridge, for a different purpose, but it is still a bridge.

This is not what has been done at the High Line. A walkway was constructed along the entire length that allows pedestrians to walk from one end to the other. However, the rails and ties were never removed, and the walkway does not, for most of its length, cover the entire width of the deck. Instead, the walkway wanders in and among the rails and ties. In some places, the walkway is made of asphalt laid level with the remaining rails. In other places, the walkway is made of metal grate and elevated above the original railbed. In others, it is made of cement blocks covering only a portion of the width of the bridge, while the remaining width is left in its "natural" state with rails, ties, and gravel ballast overgrown with self-seeded plantings. It is an interesting design choice, but "self-seeded" is a major theme for the areas of the park adjacent to the walkways. Instead of choosing to plant these areas with grass, flowers, trees, or other common landscaping items, most of them have been left exactly as they were when the railroad ceased operating.

The resulting feel is that the High Line is not a converted bridge as much as it is an elevated public park, but with some major differences. There are areas of plantings, but most of the High Line does not have the manicured flower beds typically associated with parks. The High Line also prohibits two common features of parks, which are bicycles and dogs, as well as skateboards and skates. Although it is set up as a pedestrian park, it does not serve as multiuse trails as most other converted railroad bridges do.

Probably the major attraction for tourists is the views of the city that are available from the elevated platform. The park is almost 1.5 miles long, and passes many well-known city features along the way. The northern end is a ramp that begins at the Javits Convention Center on 34th Street, a half-block from the Hudson. This area is accessible from the Number 7 subway at the Hudson Yards Station and has undergone major redevelopment with the construction of glass-sided office towers. The ramp curves up and around the storage yard for trains at the West Side Rail Yards, following the Hudson for four blocks. The bridge then curves to the east, passing through an unusual, expanded area of benches and landscaping called Pershing Square Beams. From there, the bridge again curves south, following 10th Avenue. There are landscaped plantings at the Falcone Flyover at 26th Street and an area called Chelsea Thicket at 21st Street. An overlook at 17th Street provides a distant view of the Statue of Liberty. At 15th Street, the park crosses under a brick building that is the Chelsea Market Passage, and provides access to the open-air Chelsea Market. There is a sundeck, with public art, at 14th Street. The park ends at the Whitney Museum, at Gansevoort Street.

One question associated with the High Line, for the purposes of this book, is "Is it a bridge, given that it does not cross water"? And, even if it is a bridge, does it rise to a high level of importance to tourists, given that it is not really located anywhere near the major mid-town tourist centers of New York City? Eventually, the decision to include it was based on one factor, which is its enormous popularity. Even on cold days, weekdays, rainy days, we are not talking about dozens, or even hundreds, of people. We are talking about thousands of people. These are not people using the park to commute from one location to another, nor are they local residents. These are tourists, strolling slowly, stopping at the overlooks for selfies, marveling at the architecture of the buildings, reading the informational plaques, and hanging out on the benches. The High Line is not only just one of the most densely visited tourist bridges in the world, but it is also a major addition to the list of must-see tourist sights in New York.

PIECES OF BRIDGES

As desirable as the in-place conversion of historic bridges may be to the local community, it is not always possible. Abandonment of a historic bridge is usually accompanied by the construction of a new bridge and, in many cases, the old bridge is simply in the way and has to be removed. In every case, the decision about what to do with an abandoned, damaged, or destroyed bridge depends on the price tag, requiring a conscious calculation of the costs and benefits of the various options.

In cases where the old bridge has been destroyed by flooding or an act of war, the destruction is usually not complete, but only partial. This leaves the community with the choice of rebuilding the bridge from its remaining pieces, finishing the job by demolishing what remains, or preserving the broken pieces in place.

On the Delaware River above Trenton, almost all of the bridges have, at one time or another, been destroyed by floods. Most in place today are the third- or fourth-generation bridge at their location. However, it is usually the "flimsy" parts of the bridge, meaning the wooden or iron deck and superstructure, which get destroyed, leaving the more robust parts, such as stone piers, in place. This results in funny-looking "Frankenstein" bridges that are a mixture of old and new materials and styles. An example is Lumberville-Raven Rock, where a wooden, covered traffic bridge was destroyed but replaced with a much narrower pedestrian-only bridge. In this case, the light and airy steel suspension towers and deck from the 1940s look weird sitting on the enormous stone piers from the 1850s.

There are also many cases where the remaining pieces are left in place, but converted to recreational uses. Some communities can be extremely creative in deciding what to do with the pieces of their old bridges. At the Naval Academy Bridge on the Severn River in Annapolis, a lengthy section of the old bridge was left in place and is now a popular fishing pier. At the Waldo-Hancock Suspension Bridge, the old anchor block was covered with a roof and had tables and a grill placed onto it, creating a picnic area.

On the 11th Street Bridge in Washington, DC, the deck of the old bridge was removed, but its piers were left in place and converted to pedestrian observation areas connected, by a short walkway, to the new bridge.

Another common practice, done to preserve the history of the old bridge, is to salvage prominent components, such as the date plaque or pieces of machinery, before demolition. The original 1931 date plaque from the Waldo-Hancock Bridge, along with two plaques documenting engineering distinctions awarded to the bridge, has been preserved and reinstalled at the Penobscot Narrows Bridge and Observatory. The original 1837 plaque, carved in marble and barely legible, has been reinstalled at the 1904 Riegelsville Bridge on the Delaware River. The new Route 52 Bridge in Ocean City, New Jersey, has preserved two original plaques of the World War Memorial Bridge, one dated 1932 and the other 1933. This bridge has also converted the roof of the old drawspan control building into an attractive roof for an outdoor pavilion and has preserved the drawspan control panel in a small museum located on an island accessed by the bridge.

KINZUA BRIDGE STATE PARK, MOUNT JEWETT, PENNSYLVANIA

For more than 130 years, the Kinzua Viaduct has had an eventful history, and has undergone a few different iterations of being a tourist attraction. The bridge was originally constructed of iron in 1882 to carry freight trains, and was replaced by a steel structure in 1900. At the time of construction, it was the highest and longest railroad bridge in the world. The bridge was supported by 20 open, steel lattice towers, with those over the deepest part of the valley being more than 300 feet high.

Although the height and length records were soon eclipsed by other bridges, the impressive scale of the structure attracted tourist interest even while it still functioned as a freight railroad bridge. Excursion trains originating in Buffalo and Pittsburgh brought tourists to the site to enjoy views of the Kinzua Valley. In 1959, the freight trains stopped rolling, but the tourist attraction continued. Due to its immense size and popularity, the bridge and surrounding property were acquired by the state and, in 1970, opened as Kinzua Bridge State Park. Starting in 1987, local excursion trains were run across the bridge specifically for tourists.

The tourist trains continued until 2002, at which time they were stopped to allow repairs to the bridge. However, the repairs were never completed. A tornado struck a bulls-eye right through the middle of the bridge in July 2003, destroying 11 of the 20 steel towers, and leaving the two dangling ends facing each other across almost a half-mile of empty space.

The destruction of the bridge by the tornado did not end its days as a tourist bridge. Quite the opposite. Instead, the large size of the bridge—with its enormous gaping hole in the very middle of what had been a large and apparently robust steel framework—and the mangled ruins of the collapsed towers lying in the valley became an attraction as a demonstration of the destructive power of mother nature.

The state capitalized on this, in a big way. One choice would have been to rebuild the bridge, but this would have been costly and would have erased the demonstration of the power of the tornado. Another choice would have been to remove all of the damaged pieces and restore the scenic valley to its original condition. A third choice would have been to clean up the debris of the fallen towers at the bottom of the valley, perform the minimum amount of restoration work necessary to make one of the remaining ends safe for visitors, and leave it at that.

The state did not do any of these. They did make one of the ends safe and accessible for visitors, but they did much more than that. Instead of eliminating the evidence of the tornado, they made infrastructure improvements to provide access to the remains. The largest of the intact ends, comprised of six towers, was turned into the Kinzua Sky Walk, now considered one of the more popular skywalk tourist attractions in the country. The Kinzua Sky Walk extends more than 600 feet out into the valley and is 225 feet high at the end. The end has been expanded into a comfortable viewing platform with a glass floor allowing you to look straight down more than 200 feet.

A visitor center, opened in 2016, includes interactive exhibits on the history of the bridge, as well as displays comparing and contrasting man's power to build structures, such as the viaduct, with nature's power to destroy those structures within seconds. Dozens of hiking and biking trails have been developed, linking into trails in the surrounding Allegheny

National Forest, and offering views of the skywalk towering above, as well as up-close views of the crumpled remnants of the 11 destroyed towers. Viewing areas, including some with binocular viewers, have been set up around the skywalk. Access to a viewing area within the towers of the remaining section has been developed, providing a unique view through the axis of the remaining towers.

It is quite impressive that the state, instead of erasing or ignoring the damage, turned a negative into a positive by embracing and improving what remained. One of the major, unexpected impressions on the visitor is the enormous scale of the bridge and the collapsed towers. There are multiple websites available showing pictures of the structures, but the actual scale cannot be appreciated until you use binoculars and notice the tiny people wandering among the collapsed towers from viewing points almost a mile away.

Another important observation may be made regarding the demonstration of the power of nature, which is the theme of some of the websites and exhibits. The implication seems to be that, no matter how ingenious the engineers and construction workers, the continued existence of manmade structures can be ended by overwhelming natural forces at any time. However, there are several hints given in the available information that suggests that "nature over man" is too simplistic an explanation for what happened at the Kinzua Viaduct.

The first hint is that the bridge was originally constructed of wrought-iron in 1882, but was then replaced by a steel structure only 18 years later. That is a short lifespan on such a massive structure. Lots of bridges need to be replaced when the type of traffic crossing them becomes heavier and faster. However, they are usually constructed with some room to grow. Nobody who is building a structure as a long-term investment in their company's operations would deliberately consider a design life of 18 years to be sufficient. Durations of 50 or 100 years are far more common. This suggests that the reconstruction was not needed just because trains were growing heavier and faster. It suggests that it was needed because the original design was woefully inadequate.

The second hint is mentioned on several exhibition plaques at the park. This is the fact that the speed of trains crossing the bridge was limited to five miles per hour because trains faster than this caused vibrations along the legs of the towers. Five miles per hour is incredibly slow, so a suggestion that anything faster was considered unsafe leads to an impression that the bridge structure was just that—unsafe.

The third hint is not mentioned in any of the literature but is an observation you will make yourself when you walk out to the observation platform. This is the fact that the end of the bridge sways in the wind. You can feel it, even on the shortened end, only six towers out into the valley. When the entire bridge was in place, the effect of the wind on the center of the bridge would have been much greater.

These observations suggest that the story is not simply that of an irresistible force (tornado) winning out over a seemingly immovable object (bridge). The story may actually be more common, which is that of a private company spending as little money as possible, during a time when government regulation was limited, to make a fast buck. The structure was enormous and impressive to behold, but a house of cards may also be enormous and impressive to behold, yet still fold in seconds when hit with a stiff wind.

WALNUT STREET BRIDGE, HARRISBURG, PENNSYLVANIA

Pennsylvania is home to not just one bridge that can be used to demonstrate the awesome power of nature, but two. Walnut Street Bridge in Harrisburg crosses from downtown to City Island in the middle of the Susquehanna River, a short distance upstream of Market Street Bridge. The earliest bridge to City Island was called Camelback Bridge. Several different wooden versions of Camelback Bridge existed, beginning in 1817. Damage by floods and fires over the years led to replacements, the most recent being the current Market Street Bridge, dating from 1926. A historical plaque on City Island states that Walnut Street Bridge, built in 1890, is the oldest surviving bridge over the Susquehanna River, although only a part of it survives.

On the southwestern side of City Island, opposite Wormleysburg, the original Walnut Street Bridge is no longer intact. In 1972, the Hurricane Agnes flood damaged the bridge so that it was closed to car traffic forever and used only for pedestrians and bikes. To add insult to injury, ice floes then swept away three of the spans on the southwestern side in 1996, severing the connection to Wormleysburg. The southwestern spans were never restored, so the southwestern segment today consists of nothing but the two severed ends of the bridge, with their middle missing.

Although not technically required to enjoy your visit, you are highly encouraged to find and view the YouTube video of the 1996 event, which shows the middle section of the Walnut Street Bridge being detached, slowly carried downstream, and then dramatically crunched like a tin can and sucked under when it strikes the Market Street Bridge. Make sure to watch it with the sound on—it is awe-inspiring and, because nobody was hurt, truly hilarious.

The part of the Walnut Street Bridge that can be walked today is a wrought-iron through-truss bridge that provides pedestrian access between downtown and the stadium for the Harrisburg minor league baseball team. The superstructure is a complex maze of diagonal girders and strengthening rods forming seven trusses, painted entirely black. The girders and rods seem too narrow to be strong, resulting in a light, airy appearance. The only decoration is a series of small, sun-shaped medallions at the crossings of the rods. The bridge is completely black in color, making it difficult to get good photographs. About two-thirds of the width of the deck is an open steel grid, allowing you to watch the river flowing beneath your feet. The remainder of the deck is a cement sidewalk, presumably to accommodate those who are disturbed by the openness of the grid.

RELOCATED BRIDGES

Most repurposed bridges are in their original location, but a few have been moved to make way for the new bridge. It seems unusual that such large and complex structures can be moved, but they can. Stone bridges can be dismantled, stone-by-stone, and reassembled elsewhere. Many wooden covered bridges have been moved by prying loose the wooden components and reassembling them elsewhere, much like Ikea furniture. Many small-scale steel through-truss bridges are constructed of bars and bolts, like an erector set, and can similarly be dismantled and re-erected.

Other bridges may be small enough that they can be lifted off their piers by a crane, placed onto a truck bed, and moved whole.

In some cases, relocated bridges may be re-used again to support traffic in their new location, as seen at the Four Points Bridge in Maryland. Others may be transported to be used for a different purpose, such as the Bollman Bridge near Meyersdale, Pennsylvania, which was moved to serve as a bridge on the Great Allegheny Passage Bike Trail. Carried to its extreme, Historic Bridge Park in Calhoun County, Michigan, has a collection of five historic truss bridges that were saved from demolition and moved to the park for preservation.

LONDON BRIDGE, LAKE HAVASU CITY, ARIZONA

It is completely understandable if London Bridge at Lake Havasu City, Arizona, is not high on your list of tourist bridges to visit. The entire concept just seems weird. Bridges have sat at the western edge of the Pool of London on the Thames for almost 2,000 years. In 1831, the medieval bridge was finally replaced with a "modern" stone-arch bridge. In just over 100 years, the foundation of that bridge sank into the mud to the extent that it had to be replaced. It turns out that London Bridge really was falling down. However, instead of tearing it down and salvaging any usable material, the city decided to sell the bridge. And even weirder, they found a buyer in Robert McCullough, the founder of Lake Havasu City as a retirement resort on a reservoir on the Colorado River. In 1968, McCullough spent $2.46 million to purchase the bridge. Then, he spent another $4.5 million over the next three years to have the bridge dismantled stone-by-stone, shipped to the US, transported overland to Arizona, and then reassembled in the middle of the desert.

Further distracting from the desirability of visiting London Bridge is the myth that McCullough, or the townspeople, or somebody, was rooked. According to the story, they thought they were actually getting Tower Bridge, which is so famous and iconic that it would be a major tourist attraction anywhere in the world. The myth is apparently not true, although it is likely that some segment of the population did believe they were getting Tower Bridge. Interestingly, the flip-side of this myth is the implication that getting London Bridge instead of Tower Bridge was something of a disappointment, as if London Bridge was not all that desirable in the first place.

The final straw squashing any plan to walk London Bridge is its remote location. This is not a "stop-by-while-in-the-neighborhood" bridge. You will probably need to drive there from Las Vegas, Phoenix, or Los Angeles. The closest of these is Las Vegas, well over 100 miles away. Even if you happened to be driving through this part of Arizona anyway, Lake Havasu City is 20 miles south of Interstate 40, and you would need to take more than an hour-long diversion to see it. In terms of access, this may be the most work you have to do to visit a tourist bridge. However, at your first sight of the bridge, all of your doubts will evaporate, because this is a lovely bridge placed into a nicely designed setting.

The first thing you will notice about the bridge is the decorative stonework. The bridge is constructed of five arches of about equal size and, to be truthful, is not really a complete reconstruction of the bridge as it stood in London. Instead, the bridge has a cement arch core of the same dimensions as the original London Bridge, and is then faced with the decorative stonework, balustrades, and lampposts brought over from London. The arches themselves are framed with stones with diagonally cut ends placed radially around the arch-ring to create a sunburst effect. Then, the spandrel is constructed of rough-faced, horizontal granite blocks ranging in color from dark to light gray to almost white. The deck is lined with round, carved granite balusters holding up a thick granite handrail. The sidewalks are then lined with Victorian-looking bronze lampposts that are stamped "T. Potter & Sons South Molton St. W", and appear to be the original lampposts. The deck is actually a few feet wider than the arches, with the side extensions held up by closely spaced carved, crenulated granite supports.

Another appealing feature of the bridge, especially if you have also recently visited the current version of London Bridge on the Thames, is its size. By definition, the Havasu version and the London version have to be about the same size, since one replaced the other. However, the individual stone blocks and arches seem enormous. The width of the channel that the bridge crosses seems tiny, although it is the same width as the Thames, and the bridge itself seems enormous. This may just be an optical illusion. The current London Bridge is, after all, in London, surrounded by glass office towers, with a view along the Thames for a large distance in either direction. The Havasu London Bridge is surrounded by condos and shops that are only two or three stories high. The curving channel of the arm of Lake Havasu disappears around the corner in both directions, leaving only a limited view of the water. Placed into this reduced-size setting, the bridge seems huge.

The way that McCullough chose to display the bridge is another point in its favor. The bridge connects downtown Lake Havasu City on the shore to a small island in the lake. The channel separating the island from the shore is lined on both sides with docks, shops, condos, hotels, restaurants, and parks. Three of the bridge's arches cross the channel, while the two arches on either end cross the lakefront promenade.

The channel is full of power boats, jet skis, and bikini-clad stand-up paddle boarders, and it is entertaining to watch these modern-looking transport methods passing each other under the 180 year-old stonework of the bridge. Beyond the small channel and above the shoreline shops, the view in all directions is of the barren rock mountains of the Arizona desert. Even with these incongruous touches, an attempt has been made to incorporate the London theme into the surrounding area. The bridge deck is lined with both American flags and Union Jacks, and several of the shops and restaurants have faux Olde England architecture and a "Ye Olde Shoppe" theme.

All of this is fake, obviously for the benefit of tourists and retirees only. But then, everything in this desert is fake and temporary, for hundreds of miles in every direction. Modern humans could not live here, could barely even get from one side to the other, without 100 years of dams and aqueducts providing power and water, making jet skis on Lake Havasu possible. Strangely, London Bridge is the most real thing here, even if it is out of place. It may have been moved, but for 130 years it stood at the very center of the world at the height of the British Empire. Charles Dickens probably walked across it, as did many of his characters. Queen Victoria almost certainly crossed it in a coach. Ships of the Royal Navy were moored near it during World War I. The bridge had a front-row seat for the London Blitz.

It is also undeniable that the bridge is much more attractive and interesting than its replacement. The current-day London Bridge is a nondescript cement bridge, lacking any decoration or charm. In addition, luckily for the people of Lake Havasu City, the bridge, although not as famous, may even be better than Tower Bridge, the one that they thought they were getting. London Bridge, even if it is in a fake place, is at least pleasantly designed with a uniform visual style throughout, instead of being an odd mixture of styles. Tower Bridge, with its faux castle veneer directly juxtaposed with its Industrial-Age steel structure, is as much of a tourist gimmick as bringing London Bridge to the desert.

London Bridge at Lake Havasu definitely stretches the envelope of whether it can be recommended in a book of tourist bridges. It is quite far to go to visit a bridge that is only 500 feet long and can be walked across in ten minutes. It does not help that there is little else nearby unless water sports in desert landscapes are your thing. However, chances are that you will not be disappointed, and you should definitely drop by if you are in the neighborhood.

CHAPTER 9

MULTIPLE BRIDGE TOURS

UP TO THIS POINT, ALMOST all of the dozens of tourist bridges discussed are visited by tourists and recreationists on their own, as individual bridges based on their individual attractions. However, it is also common for two or more bridges to attract tourists as a group. In some cases, this is because a large number and wide variety of bridges of different attractions are located near each other and other tourist sights, making for an attractive walking or boating tour. In other cases, a group of bridges may share a common history or construction type and, even though they are spread out over great distances, they will become the focus of a road trip.

WALKING TOURS

In Europe, multi-bridge tourist centers are found in the "Old Town" areas of major cities, all of which grew up on riverbanks long before the invention of railroads and trucks reduced the importance of rivers as major trade routes. Many of these historic, urban tourist areas are walkable, with all of the churches, museums, parks, and other attractions tightly packed within an old city center. And if that tourist center is near a river or, even better, straddles both sides of a historically important river, then it is likely that you will also find multiple historic bridges underfoot and will be crossing them several times each day.

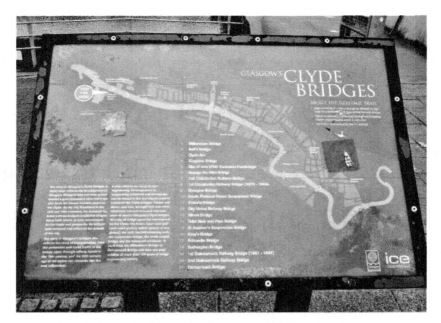

Guide Map to Glasgow Bridges at Millennium Bridge

Two of the most iconic bridges in the world, Tower Bridge and Charles Bridge, are each just one of a crowd of gorgeous, historic bridges. They may be the most well-known bridges in London and Prague, respectively, but each one is just a short walk from numerous others that should be visited. While you may not have noticed them or paid close attention, some of these others are literally under your feet as you make your way from one attraction to another in many tourist centers.

Although they may not have iconic bridges, several other prominent European tourist areas are centered on rivers or harbors, with important tourist sights to be visited on both ends of interesting bridges. Glasgow straddles the River Clyde and has many bridges, ranging from historic to modern, in the walkable central area. A map at Millennium Bridge displays the locations and lists 21 bridges crossing the Clyde near downtown Glasgow. Rome's tourist attractions are located on both banks of the Tiber and, although the bridges are few, they are among the oldest and most decorative in the world. Other cities that are among the best bridge-touring places in Europe are Dublin and Paris.

One important note—Venice has deliberately been left out of the walking tour profiles presented below. Venice is a perfect place for a bridge walking tour, so much so that a fanatical bridgespotter, Charl Durand, recently challenged himself to walk across 100 bridges in Venice in a single day. He documented the achievement in *Venice, Bridge by Bridge*, published in 2017. No description of a Venice bridge walking tour presented here could rival that of Durand, so all that can be done is to refer the reader to him and bow in his direction.

The United States is more limited in the availability of walking tours of multiple bridges. The development of urban areas in the United States proceeded quite differently from that in Europe and had an enormous effect on the configuration of tourist spots, at least with respect to walkability and bridges. Urban development in the United States occurred later, mostly after the development of railroads substantially reduced the importance of rivers as transportation systems. As a result, American cities are not as "river-centric" as European cities, and therefore lack the close association of bridges with walkable tourist areas that is found in Europe.

New York City, probably the most popular tourist city in the United States, serves as an excellent example. It is home to one of the most iconic bridges in the world, which stands on its own as a prominent tourist destination. However, the masses of tourists in New York City are almost entirely situated in Times Square, along Fifth Avenue, and in Greenwich Village. These areas are all located several miles from Brooklyn Bridge. Visitors in Times Square may choose to get on the subway to make a special visit to Brooklyn Bridge, and, given that authorities sometimes have to close off pedestrian access to stop people from getting trampled by the massive crowds, it is likely that a large number of them do. However, most of them are not in a geographic position to stroll over for a casual look. Brooklyn Bridge is just not part of a walking tour that can be combined with other New York attractions.

THAMES BRIDGES, LONDON

For maximum enjoyment of visiting bridges, it is not critical, but it is helpful, that there be something worth getting to on the other side. In the London of 30 years ago, this was not completely the case. All of the major historic and cultural attractions of London were situated on the northern bank of the Thames. Southwark, the neighborhood on the south bank between Tower Bridge and Westminster Bridge, was mostly just another part of the sprawling urban metropolis. Bridges crossed from Southwark into the City, and some of them were historic and decorated. However, one disappointing feature of London was that the construction of buildings right up to the river's edge on both banks eliminated any chance of walking along the river. This resulted in there being no good vantage point from which to view the historic buildings.

Correcting this problem on the northern bank was never an option. The northern bank has three train stations situated right on the river. More importantly, the history and iconic vista provided by many of the buildings coming directly to the river's edge, including the Tower of London and the Houses of Parliament, was never going to allow construction of a riverfront promenade on the north bank.

The Southwark bank, however, was different. There are no train stations on the Southwark bank. The only historic building that interferes with the construction of a completely uninterrupted promenade is Southwark Cathedral. Therefore, in the 1990s, a concerted effort was made to redevelop the Southwark bank and make it a desirable, visitable attraction in itself. Older, historically less important buildings were torn down to build sparkling new office buildings that incorporated the riverfront into their design. Numerous other historic buildings were remodeled into offices, shops, museums, and residences.

The best part of the Southwark bank redevelopment is the magnificent promenade called the Queen's Walk. Except for the one small diversion around the Southwark Cathedral, tourists can walk along this promenade for three miles from Tower Bridge all the way to Lambeth Bridge. This promenade can be used to access all of the historic and modern sculptural bridges across the Thames.

Tower Bridge, discussed in Chapter 1, is at the extreme eastern end of the tourist area of London, so it serves as an excellent starting point to explore the London bridges. Before starting on your multiple bridge walk, take the tour into the interior of Tower Bridge, go to the top, walk out to the western walkway, and admire the view of London, including all of the bridges you are about to walk across. Then descend back to river level, walk south toward Southwark, and turn right (west) to continue your walking tour.

London Bridge, to the west of Tower Bridge, is the most historic crossing of the Thames in London. The site is at the furthest inland reach of the Pool of London, the tidal portion of the Thames that formed the center of London's shipping industry for centuries. The Pool was the locus for the development of London as a prominent city beginning in the Roman Empire. The Pool became the location of London's docks, supporting Britain's worldwide commercial enterprises. The Tower of London was built on the north shore of the Pool as part of its defenses. The area north and west of the Tower became "the City", the commercial and banking headquarters of the British Empire. And long before that, London Bridge was built, originally by the Romans, as the furthest downstream crossing of the Thames. For hundreds of years, London Bridge was the only crossing of the Thames in the vicinity of London.

The original Roman bridge at the site was replaced numerous times. Fast-forward several centuries and the "new" London Bridge, a granite arch bridge, was constructed at the site, opening for business in 1831. Eventually, others were constructed, including Westminster Bridge in 1862, Blackfriars Road Bridge in 1869, Tower Bridge in 1894, and Southwark Bridge in 1921. Fast-forward another 40 years to the 1960s, and the "new" London Bridge was sinking into the mud and needed to be replaced. It was dismantled stone-by-stone, and loaded onto ships. The ships crossed the Atlantic, where the stones were loaded onto a train and carried out to the middle of the desert. There, they were reassembled and can be walked today. But that is a different bridge visit.

The London Bridge of today is the 1971 replacement, sitting about a half-mile west of Tower Bridge. Being located at the upstream end of the Pool of London, the bridge does not need to have a drawspan to allow passage of large ships, as does Tower Bridge. Therefore, the bridge is much lower to the water, with a clearance of about 30 feet, or high enough to only allow tour boats and barges through. The bridge is a concrete and steel arch construction, consisting of two full arches and a partial arch stretching across the river. There is no superstructure or decoration, resulting in a bridge that is mostly just serviceable in allowing traffic to flow between Southwark and the City.

London Bridge is still definitely worth visiting for the historic location, the views, and the general pleasures of walking through the appealing neighborhoods of London. The northern landing of the bridge leads directly into the heart of the City, dominated by glass-sided skyscrapers. History is still present here in the form of the Monument, Sir Christopher Wren's stone tower constructed in the 1670s, just off the end of London Bridge. The Monument was built to commemorate the Great Fire of 1666, which started close to this location. Accessible to the public for the price of a few pounds, a walk in this area needs to include an ascent of the winding staircase to the viewing platform at the top.

The closely packed bank buildings and narrow streets in this neighborhood give no indication of how close you are to the river until the moment that you step out onto London Bridge. Then, immediately, the entire Thames opens up. Until recently, the most eye-catching feature would have been the iconic silhouette of Tower Bridge on your left, a half-mile away. This has been supplanted as the dominant visual sight by the enormous Shard. Between Tower and London bridges, in the Pool, is the *HMS Belfast*, permanently docked to the Southwark bank and visitable as a tourist attraction. If you are lucky, there may be other active Navy ships in the Pool, recently entered through the opened drawspan of the Tower Bridge. Not to be missed, especially at lunchtime, is the famous Borough Market, a complex of food vendors located in the down-under space beneath the southern approaches to London Bridge.

The southern end of London Bridge may have been as far as tourists wanted to go 30 years ago. However, the redevelopment of the Southwark waterfront has made this an amazing place to wander, shop, and admire the great views of the prominent London landmarks on the north bank. Turning west on the Southwark bank takes you past numerous interesting historic sites, including Southwark Cathedral, the ruins of Winchester Palace, the thick black walls of The Clink prison, and the Golden Hind.

About a quarter-mile to the west of London Bridge is Southwark Bridge. Built in 1921, it is a nice example of the early use of steel arch bridge construction. Like London Bridge, Southwark Bridge is only about

30 feet high over the river and has no superstructure, so it is not prominently visible. However, a nice feature of this bridge is the way that the steel arches and rails have been decoratively painted to highlight its architecture. The color scheme used on Southwark is bright green and yellow, with the curved-arch girders and horizontal deck painted green and the vertical deck supports and steel rails highlighted in yellow. The color scheme is echoed in the Victorian-style lampposts. The internal structural components of the bridge are painted gray, which accentuates the bright colors on the sides of the bridge.

The landings of Southwark Bridge are relatively innocuous, leading into recent urban development without any prominent nearby landmarks on either end. The view to the east along the river includes the nearby Cannon Street railroad bridge, with the Shard hovering in the distance.

The next bridge to the west is the Millennium Footbridge, which was a prominent component of the Southwark bank redevelopment. Attracting tourists to the Southwark bank required easier pedestrian access than was available on the sidewalks of the existing roadway bridges. It required a pedestrian-only bridge, on a grand scale, directly linking one major tourist attraction to another. This link was provided in 2000 by the Millennium Footbridge.

The major tourist attraction located on the north bank in this area did not need any redevelopment. The north end of Millennium Footbridge leads up steps directly to St. Paul's Cathedral, just blocks off the river. On the south bank opposite St. Paul's was a gigantic brick power station dating from the 1940s. Although not uninteresting or unattractive, this was hardly a tourist destination. Having ceased to operate in the early 1980s, the power plant was converted to the Tate Modern, now the most visited modern art museum in the world. Just to the east of the Tate Modern, the newly constructed Globe Theatre is not only interesting as a museum, but offers performances that make this segment of the Southwark bank an attraction in the evening as well as the daytime.

To connect these icons, not just any pedestrian bridge would do. It had to be a work of art. Entirely constructed of gleaming, polished steel, Millennium Footbridge is a sort of upside-down suspension bridge. Instead of being supported from above by cables anchored on high towers, the supports pass between the anchors underneath the bridge deck. In this way, the bridge sits on a network of supports like a hammock. This unique construction keeps the visual profile of the bridge very low, so that it does not intrude on the views of St. Paul's or the Tate Modern.

As with any use of innovative technology, the grand opening of the bridge in 2000 was not without its hiccups. The movement of people on the bridge was found to create resonance, causing the bridge to sway too much to be usable. A few days after its grand opening, the bridge was closed. Back to the drawing board, dampers were added to the bridge to counteract its sway, and the bridge was re-opened in 2002.

Looking west from the Millennium Footbridge, it appears that the next bridge, the Blackfriars Railway Bridge, can be skipped. It is a rail-only bridge and is unattractive. However, what you cannot see from Millennium Footbridge is that there is another historic road and pedestrian bridge directly west, almost hidden among the shadows of the rail bridge. Like Southwark Bridge, the Blackfriars Road Bridge connects city neighborhoods that have new office and condominium complexes but do not have any prominent tourist sights. The bridge is historic, having been dedicated by Queen Victoria in 1869, and is nicely decorated. It is a cast-iron arch with decorative cast-iron railings, all done in colors of pink and white. On the southern end is a large, colorful monument to the London, Chatham, and Dover Railway, dated 1864. On the northern end is a gigantic bronze of Victoria holding her scepter and orb, dated 1896.

The next walkable bridge west of Blackfriars is Waterloo Bridge, almost a mile away. Fans of painting and art history will recognize the name of Waterloo Bridge as the subject of the numerous paintings done by Claude Monet. However, those hoping to see or walk across it will be disappointed. Monet's Waterloo Bridge was constructed on this site in 1817 and designed by John Rennie, the same architect who designed the London Bridge that now sits in Arizona. The 1817 bridge suffered the same kind of foundation settling problems as Rennie's London Bridge. A reinforcing superstructure was added to it in the 1920s, and the entire bridge was replaced in the 1940s.

Being relatively modern in construction, Waterloo Bridge is, from a distance, fairly plain and undecorated in appearance. The bridge consists of five equal-sized concrete arches sitting on narrow piers. However, on closer inspection, the bridge has some features that are interesting. First, although it appears to be made of boring, undecorated concrete, the bridge is faced with simple stonework to make a clean, elegant profile that is appealing. The dark-colored concrete of the arch supports is only slightly visible from the sides of the bridge, outlining only the edge of the arch-ring and acting as a highlight. The remainder of the spandrel, up to the deck, is faced with a light gray, finely bedded limestone that is laid vertically instead of the more common horizontal. The contrast of the light-colored vertical texture of the spandrel with the dark-colored horizontal grain of the elongated arch-ring outlines is attractive.

The location of Waterloo Bridge is also unique among the Thames bridges. Waterloo Bridge is sited on the curve where the Thames turns from a direct north-south to a direct east-west orientation. In this position, the bridge provides the best views of any of the Thames bridges. These include St. Paul's, the Gherkin, and the Shard to the east and all of Westminster to the south. This is the only bridge in London where you can take in all of these sights from a single location.

The next bridge to the south, only a few hundred feet away, is the Hungerford Railroad Bridge, also known as Charing Cross Bridge, built in the 1860s. Charing Cross Bridge leads over the Victoria Embankment directly into Charing Cross train station, and was also a subject for Monet. In this case, the railroad bridge painted by Monet still exists, although it has undergone substantial modifications in the form of a series of modern pedestrian walkways.

In 2003, the Hungerford Footbridge was replaced with two adjacent pedestrian bridges, one on each side of the railroad. These are collectively known as the Golden Jubilee Bridges in honor of Queen Elizabeth's 50th anniversary on the throne. The Golden Jubilee Bridges are complex cable-stayed bridges that are a hybrid between an addition to the Hungerford Railroad Bridge and newly constructed bridges. Both bridge decks are only about 20 feet off the side of the railroad bridge. The pylons supporting the decks with diagonal steel cables sit on both sides of each bridge. One set of pylons on the inside of the deck are attached to the piers of the railroad bridge, and the other set of pylons on the outside of the deck sit on newly constructed concrete piers. The pylons and supporting cables of the pedestrian bridges are gleaming white, contrasting sharply with the industrial red brick and black steel of the Hungerford Railroad Bridge.

In addition to Tower Bridge, London is home to another iconic bridge location that is instantly recognizable to millions of people worldwide. The next bridge to the west is Westminster Bridge. In this case, it is not so much the bridge that is instantly recognizable as the view. This is because Westminster Bridge sits a few steps away from the ornate Houses of Parliament, the iconic Big Ben clock tower, and, visible just behind those, Westminster Abbey. Most of the images you will ever see of this complex are either captured from the bridge itself, or include the bridge in the photo.

An earlier version of Westminster Bridge was constructed in 1750, becoming only the second bridge, after London Bridge, crossing the Thames near London. The current Westminster Bridge was constructed in 1862. The bridge is comprised of seven equal-sized, Industrial Age-looking arches constructed of a combination of cast- and wrought-iron. The spandrels have inset quatrefoil shapes surrounding coats-of-arms in between the arch and the deck. The railings have similar trefoil-shaped insets. The enormous lampposts, sitting on carved pink granite bases, continue this theme with intricate metalwork, including a Victoria and Albert monogram centered in a quatrefoil. The metalwork is painted entirely in a dark green except for the lampposts, which have additional highlights in gold.

Being in such a prominent location, it is understandable that both ends of the bridge are decorated with gigantic statues. The large statue on the south bank is known as the Coade Stone Lion and was made in the 1830s. It previously graced the Red Lion Brewery on the south bank, but was moved to this spot after the brewery was demolished to make way for the Royal Festival Hall. On the north landing is an allegorical bronze of Boadicea, a female leader of a revolt of the Britons against the Romans.

The iconic historic and tourist sights of London's West End, including the British Museum, theater district, Trafalgar Square, Houses of Parliament, Westminster Abbey, Downing Street, and Buckingham Palace, are all located a short walk from Westminster Bridge. The intervening area on the north bank of the Thames between Millennium Footbridge and

Westminster Bridge includes Fleet Street, the Strand, and the legal offices of the Royal Courts of Justice and The Temple, but few tourist attraction-type sights.

The redevelopment of the south bank of the Thames has substantially enhanced bridge-walking in this area. The three mile-long Queen's Walk promenade begins south of Westminster, continues around the curve of the Thames east past Millennium, Southwark, and London bridges, and ends at Tower Bridge. The new developments on the south bank opposite Westminster are as popular as those in Southwark and include the London Eye, as well as the complex of concert halls and theaters such as the Royal Festival Hall, Purcell Hall, Queen Elizabeth Hall, and the National Theatre.

Interestingly, because of the sharp curve of the river, the southern ends of Waterloo, Golden Jubilee, and Westminster bridges almost converge on a single spot, which is the London Eye, even though their Victoria Embankment ends are separated by almost a mile. This configuration places these three bridges squarely in the middle of the action, and it would be almost impossible to spend any time visiting London's historic and tourist sights without crossing all three of them to get from one important sight to another. You will not have to go out of your way to walk them, and it would be a shame to not stop to take a quick look at them while doing so.

Completing this bridge tour, from Tower Bridge to Westminster, will take your entire day and be exhausting. However, it is important to note that the bridges do not stop at Westminster. They keep on going. And although they are outside of what is considered the typical tourist center of London, they are just as gorgeous and interesting as the bridges within the center.

Five of these important bridges deserve special mention. Visible just a short distance south of Westminster Bridge are Lambeth Bridge and Vauxhall Bridge. Lambeth Bridge is beautifully painted in pastel pink contrasted with gray. Vauxhall Bridge has large bronze statues on its piers. A longer hike to the west brings you to the adjacent Chelsea and Albert bridges. The Chelsea Bridge is an interesting red and white suspension bridge. Albert Bridge is ornately decorated in pastel shades of blue and green and is the only London bridge that has its original tollhouses intact. Located a few miles to the west and probably best reached by using the Underground, Hammersmith Bridge is one of the most ornately decorated bridges in England. You will need to set aside the better part of another day to see these bridges on the fringes of the tourist area, but they are well worth it.

SEINE BRIDGES, PARIS

Your tour of the bridges of Paris is limited only by your feet and level of determination. Paris covers a large area, even when only considering the central tourist sights. If you just want to take a quick look at some of the bridges you are crossing anyway on your path from one tourist attraction to another, you can choose a mini-tour of those clustered around the Ile de la Citè. Alternatively, you can take a longer tour that includes the historic and sculptural bridges in the tourist center near the Louvre and Champs Elysèes. However, if you actually want to look at bridges for the sake of the bridges, you can venture further, either east or west, and peruse the decorated and modern sculptural bridges along a river length of almost ten miles.

Before beginning, it is interesting to note that one of the major features of the Paris bridges is that many of them are not very interesting. With this prominent location, you might expect a multitude of important historic bridges that are decorated, constructed using innovative engineering or modernistic sculptural designs, and crowded with tourists taking selfies with the Eiffel Tower in the background. And they do, at least two or three within each of these categories. However, these are also intermixed with a very large number of relatively plain-looking, gray, stone arch bridges. These are not without a few interesting features, but this is Paris, after all, and a 300 year-old stone arch bridge that attracts tourists in a smaller town barely registers a blip on the tourist radar here. There are also several interesting iron arch bridges, with decorative open spandrels, dating from the late 1800s. While these are important attractions in smaller cities, Paris has four or five of them. It is almost too much of a good thing.

The greatest concentration is on both sides of the Ile de la Citè and Ile St. Louis, which is also one of the densest concentrations of important tourist sights in Paris. In this area, you are going to be visiting the Hotel d'Ville on the Right Bank, the Latin Quarter on the Left Bank, and Notre Dame and Saint Chappelle on the islands in between. The islands are the historic center of Paris, fortified by the Romans, and the residence of royalty for hundreds of years. In all, there are 13 small bridges clustered here, including five connecting to the Left Bank, five connecting to the Right Bank, two spanning entirely across the islands from one bank to the other, and one connecting the two islands in the middle.

Seven of the bridges connected to the islands are stone arches, including the two oldest bridges in Paris, the Pont Neuf from 1607, and the Pont Marie from 1635. Pont Neuf, discussed in detail in Chapter 2 and the oldest of the Paris bridges, offers some of the most amazing views and displays some of the most unusual decoration, so it is the centerpiece of the entire bridge tour. This prominence is documented by the tens of thousands of love padlocks displayed around the Square du Vert Gallant in the center of the bridge. If you are going to visit just one Paris bridge, this is probably the one.

Although it is about the same age as Pont Neuf, Pont Marie is much smaller and plainer in appearance, with no substantial decoration. The stone arches have niches intended for the placement of small statues, but they are no longer occupied.

The other stone arch bridges connected to the islands are Pont St. Michel, Pont Au Change, Petit Pont, Pont de l'Archevêché, and Pont Louis Phillippe. Each of these locations was the site of an early bridge, in some cases dating back to AD 1000. Although they are later replacements of earlier bridges, the current bridges would still be considered "old", dating from as early as 1828 for Pont de l'Archevêché to 1862 for Pont Louis Phillippe. Many of them have medallion or wreath decorations on their spandrels, above the piers. An eighth bridge, Pont de la Tournelle, appears to be of stone, but it is stone-clad concrete, dating from 1928. It is distinguished, though, by having an enormous statue of St. Geneviève rising from its deck.

Also interesting in this central area are four early iron arch bridges, mostly dating from the mid-1800s. Again, these are historic bridge locations, with the first bridge situated at the location of Pont Notre Dame being the Grand-Pont, constructed prior to AD 887. The current Pont No-tre Dame dates from 1919 and is the most recent of the iron arch bridges. Pont d'Arcole dates from 1856 and was the first bridge in Paris to be constructed on an arch from bank to bank, with no piers in the river. Pont Au Double, from 1847, has an extremely prominent location, as it leads directly from the Left Bank into the plaza in front of Notre Dame Cathedral. The name is carried over from its predecessors at this location, which charged a toll of a double denier to cross. Pont de Sully was constructed in 1876. It is actually two separate bridges crossing the eastern tip of the Ile St. Louis and provides access to a riverfront park, the Square Barye, facing the boats coming into Paris from upstream.

All of the iron bridges have decorative cast ironwork in their open spandrels and on their railings, some more than others. The most intricate is that on Pont Notre Dame, which includes fluted columns and scrolls on the vertical supports in its open spandrel and gorgeous scrolls and leaves attracting padlocks on its railing. Pont Au Double is relatively restrained in its cast-iron ornamentation, but is distinctive for its deep copper color.

The thirteenth bridge in the group is one of the least historic of the Paris bridges. This is the Pont St. Louis, constructed in 1970 to provide a pedestrian-only connection between the two islands. It is a plain, un-adorned steel-girder bridge with little visual attraction. However, it has a few features that result in it being one of the most crowded tourist bridges in Paris.

As the only bridge that connects the two islands, the Pont St. Louis may be the most centrally located bridge in the city with respect to the funneling of pedestrian traffic from one important tourist sight to another. However, tourists use it for more than walking between the islands. Of the bridges used to access the Ile de la Citè from the Right Bank of the Seine, this is the only one that offers an unobstructed view of the flying buttresses of Notre Dame. More than a few tourists crossing it find that they must stop and stare for a while. This prominent location has also resulted in the bridge becoming the main stage for street performers in Paris. As a result, it is overrun by tourists, especially in nice weather.

You are probably not going to limit your Paris vacation to the Ile de la Citè. At a minimum, you will be visiting the Louvre and Champs Elysèes, which are located further west. Other sights in this area include the Musèe d'Orsay, Tuileries, Assemblèe Nationale, Place de la Concorde, and Grand Palais. There are six important tourist bridges between the Ile de la Citè and the Grand Palais. In this area, the two branches of the Seine that pass around the islands have rejoined, so the river is wider and the bridges are much longer.

The first bridge downstream of the Ile de la Citè, and a prominent part of the iconic view from its tip, is the Pont des Arts. This is possibly the best known of the Paris bridges, at least from depictions in movies, TV shows, and guidebooks. The current bridge was built in 1984, and appears to be a perfect example of the recent trend of building bridges in the form of modern sculpture. It has the weightless, gravity-defying look. It has the unusual engineering. It has the iconic location leading to the eastern end of the Louvre. It has the iconic views of Pont Neuf. It is pedestrian-only.

It is stunning, then, to admire it and realize it was originally built, in almost this exact form, in 1803. The bridge is a perfect example of how beautiful architecture and technology can be. A narrow, pedestrian-only bridge, the structure is a series of steel-ribbed arches. On some arch bridges, the space between the arch and the deck, known as the spandrel, is a solid wall. These are closed-spandrel bridges. On others, the space consists of vertical supports or mini-arches sitting on the main arch, and extending up to support the deck above. These are known as open-spandrels, and this space is often used for decorative purposes. On the Pont des Arts, the space is almost completely open, being spanned only by a few curved, flimsy-looking steel ribs. This web appears to be too light and fluffy to be able to hold itself up, let alone the masses of tourists crossing at any given time.

Of the six bridges situated between the Ile de la Citè and the Grand Palais, two are extremely old stone bridges. In less prominent tourist cities, a graceful series of five stone arches built in 1689, such as the Pont Royal, might be a major tourist attraction. In Paris, it is just another bridge carrying cars and trucks past the western end of the Louvre. The Pont de la Concorde, providing the ceremonial entrance into the Place de la Concorde and the Champs Elysèes, was built in 1791. These two bridges are unadorned and appear to be plain, but become much more interesting once you ponder their size and age.

Possibly the least interesting bridge in this area, situated between the Pont des Arts and the Pont Royal, is the Pont du Carrousel, but even this bridge is charming. It is a concrete bridge faced with stone, built in 1937. It is also one of the few Paris bridges on which the ends expand into an inviting pedestrian plaza graced with sculptures and decorative lampposts. Although the current bridge is not old, it displays four allegorical statues of the Seine, City of Paris, Abundance, and Industry from an earlier bridge dating from 1847. The plaza on the northern end highlights the entrance under a ceremonial arch into the Place du Carrousel, where you will find the famous glass pyramidal entrance to the Louvre.

Between the Pont Royal and the Pont de la Concorde is another sculptural, modern pedestrian bridge, the Passerelle Lèopold-Sèdar-Senghor. Named after the first president of Senegal, the Passerelle Senghor was built in 1999 of steel I-beam construction. The Passerelle Senghor is not adorned with decoration. However, the functionality of the bridge is extremely unusual.

The riverfront along the Seine in central Paris has two levels, with the quays at street level being about 20 feet higher than the walkways along the river. Except for the Passerelle Senghor, all of the Seine bridges extend from quay to quay, and the lower river level can only be accessed by occasional stairways that punctuate the walls that confine the river. The Passerelle Senghor, though, acts as six bridges in one. From a distance, you can only see the curve of the upper deck extending from quay to quay. Underneath the curve is a complicated substructure that does not obviously reveal how the deck is supported. Once you are on it, though, you can see what is going on. Below the main deck, in the middle of the bridge, is a second lower deck extending from river level on one side to river level on the other side. This lower arch has much steeper sides than the upper arch so that the apex of each arch meets in the middle of the bridge.

With this unusual construction, you can cross the bridge from quay to quay, riverside to riverside, or from a quay on one side to the riverside on the other, and vice-versa. The lower deck on the northern end is even more complex, as it does more than just exit to the right or left onto the riverwalk. In addition to right and left options, the lower deck also leads directly through an archway under the quay into the gardens of the Tuileries. While the complexity of the structure detracts from its aesthetics when viewed from a distance, the effect becomes charming once you are on the bridge and get a chance to see how it works.

The upper deck of Passerelle Senghor is deliberately designed for comfort, as a place where you just want to hang out for a while. The deck is made of wooden planks, and although it is not obvious to just read about it, this is immediately comforting on your feet the minute you step onto it. After pounding the pavement in Paris all day, the slight give of the wood is noticeably comfortable. The wood theme also extends to the numerous benches placed on the bridge, which was obviously designed to be a gathering and resting place as much as it was a way to cross the river.

The western end of this area is the Pont Alexandre III. The curious dedication of the bridge to the Russian Czar and the over-the-top decoration are discussed in Chapter 4. Like several of the other bridges in Paris, the location of Pont Alexandre III is as much ceremonial as it is functional. The highlight of the 1889 Exposition was the Eiffel Tower on the Left Bank, which was such a hit that the Parisians decided to leave it in place rather than take it down, as intended. A similar highlight of the 1900 Exposition was the modernistic glass domes of the Grand Palais and Petit Palais on the Champs Elysèes. Again intended as a temporary attraction, both buildings are still major landmarks more than 100 years later. Also built in 1900, the Pont Alexandre III effectively connected the new Grand Palais and Petit Palais to the Esplanade des Invalides, Champ de Mars, and Eiffel Tower. In this position, the sidewalks on the bridge are a terrific place to enjoy views of all of these landmarks from one place.

The Pont Alexandre III and the Grand Palais are probably not the western end of your tourist visit to Paris. From the Pont Alexandre III, you can see the Eiffel Tower beckoning to you in the distance. But that is the problem—it is in the distance. It is directly on the river and at the base of an interesting tourist bridge. Nobody could blame you if, at this point, you start trying to figure out how to use the Metropolitan to get around. If you do decide to take the subway and skip the bridges, you will actually not miss much. However, if you decide to walk the additional two miles along the river, there are a few bridges on the way.

The first, just a short walk to the other side of the Grand Palais from the Pont Alexandre III, is the Pont des Invalides. Built in 1854, it has allegorical statues of Victory on Sea and Victory on Land on its piers. The Pont de l'Alma is a relatively unattractive steel-girder bridge built in 1972. This was the location of a previous bridge in 1854, and one of the original statues from that bridge, a depiction of Zuave, a force that participated in the Battle of the Alma in the Crimea, is displayed on one of its piers at river level. The Pont de l'Alma attracts a large number of visitors to its northern end, where a replica of the flame of the Statue of Liberty was installed in 1987. However, the tourists are not attracted by the flame. They are attracted because the flame has become a memorial to Princess Diana, who died in a car crash in the tunnel below the bridge. Further along is the Passerelle Debilly, an attractive pedestrian-only steel arch bridge built in 1900.

Finally, after your two-mile hike, you will reach the Pont d'Iema at the base of the Eiffel Tower. A stone arch bridge built in 1814, this bridge has monuments on all four corners, with allegorical equestrian statues of the Gallic Warrior, Roman Warrior, Greek Warrior, and Arab Warrior. The spandrel of the bridge displays eagles surrounded by laurel crowns. However, most important is the way the bridge serves as a prominent corridor between the Eiffel Tower on the Left Bank and the Trocadero on the Right Bank. At Pont Alexandre III, the view of the Eiffel Tower is eye-catching, and at each successive bridge along the way, it becomes larger and more prominent. The view of its base, though, is always blocked by the surrounding buildings. Once you arrive at the Pont d'Iema, you can see the entire structure from base to top, and it is enormous. In a city where millions of selfies are taken every year, this may be the spot that sets the record for most selfies.

If you do decide to take the subway instead of walking to the Eiffel Tower, you will probably choose the Champs de Mars Station. If so, and if you want to squeeze in one more bridge, the Pont de Bir-Hakeim is situated near the station. This is a very decorative two-level bridge. The open-spandrel iron arch was constructed in 1878 and displays eight elaborate cast sculptures of blacksmiths and boatmen on its piers at river level. The second level, which carries trains, was added in 1904. The central pier of the bridge rests on the northern end of an island and opens into a pedestrian plaza with a large allegorical sculpture representing Renaissance France, dating from 1930. This plaza is another location with a close-up, unobstructed view of the Eiffel Tower.

There are far fewer tourist attractions on the eastern end of the tour upstream of the Ile St. Louis, and you will probably not be venturing in that direction unless you want to see a few interesting bridges. The first two to the east display some attractive decorations. The Pont d'Austerlitz, an 1854 stone arch bridge, is decorated on its spandrel, above the piers, with allegorical flags, ivy branches, faces, and lions' heads. The 1904 Viaduc Austerlitz is a railroad bridge carrying trains into the Gare Austerlitz and is not walkable. However, it is worth stopping on the quay for a look. The bridge is an iron superstructure truss, with gorgeous, molded iron decoration on the arch and carved stone decoration on the buttresses. Further on, the Pont de Bercy is similar to Pont de Bir-Hakeim. It is a decorated stone arch bridge constructed in 1864, but with a second level added for trains in 1906.

The highlights, though, and the bridges that make it worth your time to venture this far, are two modernistic sculptural bridges, the Pont Charles de Gaulle and Passerelle Simone de Beauvoir. Pont Charles de Gaulle, built in 1994, is discussed in more detail in Chapter 5. It seems plain in appearance, until you notice how it was designed to appear weightless. If you do not want to walk the two miles from the Notre Dame area, you can visit it by taking the Metropolitan to Gare Austerlitz.

The final bridge is the Passerelle Simone de Beauvoir, constructed in 2006. This bridge is similar in function to the Passerelle Senghor in that it provides access to multiple levels on a single bridge. At Passerelle Senghor, the bridge accesses both river level and quay level. At Passerelle Simone de Beauvoir, the bridge does not access river level, although there are stairs and elevators on both ends to allow this access. Instead, the National Library of France and the Parc de Bercy, on each end of the bridge, are both located on elevated bluffs that are higher than the riverside highway. As a result, the lower level of the bridge accesses the highway and quay level, while the upper level accesses the library and the park.

One unusual feature of the historic traffic bridges in Paris is that, with only one exception, they are all still carrying traffic a hundred or more years later. There are many examples, such as the Old Dee Bridge in Chester, of historic bridges from as early as the 1300s still carrying traffic 700 years later. Far more often, though, they have been closed to traffic and converted to pedestrian-only use.

Paris seems to be an anomaly in that they have continued to use almost all of their old traffic bridges. In all, there are 18 bridges in the city dating from before 1900. Three of these are extremely old, dating from the 1600s. Yet of these 18, 17 still carry traffic today. Only one, the Pont Au Double dating from 1847, has been closed and converted to pedestrian-only use after a long career carrying traffic. That closure was not due to structural weakness, but to the conversion of the entire area in front of Notre Dame into a pedestrian plaza.

Your trip to Paris is going to include a great deal of outdoor city walking. Parks, monuments, towers, gardens, cafes, boulevards, walks along the river. More than four miles of river from Notre Dame on the east to either the Eiffel Tower or Arc de Triomphe to the west, with something amazing to see almost every step of the way in between.

Moreover, these sights are evenly distributed on both banks of the river. To do all of this, you are going to be crossing these bridges anyway. Take a few minutes to stop and look at them. Many of your most amazing views of the city are found on these bridges, because they allow you to get free of Haussmann's view-blocking apartment blocks. Ponder a little about their history—Czars honoring their parents here, kings being guillotined there. Read a little bit about them in advance, so you know what you are seeing. Plan your comings and goings so you get to see all of them instead of just crossing the same one each time. While you are at it, cross underneath to admire the clever engineering and look at details of the decorations. Pause on top to look at the statues or admire the great variety of padlocks that have been attached. It will not require you to go far out of your way to check them out, and you have to find a place to sit and rest your feet anyway.

CHICAGO RIVER BRIDGES

Chicago is most definitely not an obvious location for bridge touring. In most vintage travel posters of the downtown landmarks, there is not a bridge in sight. Driving on interstate highways through the city or flying into the airports, you will not see any bridges, and you will not see any substantial rivers or harbors to be bridged. Even driving around downtown, visiting the museums, theaters, skyscrapers, and other urban attractions, you can be forgiven for not noticing that a few of the city blocks between stoplights are slightly longer than the others. Even if you look down instead of up, and it registers that there is a narrow, almost insignificant stream flowing through the middle of the city, you will probably not leap to a logical conclusion that this results in tourist bridges.

Another enigma in Chicago is that the reason for the development of an enormous city at this location is not obvious. In other cities, the reason can often be figured out with a little thought, especially after reviewing maps or considering the view from a walkable bridge. The city will have a substantial natural harbor to support shipping, like New York or London. Or the city will have natural barriers that serve a defensive purpose, such as an island in Paris or cliffs in Luxembourg. The regional topography, maybe the locations of mountain passes, would have governed the locations of major overland trade routes. Such is the case for Geneva and Lucerne. Or a river may have provided an important energy source to drive mills, as resulted in the siting of cities like Wilmington, Minneapolis, and Strasbourg. Maybe a bridge was built just because there was something pretty to look at, like at Niagara Falls.

Chicago has none of these. No natural harbor. No natural defenses. No historic trade routes. No river flow that is sufficient to drive mills. And certainly no scenic waterfalls. It is located on the shoreline of one of the Great Lakes, but the Great Lakes have hundreds of miles of shoreline with no other cities of this scale. Why did the city develop at this particular point on the shoreline?

What this location had in the 1830s was the Chicago River, only a hundred feet or so wide and a few miles long. It was flat, with a very small watershed, so the water was stagnant most of the time. It was almost completely silted in where it entered Lake Michigan. It was barely different from hundreds of other creeks and small rivers that flow into Lake Michigan from all sides. It had just one difference, really, but one that was not obvious.

French fur traders learned from the local natives that they could canoe from the lake up the river for about a mile inland. There, where two branches join, they could turn left and continue a few miles further up the South Branch to a swamp named Mud Lake. At Mud Lake, they could drag their canoes over the mud for a mile or two. At that point, they could put their canoes back into flowing water, this time in the Des Plaines River. Still not much of a river, but with an important difference. Instead of flowing east into Lake Michigan, the Des Plaines flowed west. Into the Illinois River. Then, into the Mississippi River. And then south to the Gulf of Mexico. Or, if desired, upstream on the Missouri River all the way to Montana. Or into one of many other tributaries, such as the Ohio or the Arkansas. With this short portage at Mud Lake, the Chicago River unlocked the passage between the Great Lakes and the entire mass of land between the Appalachians and the Rockies. The Great Lakes, in turn, were connected to the Atlantic Ocean through the St. Lawrence River, or through the Erie Canal to the Hudson.

In the 1830s, this connection effectively doubled the size of the country that could be easily explored and exploited. Once this was understood, Chicago turned from an insignificant backwater into a major city almost overnight. The rest of the story of the river is entirely about hydraulic engineering. Improvement of the harbor. Construction of a shallow canal, the Illinois and Michigan (I&M) Canal, across Mud Lake. The reconstruction of the I&M as a deeper, wider canal to accommodate larger ships. The use of the canal to divert sewage and industrial wastes from the growing city into the Des Plaines River instead of Lake Michigan, which served as the city's water supply. The construction of a parallel canal, the Sanitary and Shipping Canal, which reversed the flow of the Chicago River forever. Even today, the river does not flow a few city blocks to the east to discharge into the lake. It flows west to the Mississippi.

You will not see any of this while visiting downtown Chicago. Not from the Riverwalk, the bridges, or even the river tour boats. You will not see any evidence of the old canals, which are several miles west of downtown. The ocean-going ships, which used to sail directly through downtown, have long since been diverted into yet another canal, this one using the Calumet River instead of the Chicago. You will see a few canoes, but they are no longer paddled by French fur traders. To understand the role that the river played in the settling and growth of the city, you will have to read one of the available books on the subject, of which there are many.

All that remains is the narrow, sleepy little river, still flowing in the wrong direction. And bridges. Dozens of them. Almost all of them historic, dating back to before the 1940s. Almost all of them interesting for the clever engineering of their drawspans. Almost all of them embellished with gorgeous architectural flourishes. And most of them offering stunning, up-close views of 100 years' worth of early skyscraper architecture.

An important logistical note, before you begin your walking tour, is that it is going to be a long one. You are going to walk over, under, around, and through 18 bridges along a river length of two miles. At some point, you are going to get tired. They are going to start looking the same. You are going to see that the next bridge is unappealingly modern. You are going to wonder if this is ever going to end. You are going to decide that you have had a great bridge tour, but that you have seen enough. Nevertheless, keep going. Every time you think you have seen all that is worth seeing, there will be another treat just past the next bridge.

The general configuration of the river, and therefore the bridge tour, comprises two segments: the Main Branch and the South Branch. The tour begins at the lakefront, where the Main Branch enters Lake Michigan, with Grant Park along the lakefront to the south and Navy Pier extending into the lake on the north. From this point, the Main Branch of the river is oriented directly east-west, cutting downtown into northern and southern halves, but sunken 15 feet below street level. There are nine bridges along this Main Branch segment, including Lakeshore Drive, Columbus Drive, Michigan Avenue/DuSable, Wabash Avenue, State Street, Dearborn Street, Clark Street, LaSalle Street, and Wells Street.

Along the entire Main Branch, there are buildings directly on the north bank of the river. In some cases, these buildings have accessible sidewalks at river level, but in most cases they do not, so you need to walk up to the next cross-street to go around the building to go from bridge to bridge on the north side.

In contrast, the south bank of the Main Branch is bordered by Wacker Drive, with no buildings directly on the river. Along the south bank, you can walk along the river from bridge to bridge either on the sidewalk at street level, or on the Riverwalk at river level. To access the bridges to walk across them, you need to be at street level. However, the landscaped Riverwalk goes directly under all of them, so it is a wonderful experience on its own.

About a mile west of the lake, the river splits into the North and South Branches at a location called Wolf Point. There are some bridges on the North Branch, and you can visit them if you have extra time. However, the main attractions are on the South Branch, which extends south from Wolf Point. Franklin Street Bridge, diagonal to the road grid, is located directly at Wolf Point, and then the South Branch bridges include Lake Street, Randolph Street, Washington Boulevard, Madison Street, Monroe Street, Adams Street, Jackson Boulevard, and Van Buren Street.

Following the river is a little more difficult on the South Branch. In this segment, there are buildings directly on the river on both the east and west banks, so there is no single sidewalk or riverwalk that extends the entire length of the segment. The best way to walk along the river to get from bridge to bridge is sometimes on the east and sometimes on the west. However, in a few cases, there is no access along the river on either side and you need to go up to the streetlight, around the building, and then cut back to the river to continue the walk.

Now, some general similarities and differences between the bridges. They are all moveable, which was necessary in the early twentieth century when ocean-going ships still used this little river almost a thousand miles from the ocean. Most of them are double-leaf bascule drawbridges, although there are differences in the specific type of design.

A particularly pleasing feature is that, although they were constructed across a period of almost a century, they were designed with a uniformity of appearance. They are almost all the exact same size in terms of length, width, and height above the river. They are all about 200 feet long, either two or four traffic lanes wide, and about 15 feet above river level. In addition, they are mostly flat and level with the surrounding city streets, since the entire downtown area was raised above river level in the 1850s to avoid flooding. The only exceptions to this are Wells Street and Lake Street, which are double-decked to carry the "L" commuter rail tracks, and Lakeshore, which is double-decked to carry a major roadway. Also, the structure of each bridge is composed of riveted steel girders, all painted the same shade of rust-red, and framed between light-colored stone abutments on the riverbanks. Each bridge also has the name of its cross-street emblazoned on both sides in gold letters on a black background. Although this might sound boring, with the bridges deliberately designed to appear similar to each other, it actually displays a pleasing, unifying theme.

To operate the drawspans, each bridge has one or more small tender houses, usually about 15 feet square and 20 feet high, situated on the street corners. These tender houses are frequently the only part of the bridge that is visible to passing cars, and studying the variety of their architecture and decoration is one of the pleasures of the bridge tour. Each bridge has a unique story and many have more than one name. Explanations of these, along with various dedications to famous persons and events, are provided on historical plaques displayed on the sides of the tender houses.

Another difference between the bridges is the variety of the architecture in the surrounding city buildings, ranging from the sparkling white diagonals of the Wrigley Building to the sleek black glass of the Willis Tower, still known to most of us by its old name, the Sears Tower.

This bridge tour description is not going to give a detailed bridge-by-bridge account of every bridge. Similar to the river, websites and books that provide details about the bridges are available. The best source of information, though, is the McCormick Bridgehouse Museum, hidden within one of the tender houses on the DuSable Bridge. This little museum not only has informative displays discussing the river and its bridges, but is also your chance to see the inner workings of one of the tender houses. If you have come to Chicago to walk across bridges, your visit is not complete without going inside one.

The best starting point for the bridge tour is the Lakeshore Drive Bridge, which is situated where a complex of locks raise and lower boats between the river and Lake Michigan. The bridge was built in the 1930s and is a complex, industrial-looking red steel truss drawbridge flanked by four white stone and blue glass tender houses. The upper deck carries the main through-lanes of Lakeshore Drive, the primary north-south artery on the east side of downtown. The lower level is at normal street level, with exits at either end of the bridge to funnel traffic into downtown to the west, or onto the Navy Pier area to the north.

Given its prime location at the lakefront, the Lakeshore Drive Bridge deserves some exploring. A good place to start is Ogden Slip, a small branch of the river extending a few blocks into downtown, parallel to the river on its north side. This area was formerly an important space for commercial docks and has since been redeveloped into an isolated, tree-lined, parklike haven with condos and shops. The Lakeshore Drive Bridge actually has two segments. The portion over the river is the original, 1930s-vintage movable bridge, while the portion over Ogden Slip is a modern cement beam bridge. From Ogden Slip, signs lead under the cement-beam extension toward Navy Pier. Once on the lakeside, stairs lead up to the pedestrian sidewalk on the lower deck of the modern bridge. This sidewalk then connects directly to the sidewalk on the older portion of the bridge. There are no pedestrian sidewalks on the upper decks.

The walk across the bridge on the lower deck is unusual in that bridge walks are usually wide-open, outdoor experiences. In contrast, this walk is in a dark, semi-confined space among the diagonal red steel girders. Because this is a movable bridge, the deck is made of a steel mesh, and cars passing at high speed make the distinctive rumbling sound commonly heard on these bridges. However, the rumbling sound is magnified because of the confined space. There is a great view of Navy Pier, Grant Park, and the lake from the sidewalk. However, be aware that this narrow sidewalk also carries the Chicago Lakefront Trail, or LFT, a popular 18 mile-long jogging and biking trail. Any attempt to stop to admire the views or take pictures during your walk is likely to result in hurled epithets, especially on sunny summer weekends.

On the southern end of the bridge, a ramp carries the LFT down to river and lake level in Grant Park, which occupies the area between Lakeshore Drive and the lake. Doubling back toward the river, you will find that excellent views of the bridge and its tender houses, silhouetted against downtown skyscrapers, can be had from the hiking and biking paths in the park. Continuing along the waterfront back toward the bridge, there is a sculpture/pavilion-type structure made of cement walls and sky-blue steel arches extending under the bridge. This structure, built in 2000 as the Riverwalk Gateway, acts as the connection between Grant Park and the Riverwalk, which follows the river for more than a mile along the southern edge of the Main Branch. Once you pass through the Gateway, you leave the area of open-air parks along the lake and enter the sunken, semi-isolated river world surrounded by skyscrapers and bridges.

Continuing west along the Riverwalk, the first bridge you come to will be Columbus Drive Bridge. This is one of the newest of them, dating from 1982. It is sleek and modern in appearance, with smooth gray granite abutments and a tender house framing a smooth, sweeping red-steel arch that hides most of the counterweight and mechanical components of the bridge. Columbus Drive Bridge has stairs on all four corners leading down to river level. On the south end, stairs lead to the Riverwalk, and on the north end, they lead to a small riverside plaza that is the location of the Centennial Fountain.

The next bridge to the west should probably be considered the architectural and historic epicenter of the bridge tour and of Chicago as a whole. The bridge here is the Michigan Avenue Bridge, also named the DuSable Bridge after Chicago's first non-native settler. The DuSable Bridge is located at the former location of Fort Dearborn, constructed in 1803 at what was, at that time, the mouth of the river. The outline of the original fort is recorded in bronze plaques on the sidewalk around the corners of Michigan Avenue and Wacker Drive.

In the early twentieth century, Michigan Avenue was designed to be a grand boulevard, the Magnificent Mile, housing the most prominent buildings and homes in the city. The most well-known today is the Wrigley Building on the northern bank of the river. The bridge and the Wrigley Building were constructed at about the same time, in 1920, and both incorporated decorative elements. The angled tiers and clock tower of the Wrigley Building are one of the major landmarks of Chicago and, by being located directly on the river, the views are not blocked by other buildings. The best place to view the building is from the Riverwalk on the opposite bank, which also provides a great view of the bridge. The northern end of the bridge is actually a plaza that is combined with the plaza at the front entrance to the Wrigley Building and, across the street, the Tribune Tower.

The entire bridge complex is crawling with a variety of carved marble reliefs, bronze reliefs, and bronze plaques celebrating various historic occurrences and achievements in Chicago. Some of these are located on the tender houses at the ends of the bridge, some are located on the bridge itself, and some are located on the sidewalk plazas at either end. In no particular order, these include: several dedications for the original opening and multiple reopenings of the bridge; Fort Dearborn; the reversal of the Chicago River; the use of the river by Marquette, LaSalle, and Jolliet in the seventeenth century to reach the Mississippi (no fewer than three separate elaborate plaques!); the use of bridges as symbols in literature (placed by the Friends of Libraries); regeneration of the city after the Great Fire; and Chicago as the location of more movable bridges than any other city in the world. There are even bronze plaques dedicating the 1992 and 2009 renovations to Frank Paschen and Harry Paschen. No statement of who Frank and Harry are, just that the renovations in those years were dedicated to them.

In addition to being the historic center of Chicago and locus for dedications of all sorts, the DuSable Bridge is also unusual in its construction. The bridge's drawspan deck is one of four double-level drawbridges on this bridge tour. In the case of Wells Street, Lake Street, and Lakeshore Drive, the second level is elevated above normal street level to carry trains or through traffic above the street-level bustle of the city. In the case of DuSable, the second level is sunken down below normal street level, connecting the mysterious subterranean world of Lower Wacker Drive on the south side with an equivalent underworld on the north side. This lower deck is also walkable, making it necessary to cross DuSable four times to fully investigate all of the inner workings and outer views of the bridge.

The DuSable Bridge also has the most ornate tender houses on this bridge tour. Most of the tender houses on the river are simple structures with understated decoration, except for some differences in their style of roof. At DuSable, the four tender houses are small monument-like stone buildings with multiple levels of windows, topped by carved stone urns and faced with fantastic, allegorical carved stone reliefs.

Another attraction of the DuSable Bridge is the McCormick Bridgehouse Museum. The Bridgehouse Museum is entered directly from the Riverwalk, at the base of the tender house on the southeast corner of the bridge. The displays inside discuss the development of the river, its significance in providing a link between the Great Lakes and the Mississippi, and the history of the bridges.

Although the displays are informative, the biggest attraction is the ability to explore the inside of one of the tender houses. It has a very small floor area, but is six levels high. The entrance, from the Riverwalk, is on the lowest level and features an up-close experience with the motors and gears used to raise the drawspan. Two levels up, at street level, large ornate circular windows provide a unique view of the bridge toward the Wrigley Building. Three more levels up, at the top, three rectangular windows on each wall provide an elevated view of the bridge and river.

The fourth bridge from the lake, Wabash Avenue Bridge, is a good place to compare and contrast the different types of bridges on the Chicago River. To this point, Lakeshore, Columbus, and DuSable are all of relatively unusual construction. Lakeshore and DuSable are both double-level bridges and Columbus Drive, being a newer bridge, has been constructed so that its abutments and arch-shaped steel girders hide the counterweights and mechanical systems. As a result, the structure and mechanics of these are not as easy to study and compare as the rest of the bridges.

Starting with Wabash Avenue, almost all the bridges fall easily into one of two categories: the bascule trunnion bridge, or the Scherzer rolling lift bridge. In the bascule trunnion bridge, the truss support is below the deck. Therefore, the walk on these bridges is wide open, with no superstructure blocking your views or separating you from the passing traffic. On the Scherzer rolling lift bridges, the truss is partially above the bridge deck, usually situated between the roadway and the sidewalks. In general, the bascule trunnion bridges look and feel cleaner and less cluttered, although the Scherzer bridges have a certain charm with their sweeping curved steel girders above the deck.

The next three, including Wabash Avenue, State Street, and Dearborn Street, are all bascule trunnion bridges. Wabash Avenue, also named the Irv Kupcinet Bridge after a *Chicago Sun-Times* columnist, was built in 1930. State Street, also called the Bataan-Corregidor Memorial Bridge in honor of the World War II battle, dates from 1949, although bridges have been at this location since 1864. Dearborn Street is the location of the first movable bridge in Chicago, which dated from 1834. The current bridge dates from 1963, but except for the more modern appearance of the tender house, it appears exactly the same as the Wabash Avenue and State Street bridges.

The prominent feature of the walk over these three bridges is the varied architecture of the surrounding skyscrapers. At the southern end of Wabash Avenue Bridge is the Jewelers Building, a gorgeous, tiered building dating from the mid-1920s. Of the same era, just to the east toward the lake, is the Mather Tower, famous for the slender octagonal shape of its top 21 floors. For something completely different, look across to the north side of the river to the two Marina Towers, dating from the mid-1960s, which appear to have been inspired by the shape of the corncob. Some other exploration is recommended in this area. Wabash Avenue and State Street house the Chicago Theater District, with several major theaters visible both north and south of the river. There are also several jazz and blues clubs nearby. On the Riverwalk, between Wabash and State, is the Chicago Vietnam Veterans Memorial.

Starting at Wabash Avenue, the general shape of the tender houses becomes similar. They are all square in shape. The only exceptions are Madison Street and Monroe Street, which are more ornate, being eight-sided. There is always an entrance door at street level and a second level composed mostly of glass windows to allow the operator to see what is going on below. The lower floor is usually composed of a light-colored stone (white granite, sandstone, or limestone), although Dearborn Street is a red granite, and Washington Boulevard is decoratively painted red and green. The lower floor always has historical plaques, and, in many cases, a bronze bell, used in the early days to signal that the bridge was about to open. Above the second-floor windows, the older tender houses are capped by either an ornate gray metal hood or a carved stone faux-shingle roof. The exact shape and color of the caps vary from bridge to bridge, with some having convex edges and some concave, and some being more ornate than others. The tender houses on the newer bridges (Dearborn Street, Randolph Street, and Van Buren Street) have flat tops.

The next two, dating from 1928 and 1929, are Clark Street and LaSalle Street. These are both Scherzer rolling lift bridges and, therefore, have prominent curved steel girders as a superstructure. Most of the bridges have boring straight vertical bars of red steel serving as their railings. However, a few of them have an attractive, decorative design built into their railings, usually a flower motif. These are found on DuSable, LaSalle Street, Franklin Street, and Madison Street. On most of these, the design is relatively restrained, but those on LaSalle Street are gigantic, in-your-face sunflowers.

The next bridge past LaSalle Street is Wells Street Bridge, dating from 1922. This is a double-deck steel truss bridge that carries cars at street level, and trains of the "L" on an upper level. Lake Street Bridge, which dates from 1916, is just around the corner on the South Branch, and is almost identical to the Wells Street Bridge.

Between Wells Street and Lake Street, running diagonally across the Main Branch, is the 1920 Franklin Street Bridge, another Scherzer rolling lift bridge. Along with the flower-shaped designs on its railings, Franklin Street has carved granite balustrades at the ends of its tender houses. Dominating the view from the Franklin Street Bridge is the Merchandise Mart building on the north bank. At 17 stories high, the Merchandise Mart is not nearly as tall as the surrounding skyscrapers, but it covers two full city blocks, and is quite a sight. Built in 1930 as the wholesale warehouse for Marshall Field, it was, at the time, the largest building in the world in terms of floor space.

Turning the corner past the Lake Street Bridge, you enter the South Branch segment of the bridge walk. This is where the bridges might start looking similar, and you might start walking faster. Randolph Street Bridge dates from 1984 and is not particularly interesting. Washington Boulevard is a Scherzer bridge dating from 1913, and Madison Street is a bascule trunnion from 1922. Although Washington Boulevard has interesting red- and green-painted tender houses, and Madison Street has flower motifs on the railings, both bridges look suspiciously like those you saw an hour ago. However, another decorative building from the 1920s, the Civic Opera Building, makes this area worth investigating.

Along the South Branch, there are buildings between Wacker Drive and the river, so there is no sidewalk or riverwalk. The buildings on the east bank, including the Civic Opera Building, rise straight out of the water. And instead of facing the river, as they do on the Main Branch, the front entrances of these buildings are on Wacker Drive, so they effectively present their backsides to the river and the bridges. The buildings on the west bank, however, do face the river. Most prominent among these, directly opposite from the Civic Opera, between Washington Boulevard and Madison Street, is the Two North Riverside Plaza Building. Another gigantic, decorative white stone structure from the 1920s, this building has an attractive, landscaped plaza along the river. Take away the modern skyscrapers in the view and this spot must have been incredibly impressive around 1928, with the enormous white buildings hovering over the bridges.

Just past Madison Street is the 1919 Monroe Street Bridge, the last of the Scherzer rolling lift bridges. Many of the bridges you have crossed on this tour are interesting for their surroundings, views, or unique engineering. The Monroe Street Bridge, more than any of the others, is just a nice, lovely little bridge that would be worth visiting in any city. While there may be an interesting superstructure on one bridge, a decorative railing on another, and a unique tender house on a third, Monroe Street brings all of these interesting elements onto one bridge. Instead of being simple square boxes, the tender houses on Monroe Street are little multi-sided sculptures with textured stonework and ornately carved stone capitals. Being a Scherzer bridge, this is a perfect place to admire the sweeping curve of the red steel girders that separate the sidewalk from the traffic lanes. The railings are gorgeous cast-metal panels with a flower as the central motif. Unique among the Chicago River bridges, little decorative streetlamps are mounted on top of the railing posts. These are only about 18 inches high, but each is composed of red steel sculpted with a wave motif, with the open spaces filled with frosted glass.

After Monroe Street, you are approaching the end, so you might as well finish. Adams Street, Jackson Boulevard, and Van Buren Street are all bascule trunnion bridges. Jackson, dating from 1915, has a plaque indicating the Strauss Bascule Bridge Company patent number, dating from 1911. Van Buren, the end of the tour, is relatively modern, dating from 1957. However, it is worth getting there, as this is the only bridge that provides a view of the Willis Tower, and it is a great view. A view of this iconic building from anywhere else in Chicago is incomplete, because you can only see the top floors rising above the surrounding skyscrapers. Van Buren Street Bridge is perhaps the only vantage point in the entire city from which you can view the entire building, from the sidewalk to the top.

From Van Buren Street, you will see the next set of bridges further to the south and, similar to the North Branch, you can keep going if you choose. Some of those are old, many are railroad-only bridges, and others are modern. However, you will see that this is a logical ending point for the main part of the bridge tour. While the next bridge to the south, Congress Parkway Bridge, is not far, it cannot be easily accessed by walking on sidewalks along the river. The bridge structure is gray instead of rust red, and the bridge does not have the trademark gold-letter-on-black-background sign on its side. These indicate that Van Buren is the end of the bridges included within the unified design that ties the bridge tour together.

Early spring and early fall are the two best seasons for walking the Chicago River bridges, and not due to the obvious reason of favorable weather. It is because you want to visit, if at all possible, during sailboat migration season. The opening function of the bridges is seldom used anymore now that the large ships use a different route between Lake Michigan and the Mississippi. This is a common fate for moveable bridges, which are left largely disused after their original purpose is no longer needed. However, even though the commercial ships are gone, the pleasure boats are still there, and many of these are too large to sail under the bridges. These boats are kept in marinas on the lake during the season but are stored in protected shipyards along the South Branch during the winter. Every spring, typically on Wednesdays and Saturdays, the bridges open to allow flocks of sailboats out to the lake, and the process is repeated, in the opposite direction, between September and November. As long as you are intent on walking the bridges, you might as well plan your trip to catch this amazing sight.

BOAT TOURS

Almost all of the walking tours discussed above are also available as boat tours of their respective cities. So which should you do? What are the advantages and disadvantages of doing a walking tour of the bridges versus a boat tour?

The most important distinction, and the one that probably drives the decision for most casual bridgespotters, is the effort required. Walking tours require substantial effort, while boat tours require none. You can put together an amazing walking tour of just the most central of the bridges in Paris, but even that requires walking back and forth across bridges along a river length of more than a mile. The Chicago River tour is more than two miles, and London is closer to four. A complete Paris tour is about ten miles.

Adding to the level of effort is the number of bridges involved. The Budapest tour is only four bridges, while the Chicago River tour is more than 20, and the "full-Paris" is 29. Once you contemplate setting aside your day to walk across bridges, even the width of the river may become a factor, as it becomes translated into the length of the bridges. The Liffey is a narrow, almost cute river, requiring only a short amount of time to inspect each bridge. The Danube at Budapest is wide and, although there are only a small number of them, each one takes a while to see. In contrast to all of this effort required to walk from bridge to bridge, a boat tour is a relaxed, even comfortable, way to view them.

Boat tours are an attractive option for other reasons. Clearly, the novelty is a major factor. When taking your boat tour to look at the bridges, you may find one or two other people on the boat, like you, who are there to see the bridges. However, most of them are just along for the ride, to enjoy viewing the architecture of the riverfront buildings themselves. While you may be focusing on each bridge as you approach it, there is nothing wrong with enjoying the rest of the view, along with your fellow tourists, in between the bridges.

There are also some advantages to the view of certain bridges from a boat versus the view available on foot. Many bridges were constructed when passenger traffic by boat was much more common than it is today, and they were designed to be seen by those passengers. Two important examples are the sculptures on Čechův Bridge in Prague and Vauxhall Bridge in London. These sculptures are placed on the piers at boat level, facing toward the approaching boats. On both bridges, the sculptures cannot be easily seen on foot and certainly cannot be enjoyed and appreciated as the designer intended.

In fact, it is not only the decorations that may be best viewed from a boat. There are several instances where the bridges themselves *must* be seen from a boat, and where they can *only* be seen from a boat. An important example is the Cleveland Bridge, crossing the River Avon in Bath. Built in 1826, it is an important tourist bridge to walk across to see the distinctive lodges on the four corners and the ornate cast-iron railings. The view from the side is just as impressive, as it is an early example of an ornate cast-iron arch bridge. However, you will probably never see this view on foot because the land on all four corners of the bridge is private property and inaccessible to the public. The bridge can only be seen in profile by taking the boat tour.

Taken to its extreme, there are interesting bridges that are completely on private property, and you cannot see them from the side or by walking across unless you obtain permission from the property owner. Researching bridge photographs on the internet, you may find pictures of one of the most gorgeous cast-iron bridges in England, the 1824 Aldford Iron Bridge near Chester. The bridge is on private property and may require some effort and permission to visit. For access, the tourist office in Chester may be able to help.

Boat tours also have disadvantages that are remedied by seeing the bridges on foot. The most obvious of these are schedule and cost. On a boat tour, you are seeing the bridge on the schedule of the tour operator and, except in rare instances, the boat will not even stop to allow you to admire the view for a few minutes. The bridges become just a part of the passing scenery. When touring bridges on foot, you do it on your own schedule, stopping for pictures and the views whenever you want. Also, the walking tour is free. While pleasant, boat tours can be expensive in some cities.

A less obvious disadvantage of boat tours is the visibility of the bridges from the boat. Much like some bridges have features that are best seen from a boat, others have features that are worst seen from a boat. The view of a bridge from a boat is actually a little disconcerting since you are looking up at it from below, at an oblique angle. It is not the way we are accustomed to looking at them. This makes it difficult to get attractive pictures, especially if there are parts of the bridge structure or, even worse, other tourists blocking the view.

Given these challenges, there is an obvious answer to the question of foot versus boat. The answer, of course, is both. If you have the time, and the cost is not prohibitive, then you will want to explore the bridges from both angles.

RIVER CAM BRIDGES, CAMBRIDGE, ENGLAND

There is at least one bridge tour that almost must be done by boat, and that is a tour of the small bridges in the college town of Cambridge. Probably no university is as intimately associated, both historically and geographically, with its river and bridges as the University of Cambridge. Unless you have been there, you are probably completely unaware of this association because the river is not famous and, with a few exceptions, neither are the bridges. However, immediately upon studying a tourist map of the city, the relationship between the colleges, the river, and the bridges becomes apparent.

The tiny stream flowing through town is the River Cam. Like so many European cities, the settlement was founded at the furthest inland location that was deep enough to be navigable and serve as a port, but narrow enough for a bridge to be constructed. Suddenly, the name of the town is not just a name. It is also a shorthanded, but effective, set of directions for early travelers.

The main attraction in Cambridge is the historic colleges that make up the University. Most of these colleges were founded and endowed by kings, queens, and other nobility between the 1200s and 1500s, and when a king or queen established a college, they did it right, sparing no expense.

As a result, Cambridge boasts one of the largest concentrations of ornate, large-scale medieval and Renaissance buildings that you will find anywhere. There is an occasional Victorian or modern building, but the early colleges in the center of town are comprised of one magnificent old structure after another. All of them on a grand scale, and still being used 600 or 700 years later for their original purpose.

Five of these colleges, including St. John's, Trinity, Clare, King's, and Queens', straddle both sides of the River Cam. These colleges occupy the land between the main tourist drag (St. John's Street/Trinity Street/King's Parade) to the east and the river to the west, and then include pastures, fields, and, in the case of Trinity College, additional college buildings on the west side of the river, an area known as "The Backs." As a result, most of the bridges connect the main part of each campus to The Backs, and are private structures built by the colleges to serve the students and masters of each college.

The reason that they must be seen on a boat tour is not that they are completely inaccessible by foot. It is that access by foot is restricted and only available when the colleges are open to the public. This happens only during limited hours, and also requires payment of an entry fee to enter each individual college. Even then, only parts of the colleges are made available to the public, so tourist access may not include the ability to walk across the bridges. Of course, each of the colleges should be visited anyway for the architecture and history, and the bridges are an important part of the whole experience. However, to make sure you see each of them, a boat tour is necessary.

The boat tours are operated in small punts, each seating up to about 12 tourists. There are different punt-operating companies and, in fine weather, there are dozens of punts plying the tiny river, bumping into each other. The punt tours cover a stretch of river about a mile long between two popular tourist gathering places—the Mill Pond at Silver Street to the south and Quayside at Bridge Street to the north. The mill at the Mill Pond is long gone, but the weir is still there, forming a pond that is packed with punts and lined with pubs. Quayside, at the northern end of the main tourist area, has also been redeveloped with restaurants and cafes and is also lined with docks for punts. The guided punt tours are generally designed to offer views of the important academic buildings in the historic colleges between these two areas but, by definition, also pass under all of the bridges, most of which are old, decorated, and/or otherwise interesting.

The punt tour will pass underneath nine bridges. Beginning from the Mill Pond, these are Silver Street Bridge, Mathematical Bridge, King's Bridge, Clare College Bridge, Garrett Hostel Bridge, Trinity College Bridge, Kitchen Bridge, the Bridge of Sighs, and Magdalene Bridge. The three bridges located outside of the colleges, including Silver Street Bridge at the Mill Pond, Magdalene Bridge at Quayside, and the Garrett Hostel Bridge about halfway in between, are the most recent. Magdalene Bridge is the site of the original "Cam Bridge." The location was a ford used by the Romans and probably had a bridge built in the eighth century. The current bridge is an attractive cast-iron bridge dating from 1823 and rebuilt in the 1980s. Silver Street Bridge dates from the 1950s, so is not historic, but it was thoughtfully designed to incorporate a wide plaza with benches overlooking the Mill Pond. Both of these bridges carry traffic. The Garrett Hostel Bridge, hidden in an alleyway tucked between Clare and Trinity Colleges, is an attractive pedestrian-only bridge. All three are accessible to the public without entering one of the colleges.

The other six bridges are located within the colleges. Of these, King's, Kitchen, Trinity, and Clare are all old stone arch bridges which, in many cities, would be an important local attraction. In Cambridge, they are almost drowned out. Each of these connects immaculately landscaped courtyards surrounded by historic buildings on the east side of the river to idyllic gardens and pastures, populated by cows, on The Backs.

The dates of construction are 1640 for Clare College, 1711 for Kitchen Bridge at St. John's College, 1764 for Trinity College, and 1819 for King's College. The bridge at King's College is the simplest, crossing the river on a single arch, and having no carved decoration. Clare College, Kitchen, and Trinity College bridges are each composed of three stone arches with carved stone decoration of mythological figures on their balustrades. The views from all of the bridges are pleasant, but most noteworthy are the views of the famous King's College Chapel from both King's College and

Clare College bridges, and of the famous Wren Library from Trinity College Bridge.

The remaining two bridges, Mathematical Bridge and the Bridge of Sighs, are both world-famous tourist attractions. Mathematical Bridge is situated close to the Mill Pond and is so unusual that it deserves a much closer and longer look than is available from the punt. Mathematical Bridge is discussed in more detail in Chapter 6.

The Bridge of Sighs, built in 1831, is situated within St. John's College adjacent to Kitchen Bridge. The bridge is a gorgeous passageway connecting the courtyards of the college through historic riverfront college buildings. As viewed from the river, the appeal of the Bridge of Sighs is not the small arch bridge itself but the ornate stone trellis forming the windows on its sides and roof. To keep the students and masters dry as they cross from one side to another, if that were the intention, the roof would only have to be about eight feet high above the deck. Instead, it is situated about 25 feet over the walkway, leaving high open sides filled in with decorative stone arches fitted with iron grills.

There are multiple Bridges of Sighs in Europe, each with some legend suggesting that the bridge leads its crossers to some unpleasant fate on the other side. In Cambridge, the legend supposedly refers to students using the bridge to make their final trek to take their exams. The one in Venice is also a small, roofed pedestrian bridge connecting riverfront buildings and which supposedly provided prisoners their last view of Venice before they were taken to be interrogated by the Inquisition. A story told by the punt tour guides is that Queen Victoria provided the name, thinking that the bridge was a replica of the one in Venice, although they are actually quite different in appearance.

Because it connects the interiors of the college buildings, the Bridge of Sighs is not open to the public, even to those who have purchased entry into the college. If it was, it would likely be crowded with photographers interfering with the actual operation of the college. Visitors are permitted onto the adjacent Kitchen Bridge, only about 100 feet away, which provides a perfect platform for photographs.

The attractions of the colleges and the town are so enormous that the bridges, even the Mathematical Bridge and Bridge of Sighs, almost seem like an afterthought. In any other city, a collection of five stone arch pedestrian bridges dating from the seventeenth and eighteenth centuries and situated in a garden-like setting would be covered by historical plaques and prominently mentioned in the guidebooks. In Cambridge, the available maps and guides only mention the Mathematical Bridge and Bridge of Sighs in passing. The only available map or guide listing the names of all of the bridges turns out to be the *"Children's Passport,"* a cartoon-like map available from one of the punting vendors. Costing one and a half pounds, the *Children's Passport* includes a page of stickers depicting King's College Chapel, Mathematical Bridge, the Bridge of Sighs, Clare College Bridge, and several cows from The Backs, allowing kids to keep track of the sights they are seeing during their punt tour. Although it may be beneath the dignity of some adult visitors, it is the only way to follow your progress and know which bridges you are passing under on your punt tour, so you might as well embrace it.

DRIVING TOURS

The walking and boat tours discussed in the previous subsections categorize bridges according to an important common feature, which is their proximity to each other. Once you have decided to add a bridge to the list of sights to visit on your vacation, it would be a shame to miss another one or two interesting bridges that are nearby. But if you have decided to go further and make bridges the focus of your vacation, then it is common for bridge enthusiasts to choose them by a unifying theme, even if they are far enough apart that they must be visited by car.

The most common theme chosen for driving tours is probably construction type and, of all the various types, covered bridges are probably visited on multi-bridge driving tours more than any other bridge type. There are a few reasons for this. First, they are always very small in scale, so even the largest and most interesting can be fully walked, photographed, and studied in less than an hour, leaving plenty of time in the day to visit others. In addition, as discussed in Chapter 2, they tend to be found in regional clusters so that another bridge is always just a short drive away. This is the case in Lancaster and Columbia counties in Pennsylvania, Ashtabula

County in Ohio, Parke County in Indiana, and throughout northern New England. Covered bridges are also amenable to driving tours because being part of the scenery is one of their main attractions. In many cases, the scenic drive is likely to be the main object, and visiting the bridges may just be an excuse for getting in the car and driving through the woods for a few hours.

Driving tours of covered bridges can be accomplished with little work on your part, because any region that is home to a cluster of them will also have many resources, including books, websites, pamphlets, and maps available to support your visit. In most areas that are home to a concentration of covered bridges, it is likely that your hotel or local tourist bureau already has preprinted maps and directions for covered bridge tours, including short, medium, and long options. If you prefer, many of these areas have companies that offer guided tours by bus, van, or even scooter.

While the availability of these resources is useful, it can also have drawbacks. As discussed in the Covered Bridges subsection of Chapter 2, not all covered bridges are awesome. While many are important for their history and the ingenuity of their construction, they may not be particularly large or photogenic. In most of the covered bridge clusters that are amenable to a driving tour, your primary challenge is going to be to avoid spending half of the day looking at uninteresting bridges. An example is southern Vermont, where some of the most iconic covered bridges in the United States, including Cornish-Windsor and Taftsville, are mixed in with a large number of old but unattractive bridges, reconstructions of bridges destroyed in floods, and a few tourist gimmicks.

Within these clusters, it will be tempting to map out routes and try to see all of the bridges, especially since you will be driving within a few miles of each of them. However, this may not be the best approach for some areas, especially if you are only interested in one or two of the many possible attractions. Instead, you should research the possibilities on the internet in advance, to high grade your tour. There are numerous resources to do so, including Bridgehunter, apps specific to covered bridges, and state and local tourism websites. These can be used to identify which display certain construction types, which are particularly photogenic, and which are located next to other attractions such as town greens, shops, or scenic rapids on the river.

Less common than covered bridge tours, but not unknown, are driving tours of stone arch bridges, or specific types of historic iron arch or truss bridges. Stone arch bridges dating from the early 1800s are scattered throughout the eastern United States, but there are concentrations, such as in Washington County, Maryland, where they are close enough to support a day tour. Unusual through-truss bridges were built across the eastern and midwestern United States from about 1870 to the 1920s, and there are many states, such as Pennsylvania and Massachusetts, where you can hit six or eight of these in one exhausting day. A tour of these other bridge types in an area can be rewarding but, because these other types of bridges are not as well-known as covered bridges, you are going to do all of the work, including identifying the targets and plotting out efficient routes, by yourself.

In addition to a driving tour based on the theme of construction type, another common theme is a driving tour of bridges on a single river. There are many books written describing all of the bridges within a specific city, including New York, London, Paris, and Pittsburgh, and these bridges are usually amenable to walking and boat tours. However, there are also books describing all of the bridges on a specific river, including those on the Danube, Hudson, Mississippi, Connecticut, and Brazos Rivers, among others.

Driving tours based on a single river are enlightening because they reveal the history of a region, rather than just one specific city. Because the river was the trade route, it was also the communication network between cities. In this way, two cities that are separated by tens or hundreds of miles but situated on the same river may have more in common historically, linguistically, and culturally than two cities much closer to each other, but in different watersheds. In addition, driving tours along the course of a river will reveal details about the geologic history of the river valley, and how that history affected the settlement of communities and the types of bridges present today.

Finally, an antipode to a driving tour focused on various roads crossing a single river is the reverse, which is a tour focused on a single road crossing various rivers. A prominent theme discussed in this book has been how bridges affected, were affected by, and otherwise provide a key to unlocking the origin history of an area. This is not about events that happened in a specific location a few hundreds or thousands of years after the location was settled, but the factors that caused the settlement to take seed and grow in the first place. We look at the map today and see a city here, a suburb there, a small town, some farms, maybe some expansive areas of undeveloped forest or prairie or desert. We consider these patterns to be fixed and do not take time to think of how they came about.

The answer is that they came about because of trade routes, leading to the next question—who or what decided where the trade routes would be placed? The answer to that one is—a mixture of mud and gravity. More than anything else, trade routes developed where they could. They developed where it was easiest for humans on foot, riding horses, using ox carts, or sailing in boats to transport themselves and the products of their labors from Point A to Point B.

In some places, the route was a straight line from A to B. More commonly, a convoluted pattern developed because a level route is easier to traverse than one that has hills to be climbed, and because a dry route is easier to follow than one that crosses mud. If there were mountains in the way, people eventually found the easiest way to go around and over using the tools they had available. If there were rivers in the way, they eventually found the easiest way to go around and over using the bridge construction technologies available. But it was this trial-and-error process, over thousands of years, that established which route was fastest, safest, and took the least effort, and the location of that route then gave birth to the pattern of human settlements that exists today. Since the nineteenth century, humans have developed new tools to overcome mud and gravity, including the internal combustion engine, pneumatic tires, electric motors and batteries, and new bridge and tunnel construction technologies, allowing us to build new roadways almost anywhere we want.

But it is too late. The original roadway patterns and the settlements that were born from them are now established forever, to the extent that most people are not aware of their origins. Even though the footpath, or horse path, or rough stone roadbed no longer exists, remnants of the route are still there on the ground, or found on old maps, for a group of researchers, historians, and hobbyists interested in finding them. The names of some examples are familiar even if the location and significance of these routes in affecting settlement patterns are lost to most people. In Europe, the names of ancient routes such as the Appian Way, Watling Street, and Via Regia are still well-known. In the United States, most travelers have heard of the Lincoln Highway, Route 66, and the National Road. Each of these routes crossed rivers and streams at fords, on ferry boats, and, eventually, across bridges. It is the latter that allows a driving tour of the bridges along a single, historic highway to be a key to unlocking the settlement of a continent.

BRIDGES OF THE NATIONAL ROAD, MARYLAND TO OHIO

The first complication in identifying the historic bridges of the National Road, with the intention of visiting them, is deciding what defines the "National Road." The phrase is most accurately used to describe the road from Cumberland, Maryland, to Vandalia, Illinois, which was funded by the federal government between 1805 and 1838. But the road had other names, having been referred to as the Cumberland Road, United States Road, or National Pike. Also, an even older road from Baltimore to Cumberland, labeled on road signs in Maryland as National Pike or Baltimore National Pike, is sometimes referred to as National Road, even though it was not formally part of the federally authorized road from Cumberland to Vandalia. Some literature and historical signs broadly include the Baltimore to Cumberland segment as part of the National Road. Others, mostly in Ohio, more narrowly define the National Road as only the federally funded segment from Cumberland to Vandalia.

A further complication is not geographic, but time-dependent. Many of the interesting bridges on the National Road were actually constructed between 1813 and 1828, as part of the federally funded road. However, others were constructed on the same route after 1838, when the federal government turned ownership of the road over to the individual states. Today, there is no formal designation of a National Road. Most of the road became redesignated as US Route 40 in 1926, but even then many segments of the new Route 40 were realignments of the original road. Part of the Maryland portion of the road is now Interstate 68, and the segment from about Washington, Pennsylvania, and westward is now paralleled by Interstate 70.

Define it how you may, several interesting bridges of different construction types have been preserved and can be visited today. This is not a normal bridge tour that can be done in a day, because these bridges are found over a stretch of hundreds of miles. However, if you wish to combine some bridge tourism with a drive through the Appalachian Mountains, then this is a good way to see some great historic bridges.

Moving from east to west in the same direction as the early emigrants who used the road to settle the western United States, the first historic bridge you come to is Wilson's Bridge, located a few miles west of Hagerstown, Maryland, just off Interstate 70. Because it is on the Baltimore-to-Cumberland segment, Wilson's Bridge was more accurately located on the National Pike and not the official National Road. It was constructed in 1819 and was certainly used by the same oxen-drawn Conestoga wagons as the bridges further west.

Wilson's Bridge crosses Conococheague Creek near the small town of Clear Spring. Wilson's Bridge ceased to be used as part of the main highway in 1937 when US Route 40 was realigned onto a new bridge about 200 feet downstream. The original bridge continued to carry local traffic until 1972 when it was damaged by flooding from Hurricane Agnes. The bridge sat damaged for several years, but was eventually restored and became the centerpiece of a small county park with parking spaces, picnic tables, and historical markers. While it is pleasurable to walk over Wilson's Bridge, it is recommended that you also walk over the Route 40 bridge, as it is a little higher in elevation and provides a good vantage point from which to view the older bridge.

The next National Road sight is in Grantsville, about 25 miles west of Cumberland. To get to this area, take Interstate 68 west of Cumberland and follow exit signs for the Penn Alps Restaurant. The restaurant is on US Route 40, where it crosses the Casselman River over a 1930s-era steel through-truss bridge. There is quite a little complex of tourist attractions here, including the German-themed restaurant, the touristy Spruce Forest Artisan Village, and the stone arch bridge over the river, dating from 1813.

The bridge itself is physically located in Casselman River Bridge State Park. There is a small parking lot for the park on the west side of the river, and the first thing you will notice when arriving is the enormous size of the bridge as compared to the small river. The stream is only about 100 feet wide and a few feet deep. The bridge crosses on a large, single stone arch rising more than 20 feet above river level. The height of this arch seems completely unnecessary for the type of boats that could possibly have used this small stream, but historical plaques indicate that the bridge was built at a time when the Casselman River was intended to be included within the future C&O Canal. Ultimately, the canal was never completed further west than Cumberland because the invention of railroads made the canal obsolete even before it was completed. However, the gigantic Casselman River Bridge was left standing, oddly dwarfing its surroundings.

On the east side of the Casselman River, right off the end of the bridge, are the restaurant and the Artisan Village. The Village is a collection of small, historic houses from the region that have been moved to this spot for preservation. The houses are now home to workshops for sculptors, painters, and other craftspersons. From the parking lot of the restaurant, you can walk along the shoulder of Route 40 a few hundred feet to access the through-truss bridge. From there, you have an amazing view of the stone arch bridge about 1,000 feet to the north.

One subtle but interesting feature of the Casselman River deserves mention. You may not notice it right away, although you may have a slight feeling of disorientation. This is because the other streams and rivers you have crossed so far on this trip—in fact, most streams and rivers in the eastern United States—flow from north to south. In contrast, the Cassel-man River flows from south to north. Between Cumberland and Grants-ville, you have crossed the Eastern Continental Divide, separating the At-lantic Ocean drainage from that of the Gulf of Mexico. In this little corner of western Maryland and southwestern Pennsylvania, the Casselman, Youghiogheny, and Monongahela Rivers flow north toward Pittsburgh, where they join the Allegheny to form the Ohio River.

The next National Road bridge is located at Somerfield, Pennsylvania, and you will almost certainly not see it. That is because this section of the Youghiogheny River has been dammed, and the bridge normally sits below 40 feet of water in a reservoir. This is a fairly large bridge, almost 400 feet long and 40 feet high, and constructed in 1918. It is now only visible during times of extreme drought.

During the heyday of the National Road from 1815 to the 1830s, steel, which built the city of Pittsburgh, had not yet been invented. The major economic driver in the region at that time was transportation, which created growth in places where the major transportation routes intersected. Such was the case where the National Road crossed major rivers. As a result, the largest city in southwestern Pennsylvania during the early nineteenth century was not Pittsburgh, but Brownsville, where the National Road crossed the Monongahela River.

The original National Road bridge across the Monongahela at Brownsville is no longer there. The current bridge, the Brownsville Bridge, was constructed in 1914. It is historically important as a very long (more than 900 feet), single span steel through-truss bridge. It has sidewalks, and displays builder plaques from the Fort Pitt Bridge Works on both ends.

Two bridges were needed on the National Road at Brownsville. As the road approached the river from the east, it descended a steep hill from the plateau down to river level. A short brick-covered remnant of this portion of the road from 1918 can still be found in downtown Brownsville. Once near river level, the road needed to cross Dunlap's Creek, a narrow stream situated in a fairly deep gorge. The bridge over this gorge was built in 1839 and is famous as the first metal arch bridge in the United States. It was once a famous landmark of Brownsville. The image of hoop-skirted women with parasols strolling over its decorative iron arch was used in advertisements and postcards and can still be seen on display at the nearby Interstate 70 rest stop, among other inducements to visit the sights of southwestern Pennsylvania.

Brownsville has changed since 1839. The passing traffic that once made the town prosperous has long since been diverted onto high-speed highways, and you would have to go out of your way, or be lost, to end up down in the bottom of the valley in downtown Brownsville. The once-proud cast-iron bridge is still there, as attested by a historical plaque. However, the bridge has been mostly hidden behind twentieth century steel and cement restorations and expansions. From the eastern side, you can barely see the patterned cast-iron curve of the arch on just one end of the bridge. Walking over it on Main Street, you would not even know you are on a historically important bridge, except for the historical plaque.

The next bridge, at Claysville, Pennsylvania, just east of Wheeling, is a special type of bridge associated with this section of the National Road. This is the "S-Bridge," of which there are five between Claysville and Zanesville, Ohio. The S-Bridges are small stone arch bridges dating from the 1820s, the earliest days of the National Road. They are well-known due to their unusual "S" shape, which was done because it was easier to build bridges straight across a stream rather than at an angle. In these areas, the National Road approached the streams at an odd angle, made a sharp turn to cross over at a right angle, and then turned back to its original orientation, making an "S" shape. Some authors describing the S-Bridges have speculated that they must have caused traffic jams due to the abrupt turns in the road. Remember, though, that these were built in the 1820s, 100 years before traffic moved quickly enough to be slowed down by turns in the road. Instead of causing traffic jams, these bridges were carrying Conestoga wagons using the National Road to settle Ohio, Indiana, and parts further west.

The Claysville S-Bridge can be found on the corner of US Route 40 and Pennsylvania Route 221, a few miles southwest of Washington, Pennsylvania. Claysville, like most of the S-Bridges, no longer carries traffic but is preserved in a small park just off Route 40. There is a small parking lot north of the intersection, a short walk from the bridge. Claysville is one of the larger S-Bridges. It consists of two stone arches and is about 200 feet long. The roadway is wider than the other S-Bridges, probably wide enough to have supported two lanes of traffic. The roadway surface is no longer stone but is covered with grass. The masonry is of roughly rectangular sandstone blocks, but they are of various colors and grain sizes, suggesting a variety of different sources of stone for the construction of the bridge. Although there is a historical plaque, it generically discusses the construction dates for the National Road being 1805 to 1818, but does not provide a specific date for this particular bridge.

About 15 miles west of Claysville, the most spectacular bridge on the National Road is the Wheeling Suspension Bridge over the Ohio River.

Through the early years of the National Road, the Ohio River was too big to be bridged, and the road here crossed the river by ferry. The Wheeling Bridge was constructed between 1846 and 1849. This was the first long-span wire-cable suspension bridge in the United States and was the longest suspension span in the world for many years.

This is not a Roebling bridge, as John Roebling lost out on the bidding for the construction to Charles Ellet. However, it does bear a striking resemblance to the Roebling Bridge in Cincinnati and Roebling's Brooklyn Bridge. In each case, the suspension towers are massive stone arches, and the suspension cables are a combination of verticals and diagonals. The bridge was originally built with only vertical suspension cables, but the bridge deck had stability issues, including having been destroyed by a windstorm in 1854. According to the historical plaque at the eastern end of the bridge, the deck was rebuilt in 1854, and Washington Roebling provided the diagonal supporting cables for additional support in 1872.

A few miles west of Wheeling, where Route 40 passes through the town of Blaine Hill, is another location where you can walk across two different generations of National Road bridges. The main attraction here is another S-Bridge. This one is hard to find because it is at creek level at the base of a hill, and the adjacent Blaine Hill Viaduct carrying Route 40 is about 50 feet high over the creek, almost directly over the S-Bridge. You cannot see the creek or the S-Bridge when driving through town on Route 40, and there are no signs. However, on the eastern end of the viaduct, take a sharp turn around the north side and drive along the dirt road that appears to go under it. The dirt road ends at the S-Bridge, dwarfed in the shadow of the gigantic viaduct.

The S-Bridge here is fairly large, consisting of three stone arches. The S-Bridge was built in 1828 and is the longest S-Bridge on the National Road, at 345 feet. The year 2003 was the bicentennial of Ohio's entry into the union, and this Blaine Hill S-Bridge was designated as the state's official "Bicentennial Bridge." The bridge is made of yellowish, fine-grained sandstone. Although the bridge no longer carries traffic, you can walk across as well as around it on all sides. The deck is brick, a covering placed on the National Road in 1918 following World War I to improve the ability of the road to support military-related traffic in case of another war.

There are two historical plaques at Blaine Hill, one discussing the S-Bridge and the other discussing the viaduct. The viaduct dates from 1933 and consists of four large, yellow cement open-spandrel arches. A stairway near the S-Bridge leads up to the sidewalk on the viaduct. Looking down from the sidewalk effectively gives you an aerial view and a rare chance to see the odd shape of an S-Bridge.

About 30 miles west of Blaine Hill is another S-Bridge, variously referred to as the Old Washington S-Bridge, the Rhinehart Road S-Bridge, or the Salt Fork Creek S-Bridge. Although it is just a stone's throw from Interstate 70, this bridge is also hard to find. It is actually a few miles east of the town of Old Washington, hidden among unmarked back roads amid fields and scattered houses on the north side of Interstate 70. Use the exit for Ohio Route 513, go north to the intersection with the convenience store, and take a left, to the west. Follow this road for about a mile west toward Moore Woods Park, but before you get to the park, you will see the historical plaques for the S-Bridge on your right. The bridge is not preserved in a park like the other four S-Bridges. In fact, it is still part of the road, paved with asphalt, and you can drive over it. There is no dedicated parking lot, but you can pull off the road onto the grass next to the historical plaques.

The final two S-Bridges are located close to each other between Cambridge and Zanesville. Both are located in small, roadside county parks just a few feet off the north side of the current Route 40. The Peters Creek S-Bridge, also referred to in some sources as the Cambridge S-Bridge or Cassell S-Bridge, is located about six miles west of downtown Cambridge. There are historical plaques, a parking lot, and picnic tables here. The bridge is not elevated above the surrounding terrain, but you can walk over it and view it from the banks of the creek on both sides. Another treat here is what appears to be an original National Road milestone, listing the distances to Cumberland (186 miles), Zanesville (18 miles), Wheeling (56 miles), and Cambridge (6 miles).

Four miles further west on Route 40 is the Fox Creek S-Bridge, also known as the New Concord S-Bridge, which is also preserved in a small park on the north side of Route 40. Dating from 1826, this is probably the best-preserved and documented of the S-Bridges. There are signs near the Interstate 70 exit for New Concord directing you to the "Historic S Bridge." There is a historical plaque on the east side of the park discussing the older road in the area known as Zane's Trace and its relation to the later National Road. The parking lot, additional historical plaques, and another original milestone are on the west side of the bridge. A historical plaque discusses how the National Road was bricked in 1918 and states that this was the last of the bridges to be bricked. The brick roadway is still there today and can be walked. There is also a separate pathway leading underneath the bridge so you can get a view of the bridge from its north side. A plaque on that side has inscribed dates of 1826 and 1918.

The state of Ohio has done a great job in preserving and displaying its S-Bridges. There is a small National Road Museum in Zanesville where you can get information on the road. Although the National Road continued another 400 miles west to Vandalia, it does not appear that there are any other significant stone arch or suspension bridges on the road west of Zanesville. Existing books, articles, and literature do not mention additional bridges. Although both Illinois and Indiana have National Road Historical Societies with websites, these discuss historic buildings along the road but no physical remnants of the road itself or any bridges. However, the section between Hagerstown and Zanesville has preserved an amazing array of different early bridge types.

CHAPTER 10

BRIDGES NOT FOR TOURISTS

ONCE YOU HAVE WALKED ACROSS hundreds of bridges specifically to study and document the features that make them special, you will inevitably begin to see and document the opposite—bridges that are distinctly not special, do not enhance their surroundings, and do not attract tourists or other visitors. This is not a reference to the thousands of boring, everyday, working bridges that are doing their part to keep traffic moving without bothering anyone. Instead, it refers to locations where a historically important bridge has been allowed to fall into disrepair through rust or rot, or where an obvious opportunity to develop a bridge into an enhancement for the community has been missed.

One category of recreational bridges is those closed to traffic, replaced with a newer bridge, and then preserved in a park or as part of a trail. The obvious antipode to this is the historic bridges that are closed and replaced, but not preserved. In many cases, these are demolished to clear room for the new bridge, or because the cost to preserve them is prohibitive. Even rehabilitating a crumbling bridge to be safe for bicycles or pedestrians costs money, and each community weighs the costs and benefits of rehabilitation versus demolition in its own way.

One of the more prominent examples in recent years was the 2013 demolition of the Waldo-Hancock Bridge in Bucksport, Maine. The historically important Waldo-Hancock Bridge was constructed in 1931 and was one of the few remaining bridges designed by David Steinman, who also designed the Mackinac Bridge. Adding insult to injury, it seems unfortunate that its replacement, the unusual and beautiful Penobscot Narrows Bridge and Observatory, set amongst amazing scenery, was constructed without sidewalks and benches.

Another adverse side-effect of the preservation of historic bridges is the visual impact of the replacement bridge. Every time a new bridge is built to replace an older bridge, there is one obvious location to build it—right next to the old one. That is where the road is. In addition, the old bridge was built in this location for a reason, probably because the river or harbor was narrowest at this point. Therefore, this feature still makes this the most cost-effective location to build the new bridge. Examples include several of the National Road bridges (Wilson's, Casselman, and Blaine Hill), and the preserved-in-place Paper Mill Road, Ouaquaga, Nevius Street, Pineground, and Lover's Leap bridges. In some cases, the newer bridge is far enough away that it still allows for unobstructed photographs of the old bridge, such as at the Casselman Bridge. In other cases, the replacement bridge is so close that it makes photography of the historic bridge impossible.

In contrast to the groups of interesting bridges in pedestrian-friendly tourist centers such as Dublin and Paris, there are also river-centric tourist locations where you might expect to find some interesting bridges, but will be disappointed. Switzerland has three major, historic tourist centers that straddle both sides of a lovely river as it exits an enormous lake. In Lucerne, the Reuss River is crossed by two picturesque covered bridges more than 500 years old, as well as a nicely decorated pedestrian bridge from the 1890s. In nearby Zurich, the tourist areas on either side of the Limmat River are connected by numerous nineteenth and early twentieth century bridges that may be attractive, but would not entice any tourist to look at them twice. Geneva, with tourist areas on both sides of the Rhone, did a little more with its bridges. A series of modern pedestrian bridges connect the riverbanks to a small park on the Ile Rousseau and to historic buildings in the middle of the river that formerly served as waterworks or hydroelectric facilities. While these may connect tourist and cultural attractions, the bridges themselves are not old or decorative.

CHESAPEAKE BAY BRIDGE, ANNAPOLIS, MARYLAND

This book has documented a historical trajectory in the incorporation of aesthetics, recreation, and community-friendly features into the construction and operation of bridges. Two key historical developments have driven this trajectory. The first development was the invention of the automobile. For thousands of years before the motorization of North America and Europe, traffic on bridges moved at the speed of horses. The slow speed of the traffic led to community interaction and decoration. But by World War II, the bridge-crossers had closed themselves up inside their cars and increased their speed from 15 to 70 miles per hour, and all community interaction and decoration ceased.

The second historical development was more subtle, and occurred much more slowly. This was the development of an appreciation for the environment, health and fitness, historic preservation, and aesthetics that began in the 1960s and is still occurring today.

In between these two events, from the 1940s until about the 1980s, bridge construction was a desert for bridge tourists. There was little consideration of pedestrian access, community-friendly features, or aesthetics. All that mattered was speed, moving as large a volume of traffic as possible without creating traffic jams. It was in this intervening period that many of our most disappointing bridges were constructed, even in some special places. One of the more prominent examples is the Chesapeake Bay Bridge in Maryland.

The shortcomings of the Chesapeake Bay Bridge are best demonstrated by comparing and contrasting the bridge with the Delaware Memorial Bridge, which is less than 100 miles away. The Delaware Memorial Bridge is really two conventional suspension bridges, right next to each other. The location is not particularly scenic. The bridges cross Delaware Bay, and the surrounding area is completely flat. The shorelines are dominated by gigantic gantry cranes and warehouses of the Port of Wilmington on the Delaware end, and the industrial Deepwater chemical plant on the New Jersey end. The setting is so industrial that it is almost impossible to find a location to get good photographs of the bridge, because both shorelines are inaccessible to the public for miles in both directions.

In contrast, the setting of the Chesapeake Bay Bridge is much less developed. The western shore includes Sandy Point State Park, the campus of the US Naval Academy, and historic downtown Annapolis. The eastern shore includes shorefront marinas and restaurants of Kent Island. There is no comparison. The setting of the Chesapeake Bay Bridge is far more natural and attractive than that of the Delaware Memorial Bridge and is therefore deserving of the most beautiful bridge imaginable. However, that is not what happened. In fact, the exact opposite happened.

Delaware Memorial Bridge (top) and Chesapeake Bay Bridge (bottom)

Even though they were built 17 years apart in the 1950s and 1960s, the towers of the twin bridges of Delaware Memorial are completely identical in appearance, resulting in an appealing symmetry. They are visible from downtown Wilmington and from interstate highways passing through the area, providing a pleasant bright spot in what is otherwise a relatively flat, bleak, industrial landscape. None of the four towers, on its own, is particularly attractive. Where most suspension bridge towers use their interior bracing to generate a decorative geometric pattern, each of the Delaware Memorial Bridge towers simply has a large, open space with a single crosspiece bracing at the top. But the fact that there are two of them right next to each other and entirely identical, turns the twin bridge silhouette into an instantly recognizable symbol, one which is used as the logo for the Delaware River and Bay Authority, the operator of the bridge.

The main channel crossing of the Chesapeake Bay Bridge is also two conventional suspension bridges adjacent to each other. The original bridge was constructed because, by the early 1950s, populations in Baltimore and Washington were starting to use their summer vacations to go "downy ocean." Weekend trips to the beach became so popular that ferries crossing the bay to deliver city dwellers to Ocean City were becoming overwhelmed. However, the designers constructed only a two-lane bridge, with one lane in each direction. Once the bridge was constructed, development fueled by bridge-users took off on the Eastern Shore, in two different ways, both wreaking havoc on the narrow two-lane bridge.

The first was an explosion of development in Ocean City, Rehoboth Beach, Dewey Beach, and other shoreside resort towns. Once the residents of Washington and Baltimore could reach the shore in a few hours without needing to use ferries, they did so, in droves.

The second type of development occurred in Kent Island and the nearby towns in Queen Anne's County at the eastern end of the bridge. Kent Island is less than 45 miles from the downtown centers in both Washington and Baltimore, an impossible distance for commuters who need to use a ferry, but perfectly acceptable for commuters once they have a bridge. The bridge immediately turned Kent Island and Queen Anne's County from rural farming and fishing communities into suburbs of two major cities.

The result was that, by the early 1970s, a second bridge was required to handle the increased traffic. However, instead of making the second bridge identical, as was done in Delaware, the patterns of the bracing in the suspension towers do not match each other. The towers on the older, southern bridge use closely-spaced diagonal braces for support, while those on the newer, northern bridge use much more widely-spaced horizontal braces.

This may sound like a minor issue, but when contrasted with the pleasing symmetry of the Delaware Memorial Bridge, the mismatched towers of the Chesapeake Bay Bridge seem discordant. As seen in old photos of the southern bridge before the northern bridge was constructed, just one of the Chesapeake Bay bridges, on its own, was an attractive feature of the scenery. Twin bridges of either of the two styles would have been even more attractive, as demonstrated by the Delaware Memorial example. However, a pair of mismatched bridges is unfortunate, especially since the designers could have used the appealing symmetry in Delaware, only 90 miles away, as an attractive example to follow. In the photo pair above, consider that the clean, simple Delaware Memorial Bridge is doing yeoman's work in carrying eight lanes of regional interstate traffic up and down the East Coast of the United States, while the gray, industrial-looking machinery of the Chesapeake Bay Bridge is carrying only five lanes of traffic, mostly taking weekenders to the beach.

The Bay Bridge also comes up short when compared with some other prominent bridges, for instance, Mackinac. Constructed at about the same time and about the same length, both Bay Bridge and Mackinac serve a symbolic purpose in connecting the densely populated "main" part of a state to a relatively isolated, neglected fragment of the state. In Michigan, this connection is observed as an important event in state history, whereas in Maryland, uniting the populations of the state does not seem as important as getting to the beach faster on Friday night. Mackinac Bridge is celebrated, painted in unusual complementary colors, serves as a prominent symbol for the state and the city, hosts an annual walking event, and is the focus of a shorefront park, Bridge View Park, which incorporates museum displays about the bridge. Both the bridge itself and Bridge View Park operate informative, bridge-focused websites that describe the attractions of the bridge and the surrounding region and even offer bridge-related items for sale.

In contrast, the Bay Bridge is painted a depressing gray and is only used as a symbol or logo if the image can be fudged to look more attractive than the real thing. Once you realize this and start looking locally around

Annapolis, you will find that this happens quite frequently. Businesses will use a stylized version of the bridge instead of a more realistic portrayal on the sides of their trucks. The logo of the Bay Bridge Marina Yacht Club on Kent Island is lovely, showing the dark blue bridge silhouetted against a blazing, bright orange setting sun. Except they managed to show only one bridge, not two. Even the state of Maryland did this in 2019 when it released its new specialized license plates celebrating the beauty of the Chesapeake Bay. There are the well-known symbols of the Chesapeake Bay, including a wide-open water vista, seagrass, and appealing blue crab. And in the upper left corner there is the massive bridge, making Maryland one of many states to feature their most prominent bridge on its license plates. But there is only one bridge! If you look at the plate very closely you will see that the second bridge is, in fact, there in the picture, but it is shown so faintly that you really have to work to see it.

The Bay Bridge did provide a popular annual bridge walk from 1975 to 2000, and then on a couple more occasions, but it ceased altogether in 2007. A local running club sometimes hosts a 10K race across the bridge, and walkers are invited to join. Although it provides an opportunity for emphatic bridgespotters to walk across, it is not held annually, and is much more of a running event than a statewide celebration of an important landmark. Like Mackinac, the Bay Bridge is the prominent, even overpowering site visible from a popular state park, Sandy Point State Park. However, go onto the Sandy Point website and somehow, amazingly, you will find no photographs of the bridge, and the only mention of the bridge will be in the section on how to get driving directions to the park. Similarly, if you want to know current traffic conditions, the Maryland Transportation Authority operates a useful, dedicated Bay Bridge website, but it does not provide any historical information and does not celebrate the bridge in any way. In short, of all of the little ways a community can promote interest and tourism in its prominent bridges, the Chesapeake Bay Bridge has implemented none of them.

EPILOGUE

IN THE INTRODUCTION, IT WAS stated that the primary objective of the book was to offer a travel guide, to encourage you to see some interesting bridges in your community or on your travels, in a new way. That truly was the objective at the time the book was begun and, hopefully, the book still serves that purpose for a large number of bridges.

However, something else happened between Bridge Number 1 and Bridge Number 600. This was the recognition and systematic analysis of what turns out to be dozens of different features, some obvious but most very subtle, that attract people to bridges as tourists, or to pursue recreation or hobbies, or to commemorate history-changing events, or to just enjoy the vista. Just as important, as discussed in Chapter 10, was the recognition and analysis of other features, again some obvious and some subtle, that miss a clear opportunity to enhance tourism and recreation, and that may even diminish the aesthetics of their local community. Now, instead of simply providing recommendations for spending a few pleasant hours while you are on vacation, the book may also serve as an a la carte menu for communities weighing their options for disposing of their old bridges, renovating their existing bridges, or constructing new ones.

Armed with this knowledge of the features that have been used to enhance communities and attract tourists in dozens of other cities and scenic locations, it becomes easy to imagine the types of bridges that could someday be constructed to enhance the Chesapeake Bay between Annapolis and Kent Island, or dozens of other locations that deserve a better bridge. In the short term, there is little we can do to correct these disappointing mistakes, which will detract from their surroundings for a long time to come. However, these bridges are all going to require replacement at some point in the not-too-distant future, and it is hoped that some of the principles discussed in this book can be applied at that time. In other good news, new bridges are being constructed in other cities every day, and you, the reader, possess the ability to influence the ultimate decision regarding what type of bridge will be built, and what kinds of enhancements will be provided on it, in your community.

In the twenty-first century, this is no longer an uphill battle, a case of not being able to fight city hall. Laws are now on the books that obligate government officials to solicit and consider public opinion regarding public works projects. In the United States, the National Environmental Policy Act, as well as state and local laws requiring that hearings and records be open to the public, now direct how and when project information must be made available, and how and when the community can make its opinions known. Public committees and focus groups are formed and, more importantly, taken seriously. Web-based commenting systems are designed to not only capture public opinion, but to quantify it and present it to public officials in a manner making it easy for them to understand and consider. Your voice is joined with that of others, giving your opinions more weight. Social media makes this easier to do than ever before. It is now impossible for any government agency to undertake a massive public works project, such as the construction of a bridge, without also implementing an immense public involvement program. The public has spoken, and they want sidewalks, recreational features, and aesthetics that enrich their communities.

Even more important than the laws that make this community activism possible and powerful are the changes in the sensibilities of the engineers, architects, and government officials responsible for our new bridges. In the 1960s, it may not have occurred to bridge designers to add a few community-friendly features. However, except for keeping an eye on costs, which is always a major issue, most of the concepts discussed in this book would not be seriously opposed by anyone today. Nobody would object to preserving historical components, or to installing sidewalks, bike trails, decorations, benches, or plaques. Specific opinions on aesthetics may differ and will be argued, but generally, nobody is going to object to aesthetics being a major consideration in bridge design in the twenty-first century. The engineers and public officials live in the community too, and they want these enhancements as much as you do.

Having finished reading this book, you are now armed with information that you can use to improve bridge construction and preservation in your home area for yourself, for other residents, and for generations to come. Maybe, without the book, you already would have written a letter to your councilman expressing your support for a bike trail on a new bridge, or to request that an old iron truss bridge be preserved. But if you care enough to write such a letter, then you may wish to consider other ways to join your voice to those of like-minded members of your community.

One way is to learn about and follow the specific public participation procedures used by your local government. Even if you are not in direct contact with other commenters, the comment collection, organization, and response systems used by government agencies are designed to identify and combine similar comments, so that your opinion can be amplified by numbers.

More importantly, the book now provides you with additional ideas, many of them with little additional cost, regarding other enhancements to speak out about. Instead of providing generic comments about wanting a more attractive bridge, this book offers you dozens of examples in other communities that you can visit, document, research, and cite in your comments to your local government to strengthen your arguments. Armed with these tools, your comments are no longer just vague ideas that are easy to ignore, but are concrete proposals backed by specific, detailed examples from other locales.

While your own opinions may not carry the day, there is one guarantee, which is that you will find that you are not alone. The number of people sharing your interests in enhancing your local bridges is much larger than you expected. All that you have to do is walk across the Waco Suspension Bridge while staying in the hotel across the street on business, explore the

James Joyce Bridge in Dublin when visiting the House of the Dead, go for a bike ride across the Woodrow Wilson Bridge on the Washington Beltway, or bow your head for a short prayer in front of the cabinet-sized chapel on the Spreuerbrücke, and you will see other people doing the same.

Watch the people on the bridge for a little while. Realize that they are not just crossing to go to the store or office, but they are hanging out. They are speaking foreign languages, suggesting they have come to this bridge from a long distance. They are visiting the gift shop to buy the refrigerator magnet. They are posing to take selfies in front of the amazing view, which they will post to let their online companions know that they are interesting people who leave their sofa to go outside to learn and experience new things.

Maybe you will see someone moving slowly along the chain-link fencing of the Hohenzollern Bridge in Cologne, taking time to read the inscriptions on the padlocks. Perhaps you will have to wait in a short line to take your turn walking from Europe to North America on the Bridge Between Continents in Iceland. At the North Bridge in Concord, you will notice people speaking with one another in whispers and see other folks standing reverently, as if they can still hear the echoes of the shots from 1775. Or you may watch while an aging, scruffy-looking tourist with a backpack pauses in front of the stone-engraved name plaque on the Meister Eckhart Brücke in Erfurt, sets down his camera for a minute, pulls a small notebook out of his back pocket, and records Bridge Number 500 in his bridgespotting log.

REFERENCE MATERIALS

BOOKS, PAMPHLETS, AND ARTICLES

Action Artistique de la Ville Paris. *Les Ponts de Paris*. 2000.

Allen, Richard Sanders. *Covered Bridges of the Northeast*. The Stephen Green Press. 1957.

Allen, Richard Sanders. *Covered Bridges of the Middle Atlantic States*. Bonanza Books. 1959.

Baus, Ursula, and Schlaich, Mike. *Footbridges, Structure, Design, History*. Birkhäuser. 2007.

Bausch, F.A. *Bridges Crossed (and some not), A Pictorial Travelogue*. 2012.

Beattie, Andrew. *The Danube, A Cultural History*. Oxford University Press. 2010.

Burke, Kathryn W. *Images of America, Hudson River Bridges*. Arcadia Publishing. 2007.

Clare College, University of Cambridge. "Clare College, Cambridge." 2011.

Coffey, Ronnie Clark. *Images of America, Bear Mountain*. Arcadia Publishing. 2008.

Cossins, Neil, and Trinder, Barrie. *The Iron Bridge: Symbol of the Industrial Revolution*. 1979.

Costello, Mary Charlotte Aubry. *Climbing the Mississippi River Bridge by Bridge*. 1995.

Dale, Frank T. *Bridges over the Delaware River, A History of the Crossings*. Rutgers University Press. 2003.

Demetz, Peter. *Prague in Black and Gold*. Hill and Wang. 1997.

Durand, Charl. *Venice, Bridge by Bridge, A Guide to the Bridges of Venice*. 2017.

Evans, Mark. *The Poohsticks Handbook, A Poohstickopedia*. 2015.

Fox, Jackie. *Spanning a River, Reaching a Community, The Story of the Ravenel Bridge*. South Carolina Department of Transportation/Federal Highway Administration. 2006.

Gaillard, Marc. *The Quays and Bridges of Paris – An Historical Guide*. Martelle Editions. 1994.

Goldberg, Geoffrey H. *Bridges, A Postcard History*. Schiffer Publishing. 2011.

Gottemoeller, Frederick. *Bridgescape, The Art of Designing Bridges*. Second Edition. John Wiley & Sons, Inc. 2004.

Griswold, Wick. *The History of the Connecticut River*. The History Press. 2012.

Haglund, Karl. *Inventing the Charles River*. The MIT Press. 2003.

Hibbert, Christopher. *Florence, the Biography of a City*. W.W. Norton and Company. 1993.

Hill, Libby. *The Chicago River, A Natural and Unnatural History*. Lake Claremont Press. 2000.

Hinchliffe, Ernest. *A Guide to the Packhorse Bridges of England*. 1994.

Holth, Nathan. *Chicago's Bridges*. Shire Publications. 2012.

Horne, Alistair. *Seven Ages of Paris*. Alfred A. Knopf. 2002.

Hottinger, M.D. *The Stories of Basel, Berne, and Zurich*. Kraus Reprint, A Division of Kraus-Thomson Organization Ltd. 1970.

Howard, Andrew R. *Covered Bridges of Madison County, Iowa, A Guide*. 1998.

Ironbridge Gorge Museum Trust Ltd. *The Iron Bridge and Town*. 2010.

Jiràsek, Alois. *Old Czech Legends*. Forest Books. 1992.

Kennicott, Philip. "Capital Crossings". https://www.washingtonpost.com/arts-entertainment/interactive/2021/washington-dc-bridges-new-and-old/. April 1, 2021.

Knoblock, Glenn A. *Historic Iron and Steel Bridges in Maine, New Hampshire, and Vermont*. McFarland & Company Inc., Publishers. 2012.

Langer, Frantisek. *The Sword of St. Wenceslas*. 1940. In Wilson, Paul, ed., *Prague, A Traveler's Literary Companion*. Whereabouts Press. 1995.

Leech, Thomas G., and Skocik, Amanda L. Gannett Fleming, Inc. *The Bridges of the National Road – Our Nation's First Toll Road*. IBC 2004 – The Official Publication of the International Bridge Conference.

Legler, Dixie, and Highsmith, Carol M. *Historic Bridges of Maryland*. Maryland Historical Trust Press. 2002.

Martin, Pat. Prague, *Saints and Heroes of the Charles Bridge*. Penfield Books. 2003.

Massachusetts Department of Conservation and Recreation. "Rowley Reconnaissance Report, Essex County Landscape Inventory Form" https://www.mass.gov/doc/rowley/download. 2005.

Matthews, Peter. *London's Bridges*. Shire Publications. 2013.

Maynard, John F. "The History and Construction of the Hanover Street Bridge in Baltimore, Maryland". 1934

McConal, Jon. *Bridges over the Brazos*. TCU Press. 2005.

McCullough, David. *The Great Bridge, The Epic Story of the Building of the Brooklyn Bridge*. Simon & Schuster Paperbacks. 1972.

McIlwain, John. *Clifton Suspension Bridge*. 2000.

McPherson, James M. *Crossroads of Freedom, Antietam, The Battle That Changed the Course of the Civil War*. Oxford University Press. 2002.

Meacham, John. *His Truth is Marching On, John Lewis and the Power of Hope*. Merewether LLC. 2020.

Miller, Terry E., and Knapp, Ronald G., with photography by Ong, A. Chester. *America's Covered Bridges*. Tuttle Publishing. 2013.

Milne, A.A. *The House at Pooh Corner*. 1928.

Mort, Mike. *A Bridge Worth Saving, A Community Guide to Historic Bridge Preservation*. Michigan State University Press. 2008.

Newman, Rich. *Haunted Bridges: Over 300 of America's Creepiest Crossings*. 2016.

Paulson, John R., and Paulson, Erin E. *Images of America, Chesapeake Bay Bridge*. Arcadia Publishing. 2019.

Petroski, Henry. *Engineers of Dreams, Great Bridge Builders and the Spanning of America*. Vintage Books. 1995.

Petroski, Henry. *Pushing the Limits, New Adventures in Engineering*. Alfred A. Knopf. 2004.

Phillips, James S. "An Informal Look at Chicago Bridge Tending in the 19th and 20th Centuries." From http://www.scribd.com/doc/20954664/On-Operators-and-Operations. 2009.

Pratt, Robert A. *Selma's Bloody Sunday, Protest, Voting Rights, and the Struggle for Racial Equality*. Johns Hopkins University Press. 2017.

Reier, Sharon. *The Bridges of New York*. Dover Publications, Inc. 1977.

Regan, Bob. *Bridges of Pittsburgh*. With photos by Tim Fabian. 2006.

Richman, Steven M. *The Bridges of New Jersey, Portraits of Garden State Crossings*. Rutgers University Press. 2005.

Rockland, Michael Aaron. *The George Washington Bridge, Poetry in Steel*. Rivergate Books. 2008.

Rubin, Lawrence A. *Bridging the Straits, The Story of Mighty Mac*. Wayne State University Press. 1985.

Schneider, Norris F. *The National Road, Main Street of America*. The Ohio Historical Society. 1975.

Shank, William H. *Historic Bridges of Pennsylvania*. Fourth Edition. American Canal & Transportation Center. 1980.

Sherman, Sam. *Ipswich, Stories from the River's Mouth*. Morris Publishing. 2001.

Solzman, David M. *The Chicago River, An Illustrated History and Guide to the River and Its Waterways*. Second Edition. The University of Chicago Press. 2006.

Spiegler, Jennifer C., and Gaykowski, Paul M. *The Bridges of Central Park*. Arcadia Publishing. 2006.

St. John's College, University of Cambridge. "Visitor Guide."

Swift, Hildegarde H., and Ward, Lynd. *The Little Red Lighthouse and the Great Gray Bridge*. Voyager Books Harcourt Inc. 1942.

Taylor, Kate. "The Pious Undertaking Progresses: The Chantry Chapel of St. Mary the Virgin, Wakefield Bridge, in the Nineteenth, Twentieth, and Early Twenty-First Centuries." 2011.

Taylor, Rabun. "Tiber River Bridges and the Development of the Ancient City of Rome." The Waters of Rome, Number 2, June 2002.

U.S. Department of Transportation, Federal Highway Administration. "Covered Bridge Manual." Publication No. FHWA-HRT-04-098. April, 2005.

U.S. National Park Service. National Register of Historic Places Inventory – Nomination Form. "Arlington Memorial Bridge." 1980.

U.S. National Park Service. National Register of Historic Places Inventory – Nomination Form. "Brandywine Village." 1971.

U.S. National Park Service. National Register of Historic Places Inventory – Nomination Form. "Brooklyn Bridge." 1975.

U.S. National Park Service. National Register of Historic Places Inventory – Nomination Form. "Cornish-Windsor Covered Bridge." 1976.

U.S. National Park Service. National Register of Historic Places Inventory – Nomination Form. "Key Bridge." 1995.

Van Der Zee, John. *The Gate, The True Story of the Design and Construction of the Golden Gate Bridge*. Simon and Schuster. 1986.

Van Dyne, Larry. "Washington, DC: A City of Bridges," Washingtonian.com. March 2006.

Waller, Robert James. *The Bridges of Madison County*. 1992.

Watson, Wilbur J. *Great Bridges From Ancient Times to the Twentieth Century*. Dover Publications, Inc. 2006. Republication of original 1927 publication by William Helburn, Inc.

Wilson, William H. *The City Beautiful Movement*. The Johns Hopkins University Press. 1989.

BRIDGE INDEX

ABOUT THE AUTHOR

BOB DOVER IS A PROFESSIONAL GEOLOGIST with degrees from Beloit College and the University of North Carolina—Chapel Hill, and additional graduate study at Cornell University. He has more than 35 years of professional experience as a petroleum geologist and environmental geochemist, and has spent most of the past 20 years leading environmental planning efforts for transportation, solar power, nuclear power, and pipeline projects. Aside from his professional experience, his personal interest in geology is the role of topography, hydrology, and geologic materials in influencing human geography, architecture, and history.

He is a contributor of bridge photos and documentation to the historicbridges.org website, having contributed many of their Maryland bridges, as well as photo-documentation of a key bridge in the United Kingdom. Recently retired from his day job, he lives in Columbia, Maryland.

Made in the USA
Monee, IL
20 March 2023

30117268R00201